DATE DUE

One War at a Time

One War at a Time

The International Dimensions of the American Civil War

Dean B. Mahin

BRASSEY'S

WASHINGTON D.C.

Library of Congress Cataloging-in-Publication Data
Mahin, Dean B., 1925–
One war at a time: the international dimensions of the American Civil War / Dean B. Mahin.
—1st ed.
p.   cm.
Includes bibliographical references (p.   ) and index.
1. United States—Foreign relations—1861–1865. 2. Lincoln,
Abraham, 1809–1865—Contributions in foreign relations. I. Title.
E469.M28 1999   99-29912
973.7′22—dc21   CIP

Printed in the United States of America on acid-free paper that meets the American National
Standards Institute Z39-48 Standard.

ISBN 1-57488-209-0 (alk. paper)

Brassey's
22883 Quicksilver Drive
Dulles, Va. 20166

First Edition

10 9 8 7 6 5 4 3 2 1

CONTENTS

*P*REFACE

Despite the continuing flood of books on the American Civil War, the international dimensions of the war have received rather limited attention from historians. These dimensions include the official relations between the United States and other countries, the abortive efforts of the Confederacy to establish diplomatic relations with other nations, the reactions to the American conflict by important groups (political leaders, editors, shipbuilders, ship owners, cotton mill owners, workers, and others) in foreign countries, the impact of the Union blockade on the cotton supply in Europe, the British roles in the blockade running system that supplied vital arms and supplies to the Confederacy, the "*Alabama* claims" for the depredations by Confederate raiders built in Britain, and American reactions to the French military intervention in Mexico and the attempt to create an "empire" in Mexico headed by an Austrian archduke.

One War at a Time examines all of these international dimensions. It is the result of a three-year review of primary materials—the official diplomatic correspondence, the personal correspondence and diaries of key individuals in various countries, and the recollections and memoirs of these persons and others who talked to them about foreign issues—as well as a wide range of secondary sources.

Although there have been two major studies of the unsuccessful Confederate efforts to win European recognition and support, and several books on aspects of Union diplomacy, there has been no comprehensive study of the foreign relations of the United States during the Civil War. Moreover, the extensive literature on Abraham Lincoln includes no adequate examination of his role in foreign affairs. Historians and biographers have assumed with great unanimity that Lincoln lacked background and interest in foreign affairs and with only rare exceptions left the determination of U.S. foreign policies and the conduct of U.S. foreign relations to his secretary of state, William Henry Seward.

A major goal of my research was to assemble and evaluate all the available evidence on the international interests and roles of Abraham Lincoln. This evidence demonstrates that his role in U.S. foreign relations was much more substantial and important than has been assumed by historians and biographers. I have also been able to explain the objectives of Lincoln and Seward in a number of situations in which their goals were deliberately concealed by diplomatic bluffing or domestic political maneuvers.

The title of the book reflects the uncertainty Lincoln and Seward deliberately created to serve their policy objectives. The phrase "one war at a time" was widely regarded during and after the war as Lincoln's maxim for U.S. diplomacy. It indicated his strong desire to avoid a foreign war while the nation was engaged in a great internal conflict, but it also contained a threat that unacceptable actions by England and France could lead to a war with the United States during or after the Civil War. Although a foreign war was the last thing Lincoln or Seward wanted, they successfully used the threat of a war with England and/or France to restrain those nations from active intervention in the American conflict.

In diplomacy, actions by diplomats and leaders are based on their perceptions of the intentions and capabilities of other governments, of the national interests of their own countries, and of their own self-interests. Understanding their perceptions is usually just as important as understanding the realities they often misjudged. In many diplomatic episodes the only hard facts are the words of diplomats and leaders. Wherever feasible, I have used brief quotations to indicate their reactions and perceptions rather than summaries on their reactions in my words. A "reported" reaction is usually by a diplomat reporting to the foreign minister of his government. A "recorded" comment is usually an entry in a diary or journal. A "recalled" account or comment is from a memoir or recollection written some years later.

In dealing with each topic I sought the generalizations and conclusions of the historian or biographer who had made the most thorough study of that topic. As in quoting diplomats and policymakers, I pre-

ferred to quote scholars briefly rather than summarize their conclusions and generalizations. A person named and quoted but not identified in the text is usually a historian or biographer; the source of each
quote is indicated in the notes. This approach gives the reader access to
the most important conclusions of the scholars who have written on
international dimensions of the Civil War, yet keeps their conclusions
distinct from those based on my own research, for which I take full
responsibility.

During the three-year research process for this book I made full
use of the excellent facilities of the Charlotte-Mecklenburg Public
Library and the Atkins Library at the University of North Carolina at
Charlotte. Through their efficient interlibrary loan services, I utilized
books from about twenty-five other libraries. I checked unpublished
diplomatic and personal correspondence at the National Archives in
College Park, Maryland, the Public Records Office in London, and the
British Library in London. I acknowledge a great debt to my wife,
Ursula, for her support and fortitude during this long process and for
her eagle-eyed editing of the preliminary and final manuscripts. I
appreciated opportunities to obtain reactions to my conclusions from
the Piedmont Civil War Roundtable in Charlotte, the Sons of Confederate Veterans in Charlotte, and the American Civil War Roundtable
(U.K.) in London. I am very grateful to Don McKeon and his colleagues at Brassey's for their considerate teamwork.

Dean B. Mahin

CHAPTER 1

Holding Watch Against Foreign Intrusion

Abraham Lincoln and Foreign Affairs

A Lincoln biographer wrote that "the president had little to do with foreign affairs. . . . He willingly entrusted foreign policy to his secretary of state."[1] A study of Lincoln's presidency asserted that "Lincoln had little interest in foreign affairs. . . . He usually left foreign affairs in Seward's hands."[2] A British scholar wrote that Lincoln "had never shown any interest in questions of foreign policy, and he made no attempt to control Seward."[3]

These comments reflect the view of most Civil War historians and Lincoln biographers that Lincoln had limited interest in foreign relations and played only a very minor role in the establishment and implementation of United States foreign policy. This view has been derived in part from the scarcity of items related to foreign relations in the extensive collections of materials on Lincoln and in part from a few such items that seemed to indicate Lincoln's disinterest, ignorance, and/or ineptitude in the diplomatic arena. One of the most important of these was an account of the only meeting between Lincoln and Charles Francis Adams, who had been named U.S. minister to Britain. Adams went to the White House with Secretary of State William Henry Seward. The meeting was described by Adams's son:

> Presently a door opened and a tall, large featured, shabbily dressed man of uncouth appearance slouched into the room. His much-kneed,

1

ill-fitting trousers, coarse stockings, and worn slippers at once caught the eye. . . . The Secretary introduced the minister [who] proceeded to make the usual conventional remarks, expressive of obligation. . . . When Mr. Adams had finished . . . the tall man remarked . . . that it was to "Governor Seward" rather than to himself that Mr. Adams should express any sense of obligation he might feel. Then, stretching out his legs before him, he said, with an air of relief . . . "Well, Governor, I've this morning decided that Chicago post office appointment." Mr. Adams and the nation's foreign policy were dismissed together![4]

This encounter convinced Adams that Lincoln had no interest in foreign relations and that the instructions he received from Seward were determined solely by the secretary of state. During and after the Civil War, Adams, son and grandson of presidents, maintained the opinion that the sixteenth president was not up to the job. Benjamin Moran, one of Adams's secretaries in London, recorded that "Mr. Adams regards Lincoln as a vulgar man, unfitted both by education and nature for the post of president."[5] "In the history of our government," Adams stated in a public address in 1873, "no experiment has been made so rash as elevating to the head of affairs a man with so little previous preparation for his task as Mr. Lincoln. . . . It is eminently so in respect to foreign relations, of which he knew absolutely nothing."[6]

John Lothrop Motley, U.S. minister in Vienna, commented after visiting Lincoln in June 1861 that "there is doubtless an ignorance about state matters, and particularly about foreign affairs, which he does not attempt to conceal."[7] European diplomats in Washington also assumed that Lincoln played a small role in U.S. diplomacy. Rudolph Schleiden, minister from Bremen, recorded that Lincoln told him at a preinaugural dinner that "I don't know anything about diplomacy. I will be very apt to make blunders."[8] After a rare interview with Lincoln in 1863, the British minister, Lord Lyons, reported that "he does not pay much attention to foreign affairs, and I suppose did not like to talk about them without Mr. Seward."[9]

These observations by American and foreign diplomats convey an accurate picture of Lincoln as a man with a limited familiarity with diplomatic practices who was reluctant to discuss foreign issues with diplomats. But the impression that Lincoln lacked interest in U.S. foreign relations and played no significant role in the determination of U.S. foreign policies is totally incorrect.

In the nineteenth century public comments by heads of governments on foreign policy issues were rare. There were no presidential press conferences and few public occasions on which comments by the president on foreign affairs were appropriate. Although the Constitution assigned responsibility for U.S. foreign relations to the president, the secretary of state communicated with foreign diplomats in Washington and issued instructions to U.S. diplomats abroad. The president's contribution to this diplomatic correspondence was made behind the scenes and was not readily apparent.

The minimal treatment of foreign affairs by most Civil War historians and Lincoln biographers leaves the impression that, since no foreign government recognized Confederate independence or otherwise intervened in the American conflict, Lincoln did not have to worry very much about foreign relations. But the threat of European intervention was very real, as was the threat of war with Britain during the *Trent* affair and later, and the threat of war with France arising from the French intervention in Mexico. The escape of the future *Alabama* from Britain virtually eliminated international trade by ships flying the American flag. The threatened escape from Britain of two ironclad rams posed a severe threat to the Union blockade of Confederate ports and to the safety of Union ports. Lincoln was too intelligent and perceptive and too aware of his constitutional responsibilities to leave the U.S. responses to these foreign dangers entirely to a cabinet member.

Evidence of Lincoln's substantial influence on U.S. diplomacy is found in the frequent references to the president's views in Seward's dispatches to U.S. ministers, in a few important comments on diplomatic issues in Lincoln's speeches and correspondence, and in the diaries, correspondence, and recollections of persons who talked to Lincoln about foreign issues. This evidence shows that Lincoln set the major foreign policy goals of the Union government, determined U.S. responses to a series of diplomatic developments and crises, and made a number of other presidential decisions designed to reduce the chance of war with England or France. In many of Seward's dispatches he stated that the position he outlined had been directed by the president; in other cases there is separate evidence of the president's determination of the response made by Seward.

Abraham Lincoln came to the White House with a broad understanding of America's unique roles as the world's largest democracy and as the symbol of freedom and opportunity for men and women around the world. The many references in his prepresidential speeches to the nation's role as a demonstration of the viability and effectiveness of democratic self-government are reviewed in chapter 18. In the midst of the war, he evoked a national resolution "that government of the people, by the people, and for the people shall not perish from the earth."

Lincoln had a broad appreciation of the many contributions of Europeans and European culture to America and the potential role of American ideas and institutions in Europe and elsewhere. He rejected the anti-immigrant attitudes of the Know Nothing Party and was a strong advocate of European immigration to America. He saw the unsettled land in the West as "an outlet for free white people everywhere, the world over, in which Hans and Baptiste and Patrick, and all other men from all the world, may find new homes and better their conditions of life."[10] Lincoln's emphasis on popular democracy and equal opportunity for immigrants appealed to foreign-born voters, many of whom were liberals who came to America after the abortive revolutionary activities in Europe in 1848.

As president, Lincoln encouraged the flow of immigrants, which continued during the war and made an important contribution to the Union victory. The Homestead Act of 1862 provided that any citizen *or alien* could acquire title to 160 acres of land by residing on or cultivating the land for five years. Seward called this act "one of the most important steps ever taken by any government toward a practical recognition of the universal brotherhood of nations."[11] In his annual message to Congress in December 1864, Lincoln recognized that immigrants provided "one of the principal replenishing streams which are appointed by Providence to repair the ravages of internal war."[12]

The idea that Lincoln was totally ignorant of foreign countries is controverted by considerable evidence indicating a wide familiarity with the culture and institutions of the most important country in U.S. foreign relations, Great Britain. Lincoln was an omnivorous reader; his favorite authors were British. John Hay recorded that "he read

Shakespeare more than all other writers together."[13] He was delighted by the poetry of Robert Burns and other British poets. Lincoln referred to incidents in British history in two of his speeches in 1860. The most famous book on British law, *Blackstone's Commentaries on the Common Law,* had been the foundation of his legal studies; he recommended that law students read it thoroughly at least twice.[14]

An English barrister who visited Lincoln in 1864, George Borrett, recorded that the president talked knowledgeably about the British political and legal systems.[15] He was at least as well prepared as his secretary of state to deal with difficult legal questions arising in U.S–British relations—the limited power of British governments to control shipbuilding for and trade with the Confederacy, the right of neutrals to trade with belligerents, the right of belligerents to search neutral ships for contraband, the legal status of mail aboard ships captured as blockade runners, and others.

Although he admired British law and literature, Lincoln was severely critical of the antidemocratic structure and the illiberal policies of the British government at home and abroad. Resolutions he drafted for a meeting in 1852 condemned Britain's antidemocratic policies in Europe: "Her treatment of Ireland . . . forces the conclusion that she will join her efforts to despots of Europe in suppressing every effort of the people to establish free governments based on the principles of true religious and civil liberty."[16]

Lincoln shared the view of many Americans that, in light of the subjection of native peoples in the British Empire, there was a great deal of hypocrisy in the British protestations of hatred for slavery and the slave trade. Notes he prepared for the debates with Douglas in 1858 recalled the strong opposition in Britain to the abolition of the slave trade that "blazed like tallow candles for a century."[17] But President Lincoln was anxious to maintain peaceful relations with Britain. In several periods of tense U.S.-British relations, he acted to reduce the threat of war with Britain.

           ↄ   ↄ   ↄ

European diplomats in Washington thought that U.S. diplomacy was totally masterminded by Secretary of State William H. Seward. He had been a Whig governor of New York in the 1840s and a U.S. senator from New York in the 1850s. Prior to the war with Mexico that began in 1846, Seward had supported westward expansion if it was peaceful and added no new slave territory. Although he thought the war with Mexico was "odious" and "a bastard war," his opposition to it was much less intense and public than that of Congressman Abraham Lincoln.[18] In the 1850s, Senator Seward was considered an expansionist. He made several statements indicating his belief that Canada would ultimately be peacefully annexed by the United States. As governor and senator, Seward had given British leaders many reasons for considering him hostile toward Britain and other monarchies in Europe. Seward was always on the side of those abroad—in Canada, Ireland, Hungary, and elsewhere—who were seeking to overthrow governments imposed by European monarchies.

In the later 1850s Seward become the most prominent leader of the new Republican Party. He spent seven months in Europe in 1859, meeting prominent leaders in England, France, Italy, Egypt, and the Holy Land. Although Seward received 173 and a half votes for the presidential nomination on the first ballot at the Republican convention in Chicago and Abraham Lincoln of Illinois received only 102 votes on that ballot, the convention ultimately chose Lincoln as the Republican candidate. After Lincoln's election, Seward accepted the appointment as secretary of state in the belief that he could dominate an administration headed by a man who had limited experience with national government and foreign affairs.

Seward's most recent biographer, John M. Taylor, summarized his assets and liabilities for the post of secretary of state:

> Seward was recognized as one of the premier intellects in politics. He had an alert and facile mind, skilled both in assessing people and in analyzing political developments. He had a deep knowledge of history. . . . The ex-senator was remarkably well traveled. . . . Seward was the one member of Lincoln's cabinet who had a geopolitical perspective. . . . At the same time, Seward also had some serious liabilities as a diplomat. In a profession that esteems prudence above all other virtues, Seward was something of a maverick. He liked to talk and was not always discreet in conversation.[19]

In the weeks prior to Lincoln's inauguration, on March 4, 1861, the legislatures of the six most southern states voted to secede from the Union. Delegates from those states decided in Montgomery, Alabama, on February 4 to form a provisional government for the independent Confederates States of America. During this period Seward talked openly at Washington dinner tables about the idea that the North and South might be reunited by a foreign war. Such talk scared Britain's cautious minister in Washington, Lord Lyons:

> I cannot help fearing that he will be a dangerous foreign minister. His view of the relations between the United States and Great Britain had always been that they are a good material to make political capital of. . . . I do not think Mr. Seward would contemplate actually going to war with us, but he would be well disposed to play the old game of seeking popularity here by displaying violence toward us.[20]

During the five weeks between the inauguration and the firing on Fort Sumter by the Confederates on April 12, Seward continued to flirt with the idea of a "foreign war panacea" to reunite North and South although there is no evidence that he thought seriously of a war with England. On April 1, Seward wrote a rambling memo titled "Thoughts for the President's consideration." Lincoln's ability as chief executive had not yet been demonstrated, and the memo reflected Seward's lack of confidence at that time in his leadership. He wrote that "I would demand explanations from Spain and France," apparently referring to Spain's current attempt to re-annex Santo Domingo and France's moves toward the occupation of neighboring Haiti. If satisfactory explanations were not received, he "would convene Congress and declare war against them."[21] Seward biographer Glyndon G. Van Deusen wrote that the "Thoughts" memo was based on the "assumption that Seward should take over the direction of government policy—a suggestion to which no self-respecting president could possibly assent. . . . The president . . . served notice, kindly but firmly, that he was master in his own house."[22]

After the war began, Seward understood as clearly as Lincoln that the North could fight only "one war at a time." But by then it was necessary to convince England and France that war with the United States was a very real danger if either country recognized Confederate independence. The belligerent image Seward had created by indiscreet talk prior to Fort Sumter was deliberately perpetuated for some time thereafter by calculated actions taken with the concurrence of the president. On the whole, the strategy was successful, although it contributed to unfounded apprehensions in Britain regarding U.S. intentions during the *Trent* crisis, at the end of 1861.

In his first year as secretary of state, Seward's image and credibility in England suffered from varied reports of remarks he made to the British colonial secretary, the duke of Newcastle, in October 1860, when the duke was in the United States with the Prince of Wales. The best evidence regarding Seward's remarks is in a letter from the duke to the governor general of Canada in June 1861. He wrote that Seward had said "he would make use of insults to England to secure his position in the States, and that I must not suppose that he meant war. On the contrary, he did not wish war with England and he was confident we should never go to war with the States."[23] But this letter was not published until many years later, and Newcastle was partly responsible for the more belligerent versions of Seward's alleged remarks that circulated in London later in 1861, especially during the *Trent* crisis. Ephraim D. Adams noted reports in England that Seward had "expressed to the duke of Newcastle a belief that civil conflict in America could easily be avoided, or quieted, by fomenting a quarrel with England and engaging in a war against her."[24] Robin Winks wrote that during the *Trent* affair Newcastle reminded the foreign minister, Lord Russell, "of Seward's supposed threat in 1860 to find cause for war with England, adding that Seward had said he would bombard Liverpool if he became president."[25]

Before his inauguration, Lincoln apparently intended to leave foreign relations mainly to his secretary of state. Seward's son recalled that Lincoln told his father in February 1861 that "I shall leave almost entirely in your hands . . . the dealing with those foreign nations and their governments."[26] But Seward's initial interest in a "foreign war panacea," his "Thoughts" memo, and other incidents soon convinced Lincoln that Seward needed his guidance and help. Lincoln told Carl Schurz in the late spring of 1861 that "he deplored having given so little attention to foreign affairs and being so dependent upon other people's judgment, and that he felt the necessity of 'studying up' on the subject as much as his opportunities permitted him."[27]

By summer Lincoln and Seward had developed an effective relationship that persisted throughout Lincoln's presidency. It was based on Seward's gradual recognition of Lincoln's unique qualities and his acceptance of Lincoln's authority and responsibility in all spheres. "Executive force and vigor are rare qualities," Seward wrote his wife on June 5. "The president is the best of us."[28]

The idea of most historians that Lincoln paid little attention to foreign affairs is inconsistent with two well-established facts—Lincoln's great exposure to the cabinet member responsible for foreign affairs and Seward's tendency to demand the president's attention on any matter he thought was important. Seward had fewer administrative responsibilities and spent more time with the president than other cabinet members. In the evening Lincoln frequently walked over to Seward's nearby house for informal talk.

Lincoln told a committee of senators in December 1862 that it was Seward's habit to read to him his major dispatches to U.S. ministers abroad before they were sent.[29] Seward frequently conveyed to Adams and other ministers the president's reactions to their most important dispatches. Lincoln biographer James G. Randall thought these references to the president were only "a matter of mere form and usage,"[30] but Seward would hardly have selected for publication numerous dispatches containing clear statements of the president's views if these statements had not been derived from consultation with the president. Biographer Benjamin Thomas concluded that Lincoln "consulted regularly with Seward on foreign affairs."[31] Lincoln did not lack the most important skills needed in diplomacy. His experience as a lawyer, politician, legislator, and debater had honed his skills in communication, negotiation, and compromise.

Seward could draw on few of the sources of policy advice available to modern secretaries of state. The small staff of the Department of State consisted mainly of clerks. There were no policy advisers, country desk officers, or any other officers with substantive diplomatic responsibilities. The assistant secretary of state was primarily an administrator; during the Civil War the post was held by Seward's son Frederick. Neither cabinet nor Congress was a substantial influence on the administration's foreign policy. The era of informed commentary on foreign policy issues by columnists, academics, and other nongovernmental experts had not yet begun.

No cabinet member except Seward had much background or interest in foreign affairs. Aside from cabinet discussion of the U.S. response to the *Trent* crisis, in late 1861, and consultation with Secretary of the Navy Gideon Welles on diplomatic issues affecting the navy, members of Lincoln's cabinet made few contributions to foreign policy decisions.

During the Civil War, Congress was preoccupied with American issues. With only minor exceptions, congressional assent in the form of ratification of treaties or appropriation of funds was not required for the conduct of Lincoln's essentially isolationist foreign policy. Lincoln and Seward did not welcome congressional intrusion in the delicate diplomatic games they were playing with England, France, and Mexico. On several occasions they declared that it would be "inexpedient" to comply with a congressional resolution requesting recent diplomatic correspondence with a specific country. Although large collections of diplomatic correspondence were sent to Congress each December with the president's annual message, some of the most important dispatches were omitted and crucial sections were cut from other dispatches.

Actions by Congress related to foreign affairs were relatively rare during the Civil War. Most of these created problems for Lincoln and Seward, although some also provided important diplomatic opportunities. The enthusiastic congressional response to the removal of Confederate envoys from a British ship (chapter 5) made it more difficult to resolve the resulting crisis with Britain. Congressional authorizations to close Southern ports (chapter 4) and to commission privateers (chapter 12) created new tensions with Britain. But some congressional initiatives—notably the authorization of privateers and resolutions opposing the French intervention in Mexico (chapter 16)—were effectively used by Lincoln and Seward as diplomatic bargaining chips. Senate rejection of a proposal for a loan to Mexico (chapter 8) allowed Lincoln to maintain his diplomatic support for the republican government of Mexico while avoiding any actual commitment in that country.

The only member of Congress who played a significant role in U.S. foreign relations throughout the Civil War was Senator Charles

Sumner of Massachusetts, chairman of the Senate Foreign Relations Committee. One of Sumner's principal goals was to undermine respect for the secretary of state at home and abroad. His enmity toward Seward was compounded of prewar rivalry for leadership within the Republican Party, resentment that a Massachusetts congressman (Charles Francis Adams) had been appointed U.S. minister to Britain rather than himself, belief that Seward was responsible for Lincoln's initial reluctance to adopt a more radical antislavery policy, and, for a time in 1861 and 1862, belief that if Seward were discredited Sumner would be named to succeed him as secretary of state. Norman B. Ferris noted that "the Massachusetts senator's enmity toward Seward had been vented both through his close association with [British minister Lord] Lyons and directly by means of letters to English correspondents." Sumner carried on an extensive correspondence with several highly placed friends in Britain, including the duchess of Argyll, whose husband was a member of the British cabinet, and Radical leaders John Bright and Richard Cobden. "In his campaign to remove Seward from the office that he apparently desired himself," Ferris wrote, "Sumner appeared to have abandoned all his scruples."[32] Adams complained to his son in Boston that Sumner was "sowing the seeds of discord, where we ought to have a more perfect union. He is disseminating distrust in our Government when it depends upon confidence."[33]

Thanks to Sumner and other Radical Republican senators, Seward nearly lost his post as secretary of state in a cabinet crisis in December 1862 that had nothing to do with foreign policy. Seward was known to be influential with Lincoln and to oppose the extreme views of the Radical Republicans. The president met with a delegation of senators on the sixteenth and again the next night with the senators and cabinet members except Seward. Sumner was among the four senators who asked for Seward's removal from the cabinet. None of the accounts of these meetings indicates that the senators raised any objection to Seward's role in U.S. foreign relations or to the foreign policies of the administration. Seward nonetheless submitted his resignation, and Secretary of the Treasury Salmon P. Chase, who supported the Radicals, also wrote a letter of resignation. Lincoln solved the cabinet crisis adroitly by refusing to accept both resignations and demonstrating that both radical and conservative viewpoints would continue to be heard in the cabinet. Seward remained as secretary of state throughout the presidencies of both Lincoln and his successor Andrew Johnson.

૨૦   ૨૦   ૨૦

Since the American Revolution the foreign policy of the United States had been based on two principles—nonintervention by the United States in the affairs of other countries and resistance to foreign intervention in the affairs of the United States and other countries in this hemisphere. The nonintervention policy, Seward noted, had begun with George Washington: "The same principle and practice have been uniformly inculcated by all our statesmen, interpreted by all our jurists, maintained by all our Congresses, and acquiesced in without practical dissent on all occasions by the American people. It is in reality the chief element of foreign intercourse in our history."[34] The American people had concluded early in their history, Seward noted, that they should be content to contribute to human progress "by the wisdom with which they should exercise the powers of self-government, forbearing at all times and in every way from foreign alliances, intervention, and interference."[35]

These traditional policies were highly relevant to the diplomatic imperatives of the Civil War period—to prevent any type of foreign intervention in the American conflict and to avoid any U.S. entanglement with any other country that would inhibit the capacity of the Union government to put down the rebellion. The president and secretary of state were fully agreed on the main objectives of U.S. foreign policy—to prevent diplomatic recognition of Confederate independence by any European country, to limit other types of European support for the Confederacy, to avoid war with any European country, and, to the extent feasible while the Union was preoccupied with the rebellion, to inhibit the extension of European influence in the Western Hemisphere.

Lincoln viewed the Civil War as a domestic rebellion, not a war between nations. He refused to accept the idea that the Confederacy was a legitimate government. The Confederates were "insurgents" engaged in an "insurrection" against the legitimate government of the United States. Throughout the war he always referred to "rebels," "insurgents," or "rebel states," but never to "Confederates" or "Confederate states." During his first month in office Seward stated that "the most important duty of diplomatic representatives of the United States in Europe will be to counteract by all proper means the efforts of [Confederate] agents."[36] Two years later he commented that the special duty of his department was "holding watch against foreign insult, intrusion, and intervention."[37]

U.S. ministers were told that diplomatic recognition of the independence of the rebel government by any European government would constitute gross interference in the domestic affairs of the United States and would lead to war between that country and the United States. This view was strongly asserted in a dispatch in June 1861:

> Every instruction which this government has given to its representatives abroad . . . has expressed our profound anxiety lest the disloyal citizens who are engaged in an attempt to overthrow the Union should obtain aid and assistance from foreign nations, either in the form of a recognition of their pretended sovereignty or in some other . . . manner. Every instruction has expressed our full belief that, without such aid or assistance, the insurrection would speedily come to an end, while any advantage that it could derive from such aid or assistance could serve no other purpose than to protract the existing struggle. . . . Every instruction bears evidence of an earnest solicitude to avoid even an appearance of menace . . . toward foreign powers; but at the same time it has emphatically announced . . . our purpose not to allow any one of them to remain in friendship with us if it should, with whatever motive, practically render such aid or assistance to the insurgents.[38]

Lincoln and Seward believed that diplomatic recognition of the independence of the Confederacy by one or more European powers, a psychologically and politically significant form of intervention in itself, would also be accompanied by some type of military support for the Confederacy. "I have never for a moment believed that such a recognition could take place," Seward wrote the U.S. minister in London, "without producing immediately a war between the U.S. and the recognizing power."[39] "Foreign intervention," he told the U.S. minister in Paris, "would obligate us to treat those who yield it as allies of

the insurrectionary party and to carry on the war against them as enemies."[40]

Although a foreign war was the last thing Lincoln and Seward
wanted while they were engaged in a great civil war at home, they successfully used the threat of war with the United States to prevent European recognition of Confederate independence, to deter other forms of
European meddling in the American conflict, and to encourage
Napoleon III to abandon the French intervention in Mexico. The
threat was clearly implied in Lincoln's axiom, "one war at a time."
While it indicated that he did not want a foreign war while he was
engaged in a civil war at home, it suggested that a foreign war might
follow the resolution of the internal conflict in America. The British
government refrained from recognition and intervention in part due to
fear of an American attack on Canada, while Napoleon III maintained
a similar policy because he feared a war with the United States that
would terminate the French intervention in Mexico.

Most historians have attributed U.S. threats of war in the event of
European intervention solely to Seward, citing in particular Lincoln's
elimination of some of Seward's most belligerent language in a dispatch to the U.S. minister in London in the spring of 1861. Though
Lincoln's amendments to that dispatch left the door open for further
communication, they did not remove the threat of war. Lincoln understood that Seward had to engage in some adroit bluffing in the crucial
diplomatic poker game he was playing with his English and French
counterparts. But Seward's threat of war in the event of European
intervention was not just bluffing. Although there was little foundation for European fears of U.S. forays into Canada or Mexico, the danger that European intervention could lead to a transatlantic conflict
was very real and was fully recognized on both sides of the Atlantic.

CHAPTER 2

To Be Treated As Other Independent Nations

Confederate Foreign Policy

Jefferson Davis came to the presidency of the Confederate States
with a strong background in military affairs—as a West Point graduate, frontier lieutenant, colonel of volunteers in the Mexican War,
secretary of war in the cabinet of President Franklin Pierce, and chairman of the Senate Military Affairs Committee—but with little more
experience in diplomacy than Lincoln.

His primary involvement with external relations had been as an
expansionist seeking new territories that could become new slaveholding states and increase Southern power in the U.S. Congress. Prior to
the Mexican War, Mississippi was the most southwestern state except
Louisiana and a stronghold of expansionist sentiment. In 1845–46,
Mississippi Congressman Jefferson Davis had strongly supported President Polk's aggressive policy toward Mexico and the military moves
on the Rio Grande of General Zachary Taylor, father of Davis's first
wife. Just after the declaration of war with Mexico, Davis wrote a letter to a Vicksburg newspaper that provides a striking indication of his
idea of diplomacy: "Let the treaty of peace be made at the city of Mexico, and by an Ambassador who cannot be refused a hearing—but
who will speak with that which levels walls and opens gates—American cannon."[1]

After serving as a colonel of volunteers in Taylor's army, Davis was
elected to the U.S. Senate. In 1848, while the treaty that ended the

15

Mexican War and increased the size of the United States by one third was being debated in the Senate, Senator Davis sponsored a resolution insisting on the U.S. acquisition of much more Mexican territory below the Rio Grande.

As senator from Mississippi from 1847 to 1853, as President Pierce's secretary of war from 1853 to 1857, and as a senator again from 1857 to 1861, Jefferson Davis was a leading expansionist and a strong advocate of U.S. annexation of Cuba. "Cuba must be ours," he declared in 1848, "to increase the number of slaveholding constituencies."[2] He stated in 1859 that "a separate Confederacy" in the South would need Cuba "to protect its back door."[3]

Biographer Clement Eaton had some perceptive comments about Davis's approach to diplomacy:

> Davis . . . had a provincial view of the world. His personality was very undiplomatic, and he had a legalistic mind, which he applied to diplomacy. He simply couldn't understand why European nations . . . consulted their own national interests in dealing with the recently emerged Confederate States of America. . . . Although he knew that European opinion was antislavery, he could not understand that it was based on deep-seated conviction, for he himself thought that Southern slavery was a just and beneficent institution.[4]

Since the Confederacy had no diplomatic relations with any other government, there were no diplomatic crises requiring presidential decisions. But the basic foreign policies of the Confederate government were determined by Jefferson Davis just as those of the Union government were determined by Abraham Lincoln.

၌   ၌   ၌

Davis's first two secretaries of state were men who also had no background in foreign relations. The first was Robert Toombs. He had been a Georgia lawyer, legislator, congressman, and senator and was known as an able parliamentarian and debater. He was also a very strong defender of slavery and Southern rights. Burton Hendrick described Toombs as "the typical, swaggering Southern browbeater, constantly aflame with imprecations against the North, loudmouth, threatening, ferocious in his language, uncompromising and destructive in his acts."[5] Toombs has also been described as restless, blustering, tactless, argumentative, impatient, arrogant, and impetuous.[6] Toombs's instructions to the first Confederate diplomatic appointees set the stage for the initial Confederate effort to obtain European recognition and support. Thereafter there was little for the secretary to do. Soon disillusioned by his powerless office, Toombs resigned in July 1861.

The second Confederate secretary of state was R. M. T. Hunter of Virginia. He had served three terms in the U.S. House and was twice Speaker. By 1860 he was in his third term as a U.S. senator and chairman of the Senate Finance Committee. Hunter, who has been described as "a rather spineless sycophant" and a "political trimmer," was primarily motivated by ambition for higher office.[7] He waited for eight months for the beginning of official relations with European governments. After hope for European recognition waned, Hunter resigned to run for the Confederate Senate.

On March 18, 1862, Davis appointed his third secretary of state, Judah P. Benjamin, who would serve in that post for the remaining three years of the war. Benjamin was born in the West Indies of Portuguese-Jewish parents, grew up in Charleston, attended Yale, and became a successful lawyer in New Orleans. He was elected to the U.S. Senate in 1853. Benjamin was the first Confederate secretary of state with substantial international experience, although he had no experience in diplomacy. In the early 1850s he made almost annual trips to France to visit his estranged wife and daughter, who were living in Paris, and he had also visited England.[8] His law practice, which continued while he was a senator, included many cases with international dimensions.[9] In 1858, President Buchanan offered him the post of U.S. minister to Spain, but he decided to remain in the Senate.[10]

Before becoming secretary of state, Benjamin served in the Confederate government as attorney general and as secretary of war. In another time and place, Benjamin might have been a very successful secretary of state. But he was no more successful than his predecessors in achieving the paramount Confederate foreign policy goal—European recognition of Confederate independence.

Since communication with several Confederate commissioners abroad was not very time-consuming, Benjamin had time for other assignments. Some of his activities were in the "international propaganda" and "covert operations" sectors. He was also an important adviser, confidant, and alter ego to the Confederate president. Benjamin prepared most of Davis' speeches, messages to Congress, and other important documents. He often saw office seekers, journalists, congressmen, and others who had hoped to see the president.

W. H. Russell of *The Times* of London interviewed him in 1861: "Mr. Benjamin . . . is a short, stout man, with a full face, olive-coloured, and most decidedly Jewish features, with the brightest large black eyes . . . and a brisk, lively, agreeable manner, combined with vivacity of speech and quickness of utterance."[11] Burton Hendrick wrote that he "never showed . . . emotion of any kind. He was incarnated intellect and logic."[12]

In February 1861, before the inauguration of Lincoln, President Davis appointed a three-man commission to represent the new Confederate government in Europe. Although Confederate policy was to stress Federal violations of the rights of states as the primary reason for secession and to soft-pedal the slavery issue, Davis appointed one of the most radical and well-known defenders of slavery, William Lowdes Yancey, as the head of the commission. Yancey, an eloquent orator, has been described as "a doctrinaire hothead" and "the most undiplomatic of men." Ambrose Dudley Mann had prior diplomatic experience as U.S. minister to Switzerland, but has been described as windy, naive, an intellectual lightweight, and a poor judge of men and events.[13] Pierre Rost had been a Louisiana judge and was added to the commission mainly because he spoke French. If there had been a significant opportunity for these men to represent the Confederate government at European capitals, their limited diplomatic skills would have been a major impediment. But there was no such opportunity in Europe in 1861 or later.

By midsummer, when the Confederate commission had been in Europe only a few months, Yancey, discouraged and in poor health, wrote to Richmond that he wanted to resign. Secretary of State Hunter accepted his resignation on September 23 and informed Yancey and his colleagues of the appointment of two new envoys who would be ready to serve as Confederate ministers—John Slidell to France and James Mason to England. The arrival of these new envoys was delayed for four months by the incident on the *Trent* reviewed in chapter 5. The original commissioners remained in London until the new envoys arrived. Mann was sent to Brussels for a while; made trips to Paris, Madrid, and Rome; and eventually returned to London, but he never played a very important role in Confederate diplomacy.

∽   ∽   ∽

Jefferson Davis's paramount goal was maintaining Confederate independence. "We are not fighting for slavery," he told a visitor in 1864. "We are fighting for independence—and that, or extermination, we *will* have."[14] Davis's sole foreign policy goal was to obtain diplomatic recognition of Confederate independence and the military and economic support that he assumed would result from such recognition.

"Confederate hopes for recognition and intervention from Europe," Emory M. Thomas noted, "rested upon simple faith in the righteousness of the cause and in the commercial prerogatives of King Cotton. Hindsight reveals Southern optimism to have been founded upon unreal and antique assumptions. . . . Confederate diplomacy seemed to be a series of dashed hopes—great expectations followed by greater frustrations."[15]

Confederate foreign policy was based on three assumptions, each derived mainly from wishful thinking. The first was that the Confederates could ignore the slavery issue and portray themselves as fighters for liberty and freedom and the Northern leaders as tyrants seeking to impose their will on the freedom-loving South. "It was for the sacred right of self-government that [we] were forced to take up arms," Hunter proclaimed in 1861. He also expressed Davis's conviction that it was the "duty" of European governments to use their influence to end an unjust war:

> The President of the Confederate States believes . . . it to be the duty of the nations of the earth by a prompt recognition to throw the weight of their moral influence against the unnecessary prolongation of this war. . . . He has presented to their knowledge the facts to which their only

sure access is through himself, in such a manner as will enable them to acquit themselves of their responsibility to the world according to their own sense of right.[16]

As a result of Lincoln's initial reluctance to declare that the abolition of slavery was a Union objective, the Confederates were able to convince many Britons and other Europeans in 1861 and most of 1862 that the South fought for freedom and independence while the North fought for domination and "empire." This Confederate success faded in 1863 when the Emancipation Proclamation convinced Europeans that the Union was indeed fighting for the abolition of slavery.

A second assumption was that European recognition of Confederate independence would convince the North to abandon the effort to restore the Union. This view is apparent in a dispatch from Benjamin to Mason in April 1862:

> There is every reason to believe that our recognition would be the signal for the immediate organization of a large and influential party in the Northern States favorable to putting an end to the war. It would be considered the verdict of an impartial jury adverse to their pretensions. All hope of submission from a nation thus recognized would be felt to be without foundation. . . . A few words emanating from Her Britannic Majesty would in effect put an end to a struggle which so desolates our country.[17]

Jefferson Davis continued to believe during and after the war that European recognition would have insured Confederate independence. "Had these powers promptly admitted our right to be treated as all other independent nations," he proclaimed to the Confederate Congress in January 1863, "the moral effect of such action would have been to dispel the pretension under which the United States persisted in their efforts to accomplish our subjugation."[18] He included the same sentence in his memoirs in 1881.[19]

A third assumption (examined in chapter 6) was that Britain and France would conclude that diplomatic recognition and support of the Confederacy were imperative from an economic standpoint because of their dependence on Southern cotton. From mid-1861 to mid-1862 the Confederate government gave tacit approval to an unofficial embargo of cotton exports that was contrary to Confederate economic interests and could be justified only as an attempt to blackmail the Europeans to obtain their diplomatic and military support. This assumption and the policies based on it persisted until the Confederates realized during 1862 that the Europeans did not want Confederate cotton badly enough to risk war with the United States and that exports of cotton through the blockade and loans based on future cotton exports were the only sources of funds to pay for the arms and supplies the Confederacy desperately needed from Europe.

∾   ∾   ∾

Confederate propaganda in Europe was aided by the scarcity of hard news from the Confederacy. Before and during the war, most American news arrived in Europe via New York newspapers. Mail from the Confederacy to Europe through the blockade was irregular, uncertain, and slow.[20] The lack of reliable information opened a clear field for Confederate propaganda and for pro-Confederate prejudices and wishful thinking. "The Northern press has always been notorious for its unscrupulousness and mendacity," the Confederate envoy in Paris warned the French foreign minister.[21] False impressions of Confederate strength, the U.S. minister in London noted in 1862, were "very much aided by the complete darkness that surrounds the situation of the rebels."[22]

Early in 1862 the Confederate government sent a young Swiss-born journalist, Henry Hotze, to London to promote "pro-Confederate editorials in the British press."[23] He soon expanded his assignment to include the publication of a sixteen-page weekly, *The Index*. Charles P. Cullop wrote that "*The Index*, enjoying a monopoly in the collection and dissemination of southern news, [was] of great aid in educating native writers with an intimate knowledge of and sympathy for the South. Moreover, it served as an unofficial voice of the Confederacy in Europe."[24] John Slidell, the Confederate envoy in Paris, and Edwin de Leon, former U.S. consul general at Alexandria, Egypt, were both given credits of $25,000 mainly for "obtaining the insertion in public journals of Great Britain and the Continent [of] such articles as may be useful in enlightening public opinion."[25]

Several factors limited the usefulness of Confederate propaganda in Europe. In Britain members of the government and Parliament were drawn mainly from the aristocratic and commercial classes, which were sympathetic to the Confederacy. Until the Emancipation Proclamation notified Europe late in 1862 that the abolition of slavery was a major Union goal, the British public had not been very interested in the power struggle going on in America. By then the governments in Britain and France had realized that any European intervention in the American conflict would risk a war with the United States. *The Index* and other Confederate propaganda activities fed pro-Confederate arguments to those in Europe who were already sympathetic to the Confederacy, but they changed few minds and had little effect on the policies of governments.

The Confederate goal of European recognition and support was actively pursued during the first two years of the Civil War. By 1863, when it had become clear that there was almost no chance of European recognition, the Confederate government virtually abandoned diplomacy in Europe. A last desperate effort to obtain European recognition in return for a vague promise to free the slaves was made early in 1865 as the Confederacy was crumbling.

CHAPTER 3

A Powerlessness to
Comprehend

British Reactions to the American Civil War

In Britian, the upper classes—aristocrats, politicians, and business-men—tended to be sympathetic to the Confederacy, while the working classes were generally sympathetic to the Union. Upper-class reactions to the Civil War were influenced by anti-American attitudes that had persisted since the American Revolution, by ignorance and misinformation about conditions and constitutional relationships in America, and by perceptions of British geopolitical, political, and economic interests.

In the 1860s the British Empire was flourishing in Africa and Asia; its only failure had been in America. British resentment of the upstart Americans who had dared to defy British authority in 1775 had been refueled by the war between Britain and the United States that began in 1812. The memories in 1861 of older men and women in both countries of that war were just as vivid as the recollections of World War II by older Americans and Britons in 1991.

British leaders welcomed the prospect of the permanent division of the vast territory of the United States between two nations. Until the Civil War the British had been unable to apply in the Western Hemisphere the dominant principle of their foreign policy in Europe—to maintain a balance of power among the nations and prevent any one country from dominating the continent. In North America, the United States was the dominant country. Only thirteen years before the

Civil War, in 1848, its size had been increased by a third and its boundaries extended to the Pacific as a result of the treaty ending the war between the United States and Mexico. Moreover, the doctrine established by President James Monroe and expanded by President James K. Polk made it clear that the United States would not tolerate efforts by any European government to extend its control over territory in the Western Hemisphere. Many European leaders believed that the United States was a serious threat to the continued independence of Mexico and to the continuation of British rule in Canada.

The Civil War in America offered opportunities for increased British influence in the Western Hemisphere without the opposition of a single American superpower. "The English Government, at the bottom of its heart," the Russian minister to England reported, "desires the separation of North America into two republics, which will watch each other jealously and counterbalance each other. Then England, on terms of peace and commerce with both, would have nothing to fear from either; for she would dominate them, restraining them by their rival ambitions."[1] Sir Edward Bulwer-Lytton, colonial secretary in the previous Tory government, declared in September 1861 that permanent separation of North and South would be "attended with happy results for the safety of Europe." Before the war, the United States had "hung over Europe like a gathering and destructive thundercloud." But "as America shall become subdivided into separate states . . . her ambition [would be] less formidable for the rest of the world."[2]

The great majority of British observers remained convinced until very near the end of the war that the North could not win and that the Union could not be restored. There is abundant evidence of this belief in British publications and in the correspondence of British leaders. "I do not see how the United States can be cobbled together again by any compromise," the British foreign secretary wrote the British minister in Washington in January 1861. "The best thing would be that the right to secede should be acknowledged, that there should be a separation—one republic to be constituted on the principle of freedom and personal liberty—the other on the principle of slavery."[3] During the first month of the Civil War the British minister reported from Washington that all chance of reconstructing the Union was "gone forever."[4] The *Economist* thought Lincoln's goal of restoring the Union was "a futile dream": "Everyone knows and admits that the secession is an accomplished and irrevocable fact."[5] In a memorandum to Queen Victoria at the end of 1861, the British prime minister listed the "virtually accomplished dissolution in America of the great Northern Confederation" as one of the noteworthy events of the previous year.[6]

The belief that the North could not win the war was based on British experience during the American Revolution, on inadequate information reaching Britain on conditions and capabilities in both North and South, and most of all on wishful thinking by Britain's ruling classes, which welcomed the division of the American superpower and feared the consequences in Britain of the triumph of popular democracy in the North.

The British remembered that during the American Revolution Lord Cornwallis had found it impossible to control very much of the American South. *The Times* of London, Britain's most influential newspaper, doubted that it would be possible "to reduce and hold in permanent subjection a tract of country nearly as large as Russia in Europe and inhabited by Anglo-Saxons." It advised the North to "accept the situation as we did 80 years ago upon their own soil."[7]

Britons were poorly informed about the development of both North and South and were poorly prepared to evaluate the relative military potential of the two regions. The rare articles or stories about America in British publications before the Civil War typically contained gross errors and distortions as well as snide and condescending judgments about American life and institutions. Accounts of America emphasized habits, manners, dress, food, and social relationships, with little attention to population trends, industrial development, transportation systems, constitutional relationships, and potential military strength. The British had little understanding of the rapid growth of the population, industries, and railroads in the Northern states, especially in the decade just before the Civil War.

During the war no cable connected Europe and America. American news reaching Britain was two weeks old. Most news reached Europe via New York newspapers, carried by the weekly packets that arrived in Liverpool after a twelve-to-fourteen-day voyage from New York. Bulletins on battles and other important events were telegraphed to Halifax in Nova Scotia and forwarded on ships that reached England a few days earlier than the packets from New York. These bulletins were always brief and were often distorted, misinterpreted, and/or false. During the first two years of the war most of these bulletins described Union defeats, and they bolstered the upper class conviction that the Union could not win the war.

A British historian, G. M. Trevelyan, noted the cleavage along class lines of British opinions about the American conflict:

> In England the upper ranks of society sympathized generally with the South, and lower with the North. . . . The poorer classes had then many relations in the Northern United States who often wrote home to say what a fine land they had found. . . . America was therefore better understood in the cottage than in the mansion. . . . The second reason was . . . that one section was dreading and the other eagerly expecting the advent of "American democracy" in England by a further extension of the franchise.[8]

The ruling classes in Britain were comfortable with the almost aristocratic political system of the South, but feared the popular democracy of the North. Southern leadership was drawn from a plantation aristocracy with many similarities to the agrarian aristocracy that still dominated British politics and British governments. In the early 1860s the British population was about 22 million, but only about 1 million men could participate in British elections.[9] Urban workers, merchants, servants, most agricultural laborers, women of all classes, and other sizable groups had no representation in Parliament. The ruling classes feared that a Union victory in America would be viewed as a victory for popular democracy and would increase pressure for the extension of the vote in England. Charles Francis Adams, the American minister in London, felt that the real motive for the upper class sympathy for the South was "fear of the spread of democratic feeling at home in the event of our success."[10]

The British had no experience with the two most important features of the U.S. Constitution—federalism and separation of powers. Even today, British visitors are bewildered by the complex division of governmental powers in America among executive, legislative, and judicial branches in separate federal, state, and local governments. The bloody sectional war demonstrated to the British that the strange and complicated system of government devised in America in 1787 had proved to be unworkable, that Humpty Dumpty could never be put back together again. One British writer noted that most Britons were indifferent to "the attempt of some of their own seceded colonists to coerce, upon some metaphysical ground of law, others who in their turn wished to secede from them."[11]

The ruling classes in Britain were inclined to accept the Confederate leaders' portrayals of themselves as defenders of liberty and independence and their portrayals of Northern leaders as tyrants seeking to impose their will on the South. The Liberal Party in England stood for the kind of political and economic liberalism that stressed limits on the powers of government. Lord Acton, a Liberal historian, wrote Robert E. Lee after the war that "I deemed that you were fighting the battles of our liberty, our progress, and our civilization."[12]

Ironically, this idea that secession was the way to safeguard liberty required acceptance of the right of oppressed peoples, proclaimed in the American Declaration of Independence, to revolt against their oppressors. "It is curious indeed," a British journalist noted, "to hear Englishmen . . . who look on the Indian Mutiny as an act of unparalleled ingratitude, advocating the sacred right of revolution with regard to the South."[13]

The British foreign secretary, Lord Russell, shared the widely held view that the South was fighting for independence while the North was fighting for domination and "empire." Although intensely proud of their own empire, the British used the word in a pejorative sense when they applied it to America. In a speech in Newcastle in October 1861, Russell said "empire" was the main issue in America:

> We now see the two parties contending together, not upon the slavery issue, though that I believe was probably the original cause of the quarrel, not contending with respect to free trade and protection, but contending, as many States in the Old World have contended, the one side for empire, and the other for independence.[14]

An English biographer of Lincoln, Lord Charnwood, noted that there was little capacity in England during this period for the informed analysis of American affairs:

Many of the expressions of English opinion at that time betray a pow-
erlessness to comprehend another country and a self-sufficiency in
judging it. . . . Englishmen readily accepted the plea of the South that
it was threatened with intolerable interference. . . . The chivalrous
South rose in blind passion for a cause at the bottom of which lay the
narrowest of pecuniary interests. . . . But . . . our fathers, who had not
followed the vacillating course of Northern politics hitherto, did not
generally take it in.[15]

The British aristocrats' negative view of the U.S. system of government was enhanced by their negative reaction to Abraham Lincoln as
president. His immediate predecessors—Pierce and Buchanan—had
had backgrounds that seemed similar to those of British cabinet ministers. Pierce had been a congressman, a major general in the Mexican
War, and a senator, while Buchanan had been a senator, secretary of
state, and minister to Britain. But in 1860 the nation had elected a
man from the frontier whose only experience in the national government was a single two-year term in Congress.

The British minister in Washington, Lord Lyons, reported in May
1860 that the Republican nominee for president was "a rough Westerner, of the lowest origin and little education." Two months later he
still referred to Lincoln as a "rough farmer who began life as a farm
labourer and got on by a talent for stump speaking."[16] British journalists who met the president in 1861 and 1862 emphasized his rustic
and ungainly appearance. W. H. Russell of *The Times* noted the size of
Lincoln's arms and legs, his ill-fitting suit, and his "thatch of wild
republican hair."[17] Edward Dicey, correspondent for *The Spectator* and
Macmillan's Magazine, wrote a similar description in 1862 and added
that "you would never say he was a gentleman."[18]

Dicey's reports reflected the widely held British view that this rustic
frontier lawyer lacked the ability to cope with his responsibilities as president. He wrote that Lincoln "works hard, . . . does little, and unites a
painful sense of responsibility to a still more painful sense, perhaps, that
his work is too great for him to grapple with."[19] Alexander J.
Beresford-Hope, a wealthy ultraconservative, remarked that "nobody in
this country, clever as he might be at rail-splitting, at navigating a barge,
or at an attorney's desk, would, without other qualifications, ever

become prime minister of England, let alone county court judge."[20] Richard Cobden, an important Radical leader in Parliament and a stout friend of the North, thought in early 1861 that the new president was "a backwoodsman of good sturdy common sense, but evidently unequal to the occasion." Even after the Emancipation Proclamation, Cobden thought "Lincoln has a certain moral dignity, but is intellectually inferior."[21] A London correspondent reported to *Die Presse* in Vienna that Lincoln was "a plebeian, who made his way from rail splitter to representative in Illinois, a man without intellectual brilliance, without special strength of character, not exceptionally impressive—an ordinary man of goodwill." The correspondent's name was Karl Marx.[22]

The prejudices of the ruling classes in Britain against the North and Lincoln were reinforced by the newspaper that was most widely read by the British ruling classes, *The Times* of London. Lincoln recognized the newspaper's great influence when he received its correspondent, William H. Russell, on March 27, 1861: "The London *Times* is one of the greatest powers in the world. . . . I am glad to know you as its minister."[23] A British scholar, Martin Crawford, described the newspaper's persistent belief that the North could not win the war and that continued separation of North and South was inevitable:

> The longer the conflict lasted, the more convinced *The Times* became that Lincoln's government should accept disunion for what it was, a sad and irrevocable fact. . . . The critique of the American conflict which *The Times* fashioned in the late summer and autumn of 1861 would remain virtually unchanged for the duration of the war . . . Britain's leading newspaper had established itself as a committed opponent of the federal cause, with the result that its capacity for independent judgment of American affairs was substantially impaired.[24]

The staff of *The Times*, writing in 1939 of its reaction to the Civil War in America, admitted that "Englishmen in the mid-nineteenth century were neither close nor sympathetic students of American history. . . . The British public was without knowledge and without understanding of the problems and situation of the United States. *The Times* shared its readers' prejudices even while it tried to enlighten their ignorance."[25]

The Times had no monopoly on anti-Northern prejudices. The conservative London *Dispatch* compressed into a single sentence most of the upper class prejudices against the North: "The real motives of the civil war are the continuance of the power of the North to tax the industry of the South and the consolidation of a huge confederation to sweep every other power from the American continent, to enter into the politics of Europe with a Republican propaganda, and to bully the world."[26]

Upper class British political prejudices were enhanced by perceptions of British economic interests. The British saw the North as a major competitor and the South as a important supplier and customer. Northern industries, shipbuilders, and traders were the most important competitors of their British counterparts. Tariffs designed to protect industries in the North inhibited British exports to America. In contrast, the economic relations between Britain and the South were essentially those envisioned by British mercantilists in the seventeenth and eighteenth centuries—the South produced raw materials (i.e., cotton) for British manufacturers and was a major customer for British manufactured products.

By the second year of the war, the large profits made by British shipbuilders, ship owners, and merchants from trade with the Confederacy (via the blockade running system described in Chapter 11) gave the British business community a major vested interest in the continuation of the Confederate struggle for independence. British businessmen were impressed by Confederate promises of a low tariff and of an expanded postwar market for British goods. Lord Robert Cecil, an important Conservative Party leader, expressed friendship for the South as a good customer and antagonism for the North as a rival of British business.[27]

The main brake on the enthusiasm of the British ruling class for the Confederate cause was slavery in the Confederate states. Britain had abolished slavery in its colonies and led efforts around the world to eliminate the slave trade. Mark E. Neeley noted that it was strange that "the most antislavery nation on earth, Great Britain, harbored so much sentimental identification with the cause of the Confederacy."[28] If the abolition of slavery had been a Union objective from the outset of the Civil War, this goal would have been widely supported in

Britain despite the political and economic factors that generated sympathy for the South among the British ruling classes. But during the first year and a half of the Civil War, Abraham Lincoln maintained that the object of the war was to preserve the Union, not to abolish slavery. "I have no purpose, directly or indirectly, to interfere with the institution of slavery in the states where it exists," he stated in his inaugural address; "I believe I have no lawful right to do so, and I have no inclination to do so."[29]

In avoiding the slavery issue until mid-1862, Lincoln was responding to the dominant feeling in the North, to crucial strategic pressures, and to his initial understanding of the limits on his powers as president. Abolitionists were still a small minority in the North. From a strategic standpoint, it was vitally important to prevent the secession of three slaveholding states—Maryland, Kentucky, and Missouri—along the border between North and South.

Francis P. Carpenter, who painted the famous picture of Lincoln reading a draft of the Emancipation Proclamation to his cabinet, recalled Lincoln's explanation to a British antislavery orator, George Thompson, of the delay in the issuance of the proclamation:

> The people of Great Britain . . . seemed to think that the moment I was President, I had the power to abolish slavery. . . . When the rebellion broke out, my duty . . . was, first, by all strictly lawful means to endeavor to maintain the integrity of the government. I did not consider that I had a right to touch the state institution of slavery until all other measures for restoring the Union had failed. The paramount idea of the Constitution is the preservation of the Union. . . . In the last extremity, if any local institution threatened the existence of the Union, the executive could not hesitate as to his duty. In our case, the moment came when I felt that slavery must die that the nation might live.[30]

The reactions of the working class in Britain to the American Civil War were quite different from those of the British aristocracy. British workers did not care very much about a balance of geopolitical power in America or expanded trade with an independent Confederacy. They abhorred slavery in the South and passionately believed that popular democracy as practiced in the North offered a model for all countries, including Great Britain. In a series of mass meetings across the country, John Bright and other Radical leaders linked the Union cause in America with the issue of Parliamentary reform in Britain. Although the workers were unrepresented in Parliament, the ruling class could not afford to ignore their demonstrations or to take actions that would stimulate further unrest and protests in Britain.

ɛⱭ   ɛⱭ   ɛⱭ

In the mid-nineteenth century the leadership of both British political parties—the Conservatives (Tories) and the Liberals (Whigs)—was drawn mainly from persons with noble titles. In 1861 the British cabinet consisted of three dukes, two earls, one viscount, two other lords, and several baronets and knights. Only three members of the cabinet had no aristocratic title.

The prime minister, Viscount Palmerston, was seventy-seven years old in 1861. Born in 1784, just after the American Revolution, he was twenty-eight when Britain went to war again with the United States in 1812. Palmerston had served as foreign secretary in three British governments for a total of about fifteen years. His involvement with several major U.S.-British disputes had left him with the view that the Americans were pushy, ill-mannered, unyielding in their demands that their rights be respected, and totally lacking in awe of the imperial power of Britain. His continuing fears that the United States would eventually invade and annex Canada ultimately prevented him from supporting a more aggressive British policy toward the American Civil War.

One of Palmerston's biographers, Jasper Ridley, wrote that "he believed that the British constitution and social system . . . was the best in the world. . . . Palmerston was a conservative at home because he wished to preserve this system and prevent any developments in the direction of democracy. He was a liberal abroad because he wished to see this system replace the absolutist monarchies of the Continent."[31] But when he looked toward America, Palmerston was no liberal. He was hostile to the idea of a government elected by all of the citizens and, as Ridley noted, was very dubious about militant democracy in America:

Palmerston had played a very active role in the suppression of the international slave trade. . . . But though Palmerston was delighted when slaves in the intercepted slave ships were liberated by officers and gentlemen of the Royal Navy, he was not so pleased at the prospect of the slaves on cotton plantations in the Confederates states being freed by large armies . . . commanded by cigar-chomping generals in ill-fitting uniforms. And he was as conscious as Bright and the Radicals that the Union armies were the most powerful force of militant democracy since the French revolutionary armies of 1793.[32]

Oxford professor H. C. Allen wrote that Palmerston "privately . . . hoped for the success of the Confederacy because it would weaken a potential rival of Britain's—and a democratic one. But, realist that he was, he kept his personal opinions to himself and consistently adapted his public policy to the military situation. Thus, as Gladstone later said, 'Lord Palmerston desired the severance as a diminution of a dangerous power, but prudently held his tongue.'"[33]

Palmerston's attitudes and roles were as misunderstood by Americans as Lincoln's were by the British. Until several decades after the Civil War, Americans thought the prime minister had been more hostile to the Union cause than the foreign secretary. This view was based on Palmerston's insistence on the release of the Confederate envoys removed from the *Trent* (described in chapter 5), his angry correspondence with Adams about General Butler's efforts to control the Confederate ladies of New Orleans (chapter 9), his remarks in Parliament about American affairs on various occasions, and his friendship with the editor of the most anti-Northern newspaper in England, *The Times.* Seward told Welles in September 1863 that "the English ministry are our friends with the exception of the chief. His course and conduct are execrable."[34]

The foreign secretary, Lord John Russell (later Earl Russell), was a younger son of the duke of Bedford. He was born in 1792 and entered Parliament at the age of twenty-one in the second year of the War of 1812. Lord John made a memorable speech in support of the modest Reform Bill in 1831, but thirty years later he led a rather conservative faction in the Liberal Party. He was small in stature, but self-confident and strong-minded in disposition. Russell reminded Henry Adams, the young son of the U.S. minister, of his grandfather, John Quincy Adams. Burton Hendrick wrote that "there was indeed something in this aging, funereal figure, with his wizened face, pointed and protruding nose, high, slanting, partially bald forehead, his cold, unfriendly pale blue eyes, that suggested not only the physical attributes of the famous New England clan but its acrid disposition." Hendrick noted that Russell was famous for "his genial manners with his social equals and his distant, haughty treatment of the rest of the world; for his sharp and witty tongue; [and] for a mighty independence of thought and behaviour."[35]

In the British system the foreign secretary carries out the foreign policies adopted by the cabinet and is much less subject to personal direction by the head of government than is his American counterpart. Although Russell was eight years younger than Palmerston, by 1861 the two men occupied similar positions as experienced elder statesmen. Each man had previously held the position now held by the other. Russell had served as prime minister for five years beginning in 1846; Palmerston had been foreign secretary in three governments. The two men corresponded frequently when one or both were out of London, and they treated each other as equals sharing ideas rather than as superior and subordinate. G. P. Gooch, editor of Russell's later correspondence, noted that "the prime minister never carried his right of supervision to a point which wounded the pride or diminished the authority of his colleague."[36]

Russell spent most of his life as Lord John Russell, a title derived from the fact that he was a son of a duke. But in June 1861 he became an earl and was henceforth known as Earl Russell or just Lord Russell. As an earl, he had a seat in the House of Lords and could no longer be a member of the House of Commons. Palmerston remained in the House of Commons and usually answered questions on foreign affairs. Another MP, Austen Henry Layard, was appointed parliamentary undersecretary for foreign affairs to represent the Foreign Office in that House.

Parliament was usually in session for six months—from February through July. The prime minister, foreign secretary, and other cabinet members spent most of the other half of the year at their estates in the country. During these months Russell managed British diplomacy by reading the contents of the red dispatch boxes sent to him daily by the Foreign Office and by conducting an extensive correspondence with Layard (who remained at the Foreign Office), with the prime minister and other cabinet members, and with British ministers abroad. During the Civil War several important crises in U.S.-British relations arose in the fall months; the reactions of Russell and his colleagues are fully documented in their correspondence, which is available to scholars in the Public Record Office and the British Library.

Burton Hendrick noted that the publication beginning in the late 1880s of much of the correspondence of Russell and Palmerston provided a view of their positions on American issues that was quite different from that assumed during the war and for two decades thereafter:

> Charles Francis Adams . . . went to his grave with a kindly feeling for Lord John. He regarded him as an honest man and, at bottom, a friend to the Northern cause. . . . Henry Adams echoed, for many years after his father's death, the same friendly sentiments. But all of the fury of Henry Adams' nature was aroused by the publication of Spencer Walpole's *Life of Lord John Russell* in 1889. This made clear a hitherto unknown fact: that Lord John Russell was the prime mover for recognition of Southern independence in August–November 1862. . . . These disclosures completely reversed the parts which Palmerston and Russell, in the American mind, had played in this momentous crisis. For many years it was generally believed that Palmerston was the pitiless enemy of America and that Russell was an influence steadily holding him in check. The facts were exactly opposite. Russell was, at the time in question, the force working for a European coalition in favor of the South; Palmerston was the moderating voice, holding Russell in restraint and finally wrecking his plans.[37]

એ   એ   એ

The decisions of the British government relative to America were substantially influenced by the performance of the diplomats who represented the U.S. government in London and the British government in Washington.

The U.S. minister in London, Charles Francis Adams, was the son of President John Quincy Adams and a grandson of President John Adams. Most of the minister's preparation for the post was derived from his membership in the extraordinary Adams family. Both his grandfather and his father had been American minister to England before becoming president. Just after the War of 1812, while his father was minister to England, Charles Francis and his brother attended English boarding schools for several years.

For a dozen years after graduating from Harvard—including the eight years during which his father was James Monroe's secretary of state and the four years of his father's presidency—Charles Francis held no position. For eight more years, during his father's unique postpresidential service in the House of Representatives, Charles Francis's main task was editing a ten-volume collection of his grandfather's papers. His personal political career did not begin until after the death of his father in 1848. By 1861 he had spent five years as a Massachusetts legislator and two years as a U.S. congressman.

The most balanced assessment by a contemporary of Adams as minister is in the memoirs of Carl Schurz, who visited him in London in 1861:

> I left Mr. Adams with the highest impression of his patriotism, of the clearness and exactness of his mind, of the breadth of his knowledge, and his efficiency as a diplomat. . . . He was, in the best sense of the term, a serious and sober man. Indeed, he lacked some of the social qualities which it may be desirable that a diplomat should possess. . . . He was not a pleasing after-dinner speaker. . . . He lacked the gifts of personal magnetism or sympathetic charm that would draw men to him. . . . His watchfulness was incessant and penetrating . . . and his remonstrances commanded the most serious attention without being couched in language of boast or menace. The dignity of his country was well embodied in his own.[38]

In an era in which most American ministers had little specific preparation for their diplomatic assignments, Adams seemed uniquely qualified for the post in London. Thomas A. Bailey noted that since he was "educated in an English boarding school, cultured, intelligent, well bred, and reserved, he had much in common with the English ruling class, intellectually and socially. . . . He enjoyed the respect and confidence of the British government."[39] H. C. Allen, an Oxford expert on U.S.-British relations, concluded that the heavy responsibilities of the London post had been "superbly discharged" by Adams: "He had the coolness of judgment, the patience, and the wisdom indispensable to success. . . . Even before the end of the war his success had been complete and unique."[40]

Yet Charles Francis Adams was far from an ideal minister. He was at his best when insisting on American rights. His greatest contributions to U.S. diplomacy were in laying the foundation for the U.S. postwar claims against Britain for the depredations of the *Alabama* (chapter 10) and in persistently applying pressures that led to the British decision to detain the ironclad rams (chapter 12). His efforts to convey to the British government the fundamental U.S. rejection of any kind of European intervention in the American conflict (described in chapters 4 and 9) were much less effective. In any modern Foreign Service he would receive low ratings as a political reporter, intelligence officer, or public affairs officer.

Adams served as minister to Britain just before the opening of the era in which urgent diplomatic communication with Europe was conducted by transatlantic telegrams. A transatlantic cable was laid in the late 1850s, but it soon broke. During the Civil War, transatlantic communication was by steamers that departed at least weekly and usually required twelve to fourteen days for the Atlantic crossing. A dispatch that was written just after a steamer had left for England or was carried by a ship delayed by bad weather might not be received until nearly three weeks after it was written. "Our instructions," Seward noted in one dispatch to Adams, "must always be based upon the understanding we have of facts at the time the dispatches leave this department. . . . In all cases you could hardly overdraw upon the confidence of the department in your wisdom and discretion."[41]

In 1861 the British foreign secretary found the new American minister "calm and judicious" and "very quiet and reasonable."[42] Nearly four years later Russell described in the House of Lords the minister's cautious approach to his mission:

It is the habit—and the wise habit, I think—of Mr. Adams to weigh over the despatches which he receives, and when they contain complaints, to consider how he can most effectively urge these complaints, and to endeavor to perform his duty in the most conciliatory spirit possible. . . . Almost the first time I saw him he told me that he had several despatches couched in strong terms, but he did not think it discreet to read them to me, and he then went on to describe in his own language what the complaints of his government were. I think the conduct of Mr. Adams is calculated to maintain friendly relations between the two governments.[43]

The Conservative leader, the earl of Derby, agreed that Adams had "throughout exercised a wise discretion and shown himself the friend of the two countries." Yet on several occasions Adams exercised his discretion in ways that led to misjudgments by Russell of the positions of the U.S. government. In 1862 his failure to convey to Russell the determination of the U.S. government to reject any form of European meddling in the American conflict allowed Russell to believe that the war in America might be ended through some form of European mediation.

Adams was not an effective collector or reporter of diplomatic and political intelligence. During the London "season," from February to July, Adams attended a number of social functions and gave a few dinners and receptions, but he did not make much use of these events to gain information or to explain the Union position to British leaders. He rarely invited his secretaries to join in these social activities, thus limiting their opportunities to obtain useful information. Aside from superficial conversations at social functions, his contacts were mainly limited to Foreign Office officials and a few members of Parliament and others who were already pro-Union in outlook.

His reporting to Washington on British policy toward America and on British politics was scanty and sometimes inaccurate, reflecting his limited sources of information. In the fall of 1861 he accepted Russell's assurance that Britain would not join the Spanish and French in a military intervention in Mexico, although a tripartite agreement for such intervention was signed by the British several weeks later. In 1862 Adams remained totally unaware of the serious consideration by cabinet members of British intervention in the American conflict. His dispatches contained a few general comments on Tory hostility to the United States but little analysis of the attitudes and positions of the Tory leadership. His inadequate reporting and analysis of British politics allowed Lincoln and Seward to believe that there was a real danger of a hostile new Tory government at a time in 1863 when there was little prospect of a change of government and rather limited interest in American issues on the part of the Tory leaders.

In the nineteenth century a diplomat communicated with the *government* to which he was accredited but was not normally expected to communicate with the *people*. The unique situation during the Civil War demanded special efforts to communicate with the British people, but with only rare exceptions Adams confined himself to the traditional roles of a diplomat. He usually declined invitations to meetings or dinners at which he might be expected to make any remarks. A poor public speaker, he would not have been an effective public spokesman for the Union cause if he had attempted to play that role. But Adams thought the anti-Union attitudes of the British upper classes were the inevitable result of their class interests and prejudices, and that any effort to moderate or change their outlook was pointless.

While he did not share his negative view of Lincoln with British officials, Adams made no effort to counteract their similar views. He did not think it appropriate to take any step to counteract the gross misrepresentations of the president and his policies that appeared regularly in *The Times* and other British papers. His persistent underestimation of Lincoln was apparent even at a meeting of Americans in London just after Lincoln's assassination. He commented that Lincoln had "never sought to lead, but rather to follow" and hinted that Lincoln had been a reluctant and recent opponent of slavery: "He has been susceptible to the influence of the national opinion. He . . . has been brought to the conviction that slavery, which he once defended, has been our bane, and the cause of all our woe."[44]

છ   છ   છ

The British minister in Washington, Lord Lyons, had more previous experience as a diplomat than Adams but was also less than an ideal minister. He was born Richard Bickerton Pemmell in 1817 and was educated at a "public school" (Winchester) and at Christ Church at Oxford University. His father had been named the first Baron Lyons for long service in the Royal Navy and in the British diplomatic service. One sister married the duke of Norfolk, the other a German baron. His brother, a Royal Navy captain, was killed in the Crimean War.

Richard Pemmell spent thirteen years—1839 to 1852—as an attaché in his father's British legation in Athens, acquiring there a habit of speaking little but listening intently. Between 1852 and 1859 he was assigned in turn as attaché in the Kingdom of Saxony (Dresden), attaché at the papal court in Rome, chargé d'affaires at the British legation to the Duchy of Tuscany (Florence), and special British representative to the Kingdom of Naples. Upon the death of his father in 1858, Richard Pemmell became the second Baron Lyons. The next year he was appointed British minister to the United States.

The reserved and reticent bachelor minister disliked Washington society and was rarely seen at public functions. His biographer noted that Lyons "used to state in after life, with much apparent satisfaction, that during his five years in the United States he had 'never taken a drink or made a speech.' "[45] He preferred to dine at the legation with his staff and did not invite very many Americans to his legation. The antisocial minister did not have a wide circle of American contacts and was often poorly informed about men and events in America.

Lyons's experience in royal, ducal, and papal courts had not prepared him for the task of reporting on democratic politics and on the operations of the complex federal system of government in America. He reminded Russell in the fall of 1861 that the United States was not, as was Britain, "a country in which a few statesmen decided what was for the interest of the community, and guided public opinion by their superior wisdom, talents, and authority. Here the government is in the hands of what are called in America 'politicians,' men in general of second rate station and ability, who aim at little more than divining and pandering to the feeling of the mob of voters."[46]

Norman B. Ferris, author of two books on U.S.-British relations during the Civil War, thought Lyons was "cold and distant, convinced from the outset of his mission that most Americans were easily swayed by 'violent feelings,' and that they tended to be a boastful, boorish lot. In Lyons' opinion, the acts of the United States Government would usually reflect 'what will sway the mob.' The way to deal with America was with 'firmness on our side. If they thought they could attain their ends by threats and bluster, there would be no limit to their pretension.' "[47]

Lyons's most significant failure was his underestimation of both the president and the secretary of state. His descriptions of the Republican presidential candidate in 1860 as "a rough Westerner of the lowest origins" and as an unknown "rough farmer" were cited earlier in this chapter.[48] By then Lyons had had plenty of time to discover that Lincoln had been a well-known lawyer, state legislator, congressman, candidate for the U.S. Senate, and nationally known speaker and debater on slavery issues. No modern Foreign Office would tolerate such inadequate and inaccurate reporting by a diplomat on the presidential nominee of a major political party.

The minister's underestimation of Lincoln persisted throughout the war. His letters to Russell contain a number of disparaging remarks about Lincoln. He had not shown "any talents to compensate for his ignorance of everything but Illinois village politics."[49] "Neither the president nor any man in the cabinet has a knowledge of foreign affairs."[50] "The President is wholly ignorant of foreign countries and of foreign affairs."[51]

Lyons rarely saw Lincoln except at large dinners and receptions. A formal call on the president, to deliver Queen Victoria's handwritten note announcing the marriage of the Prince of Wales, demonstrated Lincoln's casual attitude about diplomatic niceties. Lincoln waved the marriage announcement at the astonished bachelor diplomat with the jocular admonition, "Lyons, go thou and do likewise!"[52] Although he knew that Lincoln had toned down one of Seward's dispatches at a crucial moment in U.S.-British relations in the spring of 1861, he saw little other evidence of Lincoln's contribution to U.S. diplomacy. Even after Lincoln had been in office for more than two years, Lyons still thought that he paid little attention to foreign affairs.[53]

The British diplomat's view of the relative roles of president and secretary of state was shaped by his own experience. In Britain, foreign policy is determined by collective decisions of the cabinet. A strong foreign secretary can have more influence over foreign policy decisions than the prime minister. Lyons's previous diplomatic experience was in the period in which British foreign policy had been dominated by the foreign secretary, Lord Palmerston, now prime minister. During Lyons's first two years in America, his idea of the American presidency had been formed by observing one of the weakest and most indecisive presidents, James Buchanan. Lyons did not fully appreciate the fact that in the American constitutional system the president has sole responsibility for determining American foreign policy, even though the secretary of state communicates that policy to both foreign diplomats in Washington and American diplomats abroad. The British minister never perceived Lincoln's role in foreign affairs, and he contributed substantially to the misjudgment of Lincoln by the British foreign secretary and prime minister.

Norman B. Ferris wrote that in the first year of the war Lyons also persistently misunderstood the motives and intentions of the secretary of state: "Lyons interpreted Seward's outspoken love of country as arrogance and his bantering sense of humor as recklessness. . . . Lyons was apt to misconstrue determined patriotism as mere contentiousness."[54] Ferris also noted that in 1861 Lyons "convinced his superior in London that the American secretary of state was an insulting, arrogant warmonger, when nothing could be further from the truth."[55]

Lyons's influence on Russell was enhanced by the uniquely British system of communication between Whitehall and British ministers abroad. Official dispatches, except for a few specifically marked "Confidential" or "Secret," were supposed to contain no comments that would not be suitable for publication in the annual "Blue Book" of diplomatic correspondence or in a "White Paper" on a specific topic or issue. British ministers were encouraged to reserve their most important judgments for confidential dispatches or private letters to the foreign secretary. These letters were considered private correspondence between gentlemen and were never published until, perhaps, many years later. Lord Lyons sent a private letter to Russell by almost every weekly packet. This mode of communication allowed him to pass on rumors from unidentified sources and judgments based on his personal prejudices with no fear that they would be seen or challenged by anyone but Russell. Lyons's confidential dispatches, which were usually circulated to cabinet members and senior officials via the Foreign Office Confidential Print, also contained many statements and judgments that were unsupported by specific evidence.

As the war went on, Lyons gradually formed a somewhat more favorable view of Seward. When Radical Republican Senators were attempting to force Seward from the cabinet in December 1862, Lyons wrote Russell that "I shall be sorry if it ends in the removal of Mr. Seward. We are much more likely to have a man less disposed to keep the peace than a man more disposed to do so. I should hardly have said this two years ago."[56] "Seward has such vanity, personal and natural," Lyons reported in 1863, "that he seldom makes a favorable impression at first. When one comes really to know him, one is surprised to find much to esteem and even to like in him."[57] But Lyons continued to misjudge Seward's viewpoints and intentions during the remainder of his mission in Washington.

Neither the British nor the U.S. government realized that Lyons was providing inadequate information and warped judgments on American affairs. Just before the war began Russell wrote Lyons that "I rely on your wisdom, patience, and prudence to steer us through the dangers of this crisis."[58] When ill health forced Lyons to give up his post in America early in 1865, Russell commended him for "the prudence, the moderation, the good temper, the discrimination, and the just regard for a friendly Government" he had shown during a trying period in U.S.-British relations.[59] "His language and conduct," Lincoln wrote Queen Victoria, "have been well calculated to promote harmony and good understanding between the two countries. . . . He has, I do not doubt, . . . assured your Majesty of the invariable friendship of the United States and of their cordial good wishes for the prosperity and happiness of your Majesty's realm."[60] Lincoln and Seward had no idea how much Lyons had contributed to the British government's misjudgment of their roles and intentions during the previous four years.

CHAPTER 4

Recognition Would Be Intervention

Union and Confederate Relations with Britain, April–November 1861

On April 16, 1861, a few days after the Confederates fired on Fort Sumter, President Lincoln proclaimed a Union blockade of Confederate ports. A blockade was recognized by international law as a legitimate action by a belligerent in a war between nations. But Lincoln insisted that the Confederacy was not a nation and that the conflict with the Confederates was only a domestic insurrection, not a war.

Congressman Thaddeus Stevens told Lincoln that, by proclaiming a blockade under international law, he had inadvertently recognized Confederate independence. Stevens's postwar recollection of Lincoln's response implied that he had not considered other options for blocking Confederate trade:

> I don't know anything about the law of nations. I'm a good enough lawyer in a western law court, I suppose, but we don't practice the law of nations up there, and I supposed Seward knew all about it, and I left it to him. But it's done now and can't be helped, so we must get along as well as we can.[1]

This recollection is suspect because of the anti-Lincoln bias of Congressman Stevens, leader of the Radical Republicans in the House. It is contradicted by substantial evidence that other options were considered and rejected by Lincoln and that he proclaimed the blockade

because it was the only way to block Confederate trade without causing a war with Britain.

Union steps to block Confederate trade had been considered for a
month before the Confederates fired on Fort Sumter on April 12.
There was no immediate prospect that the small and scattered Union
navy could prevent neutral ships from entering Confederate ports, yet
a blockade was recognized by international law only if it was "effective." The first option seriously considered by Lincoln and Seward was
described as "closing the ports"—a declaration that the Southern ports
were closed, followed by the use of available U.S. Navy ships to collect
duties or penalties from neutral ships violating the closure order whenever they were encountered on the high seas.

Lincoln asked Secretary of the Navy Gideon Welles on March 18 to
"inform me what amounts of Naval force you could at once place at the
control of the Revenue service." Welles replied on the twentieth that
only twelve ships were immediately available for service in the Atlantic
and Gulf of Mexico.[2] At dinner at the British legation on March 25,
Seward said "U.S. cruisers would be stationed off the Southern coast to
collect duties and enforce penalties for the infraction of the customs
laws." Lyons responded that this plan would have grave consequences:

> If the United States determined to stop by force so important a com-
> merce as that of Great Britain with the cotton-growing States, I could
> not answer for what might happen. . . . It was . . . a matter of the great-
> est consequence to England to produce cheap cotton. . . . If . . . British
> ships were to be . . . excluded from the Southern Ports, an immense
> pressure would be put upon Her Majesty's Government to use all the
> means in their power to open these ports.[3]

Lincoln's decision to proclaim a blockade was undoubtedly influenced by Lyons's opinion—which he also expressed to Lord Russell on
April 15—that a Union blockade of Southern ports under international law would be more acceptable to the British government and less
hazardous for the United States than the proposal to "close the ports":

> A regular blockade would be less objectionable than . . . closing the
> Southern Ports as ports of entry, or attempting to collect duties for the

U.S. by ships stationed off them. The rules of a blockade are to a great extent determined and known. . . . But if the U.S. are to be permitted to seize any ship of ours wherever they can find her within their jurisdiction on the plea that by going to a Southern port she has violated the U.S. customs laws, our commerce will be exposed to vexations beyond bearing, and all kinds of new and doubtful questions will be raised. . . . It would certainly justify Great Britain and France in recognizing the Southern Confederacy and sending their fleets to force the U.S. to treat British and French vessels as neutrals in conformity with the laws of nations.[4]

News of the blockade proclamation reached England at the end of April just as the three Confederate envoys to England—Yancey, Mann, and Rost—reached London. An unofficial meeting was arranged with Russell at his London residence. The foreign secretary listened to their arguments for British recognition of the Confederacy, asked a few questions, and promised that the recognition issue would be discussed soon in the cabinet.

On April 4, Seward had told W. H. Russell, correspondent for *The Times* of London, that he was "ready, if needs be, to threaten Great Britain with war as the consequence of . . . recognition" of Confederate independence.[5] When he heard that Lord Russell might receive the Confederate envoys, Seward began drafting a strongly worded dispatch to the new U.S. minister to Britain, Charles Francis Adams, who had just arrived in London. The draft, designed for presentation to Russell, made it crystal clear that British recognition of Confederate independence would be considered a cause for war between Britain and the United States. Lincoln thought Seward's language was too strong. Philip Shaw Paludan wrote that, in revising the dispatch, Lincoln drew on his wide experience as a negotiator in his legal practice and in politics:

Although he recognized the need for some truculence, Lincoln saw the importance of control. The dispatch left too few chances for maneuver, for diplomats and nations to reason themselves out of the crisis. Lincoln told Seward to modify his language. . . . Take out the reference to "enemies"; . . . use "regrets" rather than "surprised and grieved";

Britain's actions were "hurtful," not "wrongful"; "laws of nature" were not at stake, "the laws of nations and our own laws" were; to write that Britain's actions would "not pass unquestioned" was better than to say that the United States would not bear them. . . . Instead of handing Russell the dispatch, let Adams use it for guidance in face-to-face discussions. Lincoln's changes retained strength, letting Britain know of the nation's displeasure, but . . . they revealed . . . his desire to continue the process and allow room for negotiations.[6]

Lincoln once remarked that "it is as peacemaker that the lawyer has a superior opportunity."[7] Allen Thorndike Rice, editor of the *North American Review*, wrote in 1888 that Lincoln's revisions of the May 21 dispatch "saved the nation from a war with England":

This paper, by its erasures, its substitutions and its amendments, shows a nice sense of the shades of meaning in words, a comprehensive knowledge of the situation, and a thorough appreciation of the grave results which might follow the use of terms that he either modified or erased. . . . The work shows . . . an insight into foreign affairs, a skill in the use of language, a delicacy of criticism and a discrimination in methods of diplomatic dealing which entitled the president to the honors of an astute statesman.[8]

Although Adams was appointed minister to Britain soon after Lincoln's inauguration on March 4, he delayed his departure for six weeks in order to attend the wedding of his son, Charles Francis Jr. The minister sailed on May 1, arriving in England on May 13. On the train between Liverpool and London, Adams read in a newspaper that the British government had decided to recognize the belligerency of the Confederacy.

The duke of Argyll, a member of the cabinet, defended the government's decision in a letter to his friend John Lothrop Motley: "The rights and interests of humanity demand that the rules and principles of some admitted law should be immediately applied to all such contests, and the rules affecting and defining the rights and duties of belligerents are the only rules which prevent war from becoming massacre and murder."[9] Four years later, Russell explained the decision in the

House of Lords: "We were entitled to recognize the existence of belligerent rights on the part of both combatants. . . . There was nothing unfriendly, nothing uncourteous in the declaration. . . . It was the proper course for this country to declare at the earliest moment that it meant to take part neither with the north nor with the south but to remain entirely neutral in the contest".[10]

The Queen's Proclamation also commanded British subjects to observe the provisions of the Foreign Enlistment Act of 1818 that prohibited Britons from joining the army or navy of any belligerent, from arming or equipping any ship for use as a ship of war or military transport, from breaking any lawful blockade, and from carrying "officers, soldiers, despatches, arms, military stores or material" and other contraband to any belligerent.[11] H. C. Allen wrote that the proclamation "enjoined a strict neutrality on Britons and warned them that their failure to comply with it rendered forfeit their right to the protection of their government."[12] This risk—that if their ships were seized, the blockade runners would have no recourse to the British government—was the only penalty imposed on them by the proclamation. "It is not the practice of nations to undertake to prohibit, by previous laws, from trafficking in articles contraband of war," Russell wrote to Adams in December 1862; "such trade is carried on at the risk of those engaged in it."[13]

As a result of the British recognition of Confederate belligerency, ships flying the Confederate flag were treated in British ports like ships of any other belligerent nation. Under rules established by international law, ships of belligerents were allowed to obtain fuel, supplies, and repairs in neutral ports but could not obtain additional equipment or armament. The royal proclamation permitted the Confederate cruisers that would ravage Northern shipping to obtain vital supplies and coal during visits to British colonial ports.

The royal proclamation also encouraged the Confederates to believe that British recognition of Confederate independence would be forthcoming as soon as their armies won a major battle. The three Confederate commissioners reported on May 21—the same day Seward's blast against recognition was dispatched—that "England is in reality not averse to the disintegration of the United States and [England and France] will act favorably toward us upon the first decided success which we may obtain."[14]

In his first interview with Russell, on May 18, Adams vigorously protested the "precipitous" recognition of Confederate belligerency and expressed fear that it would soon be followed by British recognition of Confederate independence. Russell responded that the British government did not currently intend to recognize the Confederacy but that he could give no assurance as to the government's future policy.[15]

ℂ   ℂ   ℂ

Even after Lincoln's revisions, of which Adams was unaware, Adams was shocked by the strong language in Seward's May 21 dispatch. He thought his government was "almost ready to declare war with all the powers of Europe."[16] The tone of Seward's message, somewhat softened by Lincoln, was watered down even more in Adams's oral presentation to Russell on June 12. The minister's moderate tone was reflected in his report on the meeting: "The continued stay of the pseudo-commissioners in this city and still more the knowledge that they had been admitted to more or less interviews with his lordship . . . had already given great dissatisfaction to my government. I added, as moderately as I could, that in all frankness any further protraction of this relation could scarcely fail to be viewed by us as hostile in spirit, and to require some corresponding action accordingly."[17] But Adams conveyed to Russell the essence of Seward's dispatch, which was that "British recognition would be British intervention to create within our own territory a hostile state."

The May 21 dispatch included a statement that if the British continued to have even unofficial relations with the Confederate envoys, Adams must terminate further relations with the British, at least until he received further instructions from Washington. "You will . . . desist from all intercourse whatever, unofficial as well as official, with the British government, so long as it shall continue intercourse of either kind with the domestic enemies of this country."[18] The dispatch did not require him to inform Russell of this contingent instruction, and he did not do so. But Russell got the essential message that further contact with the Confederates would be fraught with dangers. He responded that British foreign secretaries had often met, as a means of obtaining useful information, with representatives of groups in revolt against governments with which Britain was at peace. Although he had seen the Confederate gentlemen twice, "I have no intention of seeing them anymore." He did not, although he met another Confederate envoy unofficially the following year.[19]

The week before he saw Adams, Russell had received a long confidential dispatch from Lyons:

> Mr. Seward . . . had ever regarded the foreign relations of the country as safe material from which to make (to use his own phrase) political capital at home. . . . The President is, of course, wholly ignorant of foreign countries and of foreign affairs. They believe that arrogant language and high-handed conduct toward the Powers of Europe are called for by that violent section of their party which is now predominant in the North. . . . That Mr. Seward, and the party to whom he has now given himself up, really desire to plunge the country, at this crisis of its fate, into a war with England or France seems impossible. They must be aware that by merely raising the blockade of the Southern ports, England or France would effectually disconcert their plans for the subjugation of the South. . . . At the bottom, no doubt, of the boasting and the arrogance of the Cabinet is a conviction that under no provocation will England or France really go to war with the United States.

Lyons thought the British government should demonstrate "absolute inflexibility of purpose," avoid any concession to American bullying, and move quickly to put Canada in "a complete state of defence."[20]

Lyons subsequently learned that Seward's original draft of the May 21 dispatch to Adams had been, as he wrote Russell on June 24, "all but a direct announcement of war" but had been extensively altered by the president:

> Mr. Seward's motives for provoking a war with England can be traced only to his view of his political position as candidate to succeed Mr. Lincoln. . . . He is thought to wish to set himself at the head of a new party . . . which should rally to itself the important Irish vote, by hostility to England. I imagine that the precipitation with which Mr.

Seward was disposed to act arose from the hope of beginning the war . . .
by an invasion of Canada.[21]

He did not explain how a war with England in 1861 could help a possible Seward candidacy that was still at least three years in the future.
The only apparent source of this totally distorted view of Seward's
motives is Senator Sumner, who was told about the May 21 dispatch
by Lincoln and saw the British minister soon thereafter.[22] Lyons admitted that "all this sounds like madness," but nonetheless gave Russell the
impression that he took it seriously.

In his first four months as secretary of state, Seward had tried to
create an image of himself in Europe as a tough and resolute statesman
determined to uphold American rights and interests. "You could not do
greater harm," he wrote Adams on July 6, "than by inducing an opinion
that I am less decided in my intercourse with the British Minister than I
am reputed to be, or less determined to maintain the pride and dignity
of our Government."[23] Two weeks later he noted in a dispatch that it
was his "earnest and profound solicitude to avert from foreign war" that
had "prompted the emphatic and sometimes, perhaps, impassioned
remonstrances I have hitherto made against any form or measure of
recognition of the insurgents by the government of Great Britain."[24]

H. C. Allen concluded that "this earlier belligerence of Seward
probably had, on balance, a salutary effect upon Anglo-American relations, because of the sobering influence it exerted upon the British
government, who became as a result more than ever determined to step
warily in the difficult circumstances arising from the American war."[25]

෴   ෴   ෴

During the late spring and early summer of 1861, there were
numerous indications of growing support in Britain for the Confederate cause. Initial support for the Union, based on traditional antislavery sentiment, was soon eroded by Lincoln's statements that the war
was being fought for reunion, not abolition. The British did not
understand or care about the obscure constitutional relationships of
American federalism. Most Britons came to believe that the war was

either a pointless domestic squabble over minor constitutional issues or, as was suggested by Confederate propaganda, an evil crusade by Lincoln against principles dear to the hearts of Britons—local autonomy and free trade.

On May 30, *The Times* proclaimed that the war in America was not a war of principle but merely a war for power, territory, and political and commercial gains:

> The real motives of the belligerents . . . appear to be exactly such motives as have caused wars in all times and countries. . . . They are essentially selfish motives—national power, territorial aggrandizement, political advantage, and commercial gain. Neither side can claim any superiority of principle. . . . We certainly cannot discover in these arguments anything to remove the case from the common category of national or monarchical quarrels.[26]

The latent sympathy of the British upper classes with the Confederate cause—based on the geopolitical, political, and economic factors reviewed in chapter 3—was brought into the open by news of the Union rout at Bull Run on July 21. A vivid account by correspondent W. H. Russell of the disorganized retreat of Union troops was printed in *The Times* in London on August 4 and was widely reprinted in British and U.S. papers. Russell's reports during a long spring trip through the Confederacy had convinced the editors of *The Times* and their readers that the Confederates were unanimously determined to maintain their independence. His report from Bull Run seemed to prove that they would be able to do so. When the secretary of war later denied Russell permission to accompany the Army of the Potomac, Lincoln refused to interfere on the ground that "this fellow Russell's Bull Run letter was not so complimentary as to entitle him to much favor."[27]

Lyons reported that the Union defeat in the first major battle of the war had severely shaken Union confidence and determination: "The discouragement to the uncompromising war party has been greater than could have been anticipated. Confidence in the military qualities of the volunteer soldiers has been shaken. The hope that the war could be terminated in a few months, by a vigorous effort, has vanished. The perseverance of the North in the contest no longer seems to be beyond question. The appearance of unanimity is almost gone."[28]

"The disgrace is frightful," Henry Adams wrote to his brother. "The exposé of the condition of our army is not calculated to do us anything but the most unmixed harm here. . . . Bull's Run will be a byword for ridicule for all time. Our honor is utterly gone."[29]

The day after Bull Run, Lincoln made a list of nine military objectives. "Let the plan for making the blockade effective be pushed forward with all possible dispatch" was the first item on the list.[30] This decision was the result of a just-completed reexamination of the "closing the ports" option that had been considered in the spring. Lyons had reported on June 14 that the U.S. government was "not willing to admit that it has not as much right to close the port of New Orleans by an act of Congress as it has to close the port of New York, or that it may not confiscate foreign vessels for a break of the revenue laws if they attempt to go to New Orleans after it has been closed by law as a port of entry, whether it be in fact blockaded or not."[31]

The Congress, convened by Lincoln in a special session on July 4, passed a bill that, as Lyons reported to Russell, "empowers the President to close the ports of entry in districts in which the customs duties cannot be collected, and subjects to forfeiture ships with their cargoes entering or attempting to enter ports so closed."[32] Lyons told Seward that "Her Majesty's Government did not consider that the United States had any right . . . to close by decrees any ports which were not in their own possession."[33] He hoped the president would not use the authority given him by Congress because "we cannot allow our ships to be stopped and overhauled, unless there is suspicion of contraband of war or an attempt to enter a blockaded port."[34]

Lincoln decided to ignore the congressional authorization to close the Southern ports because its use might lead to war with England. Senator Orville Browning recorded Lincoln's comments on the ports issue on July 25:

Our coast was so extensive that we could not make the blockade of all the ports effectual. . . . England was now assuming the ground that a nation had no right, whilst a portion of its citizens were in revolt, to close its ports or any of them against foreign nations. . . . If he asserted the right of closing such as we could not blockade, he had no doubt it would result in foreign war.[35]

Seward wrote Adams that week that "the President deprecates . . . the evil of foreign wars to be superinduced . . . upon the painful civil conflict."[36]

In mid-August, Lyons gave Seward a message from Russell that the British government "would consider a decree closing the ports of the South actually in possession of the insurgent or Confederate States as null and void, and that they would not submit to measures taken on the high seas in pursuance of such a decree." Seward replied that consideration of closing the ports had been dropped for the moment, but hinted that "there were influential persons who were anxious to moot it again."[37]

෴ ෴ ෴

U.S.-British tensions were increased in late summer by the failure of negotiations for U.S. adherence to the Declaration of Paris, a treaty signed by European maritime countries in 1856. Prior to the Paris treaty, international law had allowed a belligerent government to issue "letters of marque" authorizing privately owned ships to carry out specified naval operations against ships of the enemy country. Such "privateers" had been extensively used by the United States in two wars with Britain. The four articles of the Declaration of Paris provided that: (1) privateering is abolished; (2) a neutral flag protects goods belonging to a belligerent except for "contraband of war"; (3) goods belonging to a neutral are safe on a ship of a belligerent unless they are contraband; and (4) a blockade is binding only if it is "effective."

In 1856 the United States had been unwilling to give up the right to use privateers in future wars. But in 1861 Jefferson Davis announced his intention to issue letters of marque to privateers, and Lincoln and Seward feared that these Confederate privateers would prey on Union commerce. The week after the proclamation of the Union blockade, Seward instructed the U.S. ministers in London and Paris to open negotiations for U.S. adherence to the Declaration of

Paris. He hoped the broadened international ban on privateering would curb the use of privateers by the Confederates.

The British government rejected Union assertions that the Confederates were mere "insurgents" and that any ships they commissioned should therefore be regarded as "pirates." Howard Jones wrote that the British would not accept "the Union's efforts to . . . obligate all signatory nations to police the seas against Southern privateers while freeing the Union to tighten its blockade."[38]

On August 19 Russell informed Adams that the British acceptance of the U.S. adherence to the treaty must include a statement that "Her Majesty does not intend thereby to undertake any engagement which shall have any bearing, direct or indirect, on the internal differences now prevailing in the United States." Adams said this statement would destroy the reciprocity of the agreement and greatly increase the chances of its rejection by the Senate.[39] Russell replied that, without the British reservation, Britain would be "bound to treat the privateers of the so-called Confederate states as pirates" and that the British government refused to undertake any "engagement to interfere in the unhappy dissensions now prevailing in the United States."[40]

"I am instructed by the President to say that the proposed declaration is inadmissible," Seward wrote Adams on September 7.[41] In 1863 Lincoln and Seward successfully used hints that the United States would send privateers to prey on British blockade runners—an option authorized by a privateering bill passed by Congress—to convince the British government that it must prevent two ironclad rams built for the Confederacy from leaving Liverpool.

In mid-August Seward learned that the British had been secretly communicating with the Confederate government to obtain its adhesion to the provisions of the Declaration of Paris other than the ban on privateering. A reliable source said that Robert Mure—a cousin of the British consul in New Orleans, a former naturalized U.S. citizen, and a current Confederate colonel—would be passing through New York with dispatches to Russell from the Confederate government. Mure was detained by the New York police. He was carrying a sealed British diplomatic bag addressed to Russell, two hundred private letters to persons in Europe, and dispatches from the Confederate government to Confederate agents in Europe. One of the papers indicated that the

British government had been secretly negotiating with the Confederate government and that "the first step to recognition" had been taken by the British.[42]

Russell subsequently admitted that the British consul in Charleston, Robert Bunch, had been "instructed to communicate to the persons exercising authority in the so-called Confederate States" the desire of Britain and France "that the second, third, and fourth Articles of the Declaration of Paris should be observed by those States." He added that "the commerce of Great Britain and France is deeply interested in the maintenance of the articles providing that the flag covers the goods, and that the goods of a neutral taken on board a belligerent ship are not liable to condemnation." But Russell denied that this action constituted the first step to the recognition of the Confederacy as a separate and independent nation.[43]

Bunch sent William H. Trescot, former secretary of the American legation in London and assistant secretary in the Department of State in the Buchanan administration, to meet Jefferson Davis and his cabinet in Richmond. The Confederate president invited the Confederate Congress to adhere to the Declaration of Paris except for the ban on privateering, as requested by the British. The Congress did so on August 13.[44]

In contrast to Seward's very strong reaction in the spring to the prospect that Russell would receive Confederate envoys, his reaction to the British communication with the Confederate government was comparatively mild. Adams was instructed to request that Bunch be removed from his consular office. Russell replied that the consul could not be fired for following instructions. Although Seward threatened to cancel Bunch's "exequator"—the host government's permission to exercise consular functions—he let the matter drop.[45] Seward's mild response apparently reflected the continuation of Lincoln's cautious approach to relations with Britain.

Russell refused to expand his sporadic unofficial communication with the three Confederate commissioners in London. They reported in August that they had not received "the least notice or attention, official or social, from any member of the Government" since their arrival in England in April.[46] Nevertheless, the positive reaction in Britain to the Union defeat at Bull Run encouraged them to make a further effort to communicate with the British government. On August 14 they requested another interview with Russell. He replied that they should put in writing any communication they wished to make. They sent him a long letter outlining the reasons why Great Britain should recognize the independence of the Confederacy. Russell's reply, referring to them as the representatives of the "so-called" Confederate States, stated that Her Majesty's government could not "acknowledge the independence of the nine states which are now combined against the President and Congress of the United States until the fortune of arms or a more peaceful negotiation shall have more clearly determined the respective position of the two belligerents."[47]

Russell was not ready to recognize Confederate independence, but he was beginning to consider the idea that England and France should intervene in some way to stop the war and break the blockade. "In Europe," he wrote to Palmerston on October 17, "powers have often said to belligerents, make up your quarrels. We propose to give terms of pacification which we think fair and equitable. If you accept them, well and good. But if you refuse them . . . you must expect to see us your enemies."[48] But Palmerston replied that "our best and true policy [is] to go on as we have begun and keep quite clear of the conflict."[49]

Palmerston summarized his outlook on the American conflict on October 20—his seventy-seventh birthday—in a note to Layard at the Foreign Office: "It is in the highest degree likely that the North will not be able to subdue the South, and it is no doubt certain that if the Southern union is established as an independent State it would afford a valuable and extensive Market for British Manufactures, but the operations of the war have as yet been too indecisive to warrant an acknowledgment of the southern Union."[50]

Late in 1861 a new crisis brought the United States to the brink of war with Britain, but it was not provoked by the government of Britain or the United States. The greatest threat of foreign war during the four years of civil war in America was the result of an unauthorized action by an impetuous officer of the U.S. Navy.

CHAPTER 5

A Gross Outrage

The Trent Crisis, November–December 1861

B y midsummer of 1861 William Lowdes Yancey, head of the three-man Confederate commission sent to Europe earlier in the year, was ill, discouraged, and ready to resign. In August President Jefferson Davis decided that he needed diplomats in England and France who were ready to serve as Confederate ministers as soon as those countries recognized Confederate independence. Davis appointed two former United States senators. John Slidell of Louisiana, the envoy the Mexican government had refused to receive as U.S. minister after the U.S. annexation of Texas in 1845, was assigned to France. James Mason of Virginia, former chairman of the Senate Foreign Relations Committee, was assigned to England.

By October 1 they were in Charleston. Both men were accompanied by secretaries; Slidell had brought along his wife and three children. Their first plan was to run the blockade in the *Nashville*, a fast steamer that had been taken over by the Confederate navy. Word of these plans reached Washington, and Welles ordered a U.S. warship to search for the Confederate ship. But the main channel into Charleston's harbor was well guarded by five Union ships, and the draft of the *Nashville* was too deep to permit it to use any of the side channels. So the envoys chartered a small, shallow-draft steamer, the *Theodora*. On the rainy night of October 12, the ship escaped from the harbor by a side channel without being seen by the blockading Union squadron.

By October 16 the *Theodora* had reached the Cuban port of Cardenas. There the envoys learned that the next British mail packet, the *Trent*, would leave Havana on November 7 for Saint Thomas, in the Virgin Islands, where they could connect with the British "West Indian mail" to Southampton.

A week later a U.S. warship arrived at Cienfuegos, on the south coast of Cuba. The *San Jacinto* was returning from the African coast and had been ordered to join the U.S. naval force preparing for an attack on Port Royal, South Carolina. But on arrival at Saint Thomas on October 13, the ship's captain, Charles Wilkes, had met the captains of two Union ships who were hunting for the *Sumter*, the first of the Confederate commerce raiders. Wilkes learned that in July the *Sumter* had captured three Union merchant ships near Cienfuegos. The independent-minded captain steamed to Cienfuegos, even though there was very little chance that the *Sumter* would be in the same area in October as in July.

There Wilkes read in a newspaper that Mason and Slidell were in Havana. He decided that, if he couldn't find the Confederate raider, he would try to catch the Confederate envoys. He steamed around the island to Havana, where he learned that the envoys would leave Havana on November 7 on the *Trent*. Wilkes knew that the ship would have to use the narrow Bahama Channel, the only deepwater route between Cuba and the shallow Great Bahama Bank. He immediately saw the possibility of meeting the *Trent* in the channel and removing the Confederates.

Wilkes had a reputation as a stubborn, overzealous, impulsive, and sometimes insubordinate officer. The inadequate explanations by historians of Wilkes's motives for taking an action that would lead to a major crisis with Britain have included a fondness for "gunboat diplomacy," a desire for his first action in the seven-month-old war, an eagerness to renew the fame he had enjoyed as commander of an exploring expedition in the Antarctic, dislike of the British because a British officer used some of his information on Antarctica without giving him credit, and dislike of Slidell, with whom Wilkes had quarreled over a girl when they were schoolboys in New York. The most convincing explanation was recorded by the correspondent of *The Times*, W. H. Russell: "Intimates [say] that he did it to cut a dash and make a sensation, being a bold and daring man."[1]

The *Trent* left Havana on November 7 with Mason, Slidell, their secretaries, Slidell's wife and children, and many other passengers. About noon the next day, November 8, it was spotted in the Bahama Channel by the *San Jacinto*. Wilkes ordered a round shot and then a shell fired across the bow of the *Trent*. His executive officer, Lt. D. M. Fairfax, was ordered to lead a boarding party.

Wilkes wrote later that the *Trent*'s captain undoubtedly knew that Mason and Slidell "were carrying highly important dispatches and were endowed with instructions inimical to the United States" and that the carrying of this "contraband" rendered the vessel subject to seizure.[2] When Attorney General Edward Bates heard about the seizure of the envoys, he assumed that "their papers were also seized, and will probably give us useful . . . information."[3] But no papers were seized on the *Trent*. The captain, James Moir, refused Fairfax's request for a peaceful search of his ship. Fairfax decided not to use force to search for Confederate dispatches.[4]

The story of the envoys' papers remained untold until 1906, when Mason's daughter included his account of the *Trent* incident in a biography of her father:

> My first impression [when the *San Jacinto*'s boat approached] was to provide for the safety of our papers. I accordingly called to Mr. Mac-Farland and asked him to take the dispatch bag which contained my public papers, credentials, instructions, etc . . . and deliver it to the mail agent of the steamer, . . . and ask him to lock it up in his mail-room, and I told him . . . to make the same suggestion to Mr. Slidell. . . . Before the boat from the *San Jacinto* reached our ship, Commander Williams of the Royal Navy, who had charge of the mails on board, came to me . . . and reported that he had the dispatch bags of Mr. Slidell and myself locked up in his mailroom. . . . I . . . requested, if we were separated from them, that he would see to their delivery to some one of the Commissioners of the Confederate States . . . in London.[5]

Williams subsequently turned the Confederate bags over to a Mr. Hanckel of Charleston, who delivered them to the Confederate envoys in London. This clear violation of the prohibition in the Queen's

Proclamation against the carrying of dispatches of belligerent governments was not known until long after the war.

International law required that when "contraband" was found on a neutral ship by a boarding party from a belligerent ship, the neutral ship must be taken to the nearest "prize court" for adjudication. Fairfax raised two objections to Wilkes's initial plan to detain the ship: (1) putting a prize crew aboard the *Trent* would weaken the fighting capacity of the *San Jacinto*, which had a minimal crew and orders to participate in the Union attack on Port Royal, South Carolina, and (2) taking the *Trent* would seriously inconvenience the passengers and the recipients of the mail and specie aboard the ship. Norman Ferris, author of a book on the *Trent* affair, wrote that Fairfax also feared that seizing the ship might cause a war with Britain.[6]

Wilkes decided that, after Mason and Slidell and their secretaries were removed, the *Trent* would be allowed to proceed to Saint Thomas. The *San Jacinto* steamed north and arrived at the Union naval base at Hampton Roads in Virginia on November 15. An admiral wired the news of the capture of Mason and Slidell to the Navy Department. Wilkes was ordered to take the envoys to Boston, where they were held at Fort Warren with other Confederate prisoners.

The story of Wilkes's exploit quickly spread across the North by telegraph. "There is a storm of exultation sweeping over the land," reported W. H. Russell of *The Times*; "Wilkes is the hero of the hour."[7] Over the next several weeks, Captain Wilkes was wined and dined, applauded, and commended for his initiative by the press, the secretary of the navy, and the U.S. Congress. The appropriateness and legality of his action were defended by such experts as Edward Everett, a former secretary of state and minister to Great Britain, and Caleb Cushing, a former attorney general.[8]

The capture of the envoys was a victory of a sort over the Confederacy after seven months of war marked mainly by Union defeats. Wilkes had also turned the tables on an old enemy, England. The principal cause of the War of 1812 had been Britain's insistence on the right to search American vessels and to impress into the British navy seamen it considered to be British subjects. In the 1830s and 1840s Britain had reasserted the "right of search," applying it to ships flying the American flag that were suspected of carrying slaves from Africa.

Now an audacious American captain had twisted the tail of the British lion and given John Bull a dose of his own medicine.

At first Lincoln shared the general elation and did not realize that Wilkes's action might threaten war with Britain. A note to the former U.S. minister to Britain contained no hint of concern about the British reaction.[9] A journalist who saw Lincoln that week wrote that Lincoln had talked mainly about Wilkes's violation of long-standing American principles concerning neutral rights:

> I fear the traitors will prove to be white elephants. We must stick to American principles concerning the rights of neutrals. We fought Great Britain for insisting . . . on the right to do precisely what Captain Wilkes has done. If Great Britain shall now protest against the act, and demand their release, we must give them up, apologize for the act as a violation of our doctrines, and thus forever bind her over to keep the peace in relation to neutrals, and so acknowledge that she has been wrong for sixty years.[10]

Welles, who had not yet begun his diary in 1861, wrote in 1873 that Lincoln's "chief anxiety . . . was as to the disposition of the prisoners."[11] He recorded in 1863 that Seward had "at first approved the course of Wilkes in capturing Mason and Slidell."[12] He wrote later that "no man was more elated or jubilant than Seward at the capture of the emissaries, and for a time he made no attempt to conceal his gratification and approval of the act of Wilkes."[13]

General George B. McClellan, the new general-in-chief of the Union army, began a letter to his wife early on November 17 with assertions that "our government has done wrong in seizing these men on a neutral ship" and that the only way to avoid a war with England was "a prompt release with a frank avowal of wrong." But during the day he talked with Edwin Stanton, Buchanan's last attorney general and soon to be Lincoln's second secretary of war. That evening McClellan wrote "that our government is fully justified by all of the rules of international law and all the decisions in the highest courts."[14]

A Seward biographer, Thornton Lothrop, wrote that Seward asked McClellan about the consequences of a war with England, that the general replied that it would mean the end of all hope of reuniting the

Union, and that Seward immediately concluded that the envoys should be released if necessary to avoid war with Britain.[15] But Seward commented later that the British note delivered in December had been "our first knowledge that the British Government proposed to make it a question of offense or insult, and so of war."[16]

Russell of *The Times* saw Seward at the State Department on the eighteenth, but got no comment from him on the *Trent* affair. He recorded that "a judicious reticence" was being observed at both the State Department and the British legation.[17] For two weeks after learning of Wilkes's action, Seward did not even communicate with his minister in London concerning the *Trent* affair. On November 30, in a dispatch to Adams dealing mainly with other matters, Seward included a comment that Wilkes had acted on his own.[18]

Welles took his time about making any public comment on Wilkes's unauthorized act. He recorded later that Wilkes's action "was popular with the country, was considered right by the people, even if rash and irregular; but when and how to dispose of Wilkes was an embarrassment to me."[19] Welles's biographers have suggested that he was primarily concerned with the effect of his response on the navy. Richard S. West Jr. wrote that to refrain from supporting Wilkes would have inhibited "a type of audacity and moral courage that was vitally necessary to the Navy if the blockade were to be enforced."[20] John Niven wrote that Welles was acutely aware that "any misstep could have serious repercussions on the efficiency of the blockade."[21]

On November 30 Welles wrote Wilkes that "your conduct in seizing these public enemies was marked by intelligence, ability, decision, and firmness, and has the emphatic approval of this Department."[22] Welles noted later that "the letter was acceptable to all parties—the Administration, the country, and even Wilkes."[23] If Lincoln approved this letter, he was thinking mainly of domestic rather than British reactions.

The next week the first regular session of the Thirty-seventh Congress began. On the first day, December 2, there were numerous eulogies of Wilkes, and the House passed a resolution praising him "for his brave, adroit, and patriotic conduct."[24] Lord Lyons thought the president's wisest course would be to say nothing about the *Trent* in his annual message to Congress "so as to leave himself free to act when the views of Her Majesty's Government are known."[25] Lincoln came to the same conclusion. The message contained only a few generalizations about foreign relations; there was no reference to the *Trent* and no specific reference to relations with Britain.

> The disloyal citizens of the United States who have offered the ruin of our country in return for the aid and comfort which they have invoked abroad, have received less patronage and encouragement than they probably expected. . . . [The European nations] can scarcely have failed to perceive that . . . one strong nation promises more durable peace and a more extensive, valuable, and reliable commerce than can the same nation broken into hostile fragments. . . . I venture to hope it will appear that we have practiced prudence and liberality toward foreign powers, averting causes of irritation, and with firmness maintaining our own rights and honor.[26]

On December 4 Lincoln told a visiting British official from Canada, Alexander Galt, that he did not want any quarrel with England and had no hostile designs on Canada. When Galt asked about the *Trent* incident, Lincoln replied, "Oh, that'll be got along with." Galt thought "the American government is so subject to popular impulses that no assurance . . . ought to be relied on under present circumstances."[27] Two days later Lincoln told Senator Orville Browning that he understood that the seizure of Mason and Slidell was justified by international law and should therefore not cause any serious trouble with England.[28]

℘   ℘   ℘

Rumors of a Union effort to seize the Confederate envoys reached England nearly three weeks before the news that they had been seized in the Bahama Channel. By November 6 the *James Adger*, the Union ship that had been ordered to capture Mason and Slidell if they were on the *Nashville*, arrived in Southampton. There her captain, J. B. Marchand, read in *The Times* that Mason and Slidell had landed in Cuba. He concluded that the envoys were not on the *Nashville* and prepared to return to the United States. Marchand told a British naval officer that he had been ordered to intercept Mason and Slidell. By then word had reached London that Mason and Slidell were en route to England on a British mail packet. Rumors soon spread in London—as the Confederate commissioners reported—that Marchand had been ordered "to seize Mason and Slidell wherever he could find them at sea and that he expected to take them out of the West Indian mail packet."[29]

On November 9 the Foreign Office asked the three "Law Officers of the Crown"—the queen's advocate, the attorney general, and the solicitor general—for an urgent advisory opinion on the right of a U.S. warship to seize Confederate envoys traveling on a neutral ship. On the eleventh Palmerston met with the Law Officers, the lord chancellor, and a judge of the High Court of Admiralty.[30] In a note to the editor of *The Times*, Palmerston said he had been advised that "a belligerent has a right to stop and search any neutral ship . . . suspected of carrying enemy despatches, and consequently the American cruisers might . . . stop the West Indian packet, search her, and if the Southern men and their despatches and credentials were found on board, either take them out, or seize the packet and carry her back to New York for trial."[31]

Nevertheless, on November 12 Palmerston called in Adams and informed him that the British would be greatly offended by the removal of the Confederate envoys from a British ship. Adams replied that Marchand's orders were limited to taking the envoys from a Confederate ship. Palmerston wrote the queen that Adams had said Marchand had been ordered "not to meddle with any ship under a foreign flag," although Adams only said the orders contained no reference to the possibility that the envoys might be on a foreign ship. The note to the queen said international law allowed a belligerent to stop and search any neutral merchant ship "if there is reasonable suspicion that she is carrying the enemy's despatches, and if such are found on board to take her to a port of the belligerent, and there to proceed against her for condemnation."[32]

The subsequent British protest was based on Lieutenant Fairfax's failure to find Confederate dispatches on the *Trent* and Captain Wilkes's decision not to take the ship to a prize court. John Bigelow noted the irony that "our offense had been less if it had been greater.

The wrong done to the British flag would have been mitigated, if, instead of seizing the four rebels, we had seized the ship, detained all her passengers for weeks, and confiscated her cargo."[33]

The news of Wilkes's seizure of Mason and Slidell reached England on November 25, when Commander Williams and Slidell's family arrived on the *La Plata*. Williams submitted a report to the Admiralty on the seizure of the envoys. Accounts of the incident were published in London newspapers on November 27. Adams, a guest at a country house that weekend, hurried back to London but could say very little because he had no idea whether Wilkes had acted on instructions from the U.S. government.

The Times reported on November 30 that Lieutenant Fairfax had said on board the *Trent* that Wilkes was acting without instructions. But Palmerston and his cabinet, conditioned by Lyons's negative reports about Seward's intentions, were ready to believe that Wilkes's action might be part of a deliberate plan to provoke a war with England.[34]

A number of editorials in the British press asserted that Seward was eager for a war with Britain. The one in the *Morning Chronicle* appeared on November 28, the day before the cabinet acted:

> Abraham Lincoln . . . has proved himself a feeble confused, and little minded mediocrity. Mr. Seward, the firebrand at his elbow, is exerting himself to provoke a quarrel with all Europe, in that spirit of senseless egotism that induces the Americans, with their dwarf fleet and shapeless mass of incoherent squads they call an army, to fancy themselves the equals of France by land and of Great Britain by sea. If the Federal states could be rid of these two mischief-makers, it might yet redeem itself in the sight of the world.[35]

Several historians have speculated that, if efforts to lay a transatlantic cable in the 1850s had been successful and the public in Britain and America had learned quickly of the initial reactions to the incident on the *Trent* in the other country, Wilkes's action would have led to war between the two countries. Due to the absence of a cable, according to this view, there was time for sober reflection in both countries on the consequences of such a war. Yet a single telegram from Washington, informing the British that Wilkes had acted on his own, would have eliminated weeks of tension and uncertainty in Britain and totally changed the British perspective on the *Trent* incident.

Even without a transatlantic cable, if Seward had written promptly to inform Adams that Wilkes had acted without authorization, that fact would have reached London only a few days after news of the incident. But this important information was not sent to Adams until November 30 and did not reach him until December 17, three weeks after news of the incident on the *Trent* reached London. Charles Francis Adams Jr. described later the awful uncertainty of those three weeks:

> The natural inference was that Captain Wilkes had acted under instructions. . . . It was hardy conceivable . . . that a naval officer . . . should, out of his own head and acting on newspaper information, venture on such a performance. . . . But if the Wilkes seizure had been directed from Washington, the first and natural conclusion of Mr. Adams would be that it was in furtherance of the aggressive policy outlined in Secretary Seward's dispatches of April 27th and May 21st, and that a foreign war was to be provoked. Under such circumstances, . . . the chief thing for a diplomatic agent to guard against was any hasty action or ill-considered utterance. He could safely infer nothing, assume nothing, imagine nothing. He must possess his soul in patience, be enigmatical—and wait.[36]

If his father were to see Russell coming up the street, Henry Adams wrote to his brother, "he'd run as fast as he could down the nearest alley."[37]

Palmerston was determined to make a very strong protest against an insult to the British flag, even at the risk of war with the United States. "Where he felt British prestige was involved," a British historian noted, Palmerston was quick to "hurl thunderbolts" at the offending nation.[38] Adams commented later that "the one great dread of the prime minister, as regards American affairs, is that of appearing to be bullied. It inspired his whole course of action . . . in the *Trent* case."[39]

The Law Officers were consulted again, and now advised that the *Trent* had not violated international law by carrying the envoys and that their removal by Wilkes was clearly illegal. Russell began drafting a note protesting the seizure and demanding an apology and the release of the diplomats. Cabinet members were summoned from their country estates to meet on the afternoon of November 29. Adams was asked to come to the Foreign Office just before the cabinet meeting, but all he could do was to reiterate his statement to Palmerston on November 12 that the orders to Captain Marchand had been limited to removing the envoys from a Confederate ship.

The cabinet decided to demand an apology and the release of the envoys and to break off diplomatic relations if a satisfactory response was not received in a week after the protest was delivered. Drafts of two dispatches to Lyons were reviewed by the cabinet on the afternoon of November 30. William Gladstone, Chancellor of the Exchequer, wrote to the absent Argyll that he had "urged that we should hear what the Americans had to say before withdrawing Lyons . . . But this view did not prevail."[40] Gladstone recorded that Russell's drafts were "softened and abridged."[41]

That evening Palmerston sent the revised drafts to the queen with a note stating that the cabinet had concluded that "a gross outrage and violation of international law has been committed and that your Majesty should be advised to demand reparation and redress." Palmerston informed the queen that, according to Slidell's wife, the U.S. officers who had boarded the *Trent* said they were acting without instructions from Washington. But he also described rumors that General Scott, recently arrived in Paris, had said the seizure of the envoys had been authorized by the cabinet in Washington and that he had been sent to Paris to seek the participation of France in a war against England.[42]

Early the next morning Prince Albert, even then stricken with the typhoid that would end his life only two weeks later, found the strength to draft a royal note to the prime minister:

The Queen . . . should have liked to have seen the expression of a hope that the American captain did not act under instructions, or, if he did, that he misapprehended them [and] that the United States Government must be fully aware that the British Government could not allow its flag to be insulted, and the security of her mail communications to be placed in jeopardy, and [that] Her Majesty's Government are unwilling to believe that the United States Government intended wantonly to put an insult upon this country and to add to their many distressing complications by forcing a question of dispute upon us, and that we are therefore glad to believe . . . that they would spontaneously offer such redress as alone could satisfy this country, viz: the restoration of the unfortunate passengers and a suitable apology.[43]

These royal suggestions were quickly included in the primary dispatch to Lyons. A queen's messenger carrying the dispatches was aboard the *Europa* when it sailed for New York on the evening of December 1.

The British government's decision to demand an apology and the release of the envoys had been made before any information reached Britain regarding the reaction of the American public or government to the incident on the *Trent*. Two days after the British note was sent, the British papers carried extensive accounts from the American press of the strong support for Wilkes's action by the public in the North. Rumors of war preparations in the United States were sparked by the news that General Scott would return immediately to the United States. Scott had decided on his own to return, but it was rumored that he had been summoned by a U.S. government preparing for war.

On December 4 *The Times* carried the first report on the *Trent* affair from its correspondent in Washington. W. H. Russell reported that public sentiment in support of Wilkes was so strong that Lincoln and Seward would be unable to make any concession to the British. "There is so much violence of spirit among the lower orders of the people," Russell wrote in a letter published on December 10, "and they are . . . so saturated with pride and vanity that any honorable concession . . . would prove fatal to its authors."[44]

The same ship that brought correspondent Russell's first story brought Lord Lyons's first reaction to the *Trent* incident. He thought Americans generally regarded Wilkes's action as "a direct insult to the British flag" and that most of them welcomed it as such. Lyons recommended a show of British strength, including the sending of reinforcements to Canada.[45] An abstract of Lyons's dispatch was sent to each cabinet member.

In a private letter to Russell, Lyons wrote that he had been "told confidentially that orders were given in Washington, which led to the capture on board the *Trent*, and that they were signed by Seward without the knowledge of the President."[46] Although he admitted that he could not "vouch for the truth" of this statement, the transmittal of such a report without indicating its source or evaluating the probability of its being accurate was highly irresponsible.

The idea that Lincoln or Seward, already engaged in a great civil war at home, would foment or welcome a war with Britain was illogical and ridiculous. One of the few voices of reason was that of John Bright, who spoke at Rochdale on December 4:

> Our great adviser, the *Times* newspaper, has been persuading the people that this is but one of a series of acts which denote the determination of the Washington government to pick a quarrel with the people of England. Do you believe that the United States Government . . . having upon its hands now an insurrection of the most formidable character in the South, would invite the armies and fleets of England to combine with that insurrection and . . . render it impossible that the Union should ever be restored?[47]

By December 6 Adams expected that the *Trent* incident would lead to a rupture of diplomatic relations:

> The current of popular feeling is still running with resistless force throughout this Kingdom. . . . [There is] an almost universal demand for satisfaction for the insult and injury thought to be endured by the action of Captain Wilkes. . . . The members of the Government as a whole are believed not to be desirous of pressing matters to a violent issue, but they are powerless in the face of the opinion they have invited from the Law Officers of the Crown. . . . The passions of the country are up and a collision is inevitable if the Government of the United States should, before the news reaches the other side, have assumed the position of Captain Wilkes in a manner to preclude the possibility of explanation. . . . Ministers and people now fully believe it is the intention of the [U.S.] Government to drive them into hostilities. . . . My present expectation is that by

the middle of January at furthest diplomatic relations will have been sundered between the two countries.[48]

This pessimistic message was the last dispatch from Adams that was received in Washington before Lincoln and his cabinet had to decide whether to release the Confederate envoys.

Palmerston had long feared that someday the United States would find an excuse for the invasion and annexation of additional territory in Canada, as it had done in Mexico in the 1840s. The colonial secretary, the duke of Newcastle, had the primary responsibility for Canada. He had escorted the Prince of Wales to America in 1860, and it was to him that Seward has made his much-misunderstood comment about his plans to "insult" England. Various versions of Seward's alleged remarks circulated in London. *The Times* reported that Seward had said "that he was likely to occupy high office [and] it would become his duty to insult England." According to the *Chronicle*, Seward said "Either Mr. Lincoln or myself will be the next president of the United States. If Mr. Lincoln is chosen, I shall be secretary, and we are determined to take the first opportunity that presents itself to insult your country." Yet Seward had met Newcastle in the fall of 1860, when Lincoln had already been nominated as president but Seward had no idea that he would be named secretary of state.[49]

Seward's friend Thurlow Weed wrote him on December 5 from London that "the Duke of Newcastle is reported to say that Seward told him in America that we should have to fight England in a year or two."[50] "The impression is general," Adams wrote his son on December 20, "that Mr. Seward is resolved to insult England until she makes a war. . . . They quote what he said to the Duke of Newcastle about insulting England . . . and a part of a speech in which he talked of annexing Canada as an offset to the loss of the slave states. This is evidence that Mr. Seward is an ogre fully resolved to eat all Englishmen raw."[51] Adams thought the idea that Seward wanted a war with Britain was "a mistake founded on a bad joke of his to the Duke of Newcastle [who] has however succeeded in making everybody in authority here believe it."[52]

Newcastle advised Lewis to rush additional British regiments to Canada before the Saint Lawrence River froze for the winter. The secretary of war wrote a friend on December 10 that "we are making preparations on the assumption that there is to be a war."[53] During December the British government sent over eleven thousand men to Canada on eighteen transports.[54] Newcastle told the new British governor general in Canada, Lord Monch, that as soon as he heard that Lyons had left Washington he should call out the Canadian militia without waiting for instructions from London. Military planners recommended the seizure of Portland, Maine, to forestall an American attack on the terminus of Canada's most important railway, the Grand Trunk line.[55] The first lord of the Admiralty, the duke of Somerset, began planning a possible British blockade of the northeastern U.S. coast.[56]

On December 12 Adams reported that there was intense speculation in Britain on the consequences of a U.S. refusal to release the envoys:

> The impression is very fixed that it is the policy both of the administration and of the people of the United States to make unreasonable demands of this country. . . . It is considered absolutely necessary by a vigorous demonstration to inspire a conviction among us that it will not be trifled with. . . . Much speculation is indulged in as to the policy that will be adopted in case [the U.S. answer] should be unfavorable. Some think it will be a declaration of war. The better opinion is that it will be a recognition of the Confederates and a refusal further to abide by the blockade as ineffective.[57]

Suddenly, on December 14, the attention of the British nation was diverted by the death of Prince Albert, beloved husband of Queen Victoria. Adams thought the prince's death increased British fears of a foreign war: "It is felt rather than uttered that there is no really wise head now in England to guide in case of a storm."[58]

"If the answer [from America] is reasoning and not a blunt and offensive answer," Russell wrote Palmerston on December 16, "we should send once more across the Atlantic to ask compliance. . . . I do not think the country would approve an immediate declaration of war. But I think we must abide by our demand for the restoration of the prisoners."[59] The same day the British public was astonished to learn that Lincoln's annual message to the Congress had contained no reference to the *Trent* affair, that Congress had passed a resolution approving Wilkes's action, and that Welles had written a letter to Wilkes indicating approval of his seizure of the envoys.

The next day, December 17, Adams received Seward's November 30 dispatch indicating that Wilkes had acted without instructions. He immediately informed Russell, who seemed cheered by the news but was nevertheless determined to wait for the reaction from Washington to the British protest. In the next few days there were stories in the press that Seward had said Wilkes had acted on his own, but there was no confirmation of this fact by Russell. "How came it that this despatch," John Bright asked later in Parliament, "was never published for the information of the people of this country?"[60] Adams thought Palmerston had not wanted the dispatch to be released because it would "disarm him in his policy of browbeating America."[61]

The initial reactions of the British public and government to the incident on the *Trent* were mainly influenced by national pride. But other factors, reviewed by Donaldson Jordan and Edwin Pratt, were restraining the war fever:

> Intervention in the character of an angry belligerent suddenly siding with the slave states presented moral objections to which nine out of ten men were sensitive. . . . Economic motives were at this time preponderantly discouraging to the war fever. The business community of Liverpool, the center for cotton importation, appeared to pass into spasms of belligerency, yet . . . a good deal of it was due to the desire of speculators to raise cotton prices. . . . Heavy investments in American railway and other securities were held in the Manchester region, and a prolonged war would destroy their value. . . . England had been importing far more . . . American grain, flour, and provisions than ever before, and . . . the cutting-off of this supply was not to be lightly envisaged.[62]

ℰ⅋   ℰ⅋   ℰ⅋

The first news that the British government would demand an apology and insist on the release of the Confederate envoys was received in Washington on Sunday, December 15. Senator Orville Browning was visiting his friend the president: "Mr. Seward came in with dispatches stating that the British cabinet had decided that the arrest of Mason and Slidell was a violation of international law, and that we must apologize and restore them to the protection of the British flag." Browning said that if Britain "is determined to force a war upon us, so be it. We will fight her to the death."[63]

At a ball given the next evening by the Brazilian minister, Seward talked freely to guests including W. H. Russell of *The Times* about the terrible consequences of a war forced on the United States by Britain. "We will wrap the whole world in flames," he exclaimed. Russell thought Seward "means to show fight" but one of the guests explained that when Seward talked tough, he was usually preparing to make a concession.[64]

"I think there is a disposition here," correspondent Russell wrote to a colleague on November 17, "to back down if they can and give up the men sooner than have a foreign war on their hands." That evening he dined at Seward's. The correspondent wrote to his editor that Seward was "in very good humor and said everything consistent with the honor of the U.S. would be done to make England feel the U.S. did not mean to hurt her feelings or injure her prestige."[65] But Russell added that all the foreign diplomats in Washington thought the prisoners would not be given up: "In that case Lord Lyons and the legation will retire from Washington for the time."[66]

On Wednesday evening, December 18, nearly six weeks after Wilkes stopped the *Trent*, Lyons received Lord Russell's November 30 dispatches concerning the *Trent* affair. The primary dispatch described the removal of the envoys from the Trent as "an act of violence which was an affront to the British flag and a violation of international law." But the dispatch also included a paragraph very similar to the royal suggestions drafted by Prince Albert:

> Her Majesty's Government, bearing in mind the friendly relations which have long subsisted between Great Britain and the United States, are willing to believe that the U.S. naval officer who committed the aggression was not acting in compliance with any authority from his Government, or that if he conceived himself to be so authorized he greatly misunderstood the instructions which he had received. . . . The Government of the United States must be fully aware that the British

Government could not allow such an affront to the national honor to pass without full reparation, and her Majesty's Government are unwilling to believe that it could be the deliberate intention of the Government of the United States unnecessarily to force into discussion between the two governments a question of so grave a character and with regard to which the whole British nation would be sure to entertain such unanimity of feeling.[67]

The dispatch ended with a statement that the only action that would satisfy the British nation would be the release of the envoys and a suitable apology.

In a separate official dispatch, Lyons was instructed to wait for only seven days for a reply and, if compliance with the British demands was not forthcoming, to then depart for London with his staff and archives. This timetable was somewhat stretched, however, by instructions in a private letter from Russell. Lyons was told to brief Seward informally of the British demands and then allow a few days before the official delivery of the dispatch and the beginning of the seven-day period allowed for response.[68]

Lyons called on Seward on Thursday afternoon, December 19. Lyons made it clear "that the only redress which could satisfy Her Majesty's Government and Her Majesty's people would be the immediate delivery of the prisoners to me . . . and moreover a suitable apology for the aggression which had been committed."[69] Seward asked if there was a deadline for a response. Lyons told him "privately and confidentially" that he had seven days from the official delivery of Russell's dispatch. Seward asked for an unofficial copy of the dispatch; Lyons sent his private secretary to the State Department that evening with a copy. Seward agreed to meet Lyons again on Saturday for the official presentation of the dispatch.[70]

The British demands cost Lincoln several sleepless nights. "I lay awake all night," he told James R. Gilmore, "contriving how to get out of the scrape without loss of national dignity."[71] "I am not getting much sleep out of that exploit of Wilkes," he remarked to Attorney General Bates. "I am not much of a prize lawyer, but it seems to me pretty clear that . . . Wilkes . . . had no right to turn his quarter-deck into a prize court."[72]

John Bright had suggested international arbitration of the dispute in a December 6 letter to Senator Sumner.[73] The senator suggested to Lincoln that the issue be submitted to international arbitration by "the sovereign of Prussia or a group of learned publicists." Seward was now convinced that the United States had to give up the envoys or face a war with England. Lincoln told him to prepare the reply he thought should be sent to Lyons, while he would prepare a draft suggesting arbitration.

Lincoln had written a partial draft by Saturday, when he read it to Senator Browning.[74] It began with statements that "this government has intended no affront to the British flag or to the British nation" and that "the act complained of was done by the officer without orders from or expectation of the government." He noted that "we too, as well as Great Britain, have a people justly jealous of their rights, and in whose presence our government could undo the act complained of only upon a fair showing that it was wrong or, at least, very questionable. The United States government and people are still willing to make reparation upon such a showing." He listed a number of aspects of the case which should be submitted to "friendly arbitration." These included "the position Great Britain has assumed, including Her Majesty's proclamation" and "the knowledge which the master of the *Trent* had of . . . the object of [the envoys'] voyage, at the time he received them on board."[75]

Lincoln was searching for a way to avoid a politically hazardous decision to release the envoys, but international arbitration did not offer an escape from his dilemma. Arbitration was normally used to resolve boundary disputes and financial claims that were suitable for disinterested adjudication by a neutral arbitrator. The arbitration process was ill suited for the resolution of conflicts in which either side thought its national honor was threatened. Russell sharply censured the British minister in Russia, Lord Napier, for failing to reject the idea of arbitration in the *Trent* case when it was mentioned by Russian officials. He asserted that "either our flag must protect those who are traveling from a neutral port to a neutral port under its shelter, or the flag of Great Britain must be dishonoured" and that it had been agreed at the maritime conference in Paris in 1856 that "on questions of national honour, arbitration was inadmissable."[76]

Seward asked Lyons on Saturday to delay the official presentation of the British note until Monday, December 23. Lyons agreed to wait until Monday morning, which would allow him to inform Russell via the packet sailing on Tuesday from New York that the British protest had been officially delivered.[77]

On Sunday, Senator Sumner outlined for the president the probable consequences of a war with England:

> (1) instant acknowledgment of the rebel states by England, followed by France; (2) breaking of present blockade, with capture of our fleet; (3) the blockade of our coasts from Chesapeake to Eastport; (4) the sponging of our ships from the ocean; (5) the establishment of the independence of the rebel states; (6) opening of these states by free trade to English manufacturers, . . . making the whole North American continent a manufacturing dependency of England.[78]

Lincoln's response was that "there will be no war unless England is bent upon having one."[79]

After the official delivery of the British note on Monday morning, the United States government had only the seven days of Christmas week to prepare its response. "You will perhaps be surprised to find Mr. Seward on the side of peace," Lyons wrote to Russell that afternoon. "He knows his countrymen well enough to believe that if he can convince them that there is a real danger of war, they may forgive him for the humiliation of yielding to England, while it would be fatal to him to be the author of a disastrous foreign war."[80]

Seward's draft reply to the British note was discussed in a cabinet meeting on Christmas Day. "Seward studied up all the works ever written on international law," Lincoln recalled three years later, "and came to cabinet meetings loaded up to the muzzle on the subject."[81] Lincoln did not submit his draft proposing international arbitration. When Seward asked about it, Lincoln replied, "I found I could not make an argument that would satisfy my own mind, and that proved to me that your ground was the right one."[82]

Seward's draft began with statements that the right to search neutral merchant vessels for contraband was well established in international law, that the enemy envoys had been properly considered contraband, that Wilkes had conducted the search in a proper manner, and that he had a right to capture the contraband (the envoys). The central difficulty of the case arose from Wilkes's release of the *Trent* after the removal of Mason and Slidell. International law required that a neutral ship found to be carrying contraband be brought to a port and that the case against her be prosecuted in a court. Seward pointed out that, in objecting to the seizure of persons from a neutral ship without a proper legal process, the British government was accepting a cherished American principle for which the United States had fought the War of 1812 with Britain: "We are asked to do to the British nation just what we have always insisted all nations ought to do to us."[83]

During the cabinet meeting, the French legation sent in a dispatch that had just arrived from the French foreign minister that urged the United States to release the prisoners. Senator Sumner, who had been invited to attend the meeting, read letters from Cobden and Bright. Lincoln and his cabinet were impressed by Bright's chilling words:

> Our government is often driven along by the force of the genteel and aristocratic mob which it mainly represents. . . . I conclude this government is ready for war if an excuse can be found. . . . At a certain point the moderate opinion of a country is borne down by the passion which arises and which takes the name of patriotism. . . . The good men here who abhor war may have no influence if a blow is at once struck.[84]

Two cabinet members recorded their reactions in their diaries. Attorney General Edward Bates focused on the consequences of a refusal to release the envoys:

> I . . . urged that to go to war with England is to abandon all hope of suppressing the rebellion. . . . The maritime superiority of Britain would sweep us from the Southern waters. Our trade would be utterly ruined and our treasury bankrupt. In short, . . . we *must not* have war with England. There was great reluctance on the part of some of the members of the cabinet—and even the President himself—to acknowledge these obvious truths; but all yielded to the necessity and unanimously concurred in Mr. Seward's letter to Lord Lyons after some verbal and formal amendments. The main fear . . . was the displeasure

of our own people—lest they should accuse us of timidly truckling to the power of England.[85]

Secretary of the Treasury Salmon P. Chase recorded that he had reluctantly supported Seward's conclusions:

It is gall and wormwood to me. But I am consoled by the reflection that . . . the surrender under existing circumstances is . . . simply giving the most signal proof that the American nation will not, under any circumstances . . . commit even a technical wrong against neutrals.[86]

Lincoln's only recorded comment on the decision to release the envoys was made to General Grant and others early in 1865. His words were recalled by Horace Porter in 1897:

We gave due consideration to the case but at that critical period of the war it was soon decided to deliver up the prisoners. It was a pretty bitter pill to swallow, but I contented myself with believing that England's triumph in the matter would be short-lived, and that after ending our war successfully we would be so powerful that we could call her to account for the embarrassments she had inflicted on us.[87]

"The President is naturally and instinctively for peace," Senator Sumner wrote Richard Cobden. "He covets kindly relations with all the world, especially with England." Sumner told the president that it was important to break down British mistrust of his administration. "He said at once with perfect simplicity: 'I never see Lord Lyons. If it were proper I should like to talk with him that he might hear from my lips how much I desire Peace. If we could talk together, he would believe me.' "[88] But Lincoln did not talk to Lyons, and the British minister continued to misjudge both the president's intentions and the extent of his participation in determining U.S. foreign policy.

Seward's note was approved in another cabinet meeting on December 26. Lyons was informed that the "four persons" in custody at Fort Warren would be released. On the first day of 1862 Mason and Slidell and their secretaries were taken on a tug to Provincetown, on Cape

Cod, where they were transferred to a British warship, the *Rinaldo*. The ship headed for Halifax, where the envoys could get a steamer to England. But a terrible winter storm covered the ship with ice and forced the captain to go first to Bermuda and then to Saint Thomas, their original destination on the *Trent* in November. There they embarked on a West Indian mail steamer and arrived in London on January 29, nearly three months after leaving Charleston.

A short message from Lyons, anouncing the release of the envoys, was sent to Halifax by telegram and then to London by ship. It arrived on January 7. Lyons's dispatch with Seward's note arrived in London on January 9. The news was announced that night at London theaters, and audiences stood and cheered. The government, monarch, and public of Britain were very relieved by the end of the *Trent* crisis. Russell wrote Lyons that Seward's note and the release of the envoys constituted "the reparation which her Majesty and the British nation had a right to expect."[89] The relief of thoughtful Englishmen at the resolution of the crisis was reflected in an article in February 1862 by the renowned economist, John Stuart Mill:

> The cloud which for the space of a month hung gloomily over the civilized world, black with far worse evils than those of simple war, has passed from over our heads without bursting. . . . [A war with the United States] would have been a war in alliance with, and, to practical purposes, in defence and propagation of slavery. . . . We, the emancipators of the slave, who have wearied every Court and Government in Europe and America with our protests and remonstrances until we goaded them into at least ostensibly cooperating with us to prevent the enslaving of the negro . . . should have helped to give a place in the community of nations to a conspiracy of slave-owners. . . . Every reader of a newspaper . . . would have believed . . . that . . . at the dawn of a hope that the demon might now at last be chained and flung into the pit, England stepped in, and for the sake of cotton, made Satan victorious. The world has been saved from this calamity, and England from this disgrace.[90]

Adams noted in his diary, "I am to remain in this purgatory a while longer."[91]

Seward was very pleased by the reactions of other governments to the decision to release the envoys. He wrote to the Italian minister that the decision showed U.S. devotion to freedom of commerce:

This government, after a full examination of the subject, decided that it could not detain the persons taken from the *Trent* by Captain Wilkes without disavowing its own liberal interpretations of the law of maritime war. . . . The accidental circumstance [gave] it an opportunity to show the same devotion to the freedom of commerce as a belligerent that it had always before manifested as an interested neutral power. If at any time the government had entertained doubts of the wisdom of its proceeding in the case, they would all now disappear at once before the congratulations which it is receiving from the most generous and enlightened nations that have been passionless observers of the transaction.[92]

The Confederates had not been passionless observers of the *Trent* affair. They had been sure that Wilkes's act would lead to a war between Britain and the United States that would be very advantageous to the Confederacy. The mix of misinformation and wishful thinking that influenced Confederate reactions was reflected in the comments of the *Examiner* in Richmond in late December:

The Palmerston cabinet has been forced to immediate and decisive measures. . . . The Abolitionist element of the Northern States would go straight to revolution at the least movement toward a surrender of the captives. The arrest was made by the deliberately written orders of the Government, already avowed and published beyond the hope of apology or possibility of retraction. . . . The United States can do absolutely nothing but refuse the demands of Great Britain and abide the consequences of the refusal.[93]

General Robert E. Lee was one of the very few Confederates who had foreseen that Lincoln would give up the Confederate envoys. "You must not build up your hopes on peace on account of the United States going to war with England," he wrote his wife on Christmas Day. "Her rulers are not entirely mad, and if they find England is in earnest, and that war or a restitution of their captives must be the consequence, they will adopt the latter. We must make up our minds to fight our battles and win our independence alone. No one will help us. We require no extraneous aid, if true to ourselves."[94]

But most Confederate leaders were surprised and bitterly disappointed that Lincoln and Seward had released the envoys and resolved the crisis with Britain. An early biographer of Jefferson Davis, Frank H. Alfriend, wrote that the release of Mason and Slidell "was one of the first of numerous disappointments in store for the Southern people in the hope, so universally indulged, of foreign intevention."[95]

CHAPTER 6

Cotton Is King

Cotton in Confederate Diplomacy, Trade, and Finance

In 1860 the American South had nearly a world monopoly on the production of cotton. The Southern climate and soils were ideally suited to cotton, which requires abundant spring rain, warm and drier conditions for maturing the plant, and clear dry weather during harvest. Slaves provided the abundant labor needed for cultivation and harvesting. Southern rivers provided easy and inexpensive transportation of the cotton to Southern ports. The short staple upland cotton grown in the South was well suited to the machinery in use in mills in Britain and New England.[1]

Although the climate and soils were suitable for cotton production in a number of areas in Asia, Africa, and South America, the only other substantial cotton producer was eastern India. American cotton was better, cheaper, and more abundantly available than Indian cotton. Because of the short fibers and high dust content of the Indian product, the same machines made 10 to 20 percent less yarn from Indian cotton than from American cotton. Cloth from Indian cotton tended to be thinner, with a less satisfactory finish. The land tenure system in India limited the incentives of the peasants to increase productivity. Few navigable streams penetrated into cotton-producing areas. Despite major efforts to expand Indian exports of cotton to Britain, these exports increased by only about 20 percent between 1800 and 1859.[2] By the late 1850s cotton goods accounted for more than half of the value of British exports. Annual British cotton imports from America averaged nearly two million bales and provided 75 to 80 percent of the cotton used in British mills.[3]

Confederate leaders were convinced that Europe could never get along without Confederate cotton and that Britain and France would be forced to recognize and support the Confederacy in order to protect their vital supply of cotton. In his inaugural address on February 18, 1861, Jefferson Davis warned Europeans that Confederate cotton was "required" by Britain and other manufacturing countries and that any Union attempt to interfere with cotton exports to Europe would be severely detrimental to European manufacturing and commerce.[4] W. H. Russell reported to *The Times* from Montgomery in the spring of 1861 that Southerners "believe in the irresistible power of Cotton to force England to intervene. . . . The doctrine of 'cotton is king' to them is a lively, all powerful faith without distracting heresies or schisms."[5]

When the Civil War began in April 1861, most of the bumper 1860 crop had already been exported. The only way to accelerate the arrival of a diplomatically useful "cotton famine" in Europe was to restrict cotton exports from the Confederacy in 1861 and 1862. From the summer of 1861 to the spring of 1862 many Southern leaders—including local politicians, merchants, newspaper editors, and planters—cooperated in a massive voluntary effort to prevent additional Southern cotton from reaching Europe. Cotton planting was severely reduced, and many cotton bales were burned to prevent them from falling into the hands of blockade runners or Yankee invaders.

The embargo was never officially sanctioned by the Confederate government, which did not want to admit that the Confederacy was trying to blackmail European governments to obtain recognition. Confederate diplomats denied the existence of an embargo and attempted to blame the growing cotton shortage in Europe entirely on the Union blockade. Confederate Secretary of State Benjamin wrote on April 8, 1862, that "the suggestion so artfully insinuated by Northern agents that cotton is kept back for the purpose of coercing foreign powers into any particular line of policy can scarcely find credence."[6] But Jefferson Davis and his cabinet firmly believed that the embargo would ultimately convince European governments to recognize and support the Confederacy.

Ironically, the cotton embargo was in effect during a period in which the Union blockade was not yet very effective. Since there was little cotton to be shipped, few English vessels visited Confederate ports in the fall and winter of 1861–62. By the time the Confederate leaders realized that they must export cotton in order to pay for arms and supplies from Europe, the blockade had been tightened and ships carrying cotton were more vulnerable to capture by Union blockaders.

During the winter of 1861–62 Seward assured Britain and France that a significant volume of cotton would soon be exported to Europe through Confederate ports captured by Union forces. Lincoln thought that the United States should "show the world we were fair in this matter, favoring outsiders as much as ourselves." Although he was "by no means sure that [the planters] would bring their cotton to the port after we opened it, it would be well to show Europe that it was secession that distressed them and not we."[7] The Confederates soon demonstrated that they would rather burn their cotton than allow it to fall into Yankee hands. The French consul estimated that about a quarter of a million bales were burned at New Orleans just prior to its capture by Union forces in April 1862.[8] In August of that year the British consul in Charleston estimated that "about 1,000,000 bales have been destroyed at various places to prevent their falling into the hands of the Federals."[9]

The unsuccessful Union effort to promote cotton exports through captured Confederate ports was described in a pamphlet published in England in 1862:

No sooner did the Government succeed in regaining possession of . . . cotton markets, than it made provision for reopening of the cotton trade. The blockade . . . was removed from the ports of Beaufort in North Carolina, Port Royal in South Carolina, and New Orleans in Louisiana on the 12th of May 1862. Cotton agents accompanied the armies of the North, who were licensed to purchase cotton. . . . The United States Government assured the British government of their anxiety to grant every facility for the obtaining of cotton, and gave the rebels every facility to sell it. But the result has been what? Simply an order from Jefferson Davis to burn the cotton to starve the English.[10]

In fact, during 1862 the cotton embargo had been abandoned and the Confederate government had become very interested in exports of cotton through the blockade as a means of paying for the arms, ammunition, and supplies needed for the Confederate war effort and for supplies for the civilian economy. But throughout the war Confederates continued to burn cotton to prevent it from being used in Northern cotton mills or exported to Europe by Union merchants.

℘   ℘   ℘

When the Union blockade began, English and French warehouses held a great surplus of cotton. British mills had been producing more goods than they could sell, and inventories of cotton products were high. Shipments from the 1860 crop continued during much of 1861, while neither the Union blockade nor the Confederate embargo was very effective, and total shipments reaching Europe that year were only 8 percent smaller than in 1860.

But in 1862 the cotton famine finally hit Europe. The cotton crop in the South was only about a half million bales in 1862, compared to a normal crop of 4 to 5 million bales. The number of Union ships blockading Confederate ports increased, although the number of blockade runners also grew. Very little American cotton reached Europe in the first half of 1862, and only seventy thousand bales arrived in the second half.[11]

The cotton shortage caused severe hardships in the textile manufacturing area in Britain, in several French textile towns, and in a few other places in Europe where textiles were produced. As cotton supplies dwindled, mills reduced or ceased operations. The number of persons in Britain made destitute by the cotton shortage rose to nearly 2 million by December 1862.[12]

The British chargé in Washington, William Stuart, pressed Seward in July to allow cotton through the blockade.[13] Lincoln told Senator Browning "that England wanted us to permit her to get $50 million worth of cotton from the South . . . but that we could not let the cotton out without letting its value in, and in this way we could never succeed in crippling them much in their resources."[14]

The unemployment and destitution in the textile areas were major reasons for the serious consideration in Britain and France in the summer and fall of 1862 of some form of intervention in the American conflict (reviewed in chapters 7 and 9). One member of the British cabinet, the earl of Granville, wrote Palmerston in September that the British people had "a strong antipathy for the North, . . . strong sympathy with the South, and the passionate wish to have cotton."[15]

Nevertheless, several factors limited the political and diplomatic impact of the cotton shortage in Britain. Mill workers had no vote and no direct representation in Parliament. The twenty-six members of Parliament from cotton-milling districts represented the interests of mill owners rather than those of workers; they sat silently during discussions of proposals to intervene in America to restore the cotton supply.[16] Due to the geographic concentration of British cotton mills, the main impact of the cotton shortage was on Lancashire. Workers in other areas—notably the major ports and shipbuilding centers—benefited from the increased business generated by the Civil War in America. The British working class as a whole abhorred slavery, opposed recognition of the slaveholding Confederacy, and believed that their hopes for political reform in Britain were tied to victory of the Union in America.

Various segments of the British business community—which was well represented in Parliament—had important economic reasons for preferring the continuation of the war in America. Cotton traders enjoyed the high prices of cotton. Mill owners were not unhappy to eliminate surplus production and sell cotton products at high prices. Producers and processors of wool and flax were delighted by the increased markets and prices for woolens and linens. Shipbuilders and shipowners opposed any move that would risk naval warfare with the United States or curtail the handsome profits they were deriving from the rapidly expanding blockade running system described in chapter 11.

Neither the British government nor the British public was willing to risk war with the United States to obtain cotton. Richard Cobden commented that it would be much cheaper to feed the unemployed in Lancashire on "turtle, champagne, and venison" than to fight a war with the United States.[17]

During 1862 and 1863 Britain and France adjusted to the reduced imports of American cotton through the reduced consumption and export of cotton goods, the increased use of woolens and linen, and substantially increased imports of cotton from other countries, including India, Egypt, and Turkey. For years cotton manufacturers, emancipation societies, and imperialists had hoped for an opportunity to break Britain's dependence on slave-grown cotton from America. The Confederate cotton embargo and the Union blockade gave England a chance to expand cotton production in India. In 1862 Britain imported about 1 million bales from India.[18] In Egypt, the viceroy commanded that one-fourth of the cultivated land be used for cotton production. By late 1862 the annual Egyptian crop was expected to reach the equivalent of 600,000 American bales, although production was inhibited by the competition for labor from the company building the Suez Canal and exports were restricted by inadequate transportation facilities.[19] Cotton production in the area of present-day Turkey, which was only 15,000 bales in 1861, reached nearly 60,000 bales in 1862.[20]

Seward was delighted by the increased cotton production in other countries: "The insurrectionary cotton states will be blind to their own welfare if they do not see how their prosperity and all their hopes are passing away, when they find Egypt, Asia Minor, and India supplying the world with cotton."[21]

In February 1863 James S. Pike, U.S. minister in The Hague, reported that "the equilibrium demand and supply has been reached sooner than was anticipated. . . . England and France have reduced their consumption of raw cotton one-half. . . . The deficient product is made good by reduced consumption and the extra product of wool and flax."[22] Beginning in the second half of 1862, the cotton supply in Europe grew slowly due to increased cotton deliveries from the Confederacy by blockade runners and increased supplies from other countries.[23]

Adams reported in June 1863 that the improvement in the cotton supply had removed the major excuse that had been used by those advocating British intervention in the American conflict: "The aggregate number of operatives needing relief is steadily diminishing from week to week. . . . Another year will find the sources of cotton production so much extended as to place Great Britain in a position free from exclusive dependence on the southern states."[24]

ళ   ళ   ళ

Benjamin had seen the need for cotton exports much sooner than his colleagues in the Confederate leadership. Secretary of War Leroy Walker recalled that at the first meeting of the Confederate cabinet, in the spring of 1861, Benjamin, then attorney general, proposed an immediate, vigorous program to export cotton and import arms: "Mr. Benjamin proposed that the Government purchase as much cotton as it could hold, at least 100,000 bales, and ship it at once to England. With the proceeds of a part of it, he advised the immediate purchase of at least 150,000 stand of small arms, and guns and ammunition." But Benjamin's proposal was rejected by the Confederate cabinet on the ground that the war would not last long enough to implement it.[25]

By the spring of 1862, however, the Confederate leadership had begun to recognize several harsh realities—that its dominant role in world cotton production was crumbling due to increased production in other countries, that Britain and France were not likely to recognize Confederate independence because they feared war with the United States more than reduced cotton imports from America, and that exporting cotton to Europe through blockaded Confederate ports and loans based on future cotton exports were the only means of paying for the large quantities of European arms and supplies the Confederacy needed to maintain its war effort.

In a letter to Slidell on April 3, 1862, Benjamin offered cotton to France at a low price in return for action by the French navy to break the blockade. He offered the French government 100,000 bales of cotton at the price it cost the Confederate government—about nine cents per pound; the French could sell it at the market price in Europe, which Benjamin thought was at least twenty-five cents per pound. "This would represent a grant to France of not less than $12.5 million. . . . Such a sum would maintain afloat a considerable fleet for a length of time quite sufficient to open the Atlantic and Gulf ports to the commerce of France."[26]

Benjamin's offer never had a chance. Due to the tightening blockade, the letter did not reach Slidell until early July. Assuming that the offer would be rejected by the French foreign minister, Edouard Thouvenel, Slidell waited until he could wrangle an interview with

Napoleon III at Vichy. The emperor responded that, although it had been a mistake for France to respect the blockade, it was now too late to correct it; "to open the ports forcibly would be an act of war."[27]

But this offer to France demonstrated that the Confederate government was moving toward a new policy of using the primary Confederate economic asset—cotton—to obtain desperately needed arms and supplies. Although the British and French governments were unwilling to bargain diplomatically for cotton, British merchants and shipowners were eager to realize the combined profits derived from delivering British arms and supplies to the Confederacy and delivering high-priced cotton to Britain.

In addition to the blockade, several other factors inhibited Confederate cotton exports. Cotton production in the Confederacy, which had been severely reduced in 1861 and 1862 by the voluntary cotton embargo, was limited in 1863 and 1864 by the absence of many plantation owners, overseers, and slaves; by the devastation of war; and by the shrinking of the area controlled by the Confederacy. Wartime conditions inhibited the transportation of cotton to the Confederate ports. Very large quantities of cotton were burned to prevent them from being captured by the Yankees. Frank Owsley estimated that during the war 1 to 1.25 million bales of cotton were exported by the Confederacy through the blockade, not including cotton exported through Mexico, but that a large fraction of this cotton ultimately reached cotton mills in the North.[28] James W. Daddysman concluded that about 320,000 bales of cotton were exported to Britain via Mexico between 1861 and 1864.[29] M. B. Hammond estimated that in 1862, 1863, and 1864 England and the Continent received 535,000 bales of Confederate cotton. These estimates and other available data suggest that from 1862 to 1864 Confederate cotton represented less than 10 percent of the cotton deliveries in Europe.[30]

Nevertheless, cotton exports made a major contribution to the Confederate economy and war effort. Lincoln's frustration with the Union's inability to eliminate this trade is indicated in a letter he wrote in December 1864:

> By the external blockade, the [cotton] price is made certainly six times as great as it was. And yet the enemy gets through a least one sixth part

as much in a given period . . . as if there were no blockade, and receives
as much for it as he would for a full crop in time of peace. The effect . . .
is that we give him six ordinary crops, without the trouble of producing any but the first and . . . leave his fields and his laborers free to produce provisions. . . . This keeps up his armies at home, and procures
supplies from abroad.[31]

Those who successfully brought cotton to Europe made very large
profits. In 1863 the Confederate propaganda journal in England, *The
Index*, stated that cotton exports should be reserved for a Confederate
government monopoly so that the profits could be used exclusively to
finance priority imports:

Had the cotton been exported for its own account instead of [by] private speculators, the Confederate government might have dispensed
with foreign loans, might have bought its warlike stores at the lowest
cash rates, and supplied its citizens with commodities of prime necessity at a moderate advance on cost. Not only would it have earned the
fabulous profits pocketed by foreign merchants, but it would have
saved itself the issue of that flood of promises to pay with which it purchased imports.[32]

The Confederate government ignored such suggestions for the
same reasons that it ignored suggestions that all blockade running be
declared a Confederate government monopoly—lack of capital, lack of
the manpower and the management capability to organize a new system, disinclination to give major new tasks to the already overbur-
dened government apparatus, and fear of reducing the incentives that
were motivating British shipbuilders, shipowners, merchants, and
sailors to participate in the blockade running system on which the
Confederacy had become crucially dependent.

ɔ   ɔ   ɔ

The Confederates used cotton deliveries through the blockade and
the pledge of future cotton to finance the purchase in Britain of arms,
supplies, warships, and cargo ships for blockade running.

In the fall of 1862 a loan to the Confederacy, in the form of bonds secured by promises of postwar cotton, was proposed by Emile Erlanger of the Paris banking house of Erlanger et Cie. He proposed to sell Confederate bonds under terms highly favorable to his firm. The initial bond issue was to have a face value of 5 million francs ($25 million), but the firm would receive all of the proceeds of the sale of the bonds over 70 percent of the face value and would also receive a 5 percent commission. The Confederacy would receive only about 3.3 million francs but would incur an obligation to repay 5 million francs in capital plus 8 percent interest. The bonds were to be paid at face value within six months after the ratification of a peace treaty, an event that seemed only months away to European investors in the fall of 1862. Payment was to be made in the Confederacy in cotton valued at twelve cents per pound, allowing the bondholders to expect a very large profit when the cotton was sold in Europe at much higher prices.

Erlanger traveled to Richmond, where Benjamin insisted on a somewhat better deal. The total bond issue was reduced to 3 million francs ($15 million), the interest was reduced to 7 percent, and the price Erlanger was to pay for the bonds was raised to 77 percent of the face value. Benjamin remained unenthusiastic about the deal even after these improvements, but he accepted it because Slidell thought it would give the speculators around Napoleon a strong motive to urge French recognition of the Confederacy.[33]

The bonds were offered to investors on March 18, 1863, at 90, guaranteeing Erlanger a handsome 13-point profit over the 77 paid to the Confederacy. To the speculator who assumed that a Confederate victory was not far off, the bonds were an attractive speculation. The initial buyers apparently gave little thought to the possibilities that the Confederacy would not sustain itself or that the price of cotton would drop sharply as soon as the war was over and unrestricted cotton exports from America were resumed.

The loan was oversubscribed by the end of the first day, and the quotation on the bourse soon rose to 95.5. But then the price began to sag. Many subscribers, who had paid only an initial 15 percent, withdrew before the required settlement on April 24. John Bigelow, the U.S. consul general in Paris, and Robert J. Walker, a former secretary of the treasury who was in Europe as a Union agent, conducted a propaganda campaign against the Erlanger loan. Doubts about Confederate repayment of the loan were raised by stories that Senator Jefferson Davis had defended Mississippi's default on its bonds, most of which had been held by English investors. Doubts about Confederate victory were raised by signs that Grant was making progress at Vicksburg and by news of Lee's potentially disastrous invasion of Maryland.

Mason and Slidell reluctantly agreed to the use of about $6 million of the proceeds of the loan to boost the market for the bonds by secretly buying back some of the bonds, but these purchases raised bond prices for only a few days. After Union victories at Vicksburg and Gettysburg in the summer of 1863, the price of the Confederate bonds fell rapidly, at one point reaching 36. Yet John C. Schwab, who studied Confederate finances, concluded that Erlanger's bank made $2.7 million from the bonds. Burton J. Hendrick estimated that the Confederate treasury obtained only about $2.5 million from the bond issue but pledged $15 million in capital and 7 percent in interest.[34] If the Confederacy had won its independence, it would have been saddled with a large debt.

છ   છ   છ

The very large profits derived from the sale of Confederate cotton in Britain, in addition to profits from the sale of arms and supplies to the Confederacy, provided strong incentives for the British and Confederate firms engaged in the blockade running operations reviewed in chapter 11. These high profits enabled a major entrepreneur to make large net gains on his blockade running operations even though some of his ships and cargoes were captured or destroyed by the Union blockading squadrons.

Adams reported in the spring of 1864 that blockade runners bringing arms and supplies ordered by the Confederacy usually "carried the inward cargo on account of the so-called Confederate government, on condition of receiving cotton in exchange for it or bonds for the back trip."[35] Other blockade runners brought arms and supplies without orders from the Confederate government but with confidence that the cargo could be traded for cotton in the Confederate ports.

The Confederate government arranged for the shipment of some government-owned cotton to Bermuda, Nassau, and Havana, where it was sold to pay for arms and supplies.[36]

The Erlanger bonds seem to have been the primary source of funding for several warships built in Britain for the Confederacy, notably the *Alabama* (chapter 10). Cotton was also used by Confederate firms and the Confederate government to pay for ships refitted or built in Britain for use as blockade runners. The Confederate Ordnance Department, the only Confederate agency to own and operate blockade runners, apparently used cotton bonds to finance its purchase of four ships.[37]

Confederate cotton exports via blockade runners continued until the capture of the last Confederate ports, Charleston and Wilmington. Before Charleston was captured, on February 21, 1865, warehouses were burned by die-hard Confederates to prevent the cotton from falling into Yankee hands.[38] But cotton speculators in Europe feared that, when peace was restored, low-priced Southern cotton would swamp the European market. When news reached London of Lincoln's meeting with Confederate representatives at Hampton Roads in early February 1865, the cotton market was paralyzed.[39] In April, even before word reached London of Lee's surrender, Adams reported that there was great anxiety in financial circles in Britain: "The rapid fall which has already taken place in the value of cotton in this market . . . has already caused very heavy losses to individuals, and it is feared will bring on many more. The period when the exportation of staples of the Southern states. . .will be permitted . . . is awaited with anxiety."[40]

There was also panic among the holders of Confederate bonds. Although the bonds had been sold by a French company, most of the purchasers were British. Early in 1865 Adams discovered that many of the British bondholders believed or hoped that, in the event of a Union victory, the U.S. government would assume the Confederate obligation.[41] "No impression could be more erroneous," Seward replied. "You should authoritatively undeceive the public on this point."[42] After Lee's surrender, the Confederate bonds were merely expensive souvenirs of the misguided conviction in Britain that the Union could not win the war.

CHAPTER 7

A War with America Would Hamper My Operations

Union and Confederate Relations with France, 1861–1862

French reactions to the Civil War in America were based on quite different prewar perspectives on America than those that influenced British reactions. The British had always resented American independence from Britain; the French had provided crucial military and naval support to the American Revolution. The British were consistent monarchists; France had already had its first and second republics—after the French Revolution and from 1848 to 1852—and a well-organized liberal opposition looked forward to the Third Republic after the demise of the Second Empire. Most British visitors to America had written condescending or critical accounts of American manners, lifestyles, and institutions; Alexis de Tocqueville and other French visitors had written sympathetic descriptions of republican politics and government in America.

Serge Gavronsky wrote that the positive image of the United States persisted in France throughout the American Civil War: "The identity of the United States as the model republic had been established early in its history. . . . It had often been put to the test by inquiring visitors. . . . America as the land of liberty was an ideal so readily understood and so indisputably accepted that it . . . was believed without question."[1]

In 1861 France was in the tenth year of the Second Empire, ruled by Emperor Napoleon III. Louis Napoleon, nephew of the first Emperor Napoleon, was born in Paris in 1808, exiled with other

Bonapartes in 1816, and educated in Switzerland, Savoy, and Germany. In 1836 the first of his two premature attempts to overthrow King Louis Philippe led to exile in America; the second attempt, in 1840, resulted in six years of imprisonment in France followed by two years of exile in England. After Louis Philippe was overthrown in a popular uprising in 1848, Louis Napoleon returned to Paris and was elected president of the Second French Republic. In 1851 he dissolved the Parliament, proclaimed a dictatorship, and arranged for a plebiscite proclaiming him Emperor of the French, Napoleon III.

David H. Pinkney noted that the emperor was always deeply concerned with public opinion: "He ruled the nation by no legal right of succession, having seized power by a coup d'etat. . . . His title and authority rested only on force and on the sanction of popular endorsement by plebiscites. On these two foundations of the Empire he lavished much concern, assuring the loyalty of the army and . . . watching carefully the reactions of public opinion to imperial policies, to political debates, and to economic conditions."[2] Napoleon's foreign policy, Henry Kissinger observed, reflected his insecure position in France: "His policy fluctuated with his assessment of what was needed to sustain his popularity. In 1857 [Austrian Ambassador] Baron Huebner wrote to the Austrian Emperor: . . . 'Foreign policy is only an instrument he uses to secure his rule in France, to legitimize his throne, to found his dynasty.' "[3]

In 1861 Napoleon's position was insecure both at home and abroad. He had spent 75,000 French lives and 2 billion francs in the Crimean war (1854–56) with Russia, as allies of Britain and Turkey, but had little to show for it except the undying hatred of the Russians. The Austrians hated him for sending French armies into northern Italy in 1859, driving the Austrians out of Lombardy. But Italian liberals hated him for sending French troops to Rome to protect the pope. In Prussia, Wilhelm I and Bismarck were reorganizing and expanding the Prussian army and dreaming of a unified Germany that would be a threat to France. Napoleon's only major alliance was with England, a traditional enemy of France.

During 1861 and most of 1862 Edouard Thouvenel was the French foreign minister. He had been trained as a lawyer and a diplomat, and has been described as reserved, aloof, uncommunicative, and noncommittal. Until the Empress Eugénie convinced the emperor to replace him in the fall of 1862, Thouvenel braked Napoleon's initial enthusiasm for French recognition of Confederate independence.

Lincoln appointed William Lewis Dayton of New Jersey to the post of minister to France. Dayton had been a New Jersey senator and a state attorney general, as well as the vice presidential running mate of John Charles Fremont on the Republican Party ticket in 1856. He had no previous experience in foreign affairs, did not speak French, and used a hired interpreter during his visits to the French Foreign Office.

Dayton served as U.S. minister in Paris for nearly four years, until his death during the last winter of the war. Two writers who focused on Confederate diplomacy made derogatory comments about Dayton. Frank Owsley considered him an "ineffective" minister; Beckles Willson thought he was "prosaic, timid, and lacking in magnetism."[4] Yet he effectively communicated to the French government two very important positions of the U.S. government—total rejection of European meddling in the American Civil War and very strong disapproval of the French intervention in Mexico. Following Dayton's sudden death in December 1864, Thouvenel's successor, Drouyn de Lhuys, wrote that he had appreciated "the qualities, the talents, and the experience of Mr. Dayton" and that the emperor "bore a particular esteem for this minister."[5] His ministerial colleague in London, Charles Francis Adams, who rarely made charitable remarks about anyone, thought Dayton had been "a most able, judicious, and discreet representative abroad."[6]

Dayton was buttressed by the appointment of John Bigelow as U.S. consul general in Paris. Bigelow had edited the *Evening Post* in New York since 1848. He had traveled in Europe before the war and spoke French. His special assignment was promoting pro-Union attitudes in the French press.

The new minister was instructed to make it clear to the French government that "foreign intervention would oblige us to treat those who should yield it as allies of the insurrectionary party, and to carry out war against them as enemies." Seward also stressed that there was not "the least idea existing in this government of suffering a dissolution of this Union to take place."[7]

Dayton arrived in Paris on May 11, 1861, two days before Adams arrived in London. Like Adams, he learned immediately that the government to which he was accredited had accorded the rights of belligerents to the Confederates. In Dayton's first interview with the French foreign minister, Edouard Thouvenel insisted that recognition of the belligerent rights of the Confederate states did not constitute diplomatic recognition of Confederate independence. A few days later Napoleon assured Dayton that he desired the perpetuation of the American Union and was ready to offer his good offices if acceptable to both parties.[8] Seward instructed Dayton to tell the emperor "that if any mediation were at all admissible, it would be his own that we should seek or accept."[9]

"Foreign intervention would ultimately drive the whole people of the United States to unanimity," Seward wrote to the French minister in Washington, Count Mercier, "but the sympathies which have so long existed between the United States and France would, in that case, perhaps forever cease."[10]

The view that the Union could never be reestablished was as widely held in France as in England. "The Union is completely dissolved," *La Patrie* editorialized, "and, in our opinion, can never be restored."[11] But both domestic and international pressures inhibited Napoleon III from extending diplomatic recognition of Confederate independence.

During 1861 the three-man Confederate diplomatic commission in Europe was based in London, and Confederate contact with the French government was limited. Rost visited Paris in early June and had an unofficial meeting with Thouvenel, but the French foreign minister did not encourage Confederate hopes for French recognition.[12] During the *Trent* crisis, Thouvenel told Dayton that Wilkes's action was a clear breach of international law but that France would remain a spectator in any war between the United States and England.[13]

After John Slidell's delayed arrival in Paris in early February 1862, Slidell became a major player in a new game—the Confederate bid for recognition and support by France. Slidell was sixty-nine years old when he arrived in France. He grew up in New York City, received a degree from Columbia College, and moved to New Orleans in 1819. There he studied law and served in the state legislature and as a U.S. district attorney. During a single term in the U.S. Congress, from

1843 to 1845, he became an ally of presidential hopeful James Buchanan, senator from Pennsylvania. In the fall of 1845 President James K. Polk decided to send a new minister to Mexico to attempt to reopen the diplomatic relations suspended by Mexico in February due to the U.S. annexation of Texas. Buchanan, Polk's secretary of state, recommended Slidell for the Mexican assignment.

Slidell spent only about two months in the Mexican capital, conducted an increasingly angry correspondence with two Mexican foreign ministers, wrote dispatches that bolstered Polk's bellicose inclinations toward Mexico, and withdrew after two Mexican governments refused to receive him as minister. Through his belligerent dispatches and a meeting with Polk on his return, Slidell was a major contributor to Polk's decision—just before he heard that the war had already begun on the Rio Grande—to ask Congress to declare war on Mexico.[14]

In 1853 the Louisiana legislature elected Slidell to the U.S. Senate, where he became a member of the Foreign Relations Committee. His special interests were U.S. acquisition of Cuba as a slaveholding state and the abrogation of the treaty with Britain on the control of the slave trade.[15] In 1861 Slidell's totally unsuccessful mission in Mexico was still shrouded in secrecy and he was regarded as "the foremost diplomat of the Confederate states."[16]

Although the French foreign minister was not prepared to receive Slidell officially, he was quite willing to talk to him unofficially. Later the Confederate envoy would also have several audiences with the emperor of the French. By March 28 he had concluded that Napoleon would not recognize Confederate independence unless it could be done jointly with England. He wrote Mason that "the sooner our people know that we have nothing to expect from this side . . . and that we must rely exclusively on our own resources, the better."[17] But Slidell soon decided that this pessimistic conclusion had been premature.

On April 11 William Lindsay, the largest shipbuilder in England and a member of the British Parliament, had an audience with the emperor. Napoleon told him that he had been trying to get British agreement on steps to break the Union blockade, but Thouvenel had received only evasive answers to two notes to Lord Cowley, the British minister in Paris. Slidell reported that Napoleon told Lindsay that "he would at once dispatch a formidable fleet to the Mississippi, if England would send an equal force, [and] they would demand free ingress and egress for their merchantmen."[18]

The French minister in Washington, Count Edouard-Henri Mercier, concealed from Seward his strong Confederate sympathies. When Mercier returned to France at the beginning of 1864, Seward wrote Dayton that "the beginning of our unhappy civil war found him in close and intimate relations with the leaders of the insurrection. . . . Mr. Mercier has been slower than most of the representatives of foreign states residing here in accepting the conclusion that the Union would be saved."[19] Three decades later Lincoln's former secretaries, Nicolay and Hay, were less charitable: "The complete triumph of the [Union] was regarded in Paris as a contingency grossly improbable . . . and unfavorable to the perpetuity of a Latin Empire on this continent. His sympathies, and with them his beliefs, were therefore wholly on the side of the South."[20]

In April 1862 Mercier made a brief visit to Richmond. Except for minor contacts by consuls, it was the only direct contact with Confederate leaders by a British or French diplomat during the war. The visit was stimulated, although not specifically suggested, by dispatches from Thouvenel. The foreign minister wrote that the government in Paris was interested in offering, at the right time, some form of mediation in the American conflict. He dwelt on the great distress in some French industries due to the blockade. Thouvenel thought that, since the Confederates had won several victories and Union conquest of the South seemed impossible, the Union government might be ready to talk peace.[21]

Mercier requested Seward's permission to visit Richmond to judge for himself the ability and the determination of the Confederates to achieve permanent independence. Seward, who usually opposed any form of European meddling in the American conflict, seems to have expected that Mercier would return with a report that the Confederacy was on its last legs. He gave him a pass through Union lines. Mercier promised that in Richmond he would emphasize the futility of the Confederate war effort and urge reunion with the North, although it is doubtful that he intended to express such views in the Confederate capital.[22]

The French minister arrived in Richmond on April 16 and met the Confederate secretary of state. Benjamin told him that "we would not like to talk with anybody who entertained the idea . . . of our dishonoring ourselves by reuniting with a people for whom we feel unmitigated contempt as well as abhorence."[23] When Mercier mentioned the possibility that the Union might capture the Confederate seaports and other principal cities, Benjamin said they would find only women, children, and old men and that Confederate soldiers would withdraw to the mountains and continue the struggle. Benjamin thought Mercier left Richmond "thoroughly convinced that the war could have no issue but our independence, although he thought it might last a long time."[24]

The visit confirmed Mercier's convictions that the North could not conquer the South, that permanent separation was inevitable, and that the bloody war could be stopped only through some form of European intervention. Mercier's strong advocacy of European intervention significantly influenced the consideration of intervention by the French and British governments in the months following his visit to Richmond.

ɛɔ   ɛɔ   ɛɔ

By the summer of 1862 Napoleon's attitude toward the Civil War in America was strongly influenced by his rapidly expanding commitments in Mexico. During the previous winter a French brigade and British and Spanish units had landed at Vera Cruz, ostensibly to force the Mexican government to pay its debts. By April the British and Spanish had withdrawn, but the French had moved inland. In May a French attack on Puebla, Mexico's second largest city, had failed, and Napoleon was planning to send a larger French army to defeat the republicans and to install a European monarch in Mexico.

Samuel Flagg Bemis outlined Napoleon's motives: "Greedy for 'glory' and prestige to distract the public. . . . the . . . emperor had turned to America with revived plans for a colonial empire built up through the guise of protectorates. . . . Political chaos in Mexico seemed to offer the opportunity for setting up a puppet state there as a pedestal for the further spread of French influence and power. The Civil War played into his hands at an opportune moment by devitalizing the Monroe Doctrine."[25]

Napoleon thought an independent Confederacy would provide a buffer between royalist Mexico and the republican United States. He was also very anxious to obtain Confederate cotton. But he feared that French recognition of Confederate independence would lead to war with the United States and have a disastrous impact on his operations in Mexico. This fear was very apparent when British shipbuilder William Lindsay saw Napoleon again in late June, this time with his parliamentary colleague, John Roebuck. Lindsay recorded that the emperor rejected unilateral French recognition of the Confederacy: "If I took that measure alone it might . . . embroil me with the North. . . . A war with America . . . might seriously hamper my operations in Mexico. . . . [But] I am indeed most anxious to see this war brought to a close, for I dread the consequences of the want of cotton to my people during the next winter."[26]

On July 6 Slidell received the delayed April 3 dispatch from Benjamin that authorized him to offer the French government 100,000 bales of cotton at a low price in return for action by the French navy to break the blockade. Slidell presented this proposal to the emperor at Vichy on July 16. He reported that Napoleon made the following reply: "The policy of nations is controlled by their interests, not by their sentiments. I committed a great error and I now deeply regret it. France should never have respected the blockade. And she should have recognized the Confederacy. . . . But what can be done now? To open the ports forcibly would be an act of war."[27]

Slidell told Napoleon that Lincoln had sent the Senate a treaty that was "a subsidy of $11 million to enable Juárez to carry on the war against France." Napoleon had already heard from Mercier that "the Senate will not ratify it."[28] But the possibility that the United States might eventually provide material support to Juárez continued to worry the French emperor throughout the subsequent five years of the French intervention in Mexico.

Dayton and Bigelow were unaware that Lindsay and Slidell had received little encouragement from the emperor. Bigelow thought Napoleon was "hovering over us like the carrion crow over the body of the sinking traveler."[29] But several important factors were restraining the emperor. Deeply committed in Mexico at a time when Europe was in flux, he could not afford to risk a war with the United States. There was no assurance that French recognition of Confederate independence would substantially increase the flow of cotton to France. French liberals condemned the idea of recognition of a slaveholding state in America. In an article published in August, France's leading expert on America, Edouard Laboulaye, insisted that France must not submit to diplomatic blackmail: "To induce Europe to intervene, in spite of herself, is the hope and policy of the Confederates. . . . This help she will not have. . . . Whatever the sufferings of the manufacturing classes, and whatever the schemes of diplomatists, there is one fact which towers above everything else, and that is SLAVERY."[30]

When Slidell saw the emperor again, on October 28, Napoleon said he was considering a proposal for a six-month armistice with "the Southern ports open to the commerce of the world."[31] Meanwhile, Thouvenel had been replaced as French foreign minister. His successor, Edouard Drouyn de Lhuys, had been foreign minister from 1852 to 1855 and French minister to England. He was rotund, lethargic, and usually mild mannered. Baron Huebner remarked that he spoke with "a fluency of languages and a profusion of words which serves equally to reveal and to conceal his thoughts."[32]

Dayton asked the new foreign minister on November 6 about rumors that the British and French governments were considering an offer of mediation in the American Civil War. Drouyn de Lhuys said there had been some discussion of mediation but that no decision had been made.[33] In fact, a French proposal for an offer of tripartite mediation by the French, British, and Russian governments had been made on October 30. Mediation efforts would be carried out during a six-month period in which hostilities and the blockade would be suspended. (Consideration of Napoleon's proposal by the British cabinet in early November, and the cabinet's decision on November 11 to reject it, are reviewed in chapter 9.)

News of another bloody Union defeat, at Fredericksburg on December 13, convinced Napoleon that the time might be right for another attempt to stop the fighting in America. Mercier was instructed on January 9, 1863, to transmit to Seward a French proposal for a meeting on neutral ground of Union and Confederate commissioners without the cessation of hostilities or any European representation at the meeting.[34]

With Lincoln's concurrence, Seward emphatically rejected the French proposal. He wrote Dayton on February 2, 1863, that "this government has not the least thought of relinquishing the trust that had been confided to it by the nation" and that "peace proposed at the cost of dissolution would be immediately, unreservedly, and indignantly rejected by the American people."[35]

Napoleon had made his last attempt to intervene in the American Civil War, although this fact was not evident for some time. Confederate envoy Dudley Mann wrote from Brussels in March that "Louis Napoleon . . . cannot incur the risk of provoking the angry displeasure of the North."[36]

During Slidell's third interview with Napoleon, on June 15, 1863, the emperor denied that he had changed his mind about the desirability of French recognition of Confederate independence and promised to make another proposal soon to Britain for joint recognition. But he also said French commerce would be jeopardized by a war with the United States.[37]

Frank Owsley summarized the factors that prevented Napoleon from recognizing Confederate independence:

> He was under no circumstances willing to intervene alone or in company with weaker powers. . . . He refrained from repudiating the blockade or from recognizing the independence of the Confederacy because of his apprehension that the United States would declare war on him should he do so. . . . Prussia, Russia, Austria, Sardinia, and even England . . . would welcome such a war to close in upon him from the rear. . . . The French people were in sympathy with the North because of the fact that the South was slaveholding and because of the traditional friendship of the French for the United States, and especially because of the universal desire to see the United States grow strong as a counterpoise to England. . . . Should he bring on a war with America . . . he might lose his throne.[38]

Asked by Dayton in the summer of 1863 about the emperor's current policy toward the United States, Drouyn de Lhuys responded:

"He has none; he awaits events."[39] The events of 1863 did not encourage Napoleon to renew his interest in intervention in the American conflict. After the Union victories at Gettysburg and Vicksburg in July, the main focus of U.S.-French diplomatic relations shifted from the possibility of French intervention in the American Civil War to the possibility of eventual U.S. intervention in the French war with the republican government of Mexico. The latter issue is reviewed in chapter 16 and in Epilogue I.

CHAPTER 8

Maintaining the Independence of Mexico

Union Relations with the Mexican Republic

Aside from the threat of European intervention in the conflict between North and South and the brief but intense *Trent* crisis, the principal foreign policy challenge facing Lincoln and Seward was the French invasion of Mexico and the subsequent establishment of an imperial government in that country with an Austrian archduke as emperor. Lincoln's cautious responses to these developments were strongly influenced by his experience, in 1847–48, as a member of the Whig opposition to America's first foreign war.

Lincoln had concluded—as I did in a previous book on the origins and ending of the war with Mexico[1]—that President James K. Polk had provoked the war by sending an American army into Mexican territory. Zachary Taylor's army had been attacked in a region between the Nueces and Rio Grande Rivers that, although claimed by Texas, had always been Mexican territory. On December 22, 1847, Congressman Lincoln introduced a resolution asking Polk to prove, if he could, that the spot where he claimed in 1846 that Mexicans had "shed American blood on American soil" had in fact been American territory. In early January 1848 Lincoln voted with the Whig majority for a resolution declaring "the war with Mexico was unnecessarily and unconstitutionally commenced by the President." Lincoln defended these actions in an autobiographical sketch in 1860:

The President had sent General Taylor into an inhabited part of the country belonging to Mexico, and not to the United States, and thereby had provoked . . . the commencement of the war. . . . The place . . . had never . . . been conquered by Texas or the United States nor transferred to either by treaty. . . . Although Texas claimed the Rio Grande as her boundary, Mexico had never recognized it.[2]

By December 1847 Polk had painted himself into a corner in Mexico. He had sent the second-ranking officer of the State Department, Nicholas P. Trist, to Mexico in April to deliver his peace terms. When Polk learned in October that the Mexican president, Santa Anna, had rejected his terms, he sent orders recalling Trist. Polk had no plan to end the war: "The only new ideas about Mexico in his message to Congress that winter," I wrote in the previous book, "were the formation of a more tractable and compliant Mexican government under the protecting wing of the American army or, if peace on his terms continued to be elusive, a long-term military occupation of Mexico. Either policy, if implemented, would have involved the United States in extraordinarily difficult long-term roles and commitments. James K. Polk had set the United States on the road to disaster in Mexico."[3]

Congressman Lincoln pointed out the contradictions in Polk's annual message in a speech in the House on January 12, 1848:

As to the mode of terminating the war and securing peace, the President is . . . wandering and indefinite. First, it is to be done by a more vigorous prosecution of the war. . . . Then he suggests the propriety of wheedling the Mexican people to desert the counsels of their own leaders . . . to set up a government from which we can secure a satisfactory peace. . . . But soon he falls into doubt of this too; and then drops back into the already half-abandoned ground of "more vigorous prosecution." All this shows that the President is in nowise satisfied with his own positions.[4]

The author of the only substantial study of Lincoln's term in Congress, Donald W. Riddle, thought Lincoln's "spot" resolution and his January 12 speech were merely partisan efforts to embarrass the president.[5] Most Lincoln biographers have agreed. But my research revealed no other contemporary analysis of Polk's statements about the war that was as perceptive or accurate as that of the congressional newcomer from Illinois. Historians have paid little attention to Polk's Mexican dilemma in the winter of 1847–48 because he was soon rescued by his envoy. By the time Trist received Polk's recall order, General Winfield Scott had captured the Mexican capital, Santa Anna had been deposed, and a new civilian government was preparing to negotiate for peace. Realizing that the recall order was based on a total misunderstanding by Polk of the situation in Mexico, Trist decided to ignore it, and remained in Mexico to negotiate an acceptable peace treaty.[6]

Lincoln's opposition to America's first foreign war was the only noteworthy feature of his single term in Congress, which was his only experience in the national government before becoming president. The issues examined in his speeches in Congress—how the war began and how it might be ended—were the most important issues in American foreign relations in the two decades before he became president. His involvement with these issues, including the unpopularity of his opposition to the war among his constituents in Illinois, taught him two lessons. One was that when foreign war is threatened the president must have carefully considered foreign policies that can be supported by the majority of the American people. Another was that U.S. intervention in Mexico risked entrapment in a Mexican quagmire.

Between the war with Mexico and the Civil War, three factors inhibited U.S.-Mexican relations. One was the legacy of the war. All three of the elected U.S. presidents in this period (Taylor, Pierce, and Buchanan), several cabinet members, and the commanding general of the United States Army had been prominent officials or senior officers during the Mexican War. These men tended to view Mexico as a former enemy country still unworthy of much respect or consideration from U.S. officials.

Another inhibiting factor was the confusion in Mexico. For three years just prior to the American Civil War, Mexico was torn by its own bitter civil war between authoritarian conservatives and liberal republicans. During most of this period a conservative government headed by Miguel Miramon controlled the capital and much of central Mexico,

while a liberal government headed by Benito Juárez controlled the eastern coastal zone. Juárez was a Zapotec Indian who had been an efficient
and honest governor of the mountain state of Oaxaca. "Juárez had in a
superlative degree," Henry B. Parkes noted, "what Mexico supremely
needed: undeviating honesty and an indomitable will which would
never accept compromise or defeat."[7]

Following the custom of recognizing diplomatically any Mexican
government that was in possession of the capital, President Buchanan
initially recognized the conservative Miramon government. The U.S.
minister to Mexico, John Forsyth, negotiated a treaty for a $15 million
loan to the Miramon government, but it was rejected by the Buchanan
administration. After Miramon rejected a U.S. offer to buy Baja California and parts of Sonora and Chihuahua, Forsyth was recalled. By
1860 the liberals had captured the capital and other areas, although
substantial areas were still controlled by the conservatives.

A third factor inhibiting improved relations was the preponderant
interest of these U.S. administrations in obtaining territory and other
concessions from Mexico. Many leaders in the South were keenly
interested in the development of a transit route across the narrow Mexican isthmus of Tehuantepec that would connect the Atlantic and
Pacific Oceans. At a time when there was no railroad across the United
States, they dreamed of a railroad from New Orleans to and across the
isthmus that would make New Orleans the gateway for U.S. trade with
the Orient. Louisiana senator Judah P. Benjamin, later Confederate
secretary of state, was an investor in and attorney for the Tehuantepec
Company, formed in the 1850s.

In 1859 Buchanan recognized Juárez as president of Mexico. A
new minister, Robert M. Lane, negotiated an agreement with Juárez's
foreign minister, Melchior Ocampo. In return for a $2 million pay-
ment to the Mexican government and the payment of $2 million of
claims by Americans against the Mexican government, the United
States would obtain a perpetual right-of-way across the isthmus of
Tehuantepec and unprecedented rights to use U.S. troops to protect
the transit zone and to intervene to maintain order elsewhere in Mexico. Henry B. Parkes wrote that the Lane-Ocampo treaty was "vehe-
mently and justifiably reprobated in Mexico [as] a sacrifice of national
sovereignty."[8] Alfred and Kathryn Hanna noted that "Juárez bore until

his death a burden of censure for having agreed to terms that would have placed the United States in virtual control of Mexico."[9] When the treaty came before the U.S. Senate in the spring of 1860, Northern senators blocked ratification because they thought the treaty would primarily benefit the South.[10]

After Lincoln's election in 1860, Juárez realized that a U.S. president who had opposed the war with Mexico might be a valuable ally. Mattias Romero, the Mexican chargé d'affaires in Washington, was ordered to visit the president-elect in Springfield to make clear Juárez's desire for "the most cordial relations" with the United States.[11] Romero was the only foreign diplomat to visit Lincoln between his election and his inauguration. On January 19 and 21, 1861, he briefed Lincoln on recent developments in his country and reported that Lincoln had asked a number of intelligent questions about conditions in Mexico.[12]

ော   ော   ော

President Lincoln appointed Thomas Corwin as his minister to Mexico. He had been a Congressman, governor of Ohio, U.S. senator, and President Fillmore's secretary of the treasury. In the late 1840s he had been the most prominent opponent in the Senate of the war with Mexico. In a debate in 1847 Senator Corwin said that, if he were a Mexican, he would say to the American invaders, "we will greet you with bloody hands, and welcome you with hospitable graves."[13] By appointing another opponent of the war with Mexico as his minister to that country, Lincoln seemed to be sending a signal that his policy toward Mexico would be more sympathetic than that of his predecessors.

Several weeks after Lincoln's inauguration Seward told the British minister, Lord Lyons, that it might be necessary for the United States to adopt a new "policy of protection and intervention" toward Mexico because the Confederates were "much disposed to endeavor by force or fraud to unite Mexico to the Southern Confederacy."[14] Even if there had been no Civil War, it is unlikely that Lincoln would have approved an interventionist policy in Mexico. He had not forgotten Polk's dilemma at the end of 1847. But any thought of an interventionist policy in Mexico evaporated when the Confederates fired on Fort Sumter.

Preoccupied with a war at home, Lincoln was unwilling to commit U.S. financial or military resources to any other country. But Corwin pressed hard for U.S. financial aid, and Lincoln concealed his unwillingness to provide material support so that he could continue to provide effective moral and diplomatic support to the republican government of Mexico.

Corwin's alternating attention in 1861–62 to the separate but interrelated problems of money to pay the Mexican army and money to pay at least the interest on Mexico's foreign debts resulted in a great deal of confusion among contemporaries and historians concerning his proposals for financial assistance to Mexico. At first Corwin focused on Juárez's continuing struggle with the conservative opposition: "Had the present liberal party enough money at its command to pay an army of 10,000 men, I am satisfied it could suppress the present opposition, restore order, and preserve internal peace."[15]

On July 17, 1861, the Mexican congress suspended payments on all government debts for a period of two years. Corwin immediately anticipated that the British, French, and Spanish governments would send an armed force to occupy Vera Cruz and control the major source of Mexican government income, the customs duties collected at Mexico's most important port. Moreover, in a letter to Adams in London noted by Adams's secretary, Corwin expressed fear that "Great Britain, France, and Spain contemplate the seizure of Mexico and the establishment of a monarchy."[16]

Corwin thought the United States could prevent European intervention by paying the interest on the Mexican government's $62 million debt to Europeans. He proposed on July 29 that the United States pay the 3 percent interest—about $2 million per year—for a period of five years and that Mexico mortgage public lands in several western Mexican states as a guarantee of the repayment of this loan. He thought the loan would secure Mexican independence and prevent the acquisition of Mexican territory by the Confederacy or any European power.[17]

Seward shared Corwin's fear that U.S. preoccupation with the Civil War and the Mexican suspension of debt payments would provide Europeans with an excuse for the conquest of Mexico: "It is our wish and our purpose," Seward wrote Corwin on August 24, "that the people of Mexico shall in every case be exclusive arbiters of their own political fortunes and remain free and independent of all foreign intervention and control whatever." But he also stressed that while the United States was engaged in a civil war "we should not unnecessarily provoke debates with foreign countries."[18]

Corwin's proposal was discussed in a cabinet meeting on August 27. Attorney General Edward Bates thought there was "small likelihood" that Britain and France would agree: "All they can get by it is the payment of five years interest, but the sum total of the principal remains unpaid."[19] Postmaster General Montgomery Blair told the Mexican chargé a few days later that the Europeans had wanted for years to increase their influence in North America and would not give up the present "unique opportunity" to do so.[20]

On August 31 Romero had an appointment with Lincoln. The president listened attentively to Romero's review of the situation in Mexico and then, as Romero reported, "he summarized his understanding of it in a manner that I found highly satisfactory." Lincoln promised prompt action, but he did not tell Romero what kind of action was contemplated.[21]

Two days later Seward sent Corwin a conditional authorization to negotiate a treaty providing for U.S. payments of the interest on the Mexican bonds. Corwin was told that Lincoln "greatly desires that the political status of Mexico as an independent nation shall be permanently maintained." He was authorized to negotiate a treaty with Mexico "for the assumption by the government of the United States of the payment of the interest, at three per cent, upon the funded debt of that country." The government of Mexico was to guarantee to reimburse the United States for such payments, including 6 percent interest on the amount paid, and was to secure the guarantee "by a specific lien upon all the public lands and mineral rights in the several Mexican states of Lower California, Chihuahua, Sonora, and Sinaloa, the property so pledged to become absolute in the United States at the expiration of the term of six years from the time when the treaty shall go into effect, if such reimbursement shall not have been made before that time."[22] But Corwin was told that the treaty would be accepted in Washington only if the British and French governments agreed to refrain from intervention in Mexico as long as the interest was paid on the Mexican debts.

There are several reasons for doubting that Lincoln and Seward hoped for the implementation of the type of treaty outlined in Seward's September 2 instruction. Since Mexico had been unable to pay 3 percent interest on its debt, there was no reason to believe that it would be able to reimburse the United States for the interest payments plus 6 percent interest on the amount of the U.S. payments. Mexican default on the loan would have been highly likely, and default would probably have led to U.S. sovereignty over the mortgaged Mexican lands. The Lincoln administration opposed additional territorial acquisitions from Mexico on several grounds. Attorney General Bates's comments in the cabinet reflected the views of many Americans: "I have a decided repugnance to the absorption of the mongrel people of Mexico . . . who I think are wholly unfit to be our equals, friends, and fellow citizens."[23] In this period the administration and Congress still hoped for the restoration of "the Union as it was," that is, with slavery. In a such a reunited Union, the proposed treaty might lead to the extension of slavery into new territories acquired from Mexico.

The subsequent actions of Lincoln and Seward indicate that they were determined to avoid any major commitment in Mexico, but they thought the *proposal* of some form of U.S. financial assistance would provide important moral and diplomatic support for the Juárez government during a critical period. Since it seemed very unlikely that the British, the French, the Mexicans, and the United States Senate would agree to such a plan, they ran little risk of an unwanted commitment in Mexico.

Seward had instructed Adams and Dayton on August 24 to ascertain the reactions of the British and French governments to Corwin's proposal. Russell was on a working vacation in Scotland, and Adams had to make a six-hundred-mile round-trip by train to meet the foreign secretary. He reported Russell's response that "the proposed arrangement did not, by any means, meet the cause of complaint. Great Britain had much more to object to in the actions of Mexico than the mere suspension of the interest on her debt." Russell cited injuries to the lives and property of British residents in Mexico, including a number of murders and the theft of huge sums of money. The payment of only the interest on the Mexican bonds would leave many other European claims against Mexico unresolved. But Russell assured

Adams that Britain did not intend to intervene in the domestic affairs of Mexico and was attempting to prevent any such action by France and Spain.[24]

U.S. concern about Spanish ambitions in Mexico had been stimulated earlier in 1861 by the Spanish attempt to reannex Santo Domingo. Corwin agreed with Carl Schurz, U.S. minister to Spain, that "it is the desire of Spain to regain her dominion over this country and to establish here a monarchy."[25] While Adams was in Scotland, Russell convinced him that Britain was trying to prevent Spanish intervention in Mexico. The minister's secretary recorded that "there is no treaty between Great Britain, France and Spain for intervention in Mexico, nor does GB approve of such a scheme."[26] But such a treaty was signed by the three powers in London only a month later. The United States had not yet realized that the major threat to Mexican independence would come from France, not Spain.

Meanwhile, the threat of European intervention had shifted Corwin's focus back to Juárez's need for money to maintain his army. In the same September week that Seward sent a conditional authorization for a treaty on interest payments, Corwin sought authorization to negotiate a treaty giving Mexico a direct loan of $5 to $10 million to "enable it to keep on foot a sufficient force to save it from ultimate subjugation, perhaps to one of these European monarchies."[27]

Seward replied on October 2:

> The President is as deeply sensible as you yourself confessedly are of the importance of maintaining the integrity and independence of Mexico. . . . But . . . we are now necessarily paying out of the Treasury near a million a day. . . . We could not hope to satisfy the country that it would be expedient to send five or ten millions of money into Mexico until our own military and naval preparation shall have been perfected. . . . The proposition to advance at once to Mexico so large a sum . . . would, we apprehend, encounter serious opposition in the Senate. . . . Your first proposition on this subject [on July 29] seems to me the most feasible and expedient one—namely, that the United States shall assume the payment of interest for Mexico for a term of years upon a pledge of sufficient Mexican mineral lands and territory.[28]

This dispatch was not included in the diplomatic correspondence published in December, and Lincoln and Seward concealed their rejection of a direct loan from the Mexicans, the Europeans, and the U.S. Congress.

Adams's report on his meeting with Russell in Scotland arrived in Washington in mid-October along with a report from Dayton that Thouvenel had also rejected Corwin's proposal on the ground that the French bondholders wanted repayment of the principal, not just the interest.[29]

On October 31 representatives of England, France, and Spain met in London and signed an agreement for joint military action to collect the Mexican debts. The United States was invited to join this agreement, but Seward declined on December 4. He stressed that the United States had a deep interest in maintaining "the right of the Mexican people to choose and freely to constitute the form of its own government."[30]

In this era communication between Washington and Mexico City was very slow and uncertain. The monthly escorted British courier provided the only safe passage along the bandit-infested road between Vera Cruz and the capital.[31] While waiting for Seward's reaction to his September 7 proposal of a direct loan, Corwin drafted a direct loan treaty and discussed it with Mexican officials. Early in November he received Seward's October 2 dispatch rejecting a direct loan and continuing to support a treaty on interest payments designed to prevent European intervention. But Corwin doubted that European intervention could be avoided, so he sent his draft of a direct loan treaty to Seward on November 29 with a request for further instructions.[32]

The objective of the July plan had been to avoid European intervention in Mexico; the objective of his draft treaty in November was to support Juárez's army in a period before Mexico was at war with any European power. In the July proposal, sovereignty or title to the pledged lands was to be transferred to the United States if Mexico failed to repay the loan; the November draft contained no provision for the transfer of sovereignty or land titles.[33] Corwin had discovered that Juárez was unwilling to risk the loss of additional territory.[34]

On December 17 Lincoln sent Corwin's draft treaty to the Senate. Although he stated that the subject was "of momentous interest to the two Governments" and asked the Senate "for its advice," he provided no explanation of the rationale of the proposed treaty and no recommendation as to its acceptance.[35] The Senate Committee on Foreign Relations discussed Corwin's proposal on December 21. One committee member, Senator Browning, recorded that Corwin proposed "to loan Mexico nine million dollars to extricate her from her present difficulties with France and England, for which she proposed to mortgage lower California, [Chihuahua], Sonora, and Sinaloa. . . . I was for advising the making [of] the treaty, provided it was acceptable to France and England and would get them out of our waters till our domestic troubles were ended. But as we did not know the dispositions of France and England in regard to the matter, the subject was postponed for the present."[36] Even Lincoln's best friend in the Senate had not been told that the British and French had already rejected Corwin's original proposal.

Due to the *Trent* crisis and other preoccupations, Senate action on Corwin's proposal was delayed for nearly two months. Meanwhile, a Spanish army of six thousand men landed at Vera Cruz in December and was soon joined by a French brigade and seven hundred British marines. The effect of the tripartite intervention remained in doubt for several months. While negotiations with the Mexicans continued, the European troops moved from Vera Cruz to healthier encampments in the highlands. But Lincoln regarded the European intervention as "a war which is waged against Mexico by the combined powers of Spain, France, and Great Britain."[37] Seward wrote Corwin on February 15 that the Senate would impose two requirements on any treaty providing aid to Mexico: "First, that the aid . . . shall be in the form of an assumption of payment of interest. Secondly, that the aid . . . shall . . . be effectual in securing Mexico a release from all her complications with the allies now making war upon her."[38] Corwin understood Seward to require that "the allies are to be satisfied and leave, before the desired aid is given."[39]

On February 19 the Foreign Relations Committee recommended a Senate resolution supporting a treaty under which the United States would pay the interest on Mexico's debt and some other claims *if* the

European powers withdrew from Mexico.[40] The payments should be secured by such a mortgage or pledge that would not involve "any territorial acquisition or dismemberment of Mexico."[41] Although the draft treaty Lincoln sent to the Senate had proposed a direct loan, the committee had reacted to Corwin's July plan for the payment of interest on the Mexican bonds. Seward had apparently encouraged the committee to support a plan that he knew had already been rejected by the Europeans and that allowed the United States to avoid any commitment in Mexico.

Attorney General Bates noted in his diary on February 21 that a decision had been reached "to send General Scott as special minister to Mexico, to meet the British, French, and Spanish and try to mediate their affairs with Mexico."[42] The next day Lincoln nominated retired General Winfield Scott, as "an additional envoy extraordinary and minister plenipotentiary to Mexico."[43] Lincoln's brief message contained no explanation of the reason for this appointment. Romero thought it was "imprudent": "General Scott is very advanced in age, suffers greatly from the failings and pains of his age, and moreover, because of military habits and the custom of command, is inappropriate for the delicate mission entrusted to him. The diplomatic agents of the allies . . . could confound Scott easily."[44]

It is hardly conceivable that Lincoln and Seward thought a mission to Mexico by Winfield Scott would be both feasible and desirable. The idea of sending an aging and infirm general, who could not walk down Pennsylvania Avenue without support from two aides, was totally impractical. A plan to send back to Mexico the general who captured the Mexican capital in 1847 raised a host of questions regarding American intentions, including the possibility that the United States was planning to offer military aid to Juárez. The only apparent explanation of this mysterious nomination is that Lincoln and Seward thought the Scott nomination would raise enough questions to ensure Senate rejection of the committee resolution.

On February 25 the Senate voted 28 to 8 for a substitute resolution introduced by Senator John Sherman of Ohio, brother of General Sherman. It stated that "It is not advisable to negotiate a treaty that will require the United States to assume any portion of the principal or interest of the debt of Mexico, or that will require the concurrence of

European powers."[45] Two days later Lincoln withdrew the nomination of General Scott with the belated admission that "his infirmities are such that he could not be able to reach the capital of that country by any existing mode of travel."[46]

Seward sent Corwin the Senate resolution on February 28: "You will consider your instructions upon the subject referred to modified by this resolution, and will govern your course accordingly."[47] But the resolution did not react to the treaty draft he had sent to Washington in November, and the resolution and brief instruction did not reach Corwin until after he had signed a direct loan treaty.

Corwin had become convinced that direct financial support from the United States was essential for the survival of republican government in Mexico. He realized that the treaty raised questions about U.S. neutrality in the conflict between Mexico and the European powers that Lincoln had described as a war. Juárez's current foreign minister, Manual Doblada, assured Corwin that Mexico had not declared war against the allied powers, but he ignored the very tense relations between France and Mexico that would lead to active hostilities only a few weeks later.

The only substantive differences between the November draft and the treaty Corwin and Doblada signed on April 6, 1862, along with a second implementing treaty, were the deletion of all references to mineral rights and the increase in the amount of the loan from $9 million to $11 million.[48] Corwin signed the treaty despite clear indications that the administration in Washington would not support such a treaty and despite growing indications that such a loan would violate U.S. neutrality in Mexico's impending war with France.

Three days later the representatives in Mexico of the British and Spanish governments rejected the increasingly intransigent French demands against Mexico and ordered the withdrawal of British and Spanish troops from Mexico. The French force, which had been expanded during the winter, prepared to march on Mexico's second largest city, Puebla. Napoleon was now fully launched on a military and political intervention in Mexico that would be the dominant factor in U.S.-French relations for the next five years.

An $11 million U.S. loan to Juárez would have shattered U.S. neutrality in the war between France and Mexico. Seward undoubtedly foresaw Slidell's description of Corwin's loan treaty to Napoleon in July as "a subsidy of $11,000,000 to enable Juárez to carry on the war against France."[49] Napoleon's great fear of war with the United States was not yet evident in Washington.

On May 28 Seward wrote Corwin that there was little chance of Senate ratification of the loan treaties.[50] After receiving further arguments for the loan from Corwin, however, Seward informed him that the president thought "it is now his duty to refer the treaties, together with your argument and all other papers related to present conditions of Mexico, to the Senate, in a confidential manner, for their due consideration."[51] In a message to the Senate on June 23, Lincoln stated that the resolution in February rejecting U.S. payment of interest on the Mexican debt had been sent to Corwin but "by reason of the disturbed condition of Mexico" had not reached him until "a very recent date." Meanwhile, Corwin had negotiated two loan treaties with the Mexican government. Lincoln submitted the treaties for "any further advice the Senate may think proper."[52] The next day Seward wrote Corwin that, although the president had submitted his treaties to the Senate for "their uninfluenced consideration," the administration was not willing to take any action that would involve the United States in the conflict between France and Mexico:

> Notwithstanding the course adopted by the French agents and army in Mexico, the Government of France still reassures us that it is their purpose to be content with an adjustment of grievances leaving it exclusively to the people of Mexico to determine their own form of government. . . . We do not feel at liberty to reject these explanations or to anticipate a violation of the assurances they convey. . . . Under the circumstances at present we decline debate with foreign powers upon Mexican affairs.[53]

On July 3 the Senate Foreign Relations Committee decided, as Sumner told Romero, "that the treaty was not acceptable because France would consider it as a hostile measure." But he added that because of the committee's sympathy for Mexico's difficult situation "and out of consideration for Corwin, the treaty was not rejected. It was left pending, without approval or disapproval."[54]

Corwin tried to keep alive Mexican hopes of financial assistance from the United States. He told the British minister in Mexico, Sir Charles Wyke, in June that the loan treaty would be ratified as soon as there was any "signal success against the forces of the South."[55] He presumably made a similar promise to the Mexicans. "While it is pending and not rejected," Corwin wrote Seward on August 28, "Mexico will seem to have one friend and be left to hope; whereas, if it be rejected, she will be reduced to despair of either friendly feelings or aid from any quarter."[56]

When French forces approached the Mexican capital in June 1863, Juárez withdrew northward to San Luis Potosí. Corwin remained in Mexico City for ten more months. On April 27, 1864, when Maximilian was on his way up to the capital, Corwin began his return trip to the United States. He resigned as minister to Mexico in September 1864.

From 1863 to 1867 the United States government repeatedly stated that it was maintaining diplomatic relations with the Juárez government. "We are on terms of amity and friendship, and maintaining diplomatic relations, with the republic of Mexico," Seward wrote in November 1863.[57] But the United States had no diplomatic agent near the migratory Mexican president and was often uninformed as to his whereabouts; relations with the Juárez government were conducted through Romero in Washington.

Both of Corwin's proposals for financial assistance to Mexico in 1861–62 were motivated by a desire to prevent or minimize European intervention in Mexico and to contribute to the survival of republican government in that country. By appearing to be sympathetic to Corwin's treaty proposals, Lincoln and Seward bolstered the morale of the Mexican republicans and increased French fears that the United States would eventually provide money, arms, and perhaps even troops to support the republican government in Mexico. Consideration of the loan proposals in Washington provided a strong foundation for the suspicion in France, then and later, that the United States was only waiting for the end of the Civil War to become an active ally of the Mexican republicans. The uncertainty concerning U.S. intentions in Mexico was deliberately created and maintained by Lincoln and Seward, and it contributed significantly to two important U.S. objectives—preventing French recognition of Confederate independence and encouraging French withdrawl from Mexico. Napoleon's fear of eventual American intervention in Mexico was a major factor inhibiting him from recognizing Confederate independence and from providing material support to the Confederacy. The continuation of Lincoln's policy by Seward during and after the war contributed significantly to Napoleon's eventual decision to withdraw his military support for Maximilian's imperial government in Mexico.

Romero was very bitter about the failure of the U.S. government to provide financial and military assistance to his government. Thomas D. Schoonover wrote that Romero became an active ally of the Radical Republican enemies of Lincoln and Seward in the Congress.[58] But a letter the Mexican president wrote to his family in April 1865 suggests that Juárez understood from his own experience why a president engaged in a civil war at home would want to avoid another war with foreigners:

> I celebrate and applaud the inflexibility of Mr. Lincoln, for his triumph, even though belated, will be of more benefit to us than a quick peace with a sacrifice of humanity. . . . With time and our tenacious resistance we shall wear out the French and compel them to abandon their iniquitous enterprise of subjugating us, without foreign assistance, and that is the greatest glory I desire for my country. It is enough for us that the North destroy slavery and do not recognize Maximilian.[59]

The persistent refusal of the United States government to recognize the legitimacy of Maximilian's "empire" in Mexico, during and after the Civil War, is reviewed in chapter 16 and in Epilogue I.

CHAPTER 9

We May Wait a While

Britain Considers Intervention, 1862

During the *Trent* crisis, the strong British response to the removal of the Confederate envoys from a British packet was never interpreted on either side as an indication that, if the envoys were released, the British government would receive James Mason as a diplomatic representative of the Confederate government.

If there had been an opportunity for official relations between the British government and the Confederacy, James Mason's reputation and characteristics would have inhibited effective relations. Although slavery was a major impediment to British recognition of the Confederacy, Jefferson Davis had sent a man to Britain who was well-known for his energetic defense of slavery, for his advocacy of its extension into new areas, and for his authorship of the abhorrent Fugitive Slave Law. Mason had served for a decade as chairman of the Senate Foreign Relations Committee, but he had no previous diplomatic experience and lacked the personality and skills needed by a diplomat. Mason has been described as domineering, arrogant, crude, cold, stolid, sour, provincial, and dull-witted.[1] His habit of spitting tobacco juice—allegedly, even on the carpets of the House of Commons—offended the British.

But Mason's reputation and personality had little to do with his reception in England. The fate awaiting him there had been foretold in *The Times* on January 11, 1862, while Mason was still on the *Rinaldo*:

Mason and Slidell are about the most worthless booty it would be possible to extract from the jaws of the American lion. They have long
been known as blind haters and revilers of this country. . . . They must
not suppose, because we have gone to the verge of a great war to rescue
them, that they are precious in our eyes. . . . Let the Commissioners
come quietly to town and have their say with anybody who may have
time to listen to them. For our part, we cannot see how anything they
may have to tell can turn the scale of British duty and deliberation.[2]

The Tory spokesman in the House of Commons, Benjamin Disraeli, expressed hope that the government's policy of neutrality in the
American conflict would be continued. Palmerston reported to the
queen that he had assured the House that "Your Majesty has no intention to depart from the position of strict neutrality with regard to the
Civil War in North America."[3]

Mason asked for an unofficial interview with Russell, who agreed
to receive him at his London residence on February 10. Russell listened patiently while Mason read sections of his instructions related to
recognition and the blockade. Mason's statement that "in no possible
contingency would the Confederate States come under a common government with the North" strengthened Russell's conviction that the
war could only end in the permanent separation of North and South.
But Mason reported that "Earl Russell seemed utterly disinclined to
enter into conversation . . . as to the policy of his Government and
only said, in substance, they must await events."[4]

Although Mason was never received socially by the prime minister
or any member of his cabinet, he was a frequent guest at the London
houses and country estates of many other British aristocrats, including
a number of the wealthiest and most conservative men in England and
several members of the previous Tory government. These men were
already sympathetic to the Confederacy for the various reasons outlined in chapter 3. Mason made little effort to reach a wider spectrum
of the British leadership, and he ignored the working classes, who
strongly supported the Union.

The British response to the Union blockade of Confederate ports
was debated in the House of Commons on March 7. Palmerston
reported to the queen:

Mr. Gregory, who . . . is a great champion of the southern Confederacy, made a speech of an hour and three quarters, the object of which was to prove that the blockades established by the Federal Government against the southern ports are not effective or consistent with the law of nations and that they ought not to be acquiesced in by Great Britain. . . . The Solicitor-General . . . proved . . . that it is impossible for Great Britain not to acquiesce in these blockades, that to force them would be an act of war and would be a departure from principles which if Great Britain were a belligerent it should be obliged stoutly to maintain and act upon.[5]

Later in the spring, as the cotton famine became more severe and unemployment in Lancashire skyrocketed, Adams reported "a decided increase in the pressure for some kind of intervention" to restore the supply of cotton.[6] Adams's concern about possible British recognition and/or intervention was enhanced by a strange "private and confidential" letter in mid-June from Lord Palmerston. The prime minister strongly protested an order of a Union general who was attempting to control the insulting behavior of Confederate ladies in New Orleans toward his troops, who had occupied that city on April 25. General Benjamin F. Butler had announced that women making such insults would be "regarded and treated as common women plying their vocation," that is, as prostitutes. The order had been condemned in Britain as barbaric and outrageous. Since direct correspondence between a prime minister and a foreign diplomat was highly unusual, Adams feared that Palmerston was trying to precipitate a misunderstanding as an excuse for a change to a policy more sympathetic to the Confederacy.

In his reply Adams asked if the letter was meant as an official communication or only as a private exchange between gentlemen. Palmerston's response evaded that question but again expressed strong opinions on General Butler's acts and the president's duty to disavow them. Adams asked again for a clarification of the intent of the first note. A few days later he saw Russell, who insisted that no change in British policy was in the offing. A final note from Palmerston was sufficiently conciliatory to be considered a "substantial retreat."[7]

Meanwhile, there was more discussion in the press of some form of British intervention in the American conflict. The primary stimulus was the unauthorized amateur diplomacy of William Lindsay, a pro-Confederate member of Parliament from Glasgow who was one of Britain's most important shipowners. Lindsay went to Paris and saw Napoleon, who authorized him to tell Russell and Palmerston that the ineffective Union blockade should be disavowed by the European powers. On his return to London, Lindsay offered a motion in Parliament for British diplomatic recognition of the Confederacy. Debate on the motion was scheduled for July 18.

Just before the debate the news arrived that General McClellan, who had reached a point only twenty miles from Richmond, had been repelled by General Lee and that the Union peninsular campaign had failed. During the stormy debate, Lindsay stated that he "desired the disruption of the American Union . . . because it was too great a power and England should not let such a power exist on the American continent."[8] After a speech by Palmerston insisting that the Confederacy had not yet firmly established its independence and that Parliament should not interfere with the government's delicate efforts to keep British options open while awaiting further developments in America, Lindsay withdrew his motion.

The following week Russell replied to a note from Mason presenting the Confederate arguments for recognition: "In the opinion of Her Majesty's Government any proposal to recognize the Southern Confederacy would irritate the United States, and any proposal to the Confederate States to return to the Union would irritate the Confederates."[9] Yet a few weeks later Russell would attempt to convince Palmerston and his cabinet colleagues that Britain should recognize the Confederacy as part of a broader European effort to end the bloody war in America.

∞ ∞ ∞

Mercier, the French minister in Washington, had been an energetic advocate of European intervention for some months. Lyons, the British minister, reported that Mercier's April trip to Richmond had convinced his French colleague "that the restoration of the old Union was impossible; that . . . the war would, if the powers of Europe exercised no influence on it, last for years; that . . . in the end the independence of the

South must be recognized; and that the governments of Europe should be on the watch for a favorable opportunity of doing this in such a manner to end the war."[10]

Lyons had remained skeptical. If he had been in Washington that summer and fall, the British government's serious contemplation of intervention might have been avoided. But his health was poor, and he obtained Russell's permission to take home leave in England for an extended period that included the sticky Washington summer that was detested by all British diplomats. For five crucial months in the summer and fall of 1862 the British post in Washington was occupied by a chargé d'affaires, William Stuart, who had served as attaché and secretary in several British legations. Stuart was much more sympathetic than Lyons to the Southern cause and to Mercier's ideas about intervention.[11] One of Stuart's first letters to Russell reported on a talk with Mercier. The French minister had insisted that a joint British-French mediation was the only possible way of ending the war in America. Stuart thought the time for intervention might come soon. "By waiting for a disaster, we may find opportunity."[12]

In July, Adams asked Seward how he should respond to any offer of "good offices" by the British government. Seward's reply made it clear that the United States would not tolerate European meddling:

> If the British government shall in any way approach you directly or indirectly . . . on the subject of our internal affairs, whether . . . to dictate, or to mediate, or to advise, or even to solicit or persuade, you will answer that you are forbidden to debate, to hear, or in any way receive, entertain, or transmit any communication of the kind.[13]

Seward repeated the previous instruction that, if Britain recognized the independence of the Confederacy, Adams was to suspend his diplomatic mission.

Adams received this instruction on August 16, after Parliament had adjourned and cabinet members had left for their estates in the country. He made no immediate effort to inform the foreign secretary of Seward's total rejection of any form of European intervention. This inaction was consistent with Seward's instruction, which had been limited to prescribing Adams's reaction in the event that the British government took any step toward intervention. But Adams's failure to communicate Seward's total rejection of any European meddling allowed Russell and Palmerston to believe that some form of European intervention might end the war in America. Russell gave Adams no hint that the British government was considering intervention.[14]

Palmerston's evolving attitude toward intervention was analyzed by a biographer, Herbert C. F. Bell:

> Throughout the spring and early summer, Palmerston stood against interference in the American struggle; in the late summer and early autumn he was one of its leading advocates. . . . All that actually appears [in his letters] is a deepening conviction that the Confederacy's independence was assured, and an increasing desire to put as short a term as possible to the distress occasioned on both sides of the Atlantic by the war. . . . He seems to have been drawn slowly from his original determination to avoid risking "a bloody nose" by the effects of Southern propaganda, . . . reports of Southern success on the battlefield, and evidence . . . of the distress to be anticipated by his countrymen if the war went on. Around the middle of July he was very much engrossed in devising measures of relief for the sufferers in the cotton manufacturing areas. He turned to the idea of intervention at the beginning of August.[15]

Palmerston and Russell never understood Lincoln's unswerving determination to restore the Union. The futility of any European effort to promote an accommodation between North and South on the basis of permanent separation should have been evident from Lincoln's widely published August 22 letter to Horace Greeley:

> My paramount object in this struggle is to save the Union, and is not either to save or destroy slavery. If I could save the Union without freeing any slave I would do it, and if I could save it by freeing all the slaves I would do it; and if I could save it by freeing some and leaving others alone, I would also do that.[16]

But the publication of this letter in Britain in early September was quickly followed by the news that on August 30 the Union army had suffered another major defeat along the same Virginia creek—Bull Run—where it had been so disastrously defeated the previous summer. British leaders thought the Union defeat proved that there was no hope of preserving the Union and that the time was near for British intervention to end the bloody war.

"The Federals . . . got a very complete smashing," Palmerston wrote Russell on September 14, "and it seems not altogether unlikely that still greater disasters await them and that even Washington or Baltimore may fall into the hands of the Confederates. If this should happen, would it not be time for us to consider whether . . . England and France might not address the contending parties and recommend an arrangement based on separation?"[17] The prime minister thought that, if mediation were refused, the two nations should recognize Confederate independence. Russell wrote Palmerston the same day that "in October the hour will be ripe" for cabinet discussion of mediation.[18] Replying to Palmerston on September 17, he agreed that "the time has come for offering mediation to the United States Government with a view to the recognition of the independence of the Confederates. . . . In case of failure, we ought ourselves to recognize the Southern States as an independent state."[19]

In the third week of September the British learned that Lee had marched north from Bull Run, crossed the Potomac west of Washington, and threatened to cut off communications between Washington and the Northern states. No diplomatic move could be made until the results of this major military movement were known. "It is evident that a great conflict is taking place to the northwest of Washington," Palmerston wrote Russell on September 23; "if the Federals sustain a great defeat they may be at once ready for mediation, and the iron should be struck while it is hot. If, on the other hand, they should have the best of it, we may wait a while and see what may follow."[20]

Even before the results of Lee's invasion of Maryland were known in Europe, several members of the British cabinet doubted that Britain could intervene diplomatically in the conflict in America without being drawn into the war. In a letter to Russell on September 27 the earl of Granville, Lord President of the Council, described the dangers inherent in any offer of mediation:

I doubt whether in offering to mediate, we should do so with any bona-fide expectation of its being accepted. . . . If the South refuses . . . it would be hardly a reason for recognizing them. If the North alone refused, the question would then naturally arise whether we ought not then to recognize the South. Such a recognition . . . would not by itself remove the blockade, or supply us with cotton. It would give no physical strength to the South, but it would greatly stimulate the North and undoubtedly assist their Government in raising men and money. . . . If . . . the Confederates continue victorious, as is to be hoped, we should stand better then than now in recognizing them. In any case I doubt, if the war continues long after our recognition of the South, whether it will be possible for us to avoid drifting into it.[21]

Palmerston received Granville's letter, forwarded by Russell, at about the same time as news of the bloody battle on September 17 at Antietam Creek, near the village of Sharpsburg. The battle was considered a Union victory, although McClellan had allowed Lee's army to escape and return to Virginia. In an October 2 note to Russell, Palmerston acknowledged that Antietam was not "the great success of the South against the North" that would have provided a favorable opportunity for European intervention and that Granville's letter contained "much deserving of serious consideration." Any initiative by England and France should involve a suggestion that the parties "consider whether the war, however long continued, could lead to any other result than separation" and whether the great evils from prolonged hostilities could be avoided by an early agreement on "the principle of separation which must apparently be the inevitable result of the contest."[22]

Despite the Confederate disappointment at Antietam, Russell was determined to forge ahead with some form of intervention. "Two things however must be made clear," he wrote Palmerston on October 4. "(1) That we propose separation. (2) That we shall take no part in the war unless attacked ourselves."[23]

On October 6 Russell received a September 23 letter from Stuart indicating that he and Mercier now favored a proposal for an armistice without immediate recognition of the Confederacy or any mention of permanent separation. Mercier thought that after Antietam neither

North nor South wanted to resume hostilities and that both would therefore accept the proposal for an armistice.[24] In a speech in Newcastle on October 7, William Gladstone, Chancellor of the Exchequer, stated that the Confederate leaders "have made a nation" and that Britons could "anticipate with certainty the success of the Southern States so far as regards their separation from the North."[25] The speech gave the impression that the cabinet was preparing to recognize Confederate independence. In fact, there was no consensus among cabinet members for recognition or intervention. Even Russell, who thought something should be done, was not certain what should be done. H. C. Allen observed that "the foreign secretary was dangerously vague as to what exact action he envisaged":

> Sometimes he thought in terms of proposing an armistice, sometimes in terms of mediation, and sometimes even of recognizing the South or raising the blockade. He always professed that he contemplated making it quite clear "that we shall take no part in the war unless attacked ourselves," but it is more than doubtful that such ingenuous protestations would have availed to preserve peaceful relations with a furious North.[26]

After Gladstone's speech, Adams began to think of informing Russell of Seward's instructions to reject any proposal for European intervention and to break off his mission if the British recognized the Confederacy. But he saw some signs that Gladstone was only expressing his personal opinion, and decided to wait for further developments.[27] His son, Charles Francis Jr., stated in 1899 that Adams told William E. Forster about his instructions in strict confidence a few days after Gladstone's speech, while a guest at Forster's country house in Yorkshire.[28] Forster thought the cabinet should be informed of Seward's position before it made any commitment regarding intervention. Ephraim D. Adams wrote that Forster probably passed the gist of Adams's instructions to Russell through Thomas Milner-Gibson, president of the Board of Trade.[29] If so, Russell probably assumed that it was just more of Seward's "bluster."

During the week that Gladstone spoke in Newcastle, the British heard that Lincoln had declared on September 22 his intention to issue an Emancipation Proclamation at the beginning of 1863. Although Lincoln was primarily concerned with the effect of the proclamation in America, he also hoped that it would increase sympathy for the Union cause in Europe. "I cannot imagine that any European power would dare to recognize and aid the Southern Confederacy," he had remarked to Carl Schurz in January, "if it became clear that the Confederacy stands for slavery and the Union for freedom."[30]

Though unaware of the discussion of intervention among members of the British cabinet, Lincoln knew from the debates in Parliament in July and from the European press that the cotton famine was building pressure for some type of action by the British and French governments.[31] He told a delegation of Chicago clergy in mid-September that "to proclaim emancipation would secure the sympathy of Europe . . . which now saw no other reason for the strife than national pride and ambition [and] an unwillingness to abridge our domain and ambition. No other step would be as potent to prevent foreign intervention."[32]

His hopes for the international benefits of the proclamation have been overlooked by most historians. One exception was Princeton professor Woodrow Wilson, who wrote in 1893 that Lincoln hoped the proclamation would "imperatively prevent that foreign recognition of the Southern Confederacy which he dreaded."[33]

Lincoln was shocked by the initial reaction of British leaders and the British press that the proclamation was intended to provoke a "servile insurrection"—a bloody revolt of the slaves against their masters. Howard Jones found no evidence that Lincoln had thought the proclamation would lead to a slave revolt. "He talked only of black service in the Union army, mass flight from the plantations, and, to those slaves who remained, encouragement not to work."[34]

The upper class's reaction in Britain to the proclamation seems to have been influenced by concern about native uprisings in the British Empire and worry about the effect of emancipation in the American South on Britain's crucial cotton supply. Most upper class Englishmen had relatives or friends in the British colonies and vivid memories of native uprisings, especially the Great Mutiny in India in 1857–58.

Winston Churchill wrote that "the atrocities and reprisals of the blood-stained months of the Mutiny left an enduring and bitter mark in the memory of both countries."[35] "With the Indian horrors, real and imaginary, still fresh in their memories," Bryan Jenkins observed, "fears of servile insurrection and a massacre of white women and children in the slave states" undoubtedly played a role "in shaping and distorting the initial response of many Britons to Lincoln's proclamation."[36]

The idea that the Union might attempt to foment a slave revolt in the Confederacy had been broached by the first team of Confederate envoys,[37] discussed by Russell and Lyons in their private correspondence,[38] and mentioned by Russell in the House of Lords.[39] In a dispatch to Adams on May 28, a copy of which was given to Russell, Seward argued that European intervention would "render inevitable . . . that servile war, so completely destructive of all European interests in this country" which would "produce infinite suffering throughout the world and . . . result in an entirely new system of trade and commerce between the United States and all foreign nations."[40] These comments encouraged Russell to believe that, if the British recognized Confederate independence, the Union government might retaliate by encouraging slaves to revolt.

In a conversation with Cobden, and probably also in a talk with Russell, Adams stressed the danger that a convulsion in the Confederacy would totally disrupt cotton production. "The policy of my government had been carefully conservative. . . . But the time might come when . . . every other consideration would yield to the instinct of self-preservation. . . . The consequence might be a social convulsion in the southern states which . . . would put an end to all the prospect of obtaining any [cotton] from that quarter for years."[41]

Secretary of War Stanton recorded that, when Lincoln told cabinet members on July 13 that he was considering an emancipation proclamation, Seward expressed fear that "foreign nations will intervene to prevent the abolition of slavery, for the sake of cotton."[42] Many Britons assumed the Emancipation Proclamation would mean the almost immediate end of cotton production by slaves in America. "I begin to believe," John Bright wrote to Senator Sumner in October, "that another crop of cotton from slave labor will never again be grown on your Northern continent."[43] No British leader dared to express publicly a preference for the continuation of slavery over the suspension of cotton production in the South. But most British aristocrats believed that the Confederacy would sustain its independence, and they thus expected that both slavery and cotton production would continue there.

Palmerston was quoted by the *Post* in London on October 6 as calling the Emancipation Proclamation a "singular manifesto that could scarcely be treated seriously. It is not easy to estimate how utterly powerless and contemptible a government must have become which could sanction with its approval such . . . trash."[44] Stuart thought the proclamation was only a political move by an irresponsible leader: "There is no pretext of humanity about the Proclamation. It is cold, vindictive, and entirely political. It does not abolish slavery where it has the power; it protects 'the institution' for friends and only abolishes it on paper for its enemies. . . . It offers direct encouragement to servile insurrections."[45]

The Times was sure that Lincoln hoped to provoke a bloody slave revolt:

> Is the name of Lincoln ultimately to be classed in the catalog of monsters, wholesale assassins, and butchers of their kind? . . . When blood begins to flow and shrieks come piercing through the darkness, Mr. Lincoln will wait until the rising flames tell that all is consummated, and then he will rub his hands and think that revenge is sweet.[46]

In an October 13 memorandum to his cabinet colleagues, Lord Russell asserted that neither North nor South had obtained a decisive military superiority but that "as the war is aggressive on the part of the North and defensive on the part of the South, this result may be considered as favorable to the Southern cause." The memorandum contained very harsh criticism of the Emancipation Proclamation and of the policies he assumed would be followed in implementing it:

> Wherever the arms of the United States penetrate, a premium will be given to acts of plunder, of incendiarism, and of revenge. The military and naval authorities of the United States will be bound by their orders to maintain and protect the perpetrators of such acts. Wherever the

invasion of the Southern States is crowned by victory, society will be
disorganized, industry suspended, large and small proprietors of land
alike reduced to beggary.

Russell had accepted Stuart's and Mercier's idea that Britain and
other powers should propose an armistice to be followed by negotiations between North and South:

> It has become a question . . . whether it is not a duty for Europe to ask
> both parties, in the most friendly and conciliatory terms, to agree to a
> suspension of arms for the purpose of weighing calmly the advantages
> of peace against the contingent gain for further bloodshed and the pro-
> traction of so calamitous a war.[47]

There was strong opposition among cabinet members to Russell's
proposal. In a speech in Hereford on October 14 Secretary of War Sir
George Cornewall Lewis stated that everyone must admit that the
great war in America was still "undecided" and that "the time has not
yet arrived when it could be asserted in accordance with established
doctrines of international law that the independence of the Southern
States had been established."[48] Lewis's speech demonstrated that no
cabinet decision had been taken on mediation, and it stimulated further discussion in the press of the intervention issue. In an October 17
memo to cabinet members, Lewis asserted that the South had not yet
established its independence and that any offer of mediation would be
rejected by the North and would probably lead to war between Britain
and the United States.

Palmerston asked Lord Clarendon, a previous foreign secretary, to
consult Lord Derby, the leader of the Conservative opposition. Clarendon replied that Derby opposed both recognition and mediation:

> He said . . . recognition would merely irritate the North without
> advancing the cause of the South or procuring a single bale of cotton,
> and that mediation in the temper of the belligerents [would] be reject-
> ed. . . . As each party insisted upon having that which the other
> declared was vitally essential to its existence, it was clear that the war
> had not yet marked out the stipulations of a treaty of peace. . . . The

recognition of the South could be of no benefit to England unless we meant to sweep away the blockade, which would be an act of hostility toward the North.[49]

These similar statements by his secretary of war and the leader of the opposition made a major impression on Palmerston. The former foreign secretary still kept an eye on worrisome developments in Europe, and he was certain that war between Britain and the United States was not in Britain's national interest. On October 22, the day before the scheduled cabinet meeting, Palmerston wrote Russell that he had changed his mind about the desirability of intervention:

> All that we could possibly do . . . would be to ask the two Parties . . . whether they might not turn their thoughts toward an arrangement between themselves. But the answer of each might be written by us beforehand. The Northerns would say that the only condition of the arrangement would be the restoration of the Union; the South would say their only condition would be an acknowledgment by the North of Southern independence. . . . I am very much come back to our original view of the matter, that we must continue merely to be lookers-on until the war shall have taken a more decided turn.[50]

After receiving this letter, Russell canceled the cabinet meeting scheduled for the next day. Some members did not receive the last-minute notice and, on arrival at Whitehall, insisted on an informal discussion. Lewis and others expressed strong opposition to Russell's proposal. That afternoon Russell met with Adams, who was unaware then and later of Russell's advocacy of intervention. The foreign secretary assured the American minister that the British government was not presently inclined to change its policy of neutrality in the American conflict, but said he could make no promises as to the course the government might follow in the future.[51]

The next day Gladstone sent a memorandum to cabinet members in which he attempted to refute Lewis's contention that any mediation proposal would lead to war with the United States and argued that efforts to stop the war in America were essential to reduce the danger of a revolt by the starving cotton mill workers in Lancashire.[52] Russell agreed with Gladstone. If the North rejected good offices from the great powers of Europe, he wrote Lewis on October 26, "we should be entitled to choose our own time to recognize the Southern States."[53] But most other cabinet members supported the cautious position of the secretary of war. Home Secretary Sir George Grey thought a mediation offer would be rejected by the United States and would "increase the great risk of our having a quarrel with America on the termination of the war, which cannot but be a most serious evil to this country."[54]

❧   ❧   ❧

On October 27 the British minister in Paris, Lord Cowley, saw Napoleon, who expressed strong interest in a joint offer of mediation in the American civil war by the British, French, and Russian governments. The emperor thought the three governments should propose that mediation efforts be carried out during a six-month armistice during which the blockade of Confederate ports would be suspended. The new French foreign minister, Edouard Drouyn de Lhuys, conveyed this proposal in a dispatch on October 30 to the French minister in London, Baron Gros.

Palmerston very much doubted that the Union would agree to suspend the blockade, since the suspension would allow the Confederates to get all the supplies they needed during the period of the armistice. Moreover, he wrote Russell on November 2, that it would be impossible to draft provisions of the proposal regarding slavery and runaway slaves "which the Southerns would agree to, and people of England would approve of. The French Government are more free from the shackles of principle and of right and wrong on these matters . . . than we are." Russell admitted that there was little chance that the Union would accept the proposal, but he nonetheless believed that it should be made. He thought they should ask both parties if there were any terms on which they could agree to restore the Union; if there were none, they should be asked if there were any terms on which they could agree to separate. "It will be an honorable proposal to make, but the North and probably the South will refuse it."[55]

Historians have cited various reasons for Russell's persistence in supporting intervention. Ephraim D. Adams could find no other motive except a desire for the restoration of world peace.[56] Frank Owsley apparently felt that Russell was mainly concerned with restoring Britain's cotton supply.[57] Howard Jones cited a combination of humanitarian and economic motives.[58]

As in October, Lewis led the opposition to the intervention proposal. In a long memorandum to cabinet members, Lewis argued that the Confederates had not yet earned the right to recognition according to established principles of international law. He outlined the many dangers associated with intervention, including the strong risk of war with the United States. The memorandum was drafted in part by his stepdaughter's husband, William Harcourt, who had opposed intervention in a series of articles in *The Times* signed "Historicus." In one of these he noted that "Rebellion, until it has succeeded, is Treason; when it is successful, it becomes Independence." Harcourt argued that the Confederate rebellion had not yet proved that it was successful and that support by a foreign government of rebels still regarded as traitors "almost inevitably . . . results in war" with the government against which they were rebelling.[59]

When the cabinet met on November 11, only Gladstone and Palmerston supported Russell's motion for acceptance of the French proposal. Palmerston's lukewarm support was primarily motivated by a desire to avoid an open break with his foreign secretary that would threaten his government, a coalition of several Liberal factions. It was apparently given only after he was sure that the proposal would be rejected. Lewis informed his brother-in-law, Lord Clarendon, that "the principal objection was that the proposed armistice of six months by sea and land, involving a suspension of commercial blockade, was so grossly unequal—so decidedly in favor of the South—that there was no chance of the North agreeing to it."[60]

One of Palmerston's biographers, W. Baring Pemberton, described his reaction to the threat of war with the United States:

> An older and more cautious Palmerston now occupied the stage. At forty-seven he might have played for higher stakes, using the threat of an alliance with the South and war with the North to break the blockade, bring hostilities to an end, and, flourishing the sanction of trade concessions, achieve something toward the end of slavery. At

seventy-seven he was very willing to be persuaded by Cobden's argument that it would be cheaper to feed Lancashire's unemployed every day on "turtle, champagne, and venison" than to embark on a war with the United States. Tired, aging, uncertain of his majority, Palmerston was in no mind to lead his country to war.[61]

In a note informing the French government of the cabinet decision, Russell explained that "Her Majesty's Government are led to the conclusion that there is no ground at the present moment to hope that the Federal Government would accept the proposal suggested."[62] The note was published in the British press on November 15. That day Russell saw Adams and gave him the impression that he was pleased by the cabinet decision. Adams told Russell of the August instructions from Seward that he should refuse to listen to any proposal for European interference and that he should suspend his diplomatic mission if the British recognized Confederate independence. Russell said Adams had been right to withhold the instruction.[63] Nonetheless, most of the events described in this chapter might have been avoided if the U.S. rejection of any form of European intervention had been clearly understood by the British government.

Late in November the New York press learned that the French had proposed joint intervention with the British and that the proposal had been rejected by the British cabinet. Lyons sent Russell clippings from four newspapers, noting that "in every one of them foreign intervention is distinctly repudiated."[64] Through this report and Adams's belated revelation of Seward's instructions, Russell finally became convinced of the total rejection of European intervention by the government and people of the United States.

∾   ∾   ∾

Lincoln and Seward would certainly have rejected any offer of British or joint mediation as summarily as they subsequently rejected a unilateral offer of French mediation. There was no chance that Lincoln would have accepted an armistice. Suspension of the blockade for six months would have eliminated all the advantages the Union had derived from its massive blockade efforts in 1861 and 1862.

But a mediation proposal by the British and French would not have led to war between the United States and Britain unless it had been followed by diplomatic recognition of Confederate independence and/or other intervention. The United States was already fighting one war, and it certainly did not want another. Full consideration by the British government of the consequences of war with the United States would have led to the conclusion that Britain had much to lose, and little to gain, from such a war. War with the United States would have seriously threatened British control of Canada, British trade around the world, and the profits being derived by British manufacturers, merchants, shipbuilders, and shipowners from the "neutral" British trade with the Confederates.

In his annual message to Congress in early December, Lincoln acknowledged that his administration would be judged by the world primarily on its efforts to eliminate slavery:

> Fellow-citizens, we cannot escape history. . . . The fiery trial through which we pass will light us down, in honor or dishonor, to the latest generation. . . . In giving freedom to the slave, we assure freedom to the free. . . . We shall nobly save or meanly lose the last, best hope of earth.[65]

By Christmas there were signs that, despite the initial misunderstanding of Lincoln's motives, the Emancipation Proclamation was having a substantial favorable impact on public opinion in Europe. Seward noted that Lincoln was "disposed to take a more cheering view of our foreign relations at this time than he has allowed himself to indulge at any previous period since the civil war commenced."[66] James K. Pike reported from The Hague that "the anti-slavery position of the government is at length giving us a substantial foothold in European circles. . . . Everyone can understand the significance of a war where emancipation is written on one banner and slavery on the other."[67]

Henry Adams wrote his brother in January that the working class had demonstrated strong support for Lincoln's emancipation policy:

> The Emancipation Proclamation has done more for us here than all our former victories and all our diplomacy. It is creating an almost

convulsive reaction in our favor all over this country. . . . Public
opinion is very deeply stirred and finds expression in meetings,
addresses to President Lincoln, deputations to us, standing commit-
tees to agitate the subject and to affect opinion, and all the other
symptoms of a great popular movement peculiarly unpleasant to the
upper classes here because it rests on the spontaneous action of the
laboring classes.[68]

When Parliament reconvened in February 1863, there was strong
bipartisan support for maintaining the policy of neutrality and nonintervention. Richard Cobden wrote Sumner that Lincoln's emancipation policy had aroused the long-standing British feelings against
slavery: "Any unfriendly act on the part of our government, no matter
which of our aristocratic parties is in power, toward your cause is not
to be apprehended."[69] William S. Gregory, a leader of the Confederate
lobby, told Mason that "the most influential men of all parties" now
opposed recognition of the Confederacy.[70] Mason reported that "both
parties are guided . . . by a fixed English purpose to run no risk of a
broil, even far less, a war with the United States."[71]

In mid-February Russell informed Lyons that he saw no point of
further consideration of mediation, at least until both the Union and
Confederacy were "heartily tired and sick of the business."[72] Russell's
abandonment of his earlier support for intervention resulted from his
belated awareness that Lincoln and Seward utterly refused to accept
any form of European meddling; that the North was, after all, fighting
a war against slavery; that the cotton crisis was receding; and, perhaps
most important, that there was very little support for recognition and
intervention in the cabinet and in the Parliament.

"Unquestionably," Thomas A. Bailey wrote, "the Emancipation
Proclamation was a cardinal stroke in Northern diplomacy. It robbed
the South of its moral cause and elevated the struggle into a holy crusade against human bondage."[73] Bruce Catton observed that "no government that had to pay the least attention to the sentiment of its own
people could take sides against a government which was trying to
destroy slavery. . . . After 1862 the chance that Great Britain would
decide in favor of the Confederacy became smaller and smaller and
presently vanished entirely."[74]

But the threat of European intervention still seemed real in the first months of 1863. In February a joint resolution declared that the U.S. Congress would consider any European efforts to bring the war to an end as "injurious to its national interests" and "an unfriendly act," and that "the United States hereby announce, as their unalterable purpose, that the war will be vigorously prosecuted . . . until the rebellion shall be overcome."[75] "Europe," Attorney General Bates noted in his diary on February 26, "will be for or against us, just . . . as we win or lose success. In short, we must beat the enemy, or lose the friendship and support of Europe."[76]

In April Lincoln asked Sumner to send John Bright a resolution he had drafted that might be adopted by groups in England that supported the Union cause: "Whereas . . . an attempt has been made to construct a new nation upon the basis of . . . human slavery, . . . Resolved, that no such embryo State should ever be recognized by, or admitted into, the family of Christian and civilized nations."[77] By then, however, Lincoln's international interests had begun to shift to the danger of a war with England arising from an unfortunate naval incident and the danger of a war with France arising from the French invasion of Mexico.

CHAPTER 10

The Wolf from Liverpool

British Roles in the Construction, Escape, and Operations of the Confederate Raider Alabama

Aside from the brief *Trent* affair, the most important source of U.S.-British tension during the Civil War was the construction in Britain of a number of warships for the Confederacy. The tensions arising from the construction of several "commerce raiders," especially the future *Alabama*, are reviewed in this chapter. Successful U.S. efforts in 1863 to convince the British government to detain two ironclad rams that had been built for the Confederacy are described in chapter 12.

જ   જ   જ

On the day the Confederates fired on Fort Sumter, James D. Bulloch offered his services to Confederate Secretary of the Navy Stephen R. Mallory. Bulloch had been an officer in the United States Navy from 1839 to 1853 and commanded commercial mail steamers for eight years thereafter. Mallory commissioned Bulloch as a commander in the Confederate navy and ordered him to go to Britain and arrange for the construction there of warships suitable for the capture and destruction of U.S. merchant ships.

Several explanations have been offered for the high priority Mallory gave to the construction of commerce raiders. Burton Hendrick wrote that Mallory hoped the raiders would divert Union ships from

142

the blockade: "[If] warships . . . blockading Southern ports . . . should be detached from their Atlantic vigil and scattered to all parts of the world . . . the blockade would automatically come to an end. The pride the Northern section took in its beautiful, swift sailing ships . . . was notorious. That New England would sit by patiently and witness this noble armada disappear in flames . . . no one in the South believed."[1] Joseph T. Durkin, biographer of Mallory, wrote of the secretary's conviction that "the raids of the cruisers against Northern commerce must be made so damaging that the Federal government would be forced to withdraw numerous ships from the blockading squadrons in order to pursue the 'highwaymen of the sea.' "[2]

Yet there are several reasons for doubting that diversion of Union ships from the blockade was Mallory's primary objective in 1861. At the time the decision was made to send Bulloch to Europe, the Confederates were not very concerned about the prospective blockade. They were discouraging cotton exports in order to encourage European recognition, and had not yet realized the crucial importance of importing arms and supplies from Britain. Moreover, they thought the blockade could never be effective. Mallory, former chairman of the U.S. Senate Committee on Naval Affairs, knew how few U.S. Navy ships were available for blockade duty, and he could hardly have foreseen the subsequent rapid expansion of the blockading fleet described in chapter 11. He also knew as well as his counterpart in Washington that diverting Union ships to search for Confederate raiders would be pointless.

Durkin also wrote that Mallory thought "raiding the sea-borne commerce of the North . . . would strike an indirect but serious blow at Northern war industries."[3] In fact, imported equipment or raw materials played a minor role in the Union war effort, and the Confederate raiders rarely captured ships carrying cargoes of significant military value.

The Confederate commerce raiders were mainly engaged in a type of psychological warfare. Their primary mission was stated by John M. Taylor, biographer of Raphael Semmes, captain of two of the raiders: "to take the war to the enemy . . . in such a way as to force the Federals to sue for peace."[4]

Bulloch described in his memoirs his meeting with Mallory on May 9, 1861:

He warned me to be prudent and heedful, so as not to involve the diplomatic agents of the Confederate states in embarrassing complaints for alleged violation of neutral law or obligation, and he directed me to acquaint myself, as soon as possible after my arrival in England, with the nature and scope of the Foreign Enlistment Act and the Queen's Proclamation of Neutrality, if one should be issued. . . . He impressed upon me the wish of the Government to get cruising ships of suitable type afloat with the quickest possible despatch.[5]

Bulloch arrived in England on June 4, 1861. While he was at sea, the royal proclamation that recognized Confederate belligerency (described in chapter 4) also exhorted British subjects to comply with the Foreign Enlistment Act, the only British legislation governing the construction of ships for a belligerent. There had never been a judicial interpretation of the act. Bulloch engaged a leading Liverpool solicitor, F. S. Hull, who drew up an opinion and checked it with two eminent barristers. Hull concluded that (1) the law did not prohibit the construction—as distinct from the arming—of any ship, regardless of the use intended by the purchaser, and (2) although the law prohibited the arming of a warship within Her Majesty's dominions with intent to use the ship against a friendly state, there was no legal bar to adding British-built armaments to a British-built ship if the arming occurred outside Her Majesty's dominions.[6]

This legal advice guided all of Bulloch's relations with British shipbuilders. "Every possible precaution was practiced," he wrote in his memoirs, "both for the protection of the builders against criminal prosecutions under the Act and for that of the ships against forfeiture. In no case was any builder or vendor informed what was the purpose of the purchasers. No ship was ever supplied any portion of her equipment within her Majesty's dominions."[7]

The first Confederate commerce raider was the *Sumter*, a small propeller steamer built in the United States and partially rebuilt for service as a raider. It was commanded by Raphael Semmes, later captain of the *Alabama*. The *Sumter* captured seventeen U.S. merchant ships before it was blockaded by three Union warships at Gibraltar in April 1862 and was decommissioned and sold.

The raiders built for Bulloch in Britain were wooden sailing ships that were also equipped with powerful steam engines. "A vessel without good sailing qualities," Bulloch wrote in his memoirs, "would have been practically useless as a Confederate cruiser. She could only have made passages from one coaling station to another."[8] The raiders were usually under sail, and they used their precious coal only when necessary to overtake ships flying the U.S. flag.

The first warship built in Britain for the Confederacy was initially known as the *Oreto* but cruised as the *Florida*. She was built for Bulloch at the William C. Miller and Sons shipyard in Liverpool using a design adapted from drawings for a Royal Navy gunboat. Adams sent a protest concerning the ship to Russell on February 29, 1862, but the Commissioners of Customs reported that there was no evidence to contradict the builder's statement that the ship was to go to Italy, not America. Adams talked to Russell about the ship on March 22, but that day the vessel departed from Liverpool.

The British government's subsequent effort to prevent the *Oreto* from serving as a Confederate cruiser was described in a British court in 1863:

> Our government immediately sent orders to Nassau, whither she was understood to have gone, and when she arrived there she was watched. Upon the appearance of a delivery of stores which appeared to be her munitions of war into the *Oreto* while in our waters, although the case was doubtful and it was questionable whether the evidence would prove sufficient, still, to show our good faith, we strained a point, and acting upon some evidence, the *Oreto* was seized.[9]

Seward was delighted by the seizure. The British chargé reported that Seward told him that, as a result of the British action, the United States would not commission privateers to search for Confederate raiders and blockade runners, "although he could not assure me that such a measure might not hereafter be found necessary."[10]

Seward's delight was premature. Due to insufficient evidence, the legal action at Nassau against the *Oreto* was unsuccessful and the vessel was released. At a small island sixty miles from Nassau, the ship took on the armaments sent from England by Bulloch in another ship, the Confederate flag was raised, and she began her cruise as the *Florida*. The commerce raider cruised for more than two years, capturing thirty-eight American merchant ships, until she was captured by an American warship in the harbor of Bahia, Brazil, in October 1864.

The second ship built for Bulloch in England was destined to sail as the *Alabama* and to have a profound effect on U.S.-British relations and on the U.S. role in world shipping. The future Confederate raider was built by the Laird Brothers firm at Birkenhead, across the Mersey from Liverpool. She was 220 feet long and 32 feet wide, with a draft when fully loaded of 15 feet, and was rated at 1,040 tons. Each of the two horizontal steam engines was rated at 300 horsepower, but her trial run indicated that her maximum total power was close to 1,000 horsepower. Her bunkers could carry 350 tons of coal. She was equipped with a double set of sails, a condenser to produce fresh water from seawater, and spare equipment and supplies sufficient for a long voyage.[11]

The future *Alabama* did not attract the attention of the U.S. consul in Liverpool, Thomas Dudley, until after she was launched on May 15, 1862. She was christened the *Enrica*. Bulloch pressed the firm to complete as quickly as possible the installation of her engines and all other equipment *except* armament. Since this ship would become the most successful of the Confederate raiders and the center of a bitter controversy between the United States and Britain that raged until 1872, a careful examination is warranted of the circumstances surrounding her escape from Britain.

A decade of diplomatic correspondence concerning this ship began on June 23, 1862, when Adams wrote Russell that "a new and still more powerful war steamer . . . is fitting out for the especial and manifest object of carrying on hostilities by sea. . . . The parties engaged in the enterprise are persons well known at Liverpool to be agents and officers of the insurgents in the United States." He enclosed a report from Dudley.[12]

Russell forwarded the note and report to the Commissioners of the Customs. After consulting the collector of customs at Liverpool, S. Price Edwards, they replied on July 1 that "at present there is not sufficient ground to warrant the detention of the vessel."[13] Russell sent this reply to Adams on July 4. Adams consulted an eminent queen's counsel, R. P. Collier, whose status in the British legal community is indicated by his subsequent appointment to the government position of queen's advocate. Collier thought the evidence was "almost conclusive" and suggested on July 16 that Edwards be asked to detain the ship temporarily until further evidence could be obtained.[14] Adams asked Dudley to submit to Edwards all the evidence he had against the *Enrica*.

It was very difficult, Adams noted a decade later, "in a city swarming with [Confederate] sympathizers . . . to find persons who . . . were disposed to subject themselves to the odium attending a public declaration of the truth."[15] Nevertheless, when Dudley and his solicitor called on Edwards on July 21, they gave him six depositions. One was by a seaman who said Captain Butcher, registered as captain of the *Enrica*, had told him the ship was being built for the Confederacy. In 1872 the British member of the international tribunal at Geneva considering the "Alabama claims," Sir Alexander Cockburn, admitted that these depositions "established a strong case against the vessel, and afforded sufficient reason for seizing her."[16]

Adams observed in 1872 that it was difficult to resist the suspicion that Edwards had been "more or less in direct sympathy with the designs of the insurgents and not unwilling to accord to them all the indirect aid which could be supplied by a purely passive policy on his part."[17] Adams's son wrote in 1900 that Edwards "willfully shut his eyes, and would not be convinced by anything possible to obtain."[18]

The legal advisers of the Board of Customs thought the depositions did not provide sufficient grounds for seizure of the ship. This judgment was reported on July 22 to the secretary of the Treasury, George A. Hamilton, who sent the report and the depositions that day to the undersecretary at the Foreign Office, Austen Henry Layard, with the suggestion that Lord Russell might ask for the opinion of the legal advisers to the British government, the Law Officers of the Crown.[19] Their roles were described in a British paper presented to the Geneva tribunal in 1872:

> In England there is no ministry of justice or similar department of state
> to which recourse can be had by other departments when . . . a decision
> involving a question of law is required. This want is supplied by the

appointment of three Law Officers, as they are called. Two of these—
the Attorney General and the Solicitor General—are barristers or advocates with seats in the House of Commons who have been selected by
the ministry of the day. . . . The third Law Officer—the Queen's Advocate—is a permanent official. . . . The Law Officers have no bureau or
office set apart for their use, and no regular staff of assistants or
archives. . . . When time is pressing, it is usual for the three Law Officers to meet and confer together, after they have all read the papers.[20]

Hamilton's suggestion arrived at the Foreign Office on Tuesday
afternoon (July 22) at about the same time as another letter from
Adams enclosing copies of the six affidavits that had been submitted to
Edwards.[21] Layard talked to Russell, who agreed that the Law Officers
should be consulted. On Wednesday morning (July 23), Layard sent
the documents received from the Treasury to the Law Officers with a
request for their opinion. Although the note was marked "Immediate"
and asked for an opinion "at your earliest convenience," there was no
indication of the sense of urgency Adams had conveyed.[22] The papers
were sent to the home of the senior Law Officer, Sir John Harding, the
queen's advocate. Harding was ill, and later proved to be insane. The
documents remained at his home for five days without action. Russell
told Adams later that the delay "had most unexpectedly been caused
by the sudden development of a malady of the Queen's Advocate . . .
totally incapacitating him for the transaction of business."[23]

The same morning (July 23), Dudley's solicitor, A. F. Squarry,
delivered two more depositions about the ship to the Board of Customs in London, which immediately sent them to Layard. Squarry
called on Layard that afternoon, and was told that the papers had been
sent to the Law Officers. When Squarry said the matter was extremely
urgent, Layard promised to ask for the opinion "at once," but there is
no indication that he made any effort to accelerate the decision.[24] His
second note to the Law Officers that afternoon, transmitting the additional depositions, was not marked "Immediate" and repeated only the
previous request for an opinion "at your earliest convenience."[25]

Meanwhile, Adams had sent Collier copies of the six previous and
two additional affidavits. On Thursday (July 24) Adams received
another opinion from Collier; he wrote that if the collector of customs

did not detain the vessel "the Foreign Enlistment Act . . . is little better than a dead letter" and the U.S. government would have "serious grounds for remonstrance" against the British government.[26] Adams wrote later that Collier's opinion was "like a thunderbolt in a clear sky" because it shifted the responsibility for stopping the vessel from U.S. to British authorities.[27] Adams immediately sent Collier's opinion to Russell. He claimed later that Adams's July 24 note and Collier's new opinion did not arrive at the Foreign Office until Saturday (July 26),[28] but it seems more likely that the two-day delay was due to indecision. "I thought it my duty," Russell wrote in his memoirs, "to wait for the report of the Law Officers of the Crown, but I ought to have been satisfied with the opinion of Sir Robert Collier and to have given orders to detain the Alabama at Birkenhead."[29]

Layard sent Adams's note and attachments on Saturday afternoon to the office of the attorney general, Sir William Atherton, but they arrived after the office was closed for the weekend. The fact that the papers were sent to Atherton rather than Harding indicates that Layard was aware by then that Harding was incapacitated. The fact that they were sent to Atherton's office rather than to his home suggests that Layard was not eager for urgent action by the other two Law Officers. Sir Roundell Palmer, the solicitor general, wrote in 1869 that he saw the papers for the first time when Atherton brought them to his office late on Monday afternoon (July 28).

Atherton and Palmer agreed that immediate steps should be taken to prevent the *Enrica* from escaping. They wrote Russell on Tuesday morning (July 29) that the evidence submitted to them "makes it reasonably clear that such vessel is intended for warlike use against citizens of the United States and in the interest of the (so-called) Confederate States. . . . We therefore recommend that, without loss of time, the vessel be seized by the proper authorities."[30] When this opinion was received by the Foreign Office on Tuesday afternoon, a telegram was sent to Liverpool ordering that the ship be detained.[31]

❧   ❧   ❧

By the time the telegram arrived in Liverpool, the future *Alabama* was already on the Irish Sea. On Saturday (July 26) Bulloch had learned "from a private but most reliable source"—which he was still unwilling to identify in his memoirs in 1881—that it would not be safe for the *Enrica* to remain in Liverpool for more than forty-eight hours.[32]

Several historians have written that the tip came from the prime minister's office or from "Downing Street," but there is no evidence to support this idea. Charles Francis Adams Jr. wrote in 1900 that it was whispered that the warning came from the collector of customs in Liverpool, S. Price Edwards, but admitted that "there is no evidence whatever that such was the case."[33] Since Adams's July 24 letter and enclosures arrived at the attorney general's office after it was closed for the weekend, the information that action was likely on Monday or Tuesday could only have come from Russell or from the Foreign Office.

In November Russell told Adams that John Bright was saying privately that Russell himself had sent the warning to Bulloch. The foreign secretary implied that Bright might have heard this from Adams, but the American minister denied that he had said such a thing to anyone.[34] There is no reason to believe that, at a time when Russell was considering a delicate diplomatic intervention in the American conflict (described in chapter 9), he would have taken a step that would certainly lead to new U.S.-British tensions. It is therefore probable that the tip to Bulloch came indirectly from someone at the Foreign Office.

The Foreign Office official responsible for the correspondence about the ship was the parliamentary undersecretary, Austen Henry Layard. The hypothesis that Layard was the source of the tip to Bulloch is supported by considerable circumstantial evidence. Layard was neither a typical politician nor a typical diplomat. The son of a middle-class British civil servant in Ceylon, he achieved fame as an archaeologist in Turkey and later served in the British Embassy in Constantinople. His biographer described him as impetuous, hot-tempered, dogmatic, highly principled, single-minded, and sometimes insubordinate.[35] Russell characterized Layard in a letter to the queen as "a man of ability and of an upright character, but somewhat hasty in his opinions."[36]

Although there is no record of Layard's opinions on the American conflict, there is evidence of his substantial exposure to pro-Confederate viewpoints. William S. Gregory, later best man at Layard's wedding,

Abraham Lincoln's axiom "one war at a time" hinted that British or French meddling in the American conflict could lead to war with Washington.

Secretary of State William Henry Seward used the threat of war with the United States to prevent British and French recognition and support of the Confederacy.

National Archives

Charles Sumner, chairman of the Senate Foreign Relations Committee, opposed both Seward's initial tough stance toward Britain and later efforts by Lincoln and Seward to conciliate Britain.

Library of Congress

An 1861 cartoon about Northern fears of European intervention. Uncle Sam is routing John Bull, depicted as a poacher carrying cotton plants and wearing on his legs British-built Confederate cannons. The rooster on the fence is Napoleon III of France. Uncle Sam is saying, "John, You lost your Non-interfering Principle. I'll lay it on your back again."

British Foreign Secretary Lord Russell (shown here in middle age) proposed British diplomatic intervention to stop the bloodshed in America and restore Britain's cotton supply, but most cabinet members feared that any form of intervention would lead to an unwanted war.

British minister Lord Lyons reported to London that Lincoln had no interest in foreign affairs and that Seward was willing to risk war with Britain to advance his political career.

Secretary of the Navy Gideon Welles thought Lincoln and Seward were excessively concerned about the danger of war with Britain.

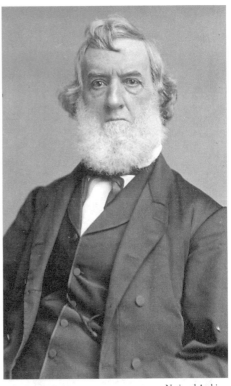

U.S. Navy Captain Charles Wilkes nearly started a war with Britain by removing Confederate envoys James Mason and John Slidell from the *Trent*, a British mail packet.

After his release by Lincoln, Confederate envoy James Mason was ignored by the British government, which realized that its recognition of Confederate independence would lead to war with the United States.

Confederate President Jefferson Davis, who had been sure Britain would intervene in the Civil War to obtain cotton, bitterly resented the British refusal to recognize his government.

The Confederate raider *Alabama* burns a captured Union merchant ship. This sketch, which appeared on the cover of *Harper's Weekly* in November 1862, contributed to Northern rage against the construction in Britain of warships for the Confederacy.

This sidewheel steamship was successively a British ferryboat, a Confederate blockade runner (the *Robert E. Lee*), and a Union warship (the *Fort Donelson*).

Confederate envoy John Slidell urged Napoleon III to recognize Southern independence and to allow the construction in France of warships for the Confederacy.

Confederate Secretary of State Judah P. Benjamin offered Napoleon III 100,000 bales of cotton at a low price if he would send a fleet to break the Union blockade, but the French emperor feared a war with the United States would interfere with French military operations in Mexico.

Before the war between Mexico and France, U.S. minister Thomas Corwin recommended financial aid to the republican government of Benito Juárez in Mexico, but Lincoln provided only moral and diplomatic support.

Mexican envoy Mattias Romero lobbied for U.S. economic and military support for the republican government in Mexico. Lincoln and Seward maintained strict U.S. neutrality in the war between Mexico and France but refused to recognize Austrian Archduke Maximilian as "emperor" of Mexico.

After Appomattox, Ulysses S. Grant wanted to send an army of Union and Confederate veterans to drive the French from Mexico, but Seward maintained Lincoln's policy of intensified diplomatic pressure for French withdrawal.

was one of the most vocal supporters of the Confederacy in Parliament. In March Gregory had spoken for nearly two hours in the House on the reasons why Britain should not acquiesce in the Union blockade of Confederate ports. As MP for Southwark, a dockland constituency in London, Layard was exposed to the pro-Confederate viewpoints of shipowners. They understood that Confederate raiders preying on U.S. shipping would provide a significant advantage to British shipping.

The hypothesis that Layard was the source of the warning to Bulloch provides possible explanations for a number of actions and inactions by Layard and Russell for which there are no other satisfactory explanations. If Layard had checked on the status of the Law Officers' opinion, after promising Squarry to do so on Wednesday, he would have discovered that Harding was too ill to deal with the matter. His apparent failure to check suggests that he was not eager for immediate action by the Law Officers. When Russell decided to send them Collier's opinion that the U.S. government would have "serious grounds of remonstrance" if the ship were allowed to escape, Layard knew it was probable that the Law Officers would recommend the detention of the ship. If sympathetic to the Confederate cause, Layard would have been motivated to pass the word to Bulloch through some "private but most reliable" person that the ship could not safely remain at her berth for more than forty-eight hours.

This hypothesis also accounts for Layard's failure to inform Russell by telegram of the ship's escape during the crucial hours when it might still have been stopped by the Royal Navy and for the absence, in Layard's note to Russell about the escape, of any expression of regret or any indication that any further action was required. It also accounts for the lateness and lack of any sense of urgency in Layard's letters conveying Russell's requests to the Treasury and the Colonial Office that the ship be detained if it came to Queenstown or Nassau.

Russell's subsequent awareness or suspicion of Layard's action would account for Russell's efforts to cover up the story of the government's handling of the *Alabama* case, for his curious comment to Lyons that the depredations of the *Alabama* were "a scandal and a reproach,"[37] and for his admission in his memoirs that the escape of the *Alabama* was "my fault as Her Majesty's Secretary of State for Foreign

Affairs."[38] As the cabinet minister in charge of the Foreign Office, Russell was responsible for any action by a Foreign Office official.

While the two Law Officers were deciding that the *Enrica* should be detained, Bulloch was carrying out an ingenious plan for her escape. On Monday (July 28) the ship was removed from the dock and prepared for a trial run, for which no custom house clearance was required. A group of guests—including the head of the Laird Brothers shipbuilding firm and his little daughter—was invited for an excursion on the river. On Tuesday morning (July 29) the ship left Birkenhead with the guests aboard and steamed down the Mersey. Bulloch then announced that he wanted to carry out night trials at sea and that the guests could return to Liverpool with him on the accompanying tug. The captain was ordered to take the ship to Moelfra Bay, on the north coast of Wales about forty-five miles west of Liverpool, and wait there for Bulloch until the next afternoon.

On Wednesday morning (July 30), at the berth of the tug, Bulloch met thirty-five to forty seamen who had been recruited on the Liverpool docks by one of his agents for a voyage to Havana. They were accompanied by a nearly equal number of women, who refused to leave their men before receiving the usual first month's pay. A customs officer arrived to inspect the tug, in response to a claim from the U.S. consul, Dudley, that she was loading munitions for the *Enrica*. The officer found no sign of munitions but reported that "a considerable number of persons, male and female, were on deck, some of whom admitted to me that they were a portion of the crew and were going to join the gun-boat."[39] He was also told that the warship was cruising off Point Lynas, a promontory just beyond Moelfra Bay.

Cockburn admitted at Geneva in 1872 that the customs officials at Liverpool, who had been ordered on Tuesday to detain the warship, missed an opportunity on Wednesday morning to follow the tug to the *Enrica* and/or to request the customs officials on the Welsh coast by telegram to search for her.[40] The customs officer only mailed a report to the Bureau of Customs in London, and the tug was allowed to depart without interference or surveillance. Bulloch took both the men and the women on the tug, met the *Enrica* at Moelfra Bay, gave them a late lunch with ample grog, and enlisted most of the men for a voyage to the Caribbean. The women were sent back to Liverpool that evening on the tug.

There were two possible routes to the Atlantic. The ship could go south through the wide but heavily traveled Saint George's Channel, passing to the south of Ireland, or it could go north through the Irish Sea and the North Channel between Scotland and Ireland. Before leaving Liverpool that morning Bulloch had received a telegram from an agent in Southampton indicating that a U.S. warship, the *Tuscarora*, had left there the previous evening, apparently en route to Queenstown, in southern Ireland. Bulloch chose the northern route through the Irish Sea, where he was less likely to meet a British or American warship. At six P.M. on Thursday (July 31) the *Enrica* reached Giant's Causeway, at the northern tip of Ireland. A fishing boat was hailed, and Bulloch and the pilot went ashore in a pelting rain. Captain Butcher proceeded to sea in accordance with his instructions from Bulloch.[41]

Meanwhile, on Tuesday afternoon (July 29) Adams heard from Dudley by telegram that the *Enrica* had escaped that morning. Unaware that Bulloch had already recruited sailors at Liverpool, he thought the ship would stop at Queenstown to pick up a full crew. Adams immediately sent a telegram to Captain Craven of the *Tuscarora*, which was at Southampton, and it sailed for that evening for Queenstown. On Thursday and Friday (July 31 and August 1) Adams sent telegrams to Craven in Queenstown with the news that the *Enrica* had been seen off Point Lynas. Adams thought this information confirmed the suspicion that she was headed for Queenstown: "You must catch her if you can, and, if necessary, follow her across the Atlantic." But Craven looked for the ship in the Saint George's Channel without success.[42]

Vigorous action by the British government immediately following the discovery that the *Enrica* had left Liverpool might have resulted in her detention while she was still in British waters. But no such action was taken. Russell had gone to his estate in the country. Layard, who might have sent Russell a telegram, chose to write a letter on the evening of July 29, which the foreign secretary did not receive until July 30. It contained no suggestion for any further action. Russell directed Layard to send a copy of the Law Officers' report to the colonial secretary, suggesting that it be forwarded to the governor of the Bahamas. Layard did so on July 31.[43] Two days later Layard complied with a direction from Russell to ask the secretary of the Colonial Office to suggest to the colonial secretary that he consider the "propriety" of instructing the governor of the Bahamas to detain the future *Alabama*. That same day—four days after Adams had sent the *Tuscarora* to Queenstown to search for the escaped vessel—Layard forwarded a request from Russell through Treasury channels that the ship be detained if it visited Queenstown.[44] No sense of urgency was conveyed by these leisurely interministerial communications.

In a cabinet meeting soon after the escape of the future *Alabama*, probably on August 2, Russell and the duke of Argyll urged that an order be sent to all British colonial authorities to seize the raider if she entered any British port. "When you brought it before the cabinet," Argyll recalled in a letter to Russell in 1872, "there was a perfect insurrection. Everybody but you and I were against the proposed step. [Lord Chancellor] Bethell was vehement against its 'legality,' and you gave it up."[45]

The future raider did not immediately proceed to any British port. Bulloch had arranged for another ship, the *Agrippina*, to carry the armament and munitions for the raider to the Portuguese Azores and to rendezvous there with the *Enrica*. The former captain of the *Sumter*, Raphael Semmes, who had been ordered to take over the new raider, also proceeded to the Azores. On August 24, 1862, Captain Semmes read his commission to the crew, ran up the Confederate flag, and gave the ship its permanent name, the *Alabama*.

≈   ≈   ≈

During the next twenty months, until April 27, 1864, the *Alabama* captured sixty-five merchant ships flying the U.S. flag. After the removal of their crews and of supplies that Semmes could use on the *Alabama*, fifty-two of these ships were burned. The rest were released after they had taken aboard crews from previously burned ships and the captains had signed bonds pledging payments by their owners to the Confederate government after the war.

The Confederate commerce raiders obtained crucially important supplies, repairs, and coal at British colonial ports. The royal proclamation in May 1861, by recognizing the belligerent status of the Confederacy, accorded ships flying the Confederate flag the same status and rights in British ports as ships from any other belligerent nation, including the United States. But rules issued on January 31, 1862, imposed limits on the use of British ports by warships or privateers of either American belligerent. No such ship was allowed to use a British port "as a station or place of resort for any warlike purpose or for the purpose of obtaining any facilities of warlike equipment." The visit of any Union or Confederate warship to a British port was limited to twenty-four hours or such longer period required by bad weather or the need for repairs or supplies "necessary for her immediate use." British officials stated at Geneva in 1872 that eleven of the twenty-five visits by Confederate ships to British colonial ports during the war had been for the purpose of repairs.

Although under sail most of the time, the Confederate raiders were usually able to overtake merchant vessels only by using steam power. Maintaining an adequate supply of coal was therefore essential. The British rules of January 1862 set limits on the amount of coal belligerent ships could obtain at British ports and provided that, without special permission, they could not obtain coal at a British port any oftener than three months.[46] But the Confederate captains often failed to mention their last visit to a British port, and British colonial officials were often glad to use their discretionary authority to be more generous than specified in the 1862 regulations.

At the Geneva tribunal the Americans maintained that the Confederate cruisers "were permitted to supply themselves with coal in British ports in greater quantities and with greater freedom and with less restrictions than were imposed upon the United States."[47] British officials admitted that an average of 175 tons of coal was taken aboard during sixteen of the twenty-five visits to British ports by Confederate cruisers. But they insisted that "such supplies were afforded equally and impartially . . . to both contending parties" and that far more coal was obtained by Union ships than by the Confederate cruisers."[48]

The British rules were intended to deny the ships of either belligerent the use of British ports as bases for sustained operations in a given area, as separate from their use for resupply and/or emergency repairs while en route to another destination. Since the Confederate raiders had to keep on the move to avoid discovery by Union warships, these British regulations created more problems for Union ships hunting for blockade runners than for the Confederate raiders.

Colonial governors and army and navy commanders in the British colonies shared the pro-Confederate attitudes of their fellow aristocrats in Britain. These officials of the British Empire were more conscious of the strategic advantages for Britain of disunion in America and more accustomed to the subservient status of dark-skinned peoples than the average Briton at home. Captain Semmes wrote in his memoirs that "the army and navy of Great Britain were with us almost to a man."[49]

John M. Taylor described the warm welcome received by the *Sumter* and the *Alabama* at British colonial ports: "At Trinidad, Semmes and his officers basked in a warm if unofficial reception, the first of many in the far-flung ports of the British Empire. . . . The raider's decks were crowded with visitors." "It seemed that every British officer at Gibraltar came to call" when the *Sumter* visited that strategic British outpost. In Jamaica the *Alabama* was "inundated by a host of local officials and citizens." It was again "overwhelmed with visitors" during its call at Saldanha Bay, in South Africa. The only cool reception Semmes received at a British port was in December 1863 at Singapore. The harbor contained twenty-six American ships idled because of fear of the Confederate raider, and the curtailed American trade had pinched the local economy. But Semmes still got the coal and supplies he needed.[50]

A series of U.S. protests against favorable treatment of Confederate cruisers in British ports began in the fall of 1861, when Seward talked to Lyons and Adams talked to Russell about the "friendly reception" given the *Sumter* at Trinidad. Adams was told that the Law Officers had concluded that there was no reason to believe that British neutrality had been violated.[51] Similar responses were made to subsequent protests.

The *Alabama* also received supplies and assistance at the ports of several other nations. Crucial help was provided at the French port of Fort-de-France in Martinique. When the *San Jacinto*, the ship Captain Wilkes commanded when he stopped the *Trent*, arrived there on

November 19, 1862, its new captain, William Ronckendorff, discovered that the *Alabama* had arrived the previous day. French officials told him that if he anchored in the harbor and the *Alabama* departed, they would enforce international rules requiring the pursuer to give the prey a twenty-four-hour head start. Ronckendorff elected to wait for the *Alabama* in international waters, a marine league from the coast. The French officials gave Semmes charts showing the best channels for his escape. A dark and rainy night allowed him to leave the harbor without making contact with the *San Jacinto.* Ronckendorff searched the coast for several days, but the Confederate raider had escaped to cruise the world and capture forty-two more Union ships before it met another U.S. Navy ship near another French port in 1864.[52]

If the era of radio communications had begun by the time of the Civil War, the depredations of the *Alabama* and its sister cruisers would have been impossible. Without radio, tracking a cruiser was impossible. News of the capture of a merchant ship by a cruiser usually reached Washington a number of weeks after the event. By the time a U.S. warship could be sent to the area where the raider had been, it was long gone. During conversations while in port, Semmes and the other raider captains often hinted that they intended to go in a certain direction when, in fact, they planned a quite different route. The cruises of the *Sumter, Florida*, and *Alabama* were eventually terminated when they were accidentally discovered by U.S. warships.

Pressure from shipping interests forced Welles to send a few warships to search for the Confederate raiders. "It is annoying," he recorded, "when we want all our force on blockade duty to be compelled to detach so many of our best craft on the fruitless errand of searching the wide ocean for this wolf from Liverpool."[53] But there is no evidence that these assignments significantly weakened the blockade.[54] Burton Hendrick wrote that "the Federal government . . . displayed far more stoicism in facing the destruction of its commerce than Mr. Mallory . . . had anticipated. . . . Lincoln never had the slightest intention of giving up the blockade, for the blockade meant the strangling of the Confederacy."[55]

The depredations of the *Alabama* and the other commerce raiders spurred a rapid "flight from the flag"—the transfer of American merchant ships to British registry. Richard Cobden commented in Parliament that "in 1860 two-thirds of the commerce of New York was carried on in American bottoms, in 1863 three-fourths was carried on in foreign bottoms."[56] A British agency listed 608 ships totaling 328,665 tons that were transferred from U.S. to British registry during 1863.[57] As the war was ending in April 1865, Adams presented U.S. figures bringing the transfer to British registry from 1861 through 1864 to a total of 715 ships totaling 480,682 tons.[58]

In the latter part of the war Confederate cruisers met very few ships flying the American flag. The *Alabama*, which had captured fifty-six U.S. ships in its first year of operation up to September 5, 1863, made only nine more captures in the remaining six months it was afloat. The *Tuscaloosa*, a ship converted into a Confederate raider after its capture by the *Alabama*, met over a hundred ships during a cruise for several months in late 1863, but only one was American.[59] During the six-week second cruise in the fall of 1863 of another Confederate raider, the *Georgia*, she did not meet a single vessel flying the U.S. flag.[60]

The role of Britons in the construction, arming, escape, and supply of the *Alabama* and other Confederate raiders was the most serious source of continuing tension between the United States and British governments during and following the Civil War. The U.S. government made it clear that it would hold the British government responsible for the depredations of the *Alabama* and other British-built raiders and would seek compensation from the British government after the war. A few months after the future *Alabama* escaped from Liverpool, Seward reviewed the British roles in the construction and arming of the Confederate raider:

> The *Alabama* is a pirate ship-of-war, roving over the seas capturing, burning, sinking, and destroying American vessels, without any lawful authority, . . . in violation of the law of nations. . . . She was purposely built for war against the United States by British subjects in a British port, and prepared there to be armed and equipped with a specified

armament adapted there for the very piratical career which she is now pursuing. . . . Her armament and equipment . . . were simultaneously prepared by the same British subjects in a British port . . . . She was clandestinely and by connivance sent by her British holders, and the armament and equipment were at the same time sent through the same connivance . . . to a common port outside of British waters, and there the armament and equipment of the *Alabama* as a ship of war were completed, and she was sent forth on her work of destruction with a crew chiefly of British subjects, enlisted in and proceeding from a port, in fraud of the laws of Great Britain and in violation of the peace and sovereignty of the United States.[61]

Most of these facts were admitted by the British government, but it maintained that at the time of her departure from Liverpool there had been no legal basis for seizing the unarmed ship. Palmerston took this position in the House of Commons on March 27, 1863: "She sailed from this country unarmed and not properly fitted out for war . . . received her armament, equipment, and crew in a foreign port. Therefore, whatever suspicions we may have had . . . as to the intended destination of the vessel, her condition at that time would not have justified a seizure."[62] Russell reiterated this position in repeated interviews and an extended correspondence with Adams.

Even the end of the *Alabama's* career evoked a mix of old and new grievances against the British. When the *Alabama* was sunk by the USS *Kearsarge* off the French port of Cherbourg in June 1864, Secretary of the Navy Welles recorded that "there is great rejoicing throughout the country over this success which is universally and justly conceded a triumph over England as well as over the Rebels."[63] Bitter memories of the British roles in the construction, arming, staffing, and supplying of the raider were mixed with outrage at the rescue of Captain Semmes and some members of his crew by boats from a British yacht, the *Deerhound*. The rescued captain and crewmen were taken to England, and the British government rejected demands that they be turned over to U.S. authorities as prisoners of war. This incident strengthened American determination to obtain compensation from Britain after the war for the costs and damages suffered by the

United States and its citizens as a result of operations of the *Alabama* and its sister raiders.

The complex story of these "*Alabama* claims," which cast a dark shadow over U.S.-British relations for seven years after the Civil War, is told in Epilogue II.

CHAPTER 11

No Obligation to Stop
a Contraband Trade

British Arms and Supplies for the Confederacy

Large and vitally important percentages of the arms and supplies used by the Confederate armies were imported from Great Britain despite the Union blockade of Confederate ports. Most of the arms and supplies were carried from Britain in British ships to a British island port—in Bermuda or the Bahamas. The majority of the ships carrying the arms and supplies on to Confederate ports were converted or built in Britain for blockade running, and were owned by British companies, commanded by British officers, and manned by British sailors.

Arms and supplies from Britain were especially crucial in the last two years of the war. They enabled the Confederacy to maintain its war effort for at least a year longer than would have been possible without these crucial imports. This vital economic and logistical support for the Confederacy was provided by British subjects despite the fact that the British government had no diplomatic relations with the Confederate government and maintained official policies of neutrality and nonintervention in the American conflict. Although blockade running was discouraged by the Queen's Proclamation at the beginning of the war, the British government made no substantial and effective effort to impede the flow of arms, supplies, and merchant ships to the Confederacy.

The predominant British role in blockade running was a result of the very strong spirit of free enterprise and free trade in Britain in the mid-nineteenth century, national and international law that allowed and protected neutral trade with belligerents, the pro-Confederate sympathies of the aristocratic and business classes in Britain, and—above all—the large profits to be made by running the blockade.

A British historian, David Thomson, wrote that free trade was the main plank in the commercial policy of the governing Liberal Party: "Palmerston represented intuitively . . . the character and outlook of the commercial and industrial middle classes."[1] Charles Francis Adams commented in 1863 that "the predominating idea of the commercial classes is trade; they care not with whom, or with what consequences, short of absolute war."[2]

No British statute made it illegal for British subjects to sell munitions to any belligerent with whom Britain was not at war.[3] Russell explained to Adams in May 1862 that owners and masters of ships carrying munitions to the Confederacy did not violate any British law:

> If captured for breaking a blockade or carrying contraband of war to the enemy of the captor, they submit to capture, are tried, and condemned to lose their cargo. This is the penalty which the law of nations has affixed, and in calling upon her Majesty's government to prohibit such adventurers you in effect call upon her Majesty's government to do that which it belongs to the cruisers and courts of the United States to do for themselves.[4]

In Parliament in the spring of 1863 the solicitor general used quotes from Secretary of State Daniel Webster and President Franklin Pierce to prove that the United States had had a policy similar to Britain's. "It is not the practice of nations," Webster wrote in 1842, "to undertake to prohibit their own subjects from trafficking in articles contraband of war. Such trade is carried on at the risk of those engaged in it under the liabilities and penalties prescribed by the law of nations."[5] "The doctrine of the United States on this subject," Russell wrote to the British chargé in Washington, "has always been the same as that of Great Britain, namely, that neutral governments are under no obligation to stop a contraband trade between their subjects and a belligerent power, and that the only penalty of such a trade is the liability of contraband shipments to be captured on the high seas by the other belligerent."[6]

Both Conservatives and Liberals in Britain believed that the power of the government to interfere with free enterprise and free trade was and should be severely limited. Moreover, it was widely believed that legal restrictions imposed on the blockade runners could not be enforced. "Selling munitions of war," Richard Cobden wrote to Senator Sumner, "is not in the power of governments to prevent."[7]

The government of the United States did not challenge the assertion that the British government had no power or obligation to prevent trade by Britons with the Confederacy. Yet there was much public resentment in the North of the vital contribution made by Britons to the military capacity of the Confederacy. The British minister in Washington, Sir Frederick Bruce, reported in 1866 that the American people "attribute the duration of the war to our recognition of the Confederates as belligerents and to the extent to which blockade running was carried out from our ports."[8]

e/o   e/o   e/o

In the fall of 1861 there were very strong protests in Britain of the Union navy's plan to bolster the blockade by sinking old ships filled with stone in Confederate harbors. The British misunderstood the intent of the plan and greatly exaggerated its potential effectiveness. There was never any intention to seal any harbor, only to block some of the secondary channels and allow the blockading ships to concentrate on the main channels. But the British jumped to the conclusion that the "stone fleet" was intended to seal permanently the Southern ports on which the British were dependent for cotton exports. The plan was regarded in Britain as ruthless vandalism, vengeful barbarism, an admission by the North that it could not defeat the Confederates by legitimate warfare, and a plot to release blockading ships to fight Britain. Russell thought the presumed plan implied "utter despair of the restoration of the union" and was "a measure of revenge and irremediable injury against an enemy."[9]

When ships loaded with stone were sunk in Charleston's harbor, the powerful tides broke up some of the sunken ships and buried others deep in the sand. The diverted currents scoured new and deeper channels. By the time Russell's protest reached Seward in January

1862, the ineffectiveness of the "stone fleet" had been demonstrated and navy officials had abandoned the plan.

The U.S. Navy had about 100 vessels when the war began, but the majority were wooden sailing ships; only 34 were steamers, and some of these were only tenders. Most of the larger warships were being repaired, were searching for slave traders on the African coast, or were in the Pacific. Through an energetic program of ship purchases and ship construction, four squadrons with nearly 300 vessels were blockading the major Confederate ports by the spring of 1862.[10] During the war the Navy Department purchased 418 vessels. About half of these were built for the navy at U.S. shipyards.[11] The rest were bought from Northern owners or were captured blockade runners purchased at auctions after they were condemned by prize courts. The Union government did not buy ships from shipyards in Europe. Lincoln told Congress in December 1863 that the U.S. Navy consisted of 578 vessels, including some still under construction, and that 75 of these were ironclad or armored steamers.[12]

Only a few Union ships searched for Confederate raiders, and almost all the rest were used in the blockade. Despite the large number of ships deployed, several factors limited the effectiveness of the blockading operations. Many of the ships were poorly suited to blockade duty because they were slow and/or performed poorly in bad weather and when heavily loaded with ordnance. Steamers were more effective blockaders than sailing ships, but their operations were restricted by inadequate coal supplies; by 1862 the four blockading squadrons needed three thousand tons of coal per week. John Niven, a biographer of Welles, wrote that these squadrons had severe manpower and morale problems:

> It was difficult . . . to recruit officers and men for this arduous but humdrum duty. The ships lay at anchor for months, and the men were tossed around in winter gales, sweltered in the humid summer months, and subsisted on a monotonous diet of salt meat and fish, with only infrequent mails and newspapers from home. The squadrons were always undermanned. There were no bounties . . . for naval volunteers. . . . The one big attraction that assured enough officers and men for blockade duty was the prospect of prize money from captured ships and cargo that were condemned and sold at public auction.[13]

❧   ❧   ❧

Blockade running was inhibited in 1861 by the widely held belief that the war would not last very long, by the large cotton supply in England at the beginning of the war, and by the cotton embargo that initially withheld an important incentive for blockade running—cotton imports into England. During 1862, however, an effective blockade running system was established. The cotton supply in Britain had dwindled, the Confederate cotton embargo had waned, and Union defeats at Bull Run and elsewhere had convinced British companies that the war would last long enough to warrant substantial investments in refitting and constructing ships for running the blockade. Arms and supplies were carried in deepwater ships from Britain to island ports that were relatively near the Confederate coast. There the cargoes were transferred to ships with the special characteristics required for successful running of the blockade of Confederate ports.

The channels leading to most of the Southern ports were rather shallow. Since the main channels were carefully watched by Union steamers, blockade runners often had to use even shallower secondary channels. Shallow-draft vessels were therefore essential. Several other characteristics of the blockade running ships reduced the chances that they would be detected by Union blockaders at sea or during their nighttime approaches to or departures from the blockaded ports. The ships selected or built for blockade running were typically long ships with low profiles and minimal masts; on some of the ships, the masts could be lowered when not in use. Some blockade runners had telescopic funnels that could be lowered to reduce the ship's silhouette. The ships were painted gray or bluish green to reduce their visibility. Various devices were used to permit silent operation and to prevent any light from being detected from hatches or compass housings. Boilers were stoked with anthracite coal, which produced little smoke. Powerful engines often enabled the blockade runners to outrun their pursuers.[14]

In 1862 a number of steamers that had formerly been used on rivers in England or Scotland or on the British and Irish coasts were converted for blockade running in the dockyards of Liverpool and Glasgow. Staterooms were removed and cargo capacity was increased.

The vessels were repainted and refitted to reduce visibility and permit quiet running at night without lights.

The British role in blockade running was described in a British publication in 1862:

> Score after score of the finest, swiftest British steamers and ships, loaded with British material of war of every description, cannon, rifles by the hundred thousand, powder by the thousand of tons, shot, shell, cartridges, swords, etc, with cargo after cargo of clothes, boots, shoes, blankets, medicines and supplies of every kind, all paid for by British money, at the sole risk of British adventurers, well insured in Lloyds and under the protection of the British flag, have been sent across the ocean to the insurgents by British agency.[15]

Adams reported in April 1863 that "almost all the disposable steam vessels in this country and some on the continent are being bought up at any cost, apparently to prosecute the business of running the blockade."[16] By then British shipyards were also busy building a large fleet of ships that were specially designed for blockade running.

The available data does not permit an accurate estimate of the number of British-built ships used as blockade runners. In his study of blockade running, Stephen R. Wise provided information on 372 ships that were used or built as blockade runners. About 200 of these were identified as having been built in Britain before or during the war.[17] In March 1864 the British Foreign Office published a list of claims by British subjects against the U.S. government, most of which arose from the capture of 397 ships by the U.S. Navy.[18] These two lists included over 500 British-built blockade runners. In December 1863, Lincoln informed Congress that the navy had captured more than 1,000 blockade runners;[19] in 1865, the secretary of the navy reported that Union blockaders had captured or destroyed 1,504 blockade runners during the war.[20] If the proportion of British-built ships among these blockade runners was as high as on Wise's list, the blockading fleet captured or destroyed at least 800 British-built blockade runners.

The great majority of the officers and seamen manning blockade runners, including those owned by Confederates, were British subjects.

The prewar American merchant marine had been based primarily in the Northeast; the Confederacy had few experienced sailors. Confederate citizens who were found on captured blockade runners were treated as prisoners of war, while British sailors on such ships were usually released as soon as their nationality could be verified. But in January 1864 Seward informed Lyons that many crewmen of captured blockade runners had escaped detention by posing as British subjects when, in fact, they were Confederate citizens. Henceforth seamen captured on blockade runners would be detained until "it can be ascertained whether in fact they are neutral aliens or are belligerent enemies of the United States."[21] This new policy resulted in a number of protests by Lyons of the detention of British subjects. Seward wrote that deception was the norm in such cases:

> Blockade runners . . . generally resort to every possible artifice and fraud which promises to conceal their true nationality, the unlawful character of their voyage, and the nationality of their vessels. They simulate flags, they erase names, they throw papers overboard or burn them, they state falsehoods, and they equivocate under oath. Whether neutrals or insurgents, when captured, they lay claim to the character of innocent traders and of neutrals and . . . generally lay claim to the rights of British subjects.[22]

The Confederate government relied mainly on private shippers to take the risks associated with blockade running. In a study of the Confederate supply system, Richard D. Goff noted that two distinct types of entrepreneurs were utilized:

> In one approach the War and Navy departments sent agents abroad to contract for supplies. The agents paid the European contractors on delivery and then arranged for large tramp steamers to carry the goods to Bermuda, Nassau, and occasionally to Havana, the agents paying the freight. At these ports other Confederate agents supervised the repacking . . . goods into smaller lots for light, fast steamers to run into Confederate ports past the blockaders. . . . The second approach was for the War Department to rely on private initiative to bring supplies. . . . Government officials bought goods from blockade runners as they arrived

and gave out contracts to private individuals to go to Europe, buy the goods, ship them to the Confederacy, and resell them to the government at some predetermined rate.[23]

The Confederate government's reliance on private shippers and traders had two unfortunate consequences. First, the government had to pay extremely high freight costs for both the transatlantic shipments and the blockade running trips to Confederate ports. Second, much of the cargo capacity of the blockade runners was used for luxury items for civilian use.

Confederate representatives in Europe urged the government to take control over blockade running. C. J. McRae, an agent of the Confederate Treasury Department, thought the government should take control over both cotton exports and blockade running. Mason agreed that steps should be taken to reduce "the immoderate profits now reaped by private enterprise."[24] Henry Hotze, the chief Confederate propaganda agent in London, also wrote that blockade running should be a government monopoly "to save the public the enormous profits now made by private speculators."[25] The Confederate government ignored these suggestions. The Confederacy lacked the money to establish a government monopoly, which would have required the purchase or lease of a large number of British-owned ships. Moreover, Confederate leaders were reluctant to tinker with a system that was providing crucial arms and supplies, albeit at high prices.

In February 1864 the Confederate Congress passed a law giving the president authority to regulate all foreign commerce, including control over exports of cotton, tobacco, sugar, molasses, rice, and military and naval stores. Importation of many luxury goods was also prohibited. Although the House deleted a provision that specifically authorized the president to require shippers to use half their cargo space for government shipments, Davis interpreted the law broadly and imposed this restriction. But the new regulations did not limit the profits to be made from blockade running, and both the number of blockade runners and the volume of trade continued to grow as long as some Confederate ports remained open.[26]

℘   ℘   ℘

The transshipment of goods at British colonial ports was an essential link in the blockade running system. The principal ports were Saint George, in Bermuda, and Nassau, in the Bahamas.

Saint George had a well-protected harbor of considerable depth, near the open sea. The harbor was accessible by ships drawing up to twenty feet of water, but only ships drawing less than twelve feet could reach the docks; vessels with deeper drafts had to be loaded or unloaded in the harbor with lighters.[27] Due to the limited port facilities, it proved difficult to maintain an adequate supply of coal at Saint George for the use of transatlantic and blockade running vessels.

Nevertheless, Bermuda had two important advantages over the Bahamas. Because the island was seven hundred to eight hundred miles from the nearest coal depots and there was no anchorage in the deep water around the island, the U.S. Navy could not maintain ships permanently around Bermuda. Saint George was thus a safer port for blockade runners than Nassau. It was also a healthier port; due to the prevalence of yellow fever in the Bahamas during the summer months, blockade runners arriving at Wilmington and other Confederate ports from Nassau were subject to long periods in quarantine.

The Confederate government established an ordnance depot at Saint George, and it was soon the major transshipment point for rifles and other ordnance. The Ordnance Bureau was the only Confederate agency that owned and operated ships used for blockade running. Colonel Josiah Gorgas, chief of the bureau, described the crucial role of imports via Bermuda in his diary on August 3, 1863:

> Our freight steamers continue to run to Bermuda, from Wilmington. This is our chief source of supply for arms, and we get our steel, tin, zinc, and various other articles wholly in this way. We also import leather, tools, hardware, medicines, saltpetre, lead, etc, in large quantities. We own four ships belonging to the Bureau and there are others running in which the War Dept. is largely interested. Thus far none of our vessels has been captured, though we have now made some fifty trips out and back.[28]

The blockade runners were very welcome in Saint George. Young ladies from the better families entertained the officers at balls, dances, and other festivities, while the seamen were welcomed at taverns and bawdy houses.

But except during periods when it was ravaged by yellow fever, Nassau, in the Bahamas, was the colonial port most frequently used by the blockade runners. It had a good harbor and anchorage. It was the closest colonial port to the Confederate ports on the Atlantic: Nassau was only 515 miles from Charleston and 570 miles from Wilmington, while Saint George was 772 miles from Charleston and 674 miles from Wilmington. Trips to these ports from Nassau required two fewer days than those from Bermuda, and the space not needed for extra coal could be used for additional cargo. During the first 100 miles of the route north from Nassau the blockade runners could stay close to other islands in the Bahamas chain and, if they met a Union ship, scurry to the safety of British waters.

The officials and people of the Bahamas were sympathetic with the Southern cause and very helpful to the blockade runners. After the American Revolution, many loyalists from southern states had settled in the Bahamas. In the 1860s their descendants still had close family, cultural, and commercial ties with the American South. British officials in the Bahamas were delighted by the rapid growth of trade and did everything they could to encourage it.[29]

Secretary of the Navy Welles was very bitter about the support of the blockade runners by British officials at Nassau:

> Almost all of the aid which the Rebels have received in arms, munitions, and articles contraband have gone to them through the professedly neutral British port of Nassau. From them the Rebels have derived constant encouragement and support. . . . Our officers and people are treated with superciliousness and contempt by the authorities and inhabitants, and scarcely a favor or courtesy is extended to them while they are showered upon the Rebels. It is there that vessels are prepared to run the blockade and violate our laws, by the connivance and with the knowledge of the colonial, and, I apprehend, the parent, government.[30]

The British foreign secretary continued to maintain that blockade runners, although risking capture of their cargoes, were breaking no law. Russell insisted that the liability of these ships to capture under the rules of international law did not mean that this trade was any less "lawful and innocent" than if there were no such liability.[31]

ɛɔ   ɛɔ   ɛɔ

Despite the larger number of Union ships available for blockade duty as the war went on, the Union navy was never able to prevent large numbers of blockade runners from reaching Confederate ports. Marcus W. Price concluded that about 85 percent of the blockade running trips into Wilmington and 65 percent of the trips into the Gulf ports were successful.[32] Even in 1864, about two of every three attempts to evade the blockade were successful.[33]

During the last two years of the war the arms, equipment, clothing, shoes, and food brought from Britain by blockade runners were essential for the maintenance of the Confederate war effort. Stephen Wise estimated that during the war the South imported at least 400,000 rifles, about 60 percent of the rifles used by Confederates; about 3 million pounds of lead, one third of the army's requirement; and 2.25 million pounds of saltpeter, two thirds of the saltpeter used by the Confederates to make powder.[34] Between October 1864 and January 1865, the Confederate Ordnance Bureau imported 50,000 rifles and carbines, over 400,000 pounds of lead, and large supplies of saltpeter for the production of powder.[35] Even at Appomattox, Lee's army was adequately supplied with arms and ammunition.

In the 1860s almost all American production of textiles and leather products was in the North; the Confederacy was highly dependent on imports of textile products, including uniforms, blankets, and tents, and of leather products, especially shoes and harness.[36]

Food imports were even more crucial. Plantation agriculture in the Southern lowlands emphasized staple crops, especially cotton, tobacco, rice, and sugar; the two largest crops—cotton and tobacco—were not foodstuffs. Most of the food produced on plantations and farms was consumed locally. Efforts during the war to expand food production for the cities and armies were retarded by the absence of many of the plantation owners and farmers; by the devastation, isolation, or capture of many agricultural areas; and by the progressive deterioration of the railroad network in rural areas. The Confederacy never developed an effective system for allocating rolling stock and maintaining track and equipment. Priority was given to rail lines that were crucial for military operations, while lines serving agricultural areas were neglected and cannibalized.[37] Since the Confederacy had no capacity to produce steel rails, rail lines could be repaired or extended only by taking rails from existing secondary lines in rural areas.

Despite the growing dependence on food imports, the quantities of food that could be procured abroad and delivered by blockade runners were limited by supply, transport, and economic factors. Britain, where most of the cargoes originated, did not produce enough food to feed itself and was highly dependent during the Civil War period on wheat imports from the United States. Only a few types of food products could survive the long transatlantic voyage. Since tinned beef, barrels of salt pork, and other preserved foods were bulky, with a low ratio of value to bulk, blockade runners preferred to use their cargo space for high-value military equipment or luxury items.[38]

The imports of both food and war material were inhibited by defects in the Confederate supply system. Richard D. Goff concluded that the effectiveness of Confederate overseas procurement was greatly limited by the primary reliance on private shippers, inadequate regulation of the blockade runners, lack of centralized control of purchasing and disbursement, and poor planning and administration.[39] Nevertheless, blockade runners continued to provide crucial support for the Confederate war effort and civilian economy until Union forces captured the last of the Confederate ports.

When the war began the Confederacy had five ports that were connected by rail lines with Confederate cities—three on the Atlantic (Wilmington, Charleston, and Savannah) and two on the Gulf of Mexico (Mobile and New Orleans). New Orleans was captured by Union forces under Admiral David Farragut in April 1862, but Mobile remained open for two more years, until taken by Farragut in August 1864. All three of the Confederacy's major Atlantic ports remained open until the last few months of the war. Union forces besieged Charleston in 1863, but the city held out and its port remained open. Savannah was taken in December 1864 when General Sherman reached the sea. His march from Atlanta cut the rail lines previously used to send supplies northward from Georgia, Alabama, and Mississippi. While Sherman was marching to the sea, General Sheridan was systematically destroying food supplies in the Shenandoah Valley of Virginia, the "breadbasket of the Confederacy."

At the end of 1864, Lee's army in Virginia was almost totally dependent on food from Europe brought by blockade runners, but the two remaining Confederate ports—Charleston and Wilmington—were under intense pressure from Union forces. The last blockade runner to reach Wilmington—the closest port to Lee's army—left there on January 2, 1865. Ten days later Colonel Gorgas recorded in his diary that "General Lee's army has but two days food left, and an order is issued today to call on the citizens of Richmond for a part of their supplies."[40] The last ship reached Charleston on February 17. With the closure of the last Confederate port, the Confederate lifeline was cut. A few weeks later, at Appomattox, the lack of food for his army was the most important reason for Lee's surrender.

Despite the determined efforts of the U.S. Navy, blockade runners kept the Confederate war effort going for at least a year longer than would have been possible if the Confederate ports had been effectively sealed. Hamilton Cochran wrote that the blockade runners also made other vital contributions to the Confederacy:

> The benefits of blockade running to the Southern cause were incalculable. The business it carried to the South, the life and activity it brought, the news it told and carried away, the sympathy it communicated, the money it left behind—all these were sinews of war, without which the war must have ceased from twelve to twenty-four months earlier than it did. Blockade runners were the connecting link between the Southern Confederacy and the outer world, substantial evidence of the sympathy of other and older nations. They were of as much moral as material value; they cheered and encouraged the Southern heart.[41]

CHAPTER 12

A Thing to be Deprecated

Britain Detains the Ironclad Rams, 1863

In its first six months at sea the *Alabama* captured thirty-three Union merchant ships and burned all but six of them. Reports of these depredations stimulated the Congress to pass a "privateering" bill. It gave the president authority to issue "letters of marque" under which privately owned ships could be armed and used for naval missions specified by the president. Since three Confederate raiders—the *Sumter*, the *Florida*, and the *Alabama*—had thus far escaped capture by the U.S. Navy, the chance that any raider could be found and captured by a single privateer was remote. But Seward proposed that privateers also be authorized to seize blockade runners.

The secretary of the navy was tempted to use privateers to punish the British for the construction of warships for the Confederacy: "If . . . rovers built by English capital and manned by Englishmen are to be let loose to plunder our commerce, let England understand that her ships will suffer." But Welles feared that "to clothe private armed vessels with governmental power and authority, including the belligerent right of search, will . . . beget trouble and . . . abuse" and that the British government would retaliate by authorizing British privateers: "A few privateers let loose among our shipping, like wolves among sheep, would make sad havoc."[1]

Seward called in Lyons on March 8 and handed him a note stating "that the departure of more armed vessels under insurgent-rebel command from English ports is a thing to be deprecated above all things."[2] "Mr. Seward said he was well aware of . . . the danger of issuing letters of marque," Lyons reported, but "unless some intelligence came from England to allay the public exasperation, the measure would be unavoidable."[3] A similar message was sent to Russell via Adams.

Lyons thought Seward hoped the threat of privateers would scare Britain and France into restricting shipbuilding for the Confederates:

> The predominating feeling in the United States at this moment is exasperation against England on account of the proceedings of the *Alabama* and still more on account of the fleet of new vessels which are commonly believed to be building in England for the Confederates. Prudent men have tried to persuade the President of the folly of issuing letters of marque, and think they have convinced him. . . . Both Mr. Seward and Mr. Chase are in favor of issuing them—Mr. Chase from genuine anger with England, Mr. Seward . . . as a means of negotiation with Europe.[4]

At the end of March Seward received a discouraging reply from Russell to a protest by Adams about shipbuilding for the Confederacy. The gist of Russell's response, Adams reported, was "the want of power to do anything at all to protect a friendly nation from the hostilities of British subjects who knowingly violate the injunctions of the Queen's proclamation."[5]

Seward read Russell's reply to the cabinet on March 31. Welles thought it indicated that "a devastating and villainous war is to be waged on our commerce by English capital and English men under the Rebel flag with the connivance of the English Government, which will . . . sweep our commerce from the ocean." But he admitted that "we are in no condition for a foreign war."[6]

On March 26 Adams saw Russell and conveyed Seward's message that implementation of the privateering bill would be unavoidable unless the British government took steps to prevent the outfitting of future cruisers. Russell claimed that he was eager to stop illegal shipbuilding but needed evidence that would hold up in court.[7]

The next day shipbuilding for the Confederates was debated in Parliament. Bright proclaimed that the very large pro-Union meeting of trade unionists in London the previous evening had demonstrated popular support for government policies more sympathetic to the North. Laird, whose shipyard had built the future *Alabama*, was cheered for a speech criticizing Bright for setting one British class against another. Palmerston insisted that Adams had provided no evidence on which the government could have prevented the departure of the *Alabama*.[8]

But the threat that the U.S. government would implement the privateering bill had strengthened Lord Russell's resolve to prevent any more potential Confederate raiders from leaving England. On March 31 he asked the Law Officers for a legal opinion on the government's authority to seize the *Alexandra*, another vessel being built for service as a Confederate raider. They approved the seizure on April 4. Russell informed Lyons that orders had been given "to watch, and stop when evidence can be procured, vessels apparently intended for the Confederate service."[9] The crucial caveat was that the ships would be stopped "when evidence can be procured."

The seizure of the *Alexandra* was immediately challenged in court, and the case was tried before a jury in the Court of Exchequer in late June. The presiding judge told the jury that if they thought there was no intent to arm the *Alexandra* in Britain, they should return a verdict for the defendants. They immediately did so. Adams was disgusted: "The presiding judge has decided the case . . . upon a construction of the enlistment act which leaves nothing of it, as a penal measure of prevention, but the name."[10] The government appealed the decision. The *Alexandra* was allowed to leave England but was seized again at Nassau. Although the government ultimately failed again to support its charges, the appeal took so long that the ship reached the Confederates too late to be of any value. Meanwhile, the government's inability to sustain in the courts its seizure of the *Alexandra* was the principal reason for the slowness of its response to a new challenge—the construction in Britain of two ironclad rams for the Confederate navy.

જ જ જ

In the parliamentary debate on March 27 Bright read a letter from Liverpool that stated that "the two rams (iron-clad) building by Lairds at Birkenhead for the Confederates are most formidable. They will each have two turrets or towers, similar to the American monitors."[11] But Consul Dudley did not focus on these ships until his agents discovered their unique feature. It was a great iron piercer, extending six or seven feet beyond the prow but three to four feet below the waterline, that could impale a wooden warship below any protective iron plate. The rams were designed to carry nine-inch rifled guns in turret batteries. Their 350-horsepower engines would produce speeds of ten knots, and the ships were expected to be highly maneuverable.[12]

The contract for the rams, like that for the *Alabama*, had been designed to avoid violations of the Foreign Enlistment Act. The contract was between the Laird shipyard and Bulloch, acting as a private citizen, with no reference to the Confederacy. The ships were to be delivered to Liverpool with only the equipment of a commercial ship. But the turrets and piercers made it impossible for these ships to pose as commercial vessels.

Bulloch worried that, as a result of pressure from the U.S. government, the British government would prevent the departure of the rams from Liverpool. With the help of a queen's counsel, he devised a plan for the nominal sale of the rams to a French shipbuilder, Bravay and Company. Bravay bought the unfinished ships but arranged for their completion according to Bulloch's specifications. The French shipbuilder made a secret commitment to sell the ships to Bulloch after they were beyond British jurisdiction at the sale price plus a commission.[13] Laird Brothers cooperated in the deception by concealing the original contract with Bulloch.[14]

When Adams heard about the Laird rams, he realized that they would pose a severe threat to the ships of the Union blockading squadrons, most of which were built of wood. The first of a series of protests by Adams to Russell about the rams was written on July 11, 1863: "All the appliances of British skill to the arts of destruction appear to be resorted to for the purpose of doing injury to the people of the United States. . . . It is not unnatural that such proceedings should be regarded by the government and people of the United States with the greatest alarm, as virtually tantamount to a participation in the war by the people of Great Britain."[15] The Foreign Office sent Adams's letter to the Law Officers, who accepted the opinion of the collector of customs at Liverpool that the rams were being built for

Frenchmen. They advised that the government "ought not to detain or in any way interfere with the steam-vessels in question."[16]

Meanwhile, Adams was informed of Lincoln's view that the decision in the *Alexandra* case had left the United States "without any guarantee whatever against the indiscriminate and unlimited employment of capital, industry, and skill by British subjects, in building, arming, equipping, and sending forth ships-of-war from British ports to make war against the United States." Seward's July 11 dispatch also contained a threat that, if the British continued to allow Confederate raiders to use British ports, the U.S. Navy might be authorized "to pursue these enemies into the ports which . . . become harbors for the pirates. . . . The President very distinctly perceives the risks and hazards which a naval conflict thus maintained will bring to the commerce and even to the peace of the two countries."[17] Adams did not communicate this threat to Russell; he feared that doing so might "close all further possibility of preserving the peace between the two countries."[18]

∞   ∞   ∞

During the second half of July the news of the Union victory at Gettysburg and the Confederate surrender at Vicksburg had a profoundly sobering effect on British opinion about the war in America. Adams wrote his son that the news had been greeted in the salons of London with great disappointment, consternation, and "tears of anger mixed with grief."[19]

Adams took his family to Scotland and the Lake District for the month of August. For a few days Adams and his wife were guests of the duke of Argyll at Inveraray. Adams told Argyll that the French consul in Liverpool had denied that the rams "were being built on French account," and he convinced the duke that "the assertion that they were so built is of itself a strong indication of fraud."[20] Argyll commented later that he "had urgently pressed the duty and necessity of detaining the ships."[21]

Returning to London for a few days in mid-August, Adams sent Russell another letter and two additional affidavits about the rams provided by Dudley.[22] Russell suspected that the story that the rams were being built for Bravay was a deception, but he could not prove it. On August 22 he sent a telegram to the British minister in Paris, Lord Cowley, asking him to find out if the ironclads were intended for the

French government. Cowley replied that they were not. Russell then asked the British consul general in Alexandria, Robert Colquhon, by telegram for verification of Bravay's claim that the rams were being built for the viceroy of Egypt. Colquhon replied that ironclads had been ordered from Bravay by the previous viceroy prior to his death at the end of 1862 but the order had been canceled by his successor.[23]

On Tuesday (September 1) Russell responded to Adams's August 14 letter submitting depositions about the rams:

> Her Majesty's government are advised that the information contained in the depositions is in a great measure mere hearsay evidence and generally is not such as to show the intent or purpose necessary to make the building or fitting out of these vessels illegal under the Foreign Enlistment Act. . . . Her Majesty's government are advised that they cannot interfere in any way with these vessels."[24]

Yet in letters on Tuesday to the Home Office and Treasury, Layard stated that "so much suspicion attaches to the ironclad vessels at Birkenhead that if sufficient evidence can be obtained to lead to the belief that they are intended for the Confederate States of America, Lord Russell thinks the vessels ought to be detained until further examination can be made."[25]

On Wednesday (September 2) Russell reiterated to Layard his opinion that the rams "ought not to be allowed to go out of the port of Liverpool till the suspicion about them is cleared up."[26] Layard wrote Russell that he had had a long talk about the rams with Solicitor General Roundell Palmer, who suggested that the customs officers be asked to detain the rams temporarily until sufficient evidence could be furnished as to their ultimate destination.[27]

"I quite agree in the course suggested by Roundell Palmer," Russell replied on Thursday (September 3). "I have made up my mind that the vessels ought to be stopped, in order to test the law and prevent a great scandal. Write at once to the Treasury to advise that the vessels be prevented from leaving the port of Liverpool till satisfactory evidence had been given as to their destination."[28] This order was also sent by telegram to Layard. That afternoon Layard wrote to the Treasury requesting that it "give directions to Customs Authorities at Liverpool to stop the Iron Clad Vessels at Messrs. Laird's Yard at Birkenhead, as soon as there is reason to believe that they are actually about to put to sea and to detain them until further orders."[29]

Russell also wrote to Palmerston on Thursday:

> The conduct of the gentlemen who have contracted for the two iron-clads at Birkenhead is so very suspicious that I thought it necessary to direct that they should be detained. The Solicitor General has been consulted and concurs in the measure as one of policy, though not of strict law. We shall thus test the law, and if we have to pay damages, we have satisfied the opinions which prevail here as well as in America that the kind of neutral hostility should not be allowed to go on without some attempt to stop it.[30]

"I think you are right in detaining the ironclads," Palmerston replied on Friday (September 4), "though the result may be that we shall be obliged to set them free. . . . To justify seizure we must . . . prove that they are intended for the use of the Confederates."[31]

Nearly a week went by before Adams was informed of the decision to detain the rams. Asked in the House of Lords in February why he did not tell Adams about the decision on September 3 or 4, Russell replied that "Mr. Layard had written a letter to the Treasury . . . and he had to wait for their answer."[32]

On Thursday morning (September 3) Adams returned to London and sent Russell a note with additional depositions concerning the rams: "It is my painful duty to make known to your lordship . . . the grave situation in which both countries must be placed in the event of an act of aggression against . . . the United States by either of these formidable vessels."[33] Adams wrote again to Russell on Friday morning (September 4) to record "a last solemn protest against the commission of an act of hostility against a friendly nation."[34] That afternoon he received Russell's unaccountably delayed September 1 letter saying that the government could not find sufficient evidence to justify detaining the rams. "I clearly foresee that a collision must now come," Adams noted in his diary. "The prospect is dark for poor America."[35] After a sleepless night, he wrote another note to Russell on Saturday morning (September 5) that contained a sentence that would be quoted frequently by historians: "It would be superfluous in me to point out to your lordship that this is war."[36]

After Layard saw this note on Saturday afternoon, he wrote a note to Stuart, the British chargé in Washington while Lyons was on a trip to Canada. He was authorized to inform Seward that "we have given orders today to the commissioner of customs at Liverpool to prevent the iron-clads leaving the Mersey."[37] Benjamin Moran, one of Adams's secretaries, wrote later that the note to Stuart was intended "first, to appear to Mr. Lincoln as having acted spontaneously . . . and secondly, to be able to say in Parliament when questioned that H. M. Government had not been 'bullied' into stopping the rams by Mr. Adams, but had acted . . . from its own convictions, regardless of outside pressure."[38]

On Saturday afternoon Adams received a note Russell wrote on Friday indicating that the matter of the rams was receiving "serious and anxious consideration." But Adams was not informed of the decision to detain the rams until Tuesday (September 8). That morning the *Post* reported that the government was taking action to detain the rams. That afternoon he received a third-person note from the Foreign Office: "Lord Russell presents his compliments to Mr. Adams, and has the honor to inform him that instructions have been issued which will prevent the departure of the two iron-clad vessels from Liverpool."[39]

This news was greeted by the staff of the U.S. legation in London with the same elation as that of the Confederate surrender at Vicksburg. The minister had not felt a greater sense of relief even when he heard of the resolution of the incident on the *Trent*.[40] "I have more hopes of our prospect of being able to preserve friendly relations," he wrote Seward, "than at any moment since my arrival in England."[41]

Some days later the Law Officers delivered a definitive opinion that the government did not have legal grounds for detaining the ironclads. Palmerston came up with the ultimate solution, which was for the Royal Navy to buy the ships. "We are behind in iron-clads especially in rams, which would be useful for Channel service in the event of war and would tend to be peacemakers."[42] The Foreign Enlistment Act had again proved to be an inadequate legal basis for enforcing the neutrality policy of the British government. Although possible revisions of the act were discussed in the cabinet, they were strongly opposed by some cabinet members on the ground that they would give the impression that Britain was responding to Yankee pressure.[43]

All the parties involved with the rams—Union, Confederate, and British—shared a common conviction that if these ships entered Confederate service they would have a devastating effect on the Union blockade of Confederate ports and would pose a serious threat to Union ports. The *Alabama*'s depredations and the news of the building of additional warships for the Confederacy in Britain had built up fears of attacks by Confederate raiders on the unguarded Northeastern ports. The governor of Massachusetts and the Boston Board of Trade appealed to Welles in May for protection for Boston. Delegations from Maine and Connecticut visited Welles in July to appeal for the assignment of warships to guard their coasts.

After news of the awesome rams was received, fear of Confederate attacks reached panic proportions along the Northeast coast. Two New York newspapers, the *Times* and the *Evening Post*, demanded that a steam frigate be detached for the defense of New York City.[44] The secretary of the treasury urged Welles to send U.S. warships to capture the rams off the English coast before they could reach the United States.[45]

Seward wrote Adams of his anxiety about "the new invasion which is threatened":

> The navy . . . neither have now nor can seasonably have vessels that can be spared from the siege of Charleston, adequate to resist the formidable rams which . . . are within a few weeks to come forth against us from Laird's shipyards. . . . [They] must therefore be expected to enter Portland, Boston, New York, or, if they prefer, attempt to break the blockade at Charleston, or to ascend the Mississippi to New Orleans. Can the British government suppose for a moment that such an assault . . . can be made upon us by British-built, armed, and manned vessels, without at once arousing the whole nation, and making a retaliatory war inevitable. . . . For the interest of both countries and of civilization, I hope they will not let a blow fall . . . that will render peace impossible.[46]

When Seward received copies of Adams's early-September notes to Russell, he wrote him that the notes had been "distinctly and unreservedly approved" by the president.[47] After Lincoln heard about the British government's order to detain the rams, he sent instructions to Adams to express appreciation for the "eminently gratifying" decision.[48] In June 1864, after the rams had been sold to the Royal Navy, Adams was instructed to assure Russell of the president's "lively satisfaction in the removal of an unhappy occasion of disagreement between the two countries."[49]

The Confederates were bitterly disappointed by the British decision to detain the rams. Mallory had written on March 27, 1863, that the acquisition of the ships "is an object of such paramount importance that no effort, no sacrifice, must be spared to accomplish it."[50] A year later, when Mallory heard that the rams had been sold to the Royal Navy, he thought their loss was "a great national misfortune."[51] Many historians have accepted the view that the rams posed a very serious threat to the Union. Thomas A. Bailey wrote that "if the rams had put to sea, the South would probably have won its independence, and the North, already angry over the *Alabama* affair, would almost certainly have declared war on Britain."[52]

Although Bulloch seems to have realized that the rams were too large to enter the shallow waters along the Atlantic coast or for effective use on the Mississippi, he thought they could "sweep the blockading fleet from the sea-front of every harbor from the capes of Virginia to the Sabine Pass" and could attack unprotected ports in the Northeast.[53] The performance of the rams in the Royal Navy indicates that Bulloch had greatly overestimated their capabilities. British officers reported that the ships performed poorly in heavy seas with difficult steering, excessive rolling, and decks constantly awash. Warren F. Spencer wrote that the potential role of the rams was actually much more limited than was supposed in 1863:

> No one knew their real capabilities and limitations. . . . It was ignorance that created the myth of the rams' awesomeness. The myth . . . lifted to their highest peaks the expectations of the Confederate officers in Europe. It created the most dangerous moment in British-United States relations since the *Trent* affair. It forced the English ministry to depart from its own liberal principles of government by law and to seize the ships according to policy. . . . The

Southerners . . . were not just disappointed but crushed. . . . Their country had suffered a severe, perhaps irreversible blow. . . . When the Laird rams are studied in detail it is clear that acting alone they could not have punished the North; they merely would have been troublesome.[54]

CHAPTER 13

Questions of Great Intricacy and Importance

Lincoln Conciliates Britain, 1863

During 1863 Abraham Lincoln took a number of steps that he thought would ease tensions between the United States and Britain and reduce the chances that Palmerston's Liberal government would be replaced by a Conservative government more hostile to the United States.

        ℰℬ   ℰℬ   ℰℬ

Early in the year the main sources of U.S.-British tension were the actions of the Caribbean flotilla commanded by Acting Rear Admiral Charles Wilkes, the same man who had taken the Confederate envoys off the *Trent* in 1861. In February, Wilkes's ships seized two British merchant ships that were en route from one neutral port to another but were carrying goods that appeared to be intended for the Confederacy. The *Springbok* was seized while en route from London to Nassau with a cargo of bayonets, army and navy buttons, army cloth, army blankets, and other military supplies. The *Peterhoff*, seized off Saint Thomas, was ostensibly bound for the Mexican port of Matamoros, on the lower Rio Grande, with a cargo of gray blankets, boots, horseshoes, and other military equipment. A crew member claimed, however, that the cargo was to be landed at the Confederate port of Brownsville, Texas, across the river from Matamoros.

Henry Adams wrote his brother that the seizure of neutral ships en route between neutral ports had created a tremendous stir in England: "The owners . . . set up a tremendous cackle, and . . . all the newspapers cackled, and deputations of blockade runners went to the Foreign Office and in short the whole blockade running interest, the insurance companies and underwriters, the ship-owners, and all their relations, friends, and acquaintances, were exasperated and acrimonious."[1] These captures triggered four controversies—the use of a neutral port by the U.S. Navy, the legitimacy of British trade with Matamoros, the doctrine used to justify the seizures, and the fate of mails found on seized ships.

The senior British admiral in the western Atlantic, Alexander Milne, protested that "the *Peterhoff* was chased from a neutral port, and captured the same day, the belligerent captor making the neutral port a position from whence to watch neutral vessels."[2] Lyons convinced Seward that the U.S. Navy's use of neutral ports should be curtailed. In July, Lincoln sent Welles a letter, apparently drafted by Seward, proposing the following new orders to naval commanders: "You will avoid the reality, and as far as possible, the appearance of using any neutral port to watch neutral vessels and then to dart out and seize them on their departure. . . . Complaint has been made that this has been practiced at the port of St. Thomas, which practice, if it exists, is disapproved and must cease."[3]

The U.S. and British governments viewed the rapidly expanding British trade with Matamoros from opposite perspectives. Seward stressed in a note to Lyons that the United States was concerned about both arms deliveries to the Confederates and cotton exports via the Rio Grande:

Suddenly . . . as in the tales of the Arabian Nights under the waving of a wand . . . that trade rose from a petty barter to a commerce that engaged the mercantile activity of Liverpool and London. Simultaneously roads across the interior of Texas were covered with caravans, the cotton of disloyal citizens in the insurrectionary region became . . . the property of the treasonable conspiracy against the union, and it was hypothecated . . . for a foreign loan to satisfy obligations contracted by them in the fitting out . . . of naval expeditions to destroy the commerce of the United States.[4]

But Lyons protested that the U.S. Navy was interfering with legitimate British trade with Mexico:

> It is an impression, widely and deeply felt, that it is the intention of the American government, by captures without cause, by delays of adjudication, by wanton imprisonment of masters and part of the crew of captured vessels, to put a stop to the British trade to Matamoros altogether. . . . The trade to Matamoros is, however, a perfectly legitimate trade. . . . How is it possible to say before hand that certain goods will be consumed in Mexico, and certain other goods will be carried into the so-called Confederate states? . . . If . . . it should appear that . . . the British trade were deliberately and systematically made subject to vexatious capture and arbitrary interference, it is obvious that Great Britain must interfere to protect her flag.[5]

Both the *Springbok* and the *Peterhoff* were taken to a prize court in New York, where attorneys applied the "doctrine of continuous voyage" that had been used during the Napoleonic Wars to justify the seizure of cargoes that were en route to a neutral port but were destined for delivery to an enemy. The doctrine's use during the Civil War was attacked by British shipowners but not by British officials; they thought wider acceptance of this doctrine would prove very useful for Britain in the future, as it did during World War I.

The administration of the British Empire and Britain's foreign commerce were dependent on reliable delivery of international mails. During the *Trent* incident, Russell stressed that inteference with the operation of any mail packet would be a "noxious and injurious" act adversely affecting many private and government interests.[6] The British insisted that the mail aboard a cargo ship must also be protected, even if its cargo were contraband, and demanded that the mail on the *Peterhoff* be released without opening it. Seward maintained that "mails are sacred," an international "institution" with which the U.S. Navy could not interfere. Welles claimed that U.S. statutes and international law required that mail found on a captured vessel must be turned over to the prize court for disposition.[7] Lincoln ordered the release of the captured mails. He told Welles "his object was to 'keep the peace,'" for we could not afford to take upon ourselves a war with England and

France, which was threatened if we stopped their mails."[8] Welles thought Lincoln had been "humbugged" by Seward, whom he believed to be "daily . . . wailing in his ears the calamities of a war with England."[9]

∽ ∽ ∽

For some weeks in the summer of 1863 Lincoln was very concerned about the possibility that Palmerston's Liberal government would be replaced by a more hostile Tory government. Lincoln hoped for a continuation of the present British government despite his frustration with the attitudes of the foreign secretary, Lord Russell. Lincoln never knew that in the cabinet Russell had advocated European intervention in the American conflict. But Russell's anti-Union opinions—that the Union was fighting only for "empire," that the Union could not win the war, and that Confederate independence was inevitable—were well known. In the spring of 1862 Adams reported that, in Russell's speech to the House of Lords, "the final disruption of the United States and the ultimate recognition of the seceding States . . . are visible in every word."[10] Adams wrote that Russell had "expressed the belief that this country is large enough for two independent nations and the hope that this government will assent to a peaceful separation from the insurrectionary states."[11]

Carl Sandburg, who cited no sources in his biography of Lincoln, wrote that someone showed Lincoln these reactions to the Emancipation Proclamation by Russell in his January 17 letter to Lyons: "The proclamation *professes* to emancipate all slaves in places where the United States authorities cannot exercise any jurisdiction or make emancipation a reality; but it does not *decree* emancipation of slaves in any states or parts of States occupied by federal troops. . . . There seems to be no declaration of a principle adverse to slavery in this proclamation. It is a measure of war of a very questionable kind."[12]

No motive by Lyons for allowing these reactions to reach the president can be identified. Yet Sandburg's story is supported by a comment by Senator Sumner to Richard Cobden on April 26—"I am tempted to tell you how our imperturbable President felt on reading the Letter about his Proclamation"[13]—and by two letters Sumner wrote just after

Lincoln's death. The first was to the duchess of Argyll: "I have never known him to speak harshly of but one man, and this was an eminent Englishman who has so misstated him and our cause." The duchess assumed that he meant Russell.[14] Sumner was more specific in a letter to John Bright: "President Lincoln never expressed himself with bitterness about anybody, except the British Minister for Foreign Affairs."[15]

Nevertheless, there is substantial evidence that Lincoln believed that the continuation of the Liberal government in Britain was better for the United States than its displacement by a Tory government. He agreed with the statement of *The Index*, the Confederate propaganda organ in England, that while the Palmerston government remained in power "the cabinet at Washington has nothing to fear, and the Confederate States nothing to expect."[16] Lincoln and Seward had heard from many sources that most members of the Conservative Party were hostile to the Union. Adams commented that the main body of the party "continues to be animated by the same feelings to America which brought on the [American] revolution and which drove us into the war of 1812."[17]

But several factors were inhibiting a Tory effort to replace the Palmerston government. The Tory leaders feared that, if they formed a government, it would have a very narrow majority. They thought their best chance would come after Palmerston's death or retirement.[18] Queen Victoria, still "forlorn" after the death of Prince Albert at the end of 1861, hoped there would be no cabinet crisis in 1863.[19] The limited interest of the Tory leaders in challenging the government's policy toward America was described by Ephraim D. Adams:

> Lord Derby, able but indolent, occasionally indulged in caustic criticism, but made no attempt to push his attack home. Malmesbury, his former Foreign Secretary, was active and alert in French affairs, but gave no thought to relations across the Atlantic. Disraeli, Tory leader in the Commons, skillfully led a strong minority in attacks on the Government's policy, but never on the American question, though frequently urged to do so by friends of the South.[20]

The attitudes of the Tory leaders on the American question were poorly understood by the leaders of the pro-Confederate bloc in Parliament. For a while in the late spring and early summer of 1863 the military situation in America—the Union defeat at Chancellorsville, the stubborn Confederate resistance at Vicksburg, and Lee's plans to march northward into Pennsylvania—seemed to offer an opportunity to appeal for Tory support for recognition. The Confederate lobby was also encouraged by the reactions in Britain to the death of General "Stonewall" Jackson. *The Times* described Jackson as "a brave man fighting for his country's independence." The *Morning Herald* thought "this immeasurable loss will add to the warmth of popular feeling for the men who have striven so long in a just cause."[21]

In late May, John Arthur Roebuck, MP for Sheffield, submitted a resolution requesting the government to join with foreign powers in recognizing Confederate independence. Roebuck had grown up in Canada and acquired there "a cordial detestation of the Yankees." He has been described as restless, trivial, vain, dogmatic, and a firebrand. Adams thought he was "rather more than three quarters mad,"[22] but Mason considered him "a statesman of great intelligence and experience."[23] Debate on Roebuck's motion was scheduled for June 30.

Slidell saw Napoleon on June 13 and talked of efforts being made to force the British cabinet to "act or give way to a new ministry." The emperor said the French minister in London, Baron Gros, would be instructed to inform Russell of France's readiness to discuss joint recognition of the Confederacy by Britain and France. Roebuck and Lindsay hurried to Paris, and met with the emperor on June 25. Slidell reported that France was now "not only willing but anxious to recognize the Confederate States with the cooperation of England."[24] But no such instructions were received by Baron Gros prior to the debate in Parliament.

In the debate on June 30, Roebuck asserted that he had been commissioned by the emperor to urge Britain to recognize the Confederacy. The Confederate lobby had expected Disraeli to support Roebuck's motion, but he did not.[25] Ephraim D. Adams wrote that Roebuck and the Confederate lobby made two tactical errors: "First, in the assertion that a new French offer had been made when it was impossible to present proof of it; and second, in bringing forward what amounted to an attempt to unseat the Ministry without previously committing the Tories to a support of the motion. Apparently Disraeli was simply letting Roebuck 'feel out' the House."[26] The debate showed that neither the Tory leadership nor most Tory members were ready to force a vote of confidence on the recognition issue. Most MPs resented Napoleon's pressure for recognition. James McPherson observed that "the notion of allowing the Frogs to dictate British foreign policy was like a red flag to John Bull."[27]

But Adams reported that there was still a strong movement in Parliament "to take some action or other in favor of the rebels." "The only effective answer . . . is success in the war," he wrote on July 3, 1863.[28] News of the great battle at Gettysburg, which ended that day, did not reach Britain until just after the withdrawal of the Roebuck motion.

Since Palmerston was ill on June 30, the vote on Roebuck's motion had been deferred. Meanwhile, there had been sharp criticism in the French liberal press of Napoleon's willingness to recognize the Confederacy jointly with Britain. Palmerston appealed to Roebuck and Lindsay on July 9 to refrain from further discussion of their conversation with Napoleon, on the ground that it might impair British relations with France. But the next day Lindsay gave a long account in Parliament of his meeting with Napoleon. *The Times* appealed to Roebuck on July 13 to withdraw his motion. By then Roebuck and his supporters had realized that the motion would be defeated by a large majority, and it was withdrawn that evening.[29]

❧   ❧   ❧

During the six weeks between the proposal and the withdrawal of the Roebuck motion, there had been extensive comment and speculation about the recognition issue in the press in Britain and America. The controversy surrounding the Roebuck motion was mainly responsible for a level of anxiety in Washington about a possible change of government in Britain that was unwarranted by the actual British political situation.

Welles recorded on July 17 that newspapers contained "an intimation that should Roebuck's motion for a recognition of the Confederacy prevail, Earl Russell would resign" and that in the cabinet meeting that day Seward had "expressed great apprehension of a breakup of the British ministry."[30] A week later Lincoln's previously cited letter to

Welles, proposing new restrictions on the use of Saint Thomas by U.S. Navy ships searching for blockade runners, ended with the curious statement that the proposed order would "contribute to sustain a considerable portion of the present British Ministry in their places, who, if displaced, are sure to be replaced by others more unfavorable to us."[31] Although the connection between U.S. Navy operations at Saint Thomas and a possible British cabinet crisis is hardly evident, the letter illustrates the extent of Lincoln's concern about the possibility of a change of government in Britain.

When Seward heard that the Roebuck motion had been withdrawn, he sent Adams this message from the president:

> I am authorized to tender to Great Britain assurances of the desire of the United States for the removal of every cause of alienation, and for the re-establishment of the relations between them on the foundations of common interest. . . . We invite her to weigh these advantages against the promised benefits of any hostile alliance that she can form against us. We are yet friends, though that friendship has been severely tried. If we must become enemies, the responsibility of that unhappy and fearful event will rest on her Majesty's government and the people of Great Britain.[32]

On the same day Adams reported on the British reaction to the Confederate surrender at Vicksburg: "The feeling of regret at the course of events is very general. At the same time there is mixed with it a little of self-gratulation at the escape from committal on Mr. Roebuck's motion."[33] Three weeks later, while still waiting for the British government's response to his protests on the rams, Adams was cautiously optimistic:

> The hopes of the rebel sympathizers . . . have been seriously dashed by the military events of July. The most decisive proof of this is to be seen in the fall of the Confederate loan [which] had gone down to thirty percent discount. While the popular opinion continues in this state, there is no likelihood whatever of any change in the ministerial policy. . . . The policy of the United States should be, so far as possible, to avoid every cause of collision with this country.[34]

Lincoln and Seward continued to worry about the possibility that some incident would shatter the fragile structure of U.S.-British accommodation. Welles thought the orders restricting the Navy's use of Saint Thomas resulted from Seward's "constant trepidation lest the Navy Department or some navy officer shall embroil us in a war, or make trouble with England."[35] He recorded that, in a conversation on August 21 about the proposed instructions, Lincoln said "he thought it for our interest to strengthen the present [British] ministry, and would therefore strain a point in that direction."[36]

Seward's conciliatory attitude toward Britain may have been enhanced in late August by a unique opportunity for informal conversations with Lyons. Aware that perceptions by the European diplomats of the relative strength of North and South were inhibited by their limited knowledge of America beyond Washington, the secretary of state and former New York governor and senator invited the diplomatic corps to join him on a "diplomatic excursion" through New York State. Most of the ministers—including Lyons, Mercier, and the Russian minister, Stoeckl—participated in at least a part of the two-week tour. Traveling in a special railroad car provided by the War Department, they visited New York City, Albany, Syracuse, Utica, the Finger Lakes, Buffalo, and Niagara Falls.[37] The prosperous cities, busy canals and harbors, extensive rail network, booming industries, and productive farms of upstate New York gave the European diplomats a new outlook on the ability of the North to sustain the conflict. The long hours on the train provided an unprecedented opportunity for informal talk between the secretary of state and the European diplomats. There is, regrettably, no record of Seward's conversations on the train. While Seward was away, John Hay wrote that "the Tycoon is in fine whack. I have rarely seen him more serene and busy. He is managing this war, the draft, foreign relations, and planning a reconstruction of the Union, all at once."[38]

The conciliatory efforts of Lincoln and Seward toward Britain in the summer and fall of 1863 were motivated in part by a desire to counteract anti-British statements by the chairman of the Senate Foreign Relations Committee, Senator Sumner. In 1861 the senator had been very critical of Seward's strong warnings to the British and had encouraged Lincoln to soften the strongly worded draft of Seward's May 21 dispatch to Adams. By mid-1863, however, Sumner thought

Seward was too willing to accede to British demands; he strongly disapproved of the decision to return the mails captured on the *Peterhoff*, and he thought the United States should take a more aggressive line with the British on the construction of ships for the Confederacy in Britain and the reception of Confederate raiders in British colonial ports.

David Donald, biographer of Sumner, described the severe criticism of British policy in Sumner's four-hour speech at the Cooper Union in New York on September 10:

> Believing that the most serious threat to peace lay in the likely escape of the Laird rams, he devoted his speech largely to a review of the British policies which had led up to this anticipated breach of international law. . . . He accused the British government of "flagrant oblivion of history and duty." . . . The speech is an indictment, not a plea for reconciliation. If Sumner sought to bludgeon the British into being peaceful, he showed a remarkable misconception of their national temper.[39]

The British were outraged by Sumner's speech. Russell thought Sumner had "taken infinite pains to misrepresent me in every particular," and he tried to counteract Sumner's criticism by a speech in Scotland in October.[40] The duke of Argyll thought Sumner had made "a very foolish and inexpedient speech," but admitted to Gladstone that Sumner had made a strong case against shipbuilding for the Confederacy in Britain and the use of British ports by the Confederate raiders.[41]

Sumner's speech was made while news of the British government's decision to detain the Laird rams was on its way across the Atlantic. The British decision evoked a strong statement—by Seward to Adams on September 23—of Lincoln's determination to maintain peaceful relations with Britain:

> The President . . . thinks that he apprehends in some degree the firmness and fidelity to just principles which the cabinet of London has exercised. Nor does he for a moment doubt that a sincere desire to cultivate the friendship of the United States has had its proper influence in the determination at which the cabinet arrived. You will, therefore, specially inform Earl Russell that the government of the United States will hereafter hold itself obliged, with even more care than heretofore, to endeav-

or to conduct its intercourse with Great Britain in such a manner that the civil war in which we are unhappily engaged shall, when it comes to an end, leave to neither nation any permanent cause for discontent.[42]

In a letter to the president on September 30, Welles acknowledged Lincoln's "strong desire to conciliate Great Britain and to make all reasonable concessions to preserve friendly relations with her."[43]

୧   ୧   ୧

The British government's conclusion that strict neutrality in the American conflict was the only safe policy was buttressed by a confidential dispatch from Lyons in November on America's military capabilities in the event of a war with Britain:

> At the commencement of a war with Great Britain, the relative positions of the United States and its adversary would be very nearly the reverse of what they would have been if a war had broken out three or even two years ago. Of the two Powers, the United States would now be the better prepared for the struggle. . . . Three years ago Great Britain might at the commencement of a war have thrown a larger number of trained troops into the British Provinces on the continent than could have been immediately sent by the United States to invade those provinces. . . . The United States could now without difficulty send an Army exceeding in number by five to one any force which Great Britain would be likely to place there.[44]

But Lincoln's concern in this period, as James G. Randall noted, was that some "small incident might get out of hand and lead to untold consequences. His eye was on the cause of American survival, which he identified with the cause of democracy in the world. While others were legalistic or litigious, he was careful not to be drawn into needless bickering and diverted from the great task as he saw it."[45] This spirit was evident in Lincoln's annual message to Congress on December 8, 1863:

> We remain in peace and friendship with foreign powers. The effort of disloyal citizens of the United States to involve us in foreign wars, to aid

an inexcusable insurrection, have been unavailing. Her Britannic Majesty's Government . . . have exercised their authority to prevent the departure of new hostile expeditions from British ports. The Emperor of France has, by a like proceeding, promptly vindicated the neutrality which he proclaimed at the beginning of the contest. Questions of great intricacy and importance have arisen out of the blockade and other belligerent operations, between the government and several of the maritime powers, but they have been discussed, and, as far as was possible, accommodated, in a spirit of frankness, justice, and mutual good will.[46]

As 1863 ended, several Union officials recorded their explanations for the more cautious policy of the British government during 1863. Lincoln thought the danger of a European war arising from the Schleswig-Holstein question had increased the British government's desire to minimize the danger of war with the United States. The president believed, Seward wrote Adams on December 17, that in a time of crisis in Europe "her Majesty's government cannot fail to see the importance of removing all existing causes of discontent between their own country and the United States."[47] "England . . . is becoming more disinclined to get in difficulty with us," Welles wrote in his diary; "A war would be depressing to us, but it would be, perhaps, as injurious to England."[48] At the U.S. legation in London, Moran acknowledged that "notwithstanding the [British] national hatred for us and [their] anxious wish for our destruction, their conduct has been on the whole better than it was last year. This may be attributed to . . . [European] complications, the supply of cotton from new sources, and the growing conviction that we will put down the rebellion."[49]

"The President has never failed to forecast the dangers of alienation between Great Britain and the United States," Seward wrote Adams in mid-January, "hence . . . his promptness in seeking to adjust the reasonable claims of British subjects, and meet the just expectations of her Majesty's government. . . . It is his purpose to pursue this course to the end of his administration and . . . to impress upon the habitual policy of the government a friendly and even fraternal disposition toward Great Britain, so that the two nations may go harmoniously together, favoring everywhere the development of just principles of free, responsible government, and the progress of a humane civilization."[50]

CHAPTER 14

To Make Europeans Understand

Other European Reactions to the American Civil War

The people of Europe were not well informed about the background or the progress of the American Civil War. No European country except Switzerland had experience with democratic federalism. Most Europeans had little understanding of the complex American political-governmental system, the evolution of the slavery issue in America, and the complex issues that had led to the American conflict.

During the first year and a half of the war there was great confusion in Europe about the causes of the war and the objectives of the Union government. Carl Schurz, U.S. minister in Madrid, reported in September 1861 that Lincoln's initial policy of avoiding the slavery issue had eroded the initial support for the Union cause among the "liberal masses" in Europe: "It was exceedingly difficult to make Europeans understand . . . why the free and prosperous North should fight merely for the privilege of being reassociated with the imperious and troublesome Slave States. . . . As soon as the war becomes distinctly one for and against slavery, public opinion will be . . . overwhelmingly in our favor."[1]

After the Emancipation Proclamation, European opinion on the American conflict was divided mainly along ideological lines. Henry Sanford, U.S. minister in Brussels, wrote in 1864 that the opinions of most European newspapers on the American war depended on the ideology of the political parties or factions that supported them:

197

The deep interest with which our struggle is regarded in Europe, both by the party of liberal progress and those hostile to it, becomes every day more apparent. . . . The former see in our success the vindication of the principles they profess. . . . Their opponents . . . seem to dread our success as likely to prepare the way for trouble and revolutions in Europe . . . and think no effort should be spared to avert it, hence the bitter, unscrupulous, and mendacious course which their organs in the public press have pursued toward us.[2]

Continental newspapers contained very little news from America, and the items carried were often oversimplified, inaccurate, or slanted. Bulletins about the war were sent by telegram from New York to Halifax, Nova Scotia; carried across the Atlantic by ship; and then transmitted to European capitals by telegraph from Queenstown, in southern Ireland. Although such "telegraphic" news reached Europe a few days earlier than the New York newspapers carried by the weekly packets, the bulletins were always brief and often sensational and distorted.

John Lothrop Motley, the U.S. minister in Vienna, reported in 1864 that most European readers typically got little more American news than "two or three lines twice a week in the corner of a local newspaper, containing generally the most malicious or most improbable fiction that can be culled from the telegraphic budget. . . . Our dispatches and American journals never arrive until a new telegraphic fiction or enigma has already destroyed their value." Motley recommended that the State Department send by each steamer a telegraphic news summary that could be wired to U.S. ministers in Europe when the ship reached Queenstown.[3] Such a news digest would have resembled the Wireless File of news sent daily to U.S. embassies abroad in the second half of the twentieth century. But Seward didn't think his department should get into the news business.

Several U.S. diplomats in Europe—notably John Bigelow, in Paris, and Henry Sanford, in Brussels—endeavored to promote pro-Union articles in the European press, but there was no ongoing Union propaganda outlet in Europe comparable to *The Index*, the Confederate paper published in London. Until very near the end of the war, the dominant opinion in the European press was that the Union could not win the war and that the permanent independence of the Confederacy was inevitable. George S. Fogg, the U.S. minister in Switzerland, observed in 1862 that nearly all the European newspapers were "ravens croaking and prophesying our ruin."[4]

The European press had little influence on the foreign policies of conservative monarchs, who did not worry very much about public opinion. Seward recognized in the spring of 1861 that some of these governments might welcome the permanent division of the American superpower into two countries.[5] But no European government recognized Confederate independence or took any other substantial step to intervene in the American Civil War. The reasons for governmental restraint varied from country to country. They included the desire to retain a unified United States as a powerful potential ally (Russia), fear of war with the United States (Britain and France), fear of U.S. interference with the nation's dependencies in North America (Britain, France, and Spain), reluctance to take the side of a slaveholding country (Britain and France, among others), refusal to recognize any revolutionary or insurgent regime (Russia, Prussia, Austria, and Spain), and preoccupation with European issues and dangers (Britain, France, Russia, Prussia, Austria, Italy, and Denmark, among others).

During the Civil War the United States adhered to its traditional policy of noninterference in the internal affairs of European countries and in the quarrels between Europeans. "In our whole history," Seward wrote one minister, "there is not one recorded act inconsistent with [our] unswerving policy of noninterference in the domestic affairs of other nations."[6] Seward usually responded to reports from Europe only if they contained European reactions to the American conflict or dealt with European activities or policies in North America. In such cases he often provided U.S. ministers in smaller countries with ringing statements of U.S. policy that hardly applied to the country to which the recipient was accredited but were useful additions to the annual volumes of diplomatic correspondence sent to Congress each December with the president's annual message. He insisted in a dispatch to Sanford in Brussels that the North could not be diverted from its determination to reunite the Union "by any foreign persuasions, intimidation, or constraint. . . . It cannot be made to permit the . . . sacrifice of a particle of its sovereignty or of its independence."[7]

The most crucial U.S. foreign relations during the Civil War were with Great Britain and France. U.S.-British relations are described in detail in eleven chapters of this book, while U.S. relations with France are examined in four chapters. The highlights of U.S. relations with other European countries are reviewed in the remainder of this chapter.

The German States

In 1860 German Americans were the largest group of foreign-born people in the United States except for the Irish. Most of the 1.3 million German Americans were in the North. Lincoln had many friends and political allies in the German community, and Germans cast important votes for Lincoln in 1860. Some 200,000 Germans joined the Union army. The Germans in America communicated their strong support for the Union cause to their friends and relatives in Germany. The 44 million German-speaking people in central Europe were divided among thirty-four independent nations, each ruled by a monarch, prince, or duke. Many of the German rulers were indifferent to developments in America.

In 1869, while U.S. minister in Berlin, historian George Bancroft prepared an appraisal of the policy during the Civil War of Prussia, the largest of the German states:

> The King from the first took the ground . . . that the right was with the established government of the United States . . . and that the wrong was with the seceding states which placed themselves in rebellion against their just government. . . . On the part of Prussia there was no concession of belligerent rights to the South. . . . There grew up in the aristocratic squirality a sympathy for the South . . . as the land of gentlemen. . . . When some of this faction of the Prussian landed aristocracy gave a dinner to two officers of the Southern Confederacy who happened to be in Berlin, the King expressed his extreme displeasure. . . . Baron Gerolt, the Prussian Minister at Washington, always in his dispatches supported the right of our government and steadfastly held the belief that it would succeed in putting down the rebellion. . . . The King . . . said to me that Prussia . . . had never failed on its part to cultivate the most friendly relations with the United States of America.[8]

Robert J. Walker, a former U.S. secretary of the treasury, visited a number of German cities to promote sales of U.S. bonds. He wrote in 1867 that Germans "took several millions of our loan."[9] The bonds were excellent investments. They were purchased at low prices due to a favorable exchange rate, and the principal and interest were paid in gold. They also gave the investors a strong interest in a Union victory.

Russia

The czar of Russia, Alexander I, the most autocratic of the European emperors, was the most steadfast friend of the United States among the European monarchs. He thought a strong and unified United States, friendly to Russia, would provide an important geopolitical balance to the power of Great Britain. The Russian vice chancellor, Prince Gorchakow, assured the U.S. chargé d'affaires, Bayard Taylor, in the fall of 1862 that Russia would not participate in any form of European intervention in the American conflict:

> Russia alone has stood by you from the very first, and will continue to stand by you. . . . We desire, above all things, the maintenance of the American Union as one indivisible nation. . . . Proposals will be made to Russia to join in some plan of interference. She will refuse any invitation of the kind. . . . You may rely upon it.[10]

The Russian government rejected Napoleon III's proposal that France, Russia, and Britain make a joint armistice proposal to the two warring parties in America.

A year later Russian fleets were warmly welcomed at U.S. ports on the Atlantic and the Pacific. In New York the Russian admiral and his officers were feted in a series of high society parties; in Washington they were entertained by the president, the secretary of state, and the secretary of the navy. There were rumors that, in the event of war between Britain and the United States, Russia would provide naval aid to the United States.[11] In fact, the czar was primarily concerned about the possibility of war between Russia and Britain arising from the Russian suppression of a revolution in Poland. Russia's Atlantic fleet was normally icebound in the Baltic ports during the winter. By sending it to America, the czar kept it available for use against Britain.[12]

During the Civil War a plan was developed for telegraphic communication with Europe via a mainly overland line from California to western Canada, Alaska, the Bering Strait, and Asiatic Russia. The *New York Times* commented in 1861 that "the bubble of the Atlantic submarine line has long ago burst, and it is now seen to be cheaper and more practicable to extend a wire over five-sixths of the globe on land, than on one-sixth at the bottom of the sea."[13] A charter the czar signed in 1863 allowed an association of American companies to build a line from Lake Baikal, in Siberia, to the Bering Strait and through Russian Alaska to Canada. In his annual message to Congress on December 6, 1864, Lincoln noted that "the proposed overland telegraph between America and Europe by way of Behrings' Straits and Asiatic Russia, which was sanctioned by Congress at the last session, has been undertaken under very favorable circumstances by an association of American citizens, with the cordial goodwill and support as well of this government as of those of Great Britain and Russia."[14] When the Atlantic cable was completed in 1867, the plan for a telegraphic connection to Europe through Asia was abandoned.

Austria

The Lincoln administration's relations with the Austro-Hungarian Empire got off to a poor start. The imperial government refused to accept former Massachusetts Congressman Anson Burlingame as U.S. envoy to Vienna because he had given moral support to anti-Austrian revolutionaries in Hungary and Italy. Lincoln sent Burlingame to China and eventually named a German-speaking historian, John Lothrop Motley, as U.S. minister to Austria.[15]

Motley reported that there was more sympathy with the North in Vienna than in any other city in Europe. The imperial government, which presided over a "federal" state composed of diverse ethnic groups, was sensitive to the dangers of secession.[16]

The decision of the emperor's brother, the Archduke Maximilian, to accept a Mexican throne, although deprecated in the United States, had little impact on U.S.-Austrian relations. Relations between the emperor and his brother were strained, and Austrian diplomats were instructed to stress that Maximilian's role in Mexico was his personal affair, for which the imperial government in Vienna had no responsibility.

Spain

Lincoln appointed as minister to Spain a German American politician, Carl Schurz, who had participated in revolutionary movements in Germany before emigrating to the United States. The ex-revolutionary was not warmly received by the Spanish aristocrats. By December he had decided that he would prefer the more active role of Union general. Secretary of Legation Horatio J. Perry had been in Spain since 1848, and he acted as chargé d'affaires until another German American, Gustavus Koerner, was appointed minister to Spain in August 1862.

Schurz and Perry convinced the Spanish officials that the previous advocates of U.S. annexation of Cuba had been Southerners. Confederates were more welcome in Havana than in Madrid. Cuban sugar plantations were operated by slaves, and the planters were sympathetic to the Confederate cause. The Confederate government sent an agent to Havana in the summer of 1861 to promote the use of Havana as a transshipment point by blockade runners, but the Cuban port was never as important in the blockade running system as Saint George, in Bermuda, and Nassau, in the Bahamas, both of which were closer to the Confederate Atlantic ports.

For a while in the fall of 1861 the U.S. government was very concerned about the Spanish intervention in Mexico described in chapter 8. But the Spanish, who had hoped for a Spanish prince on a Mexican throne, were not happy with Napoleon's choice of an Austrian archduke as emperor of Mexico, and they withdrew from Mexico in April 1862.

A Spanish intervention in Dominica, on the other hand, continued throughout the Civil War period. San Domingo had won its independence from Spain in 1821, and Dominica, the eastern half of the island, had separated from Haiti in 1844. When rumors of Spanish plans to reannex Dominica reached Seward, he informed the Spanish minister that reannexation would be resisted by the United States.[17] Spain ignored the warning, sent 28,000 troops to the island, and spent the next four years battling the Dominicans and yellow fever. Welles recorded that Lincoln told one of his folksy stories to underline his unwillingness to take sides in the struggle between the Spanish and the predominately black Dominicans:

The President remarked that the dilemma reminded him of the interview between two negroes, one of which was a preacher endeavoring to admonish and enlighten the other. "There are," said Josh, the preacher, "two roads for you, Joe. Be careful which you take. One ob dem leads straight to hell, de odder go right to damnation." Joe opened his eyes under the impressive eloquence and awful future and exclaimed: "Josh, take which road you please; I go troo de wood." "I am not disposed to take any new trouble," said the President, "just at this time, and shall neither go for Spain nor the negro in this matter, but shall take to the woods."[18]

Early in 1865 Spain kept her promise to "relieve herself of the burden of that dependency."[19] When the Spanish foreign minister proposed that the great powers guarantee the independence of the island of San Domingo, including Haiti, Seward replied that it was "a fixed principle of this government not to enter into entangling alliances of any kind with foreign nations."[20]

Italy

The Civil War began just as Italian unification was being achieved. During the 1850s King Victor Emmanuel of Sardinia aspired to unify Italy under a constitutional monarchy. In 1859 Napoleon sent French troops to help the Sardinians drive the Austrians out of Lombardy. Popular revolutions drove the Hapsburg princes out of Tuscany, Parma, and Modena and eliminated papal authority in Romanga. Red-shirted patriots took over Sicily and Naples. In February 1861, just before Lincoln was inaugurated, representatives of 22 million Italians met in a parliament in Turin. On March 17 Victor Emmanuel assumed the title of king of Italy. Of the major Italian cities, only Rome and Venice did not yet belong to the new Italy. The United States government remained aloof from these rapid changes. Seward described U.S. policy with regard to Italy in October 1862 as one of "absolute abstinence from all intervention in its domestic affairs."[21]

In September 1861 the hero of Italian liberation, Giuseppe Garibaldi, was offered a commission as a major general in the Union army. Seward wrote later that the offer was made "by the President's direct authority."[22] Garibaldi had lived in New York for several years, and later described himself as a U.S. citizen. The only apparent explanation for the offer is that Lincoln thought a Union command for Garibaldi would rally support for the Union cause among European liberals.

The offer backfired. Garibaldi replied that he would be interested in a commission only if he were given the supreme command of the Union army and the war had been clearly defined as a crusade for the emancipation of the slaves.[23] Later, Garibaldi wrote of "an appeal to all the democrats of Europe" to support a crusade for the "enfranchisement" of the slaves."[24] Garibaldi was considerably ahead of Lincoln's evolving policy with regard to the slaves. By then Lincoln and Seward undoubtedly shared the view of James S. Pike, U.S. minister to The Netherlands, that Garibaldi was a "wolf whom it is not safe either to hold or to let go."[25]

Netherlands

Henry C. Murphy, the outgoing U.S. minister, reported in May 1861 that Dutch opinion on the American Civil War was influenced by the successful effort of Belgium in 1830 to obtain its independence from The Netherlands. The Dutch had resisted the rebellion with all their power and might have succeeded but for intervention by the British and French; in the end Belgium was lost, and the Dutch were left only with a large debt. "There are not a few," Murphy reported, "who regard the present position of the United States as an expensive and useless effort."[26]

Soon after the British proclamation recognizing Confederate belligerency, the Dutch government issued a similar proclamation. In the fall of 1861 the new U.S. minister, James S. Pike, was instructed to protest the hospitality accorded to the Confederate raider *Sumter* in several Dutch ports in the Caribbean.[27] The Dutch Foreign Office replied that orders had been sent to Dutch ports requiring that both Confederate and Union ships remain no more than forty-eight hours and be given no more than a twenty-four-hour supply of coal.[28]

In 1863 the Emancipation Proclamation contributed to warmer U.S.-Dutch relations, and Union victories at Gettysburg and Vicksburg restored U.S. military prestige. Sarcastic and insulting remarks about the United States disappeared from the Dutch press, and Dutch bankers began to buy U.S. bonds. In January 1864 the king assured

Pike of the "sincere sympathy with the United States government as an old and faithful friend of Holland."[29]

Belgium

American relations with Belgium were overshadowed by the Belgian monarch's support for the establishment of a European monarch in Mexico. Carlotta, wife of the Austrian archduke who became Emperor Maximilian in Mexico, was the daughter of King Leopold I of Belgium. In the summer of 1864 a corps of Belgian volunteers known as the "Empress Guard" was established to protect the Belgian princess who was now empress of Mexico. "It was with much pain," Seward wrote, "that this government saw the Belgian King lend recognition and a legion to establish in a neighboring country . . . a system antagonistic to and incompatible with the permanent security and welfare of the United States."[30]

U.S.-Belgian relations remained cool throughout the Civil War. In September 1864 the U.S. minister in Brussels, Henry Sanford, reported that the Belgian government was thinking of sending its minister in Washington, Blondell de von Cuelebroeck, on a temporary mission to Mexico.[31] Seward replied that if the Belgian minister was sent to "recognize a foreign imperial revolutionary government in Mexico" and subsequently returned, his residence in Washington would be "less agreeable" than previously.[32]

Switzerland

Swiss reactions to the Civil War were influenced by the unique Swiss experience with popular democracy and republican federalism and by Switzerland's own brief civil war in 1846. The Swiss federal constitution established in 1848 was patterned after the U.S. Constitution, the only available model of republican federalism. The bicameral Swiss legislature reflects the compromise between large and small states in the U.S. Constitution; the cantons are equally represented in one chamber, while the second chamber consists of representatives elected in districts with equal populations.

Seward instructed George S. Fogg, the U.S. minister to Switzerland, to emphasize the common experience of the United States and Switzerland with federal systems of government:

Tell the Swiss republic . . . that with God's blessing we will preserve this model of federal republican government by which they have reformed their institutions, and we invoke them to retain their own with no less fidelity. So Switzerland and the United States shall in all ages be honored as the founders of the only true and beneficent system of human government—a system that harmonizes needful authority with the preservation of the natural rights of man.[33]

Swiss President Knuessel told Fogg that the Swiss understood better than most Europeans the nature of the crisis in America:

Switzerland, from the sincere sympathy which she has for the welfare of the Union, looks with anxiety upon the issue of the events which now shake that country. Switzerland passed through a similar crisis fourteen years ago, which threatened to tear asunder the then loose connection of the twenty-two cantons. Strengthened internally and abroad, she now stands there, esteemed by the nations. May God grant that the connection of the States of the United States of America may also emerge renewed and strengthened out of this crisis.[34]

At first many Swiss shared the common European view that Union victory was impossible and Confederate independence would be sustained. But by 1863 the "croaking ravens" had been silenced by the Emancipation Proclamation and the Union victories at Gettysburg and Vicksburg. Fogg reported that the war was "everywhere understood to be a struggle between freedom and despotism."[35]

CHAPTER 15

Alone on the Earth

The Twilight of
Confederate Diplomacy, 1863–1865

During 1862 Confederate leaders had gradually realized that Britain and France did not want Confederate cotton badly enough to risk war with the United States. By the end of the year reactions in Europe to the Emancipation Proclamation had demonstrated that slavery in the Confederacy was a major bar to European recognition and support. "The feeling against slavery in England is so strong that no public man there dares extend a hand to help us," William L. Yancey admitted in a speech after his return from a frustrating year as a Confederate commissioner in London. "We have got to fight the Washington Government alone. There is no government in Europe that dares help us in a struggle which can be suspected of having for its result, directly or indirectly, the fortification or perpetuation of slavery."[1]

The Confederate leadership bitterly resented the failure of the British and French governments to provide the recognition and support they had expected. This resentment led to an attitude of defiant self-reliance just as the Confederacy was becoming highly dependent on arms, supplies, and food from Europe. "Rest not your hopes on foreign nations," Jefferson Davis told the Mississippi legislature at the end of 1862; "This war is ours; we must fight it out ourselves."[2] "When we have achieved the victory and won our independence," former Confederate Secretary of State Hunter proclaimed, "we shall owe them only to God and ourselves and [will be] under no obligation to any other nation for alliance and assistance."[3] Confederate leaders, the *Daily Examiner* in Richmond reported in April 1863, "have been forced to the stern conclusion that their country is alone on the earth, that they have no friend but God, who is afar off, and no hope but in their own swords."[4]

In June 1863 the Confederate Senate adjourned without confirming the appointment of L. Q. C. Lamar as Confederate commissioner to Russia. Confederate Secretary of State Judah P. Benjamin informed Lamar that the Senate inaction was a result of "the conviction entertained by Senators that it was inexpedient to appoint any more agents abroad until the recognition of our independence." He added that "a deep-seated feeling of irritation at what is considered to be unjust and unfair conduct of neutral powers toward this Confederacy prevails among our people."[5]

No one was more bitter about Europe's rejection of the Confederate bid for recognition than Jefferson Davis. "The course of action adopted by Europe," he wrote in his memoirs, "while based on an apparent refusal to . . . side with either party, was . . . an actual decision against our rights and in favor of the groundless pretensions of the United States. It was a refusal to treat us as an independent government. . . . One immediate and necessary result . . . was the prolongation of hostilities."[6] Benjamin stated in a dispatch in 1863 that the lack of British recognition demonstrated that "the continuation of the war is desirable in the interest of Great Britain."[7] Nowhere in Davis's memoir or in Benjamin's correspondence is there any recognition of the fact that arms, supplies, and food from Britain enabled the Confederates to continue the hostilities for a year or two longer than would have been possible without this crucial support.

        ✂   ✂   ✂

After the Union victory at Gettysburg and the simultaneous Confederate surrender at Vicksburg in July 1863, the Confederates realized that any chance of British diplomatic recognition had evaporated. Mason reported that "the hopes and expectations of our friends in Europe have been much depressed by the late intelligence."[8] Slidell thought the news of the Union victories "cannot fail to exercise an unfavorable influence on the question of recognition."[9]

Even before receiving these reports, Davis and Benjamin had decided to terminate Mason's mission in England. On August 4 Benjamin notified him that since the British government "entertains no intention of receiving you as the accredited minister of this government,...your continued residence in London is neither conducive to the interests nor consistent with the dignity of this Government."[10] Mason agreed that "from England we, long since, had nothing to expect."[11] He informed Russell of his withdrawal on September 21. Mason moved to Paris, receiving there a new Confederate commission as "Commissioner to the Continent" with only vaguely defined duties. At the U.S. legation in London, Benjamin Moran noted that Mason's mission in London had been "fruitless of everything but evil to the rebels. Mr. Mason was the unfittest man they could have sent here, and has proved an ignominious failure. His antecedents were bad, his associates were questionable, and his manners vulgar."[12]

The termination of the Confederate mission in Britain was soon followed by the expulsion of British consuls from the Confederacy. When the Civil War began, there were British consuls in six Southern cities—Richmond, Charleston, Savannah, Mobile, New Orleans, and Galveston—as well as eight Northern cities.[13] Each consul was authorized to perform consular functions in a specified area by a document known as an "exequatur" issued by the State Department in Washington. The British government wanted the consuls to remain in Confederate cities. They continued to provide some protection for British citizens and British commercial interests. Their reports, although delayed by the blockade, were the British government's best source of information on events and attitudes in the Confederacy. For the first two years of the war the Confederate government allowed the British consuls to remain at their posts and continue their functions, apparently in the hope that they would send reports to London on Confederate strength and determination that would bolster the Confederate case for British recognition.

By the fall of 1863, however, there had been several controversies concerning the status and activities of the British consuls. The Confederates resented the fact that the consuls were still supervised by Lord Lyons in the enemy capital, Washington. In March, James Magee, the British consul in Mobile, was fired by Lyons for using a British warship to send $155,000 in coin to England, ostensibly for payments on prewar Alabama bonds. Lyons thought Magee had cooperated with a Confederate plan to send specie to England to pay for munitions. In May Benjamin refused to accept the transfer of Frederick Cridland from Richmond to Mobile on the ground that Lyons had no authority over British consuls in Confederate ports. Benjamin wrote Mason that "the British minister accredited to the government of our enemies assumes the power to issue instructions and exercise authority over the consuls residing within this country. . . . This course of conduct plainly ignores the existence of this government." In June the Confederate government issued an order forbidding direct communication between Lyons and the consuls in Confederate cities.[14]

The British consul in Richmond, George Moore, was expelled by the Confederate government in June after Benjamin received a copy of a letter written by Moore: "I have lived thirty-two consecutive years in despotic countries, and . . . I have met in those foreign countries more official courtesy and consideration from the local authorities, on my representation of grievances, than I met [here] at the hands of my own blood and lineage."[15]

The Confederates also resented frequent attempts by British consuls to obtain release from the Confederate army of draftees who claimed British citizenship. The letter that led to Moore's expulsion had concerned two such cases. The acting consul in Savannah, Allan Fullerton, protested the drafting of unnaturalized foreigners for militia duty and issued a statement ordering British nationals in the militia to throw down their arms if they came into contact with Union troops. The acting consul in Charleston, H. Pinckney Walker, pestered South Carolina officials for the release of British members of the "Arsenal Guard" in Charleston and also encouraged them to lay down their arms if they met U.S. soldiers.[16]

On October 8, 1863, while Davis was visiting the Confederate forces in Tennessee, Benjamin convened the Confederate cabinet and obtained a unanimous vote to expel the remaining British consuls. Benjamin informed Fullerton and Walker that their advice to drafted British citizens was intolerable: "This assumption of jurisdiction by foreign officials within the territory of the Confederacy and this encroachment on its sovereignty cannot be tolerated for a moment."[17]

Benjamin thought "public sentiment . . . would have been quite restive under their continued residence here."[18]

Confederate leaders were furious that British authorities did nothing to inhibit the flow of immigrants to the United States from Ireland, which reached 94,000 in 1863. On arrival, many of the Irish immigrants joined the Union army. In the fall of 1863 Confederate envoy Dudley Mann was sent to Rome to deliver a letter from Davis to the pope. It appealed for papal intervention to impede the flow to the United States of Irish and German Catholics who, Davis said, were being lured by promises of high wages and then tricked into joining the Union army. The papal reply was vague and disappointing, but it was addressed "to the Illustrious and Honorable Jefferson Davis, President of the Confederate States of America." This letter from the pope was the closest Jefferson Davis ever came to European recognition as the head of an independent nation. He kept it on his wall after the war, and his daughter told a visitor that it was "one of dear papa's most valued souvenirs."[19]

The depth of Jefferson Davis's frustration with the lack of British recognition was indicated by his bitter reaction in April 1864 to a letter from Lord Lyons. He had transmitted a protest by Russell "against the efforts of the authorities of the so-called Confederate States to build war vessels within Her Majesty's dominions to be employed against the government of the United States." Davis dictated an angry reply protesting the "studied insult" of referring to the "so-called" Confederate States. Davis proclaimed that "a neutrality most cunningly, audaciously, fawningly, and insolently sought and urged, begged and demanded by one belligerent, and repudiated by the other, must be seen by all impartial men to be a mere pretext for aiding the cause of the one at the expense of the other, while pretending to be impartial."[20]

          ↄ   ↄ   ↄ

Confederate hopes for help from France persisted during 1863. When it became evident in 1864 that they would not be realized, they were replaced with a bitterness toward France even greater than that toward Britain. The main cause of this bitterness was the emperor's ultimate refusal to allow the delivery to Confederates of several warships that had been built in France for the Confederacy.

John Bigelow, U.S. consul general in Paris, recalled that Napoleon had been "disposed to protract the war in America at least until Maximilian's supremacy in Mexico was assured, and for that purpose was prepared to render the Confederates any assistance in his power that would not compromise his relations with the United States."[21] During Slidell's second meeting with the emperor on October 28, 1862, Napoleon had hinted that the secret construction of warships for the Confederacy in France might be allowed. In January 1863 Arman, the largest shipbuilder in France, came to Slidell and offered to build and arm warships for the Confederacy.

Bulloch, who feared that the Laird rams would not be allowed to leave Liverpool, was eager to transfer the Confederate shipbuilding program to France. He went to Paris in April and drew up contracts for the construction of four wooden corvettes—two at Arman's shipyard at Bordeaux and two at the yard of another shipbuilder, M. Voruz, at Nantes. The minister of the marine approved the construction and arming of the corvettes on June 6, 1863.[22] At the end of June Bulloch received authority from the Confederate secretary of the navy, Mallory, based on a secret act of the Confederate Congress, to proceed with the construction of ironclad warships in France. Bulloch soon signed a contract with Arman for the construction of two ironclad rams. The construction of the four corvettes and the two rams proceeded rapidly. Drouyn de Lhuys preferred to remain uninformed about this violation of French neutrality.

On September 10, 1863, a M. Petermann, a confidential clerk in Voruz's shipyard, walked into Bigelow's office in Paris. He asked for 15,000 francs for twenty-one letters and documents proving that the corvettes and rams were being built for Bulloch. Dayton authorized the payment and took the documents to Drouyn de Lhuys. The foreign minister claimed that he knew nothing about the contracts with Bulloch and promised that France would maintain its neutrality.[23] After an extended exchange of notes between Dayton and Drouyn de Lhuys, the French government informed Arman in February 1864 that the ironclads could not be armed in France and must be sold as commercial trading vessels.[24]

For several months Arman and Bulloch schemed to evade the government order. Bulloch reported to Mallory on February 18, 1864, that Arman had "promised that a nominal sale of the vessels should be made to a Danish banker, and that there should be a private agreement providing for a redelivery to us at some point beyond the jurisdiction of France." Bulloch initially rejected this plan as "one of simple deception," although it involved no greater deception than his nominal sale of the British-built rams to Bravay.[25] He subsequently agreed to a plan proposed by Arman under which the first ram would be legitimately sold to the Danish government, then at war with Prussia. After the legitimacy of this sale had been verified by the United States, the second ram would be allowed to leave France pursuant to an ostensibly similar sale but would, in fact, meet Bulloch's agents at a designated rendezvous.[26]

While Bulloch and Arman were scheming, the U.S. government was putting intense pressure on the French government to prevent the corvettes and rams from falling under Confederate control. Seward made it very clear that if the ships passed into the hands of the Confederates the intense public exasperation might lead to war with the United States.[27]

On June 9, 1864, Bulloch received a letter from Arman indicating that the minister of the marine had forced him to sell the corvettes and the rams to northern European governments and to provide proof that the sales were legitimate. Bulloch was appalled by this action by the same minister who had approved the construction and arming of the ships for the Confederacy just a year earlier: "I certainly thought this kind of crooked diplomacy had died out since the last century."[28] Mallory replied that he was "prostrated" by the news: "among all the bitter experiences of the war this disappointment stands forth, representing . . . a violation of faith."[29]

Bigelow wrote in 1888 that Bulloch had misunderstood the scope of Napoleon's original commitment:

> He assumed . . . that the emperor was pledged to allow Arman's ships to be built for and delivered to the Confederates and was guilty of a breach of faith in refusing them exit under the Confederate flag. . . . In this conviction . . . he was entirely mistaken. . . . The emperor . . . promised that the ships might be built and allowed to sail *if their real destination was concealed,* if they could be got out of French waters

without compromising his neutrality. . . . But the secret of the destination of the ships was not kept. When the documentary evidence that they were destined for the Confederate States was placed in the hands of his Minister of Foreign Affairs, he was no longer bound to let them go. . . . To let the vessels sail would have been not only a violation of his neutral obligation, but, practically, a declaration of war upon the United States.[30]

Meanwhile, Slidell's influence in Paris had come to an end. When the Archduke Maximilian, who was about to become emperor of Mexico, visited Paris in March, he refused Slidell's request for an appointment. Bigelow recalled in his memoirs that sometime that spring Slidell had made himself persona non grata by uttering insulting remarks about Maximilian and Napoleon while playing cards with the minister of the interior, Persigny, and the duc de Morny, Napoleon's half brother. The incident was reported to Napoleon, who denied Slidell's subsequent request for an audience. When the designated Confederate envoy to Maximilian in Mexico, William Preston, visited Paris in midsummer, he told Mercier he would send a request through Slidell for an audience with Napoleon. "In that case," replied Mercier, "you will only meet with failure, as Mr. Slidell is now persona non grata to his Majesty." Mercier cited Slidell's insulting remarks at the card club as the reason for the emperor's attitude.[31]

Slidell's only subsequent encounter with Napoleon was in September 1864 at the races in the Bois de Boulogne. The emperor asked him about the news that Sherman had captured Atlanta. Slidell reported that he replied that "the only effect of Sherman's advance was to increase the distance from his base of supplies and make his communications more liable to interruption; [and] that I did not think it at all improbable that we should soon hear of his falling back upon Chattanooga."[32]

ꞔ   ꞔ   ꞔ

At the end of 1864 Jefferson Davis authorized a last, desperate appeal for European recognition. Duncan F. Kenner, a Confederate congressman from Louisiana and a close friend of Benjamin and

Slidell, was sent on a secret mission to the British and French governments. Kenner carried letters from Benjamin to Mason and Slidell that stressed that "the sole objective for which we . . . consented to commit all to the hazards of this war is the vindication of our right to self-government and independence. For that end no sacrifice is too great, save that of honor."[33] The envoys were told that the sacrifice the president had in mind would be communicated to them by Kenner.

Most historians and Davis biographers have stated that Davis's secret message was that, in return for recognition of the independence of the Confederacy by the British and French governments, all the slaves in the South would be immediately emancipated. But there is no record of such a sweeping commitment by Davis. Eli N. Evans, the most recent biographer of Benjamin, described a much more limited message authorized by the Confederate president:

> No record exists of the crucial meeting that occurred between Benjamin and Davis in which Benjamin laid out the details of his plan to emancipate the slaves in exchange for European intervention in the war. . . . Davis balked. He would not agree to free them all at once, just like that, as Lincoln had. He wanted to ensure a fair and reasonable adjustment on both sides. . . . Davis would go to Congress with a bill to let the slaves go free if they would fight for the South. . . . Kenner was to sound them out as to what effect emancipation would have— "not suddenly and all at once, but so far as to insure abolition in a fair and reasonable time."[34]

The quotation in the last sentence above is from Mason's report in March on the Kenner mission, and it may reflect Mason's viewpoint rather than Davis's original instruction. The proposal at this late stage of the war to link recognition with emancipation demonstrates the limited understanding by Benjamin and Davis of the complex reasons why European recognition had been withheld.

The Kenner mission was doomed to failure from the start. Due to the impending closure of the last Confederate port, Wilmington, Kenner had to travel incognito via New York and did not arrive in Europe until early March. As Sherman marched north from Georgia and Grant tightened the pressure on Richmond, Europeans began to real-

ize that a complete Union victory was not far ahead. The Emancipation Proclamation had already proclaimed the freedom of all the slaves
in the Confederacy. On January 13 the U.S. House of Representatives
approved the Thirteenth Amendment to the Constitution, which,
upon ratification, would abolish slavery everywhere in the United
States. These events eliminated any possibility that the Europeans
would be impressed by a vague offer of eventual emancipation of slaves
within a Confederacy that already appeared to be on its last legs.

When Kenner arrived in Paris in the first days of March, Mason
and Slidell were appalled by the offer of eventual emancipation in
return for recognition. At first Mason refused to cooperate, but Kenner
made it clear that Mason's refusal would lead to the termination of his
mission in Europe.[35] Mason reluctantly returned to London and
obtained an appointment with Palmerston on March 14. The
slave-owning envoy rehashed the old Confederate arguments for
British recognition, but he could not bring himself to present directly
the emancipation-for-recognition proposal.

Palmerston replied that Her Majesty's government had always
intended to maintain a strict neutrality in the American conflict and,
Mason reported, "had not been satisfied at any period of the war that
our independence was achieved." The prime minister added that the
current situation in the Confederacy—"our seaports given up, the
comparatively unobstructed march of Sherman, etc.—rather increased
than diminished previous objections."[36]

Mason asked a Conservative leader who was sympathetic to the
Confederate cause, Lord Donoughmore, to take soundings of reactions
in Parliament to a proposal for recognition of Confederate independence combined with a Confederate promise of gradual emancipation
of the slaves. A few days later Donoughmore returned with the conclusion that "the time has gone by" and that it was much too late for any
change in British policy.[37] It was indeed too late. Mason's report on the
conversation with Donoughmore was written two days before the
Confederate government fled from Richmond.

CHAPTER 16

This Government Avoids Intervention

Union and Confederate Reactions to the French Invasion and Imperial Government in Mexico, 1862–1865

The American Civil War began only thirteen years after the end of the war between Mexico and the United States. In the last months of that war there had been many advocates—in the United States and in Mexico—for the U.S. annexation of all of Mexico. The treaty ending the war gave the United States a clear title to about half of Mexico's territory prior to the Texas revolution that began in 1836.

The issue of slavery in the former Mexican territories had nearly led to civil war before it was resolved by Henry Clay's great compromise in 1850. Northern leaders were determined to block the admission of slavery into any new territories. Southern leaders had realized that the creation of additional slave states was not feasible and that U.S. acquisition of additional territory that might become free states would threaten Southern power in the U.S. Congress. Aside from the minor boundary adjustment accomplished by the Gadsden Purchase in 1853, Americans showed little interest in the 1850s in further territorial acquisitions from Mexico.

But European leaders doubted that American territorial ambitions had been satisfied. They believed that, as soon as a suitable opportunity arose, the United States would attempt to absorb most or all of Mexico. After his arrival in Washington in 1859, Lord Lyons's reports to London contained several references to the American desire "to get hold of Mexico and Cuba."[1] Adams reported in 1861 that most Europeans thought the United States was "disposed to resist all foreign intervention in Mexico . . . because it is itself expecting, in due course of time, to absorb the whole country for its own benefit."[2] In 1862 he noted that the dread of further U.S. expansion "seems to haunt the minds of British statesmen."[3]

The European belief in American designs on Mexico was sustained by efforts by both Union and Confederate governments to convince Mexicans that their opponents planned to invade Mexico. One assignment of Thomas Corwin, U.S. minister to Mexico, was to persuade the Mexican government that its safety depended on the restoration of the Union, since an independent Confederacy would soon attempt the conquest of Mexico. "Well informed Mexicans," he reported, "seem to be aware that the independence of a Southern Confederacy would be the signal for a war of conquest with a view to establish slavery in each of the 22 states of this republic."[4] In May 1861 the Mexican chargé in Washington, Mattias Romero, suggested to Seward a treaty in which the United States would guarantee the Mexican boundaries in order "to prevent the introducing and spreading of slavery in the Mexican republic." Seward ignored the suggestion.[5]

The Confederates hoped to convince Mexicans and Europeans that only an independent Confederacy could guarantee Mexico against invasion from the United States. John K. Pickett, the Confederacy's ineffective agent in Mexico in 1861, was instructed to plant this idea.[6] Hunter's instructions to Slidell in September 1861 stressed that Confederate independence would create a balance of power in North America and eliminate "schemes of conquest or annexation" by Mexico's neighbor.[7]

A French pamphlet attributed to a spokesman for Napoleon stated that "the Confederate States will be our allies and will guarantee us against attack by the North."[8] In January 1864 William Preston, the Confederate envoy selected for the court of the new Mexican emperor, was instructed to stress that, if the Union conquered the Confederacy, it would then annex Mexico.[9] Slidell made the same points to Maximilian's aides in Paris a few weeks later. Both Union and Confederate claims that the other side hoped to annex Mexico were totally unfounded. But the propaganda from both sides kept alive the belief in Europe that Americans still had territorial ambitions in Mexico.

After French forces failed to take Puebla in May 1862, Napoleon ordered an entire army corps to Mexico under a new general, Elie Forey. Napoleon's desire to thwart U.S. expansion was evident in a letter to Forey on July 3, 1862:

> It is in our interest that the republic of the United States shall be powerful and prosperous, but it is not at all to our interest that she should grasp the whole Gulf of Mexico. . . . If . . . Mexico preserves its independence and maintains the integrity of its territory, if a stable government be there established with the aid of France, we shall have restored to the Latin race on the other side of the oceans its force and its prestige. . . . We shall have established our benign influence in the center of America.[10]

Other European leaders also regarded Napoleon's plan to install a European monarch on a Mexican throne as a means of thwarting the ultimate domination or absorption of Mexico by the United States. King Leopold I of Belgium thought Napoleon's plan would "raise a barrier against the United States."[11] The British prime minister, Lord Palmerston, wrote that a monarchical government would "stop the North Americans . . . in their absorption of Mexico."[12]

Lincoln and Seward, preoccupied with civil war at home, had no option but to maintain strict neutrality in the war between France and the republican government of Mexico. But U.S. disapproval of the installation of a European monarch in Mexico was expressed in a series of dispatches to William Dayton, the U.S. minister to France. The first of these, in March 1862, said the president thought that "no monarchical government which could be founded in Mexico in the presence of foreign navies and armies . . . would have any prospect of security or permanence." Seward stressed the "cordial good wishes" of the American people "for the safety, welfare, and stability of the republican system of government in that country."[13]

But Seward wrote Corwin that the administration was not willing to take any action that could involve the United States in the conflict between France and Mexico:

> Notwithstanding the course adopted by the French agents in Mexico, the government of France still reassures us that it is their purpose

to be content with the adjustment of grievances, leaving it exclusively to the people of Mexico to determine their own form of government. . . . We do not feel at liberty to reject these explanations or to
anticipate a violation of the assurances they convey. . . . Under these
circumstances at present we decline debate with foreign powers upon
Mexican affairs.[14]

Similiar instructions were sent to Dayton: "This Government,
relying upon the explanations that have been made by France, . . .
avoids intervention between the belligerents."[15]

The French intervention in Mexico developed slowly. General
Forey remained at Vera Cruz for seven months and did not enter the
Mexican capital until June 1863. The capture of the Mexican capital
by a predominately French army was a shock to Lincoln and his cabinet. "The Mexican Republic has been extinguished and an empire has
risen on its ruins," Welles recorded on July 27. "But for this wicked
rebellion in our country, this calamity would not have occurred."[16]

At the end of August Seward received a letter from J. M. Arroyo,
describing himself as "Secretary of State and Foreign Affairs of the
Mexican Empire," that reviewed recent constitutional changes in Mexico. An assembly of notables had declared that "the Mexican nation
adopts, as its form of government, a limited hereditary monarchy with
a Catholic prince" and that "the imperial crown of Mexico is offered to
his imperial and royal highness the Prince Ferdinand Maximilian,
Archduke of Austria."[17] No one in the United States would have welcomed a minor European prince as monarch in Mexico. The choice of
Maximilian, scion of one of the most powerful and conservative royal
families in Europe, compounded the very negative reaction in Washington to the events in Mexico.

The U.S. minister in Vienna, John Lothrop Motley, described the
young archduke in two private letters. "The Archduke Maximilian," he
wrote his mother, "is next brother to the Emperor of Austria, and
about thirty years of age. He has been a kind of Lord High Admiral
[and] was Governor General of Lombardy. . . . He is considered a
somewhat restless and ambitious youth." Maximilian's wife, Carlotta,
daughter of the king of Belgium, was even more ambitious. Motley
wrote a friend that Maximilian "firmly believes he is going forth to

Mexico to establish an American empire, and that it is his divine mission to destroy the dragon of democracy."[18]

The archduke hesitated for some time before deciding to accept the Mexican throne and did not arrive in Mexico until June 1864. For nearly a year the part of Mexico controlled by the French and their conservative Mexican allies was governed by a "regency" consisting of two Mexican generals, Juan Almonte and Mariano Salas, and the newly appointed archbishop of Mexico, Pelazio Antonio Labastida. The two generals had been closely associated with Santa Anna during the U.S.-Mexican war in the 1840s. The participation of an archbishop in a government violated American ideas of the separation of church and state.

Dayton reported that the French foreign minister insisted that the French army would be withdrawn from Mexico as soon as a stable Mexican government was established:

> Mr. Drouyn de Lhuys took occasion again to say that France . . . did not mean to appropriate permanently any part of the country, and that she would leave it as soon as her griefs were satisfied and she could do so with honor. . . . I took occasion to say that in quitting Mexico she might leave a puppet behind her. He said no, the string would be too long to work.[19]

Dayton was very skeptical about these assurances. He observed in a note to Seward that "truthfulness is not . . . an element in French diplomacy or manners. No man but a Frenchman would ever have thought of Talleyrand's famous *bon mot* that the object of language is to conceal thought."[20]

In September, Dayton was instructed to tell Drouyn de Lhuys that Lincoln was concerned about the discrepancy between French promises and French actions in Mexico:

> The United States government has hitherto practiced strict neutrality between the French and Mexico . . . because it has relied on the assurances given by the French government that it did not intend permanent occupation of that country or any violence to the sovereignty of its people. The proceedings of the French in Mexico are regarded by many

in that country, and in this, as at variance with those assurances. . . . The President thinks . . . you should . . . suggest to [Drouyn de Lhuys] that the interests of the United States and, as it seems to us, the interests of France herself require that a solution of the present complications in Mexico be made, as early as may be convenient, upon the basis of the unity and independence of Mexico. . . . The United States . . . are deeply interested in the re-establishment of unity, peace, and order in the neighboring republic and exceedingly desirous that there may not arise out of the war in Mexico any cause of alienation between them and France.[21]

Seward's instructions to other U.S. ministers in Europe, as understood by the minister in Lisbon, were to "abstain from discussion of the important questions connected with the present situation of Mexico until a more appropriate time and opportunity shall be presented by events."[22] The U.S. minister in Berne agreed that the United States had no other option: "Our nation has work of its own which cannot wait. Its *present* duty is to save itself. Its *future* may be to save its neighbor, and vindicate the supremacy of republican institutions upon the American continent. . . . But . . . we cannot now afford to throw down the gauntlet to any new foe."[23]

ℰ   ℰ   ℰ

Lincoln and Seward were very concerned about threats to the United States arising from the French intervention and the plan to install a European monarch in Mexico. These seem to include recognition of Confederate independence by the new Mexican government, military cooperation with the Confederates by the French and/or imperial Mexican armies, and the establishment of some type of French influence in Texas.

Rumors that Napoleon had designs on Texas had been circulating for over a year. The Austrian minister in Washington, Chevalier Huelsemann, reported in January 1863 that the French consuls in Galveston and Richmond had gotten into trouble with the Confederate government because of their "imprudent ardor to foment a revolution in Texas against Mr. Jefferson Davis." Huelsemann thought

Napoleon hoped to foster an independent "buffer" state in Texas under French protection.[24]

Seward told several cabinet members at the end of July that "Louis Napoleon is making an effort to get Texas."[25] "Political rumor," Seward wrote Dayton in September, "one day ascribes to France a purpose to seize the Rio Grande, and wrest Texas from the United States; . . . another day we are warned of coalitions to be formed, under French patronage, between the regency established in Mexico and the insurgent cabal at Richmond."[26] On the day Seward wrote these words, another rumor about French designs on Texas was reported in a Vienna newspaper:

> The French government is supposed to have arranged with the American Southern States for the cession of Texas. It is confidently assumed that the overwhelmingly German population of Texas would readily submit themselves to a German prince. It is apparently not feared that in consequence of this cession a war would arise between France and North America. Should, however, the North of America . . . be willing to burden themselves with such a war . . . then France would not object, perhaps even wish for it, in order at least to be able to interfere with armed force in favor of the South.[27]

Every assumption and conclusion in this article was incorrect, including the misrepresentation of the numbers and attitudes of the Germans in Texas. Motley, U.S. minister in Vienna, was sure that they "did not emigrate from their fatherland because [they were] fanatically attached to monarchical institutions" and that they were "strong and sincere democrats."[28]

Rumors of French ambitions in Texas persisted during the winter of 1863–64. When Dayton asked the French foreign minister about these rumors in March, Drouyn de Lhuys assured him that they were "without the slightest pretense of foundation" and that "France would not take Texas as a gift, even if it were accompanied with a handsome *douceur* [bribe]. . . . She does not want it, and would not have it."[29] By then the United States army was engaged in the last of four operations designed to establish a U.S. military presence in Texas.

Lincoln's concern about a French threat to Texas began in late July 1863 when news arrived in Washington of the French occupation of the Mexican capital. "Can we not renew the effort to organize a force to go to Western Texas?" Lincoln asked the secretary of war on July 29; "I believe that no local object is now more desirable."[30] On August 5 he wrote to General Nathaniel Banks in New Orleans that "recent events in Mexico render early action in Texas more important than ever."[31] The next day John Hay recorded that the president was "very anxious that Texas should be occupied and firmly held in view of French possibilities. He thinks it just now more important than [capturing] Mobile."[32] On August 9 Lincoln wrote General Grant that "in view of recent events in Mexico, I am greatly impressed with the importance of reestablishing the national authority in Western Texas as soon as possible."[33] Grant replied that, although he had hoped to move on Mobile, he understood "the importance of a movement into Texas just at this time."[34] General Henry Halleck informed Banks on August 10 that Seward believed it was necessary that "the flag be restored to some one point in Texas."[35] In January, Halleck wrote Grant that "it was deemed necessary as a matter of political or state policy connected with our foreign relations, and especially with France and Mexico, that our troops should occupy and hold at least a portion of Texas. The President so ordered."[36]

Fears arising from the French intervention in Mexico provided the principal motivation for four Union military moves at or near the Texas borders in late 1863 and early 1864—the unsuccessful attempt in September 1863 to invade eastern Texas via the Sabine River; the occupation of Brownsville, on the Rio Grande, in November; the unsuccessful attempt to take Galveston at the end of the year; and the disastrous expedition up the Red River toward eastern Texas in the spring of 1864. They were the only military movements during the Civil War that were made primarily because of external threats. These movements made no contribution to Lincoln's primary military objectives—crushing the Confederate army and ending the rebellion. After the surrender of Vicksburg in July 1863, the isolated Confederate forces in Texas played only relatively minor roles in Confederate military operations. Bruce Catton wrote that the effort to invade Texas was a "substantial error" and "a move in the wrong direction."[37] But Lincoln and Seward hoped to establish at least a Union "toehold" in Texas that would be a psychological barrier between the Confederacy and the

French and imperial forces in Mexico and would increase the difficulties and dangers of any French support for the Confederacy.

Governors and supreme court judges of Texas, Louisiana, and Arkansas, meeting in mid-August, recommended that the Confederate trans-Mississippi commander, General Edmund Kirby Smith, appoint a "commissioner to confer with French and Mexican authorities in Mexico." Although Kirby Smith made no effort to communicate with French or imperial authorities in the Mexican capital, he asked the Confederate envoy in Paris to urge the French to occupy *both* banks of the lower Rio Grande. He wrote Slidell on September 1 that a Yankee invasion of Mexico could be avoided only if the French helped the Confederacy to maintain its independence and to provide a buffer between the United States and Mexico. Napoleon should "take immediate military possession of the east [Texas] bank of the Rio Grande."[38] This Confederate hope was shattered in early November by the occupation of Brownsville, the only Texas settlement on the lower Rio Grande, by 6,700 Union troops.

In a memorandum for Napoleon on December 4, Slidell urged the immediate occupation of Matamoros, the Mexican port across the river from Brownsville, by French troops to counteract the expected activities of the Union troops at Brownsville: "The Texas bank of the Rio Grande will now be the point of departure of Federal emissaries to excite the population of northern Mexico in favor of Juárez, furnishing subsidies of money and munitions of war. Men, too, will be forthcoming when required to sustain the cause of democracy against imperial institutions."[39] In fact, General Banks was instructed by Seward to avoid any interference in Mexican affairs: "You will not enter any part of Mexico, unless it be temporarily and . . . clearly for the protection of your own lives against aggression from the Mexican border. . . . These directions result from the fixed determination of the President to avoid any departure from lawful neutrality and any unnecessary and unlawful enlargement of the present field of war."[40]

The Union occupation of Brownsville did not eliminate Confederate trade with Europe via Matamoros. The Confederate cotton trade moved upriver to other border towns, including Eagle Pass, three hundred miles upstream from Brownsville. Wagon trains loaded with cotton were brought down to Matamoros on the Mexican side of the Rio Grande, just out of reach of Banks's troops.

In the spring of 1864 an unsuccessful attempt was made to launch an invasion of Texas from the east by sending a Union military and naval force up the Red River in Louisiana. General Banks's army of about forty thousand men was accompanied by a fleet of gunboats under Admiral David Porter. After defeats by Confederates at Mansfield and Pleasant Hill, Banks retreated quickly. Porter's gunboats were nearly stranded by low water in the river until a regiment of lumberjacks built temporary dams that allowed the boats to escape. After the disaster on the Red River, there were no further Union moves toward Texas.

A dispatch from Bigelow in Paris urging that the United States take a stronger position of opposition to the French occupation of Mexico arrived soon after news of Banks's debacle on the Red River. Seward's reply showed his disappointment at the failure of the expedition: "With our land and naval forces in Louisiana retreating before the rebels instead of marching toward Mexico, this is not the most suitable time for offering idle menace to the Emperor of France. We have compromised nothing, surrendered nothing, and I do not propose to surrender anything. But why should we gasconade about Mexico when we are in a struggle for our own life?"[41]

After the failure of the Union efforts to establish a significant "toehold" in Texas, Lincoln and Seward were determined to avoid any confrontation with the French forces in Mexico. "On no account and in no way," Seward wrote in September to the commander of Union forces in the Gulf region, "must the neutrality of the United States in the war between France and Mexico be compromised by our military forces."[42]

eɔ   eɔ   eɔ

In contrast to the cautious Union neutrality, Confederate officials were eager to become allies of Maximilian as soon as he was installed as emperor of Mexico. Confederate moves toward relations with Maximilian were unencumbered by earlier relationships with Juárez. A brief Confederate effort in 1861 to establish relations with Juárez had been a total disaster. The Confederate diplomatic agent in Mexico, John K. Pickett, was a former army officer and soldier of fortune who has been described as undiplomatic, imprudent, temperamental, adventurous, and swashbuckling. He was the Confederacy's most inappropriate and least successful envoy. By the time Pickett arrived in Mexico, Corwin was already talking with Mexican officials about U.S. help with Mexico's severe financial crisis. Pickett's dispatches to Richmond were seized by Mexican authorities and sent to Juárez. By mid-fall Pickett had begun to court the Mexican conservatives. But he got into a fistfight with a Yankee and spent thirty days in a Mexican jail. He was released after bribing a judge and was escorted out of the country. After this disastrous mission, the Confederate government made no further effort to establish relations with the republican government of Mexico.

During his abortive mission to Mexico in 1845–46, Slidell had sent alarmist reports to President James K. Polk about schemes by monarchists in Mexico to set a European prince on a Mexican throne. But sixteen years later, as a Confederate envoy in Paris, Slidell saw an opportunity to curry favor with Napoleon by supporting his plans for a monarch in Mexico. Slidell's remarks on Mexico during his first meeting with Napoleon at Vichy in July 1862 were reiterated in a letter to Thouvenel:

> Although the undersigned has no instructions from his government in relation to the military expedition which his Imperial Majesty has sent to Mexico, he does not hesitate to say that it will be regarded with no unfriendly eye by the Confederate States. They can have no other interest or desire than to see a respectable, responsible, and stable government established in that country. . . . Confident that his Imperial Majesty has no intention of imposing on Mexico any government not in accordance with the wishes of its inhabitants, they will feel quite indifferent as to its form.[43]

Slidell also told the emperor that "as the Lincoln government was the ally and protector of his enemy Juárez, we could have no objection to make common cause with him against the common enemy."[44]

During the fall of 1863 there were several indications that Maximilian intended to recognize the Confederacy after his arrival in Mexico.[45]

Slidell reported in December that an emissary from Maximilian said the archduke was sympathetic with the Confederate cause and would soon establish friendly diplomatic relations with the Confederacy.[46]

Jefferson Davis was delighted by the prospect of recognition by the new government in Mexico. "If the Mexican people prefer a monarchy to a republic," he told the Confederate Congress on December 7, "it is our plain duty cheerfully to acquiesce in their decision. . . . The Emperor of the French has solemnly disclaimed any purpose to impose on Mexico a form of government not acceptable to the nation."[47] He did not wait for Maximilian's arrival in Mexico to appoint an envoy to his new court. On January 7, 1864, William Preston, Buchanan's minister to Spain, was commissioned as minister plenipotentiary and envoy extraordinary from the Confederate States of America to the imperial court of Mexico. Preston was instructed to tell the imperial government of Mexico that "the future safety of the Mexican Empire is inextricably bound up with the safety and independence of the Confederacy" and to stress that the U.S. government, which "has become so debased as to be under the control of the lower classes," intended "if successful in their designs on us, to extend their conquests by the annexation of Canada on the north and Mexico on the south."[48] Preston went to Havana so that he could reach Mexico quickly after Maximilian arrived there and confirmed officially his willingness to receive a Confederate envoy. Slidell eagerly awaited a chance to meet Maximilian during his visit to Paris in early March 1864.

But prior to or during his Paris visit, Maximilian became convinced that recognition of the Confederacy was not a good idea. The U.S. consul in Trieste, Richard Hildreth, who was the U.S. official nearest Maximilian's estate at Miramar, may have convinced him that recognition of the Confederacy would lead to bitter hostility by the United States. Joan Haslip, a biographer of Maximilian, wrote that the consul raised the specter of eventual American intervention in Mexico: "In a well-meant attempt to dissuade him from what he termed 'this mad adventure,' the Consul warned him that if Napoleon did not withdraw his troops on his own, 'an American army of experienced veterans would be landed in Mexico, strong enough to enable the Mexicans to throw out the intruders.' "[49] The Austrian foreign minister, Count Rechberg, may have suggested to Maximilian, as he did to

Motley in September, that past U.S. efforts to acquire Mexican territory had been initiated by Southerners and that as emperor of Mexico he would have more to gain from diplomatic relations with the United States than with the Confederacy.[50]

During his visit to Paris in early March 1864 Maximilian apparently became convinced that, if he avoided contacts with the Confederates, his Mexican empire would eventually be recognized by the United States. Several newspapers had suggested this possibility, and the *Globe* in London reported that Dayton had indicated that the U.S. government was ready to recognize Maximilian's government in Mexico. Maximilian's belief in this prospect seems to have come primarily from Mercier, the former French minister in Washington, who met Maximilian in Paris.

Slidell reported Mercier's claim that "at his parting interview with Lincoln he was told . . . to say to the archduke that his Government would be recognized by that of Washington without difficulty on the condition, however, that no negotiations should be entered into with the Confederate states."[51] There is no evidence that Mercier actually met Lincoln in the period before he left Washington at the end of 1863, and there is no other evidence that Seward and Lincoln ever considered recognizing Maximilian as emperor of Mexico. Mercier was probably acting on orders from Napoleon. Confederate commissioner Ambrose Dudley Mann heard in Brussels that "Louis Napoleon has enjoined upon Maximilian to hold no official relation with the Confederate government."[52]

Slidell asked for an appointment with Maximilian, but the archduke refused to see him. He met Maximilian's aide and several Mexicans who were in Paris with Maximilian. He told them that without the active friendship of the South, Maximilian would be powerless to resist aggression from the North. But Slidell doubted that this argument would be effective. He reported to Benjamin that "it would be impossible to exaggerate the unpopularity of the Mexican expedition among all classes and parties in France." He thought Napoleon's desire for an early withdrawal from Mexico might "account for the evidently increased desire to avoid giving umbrage to the Lincoln government."[53]

❧   ❧   ❧

While Maximilian was preparing to depart for Mexico, opposition to the French intervention and to the installation of a European monarch in Mexico was intensifying in the United States. "The war of France against Mexico," Seward noted in a dispatch to Adams in London, "wears upon the American people."[54] Congressional opposition to the French intervention and impending monarchy was encouraged by Mattias Romero, who resigned as Mexican chargé early in 1863 but soon returned as Mexican minister with a new mandate and budget to carry on a lobbying program. Thomas D. Schoonover, who translated a collection of Romero's dispatches, wrote that the Mexican envoy thought "his chief responsibility was to lobby for moral and material support against the French":

> He hoped to change opinion and policy over the long run by constant, slow pressure. . . . Romero also persisted in meddling in domestic politics. He supported various efforts to oust Secretary of State William H. Seward who . . . successfully opposed taking aggressive steps to compel the French to withdraw from Mexico. Romero generally cooperated with the Radical efforts to defeat Lincoln in the election of 1864. . . . Romero's interaction with such Radical leaders as Benjamin Wade, Henry Winter Davis, and Zachariah Chandler . . . supplied these House and Senate opponents of Seward, Lincoln, and Johnson with resolutions and information for their speeches and debates . . . Romero worked with the Radical leaders in part because he hoped to . . . awaken American public opinion against the French intervention.[55]

In January 1864 Senator James McDougall of California proposed a joint congressional resolution declaring that the French intervention in Mexico was "an act unfriendly to the republic of the United States of America" and that if the French did not withdraw from Mexico by March 15 "it will become the duty of the Congress of the United States to declare war against the Government of France."[56] This belligerent resolution was tabled by the Senate in early February. Lyons reported that Seward told him he was personally in favor of a U.S. effort after the Civil War to help Juárez drive the French from Mexico.[57] All the other evidence indicates that Seward strongly opposed any U.S. intervention in Mexico. Seward probably thought that the

British, hoping to avoid a U.S. intervention that would have a negative impact on the substantial British economic interests in Mexico, would encourage Napoleon to withdraw his troops from Mexico.

During Maximilian's visit to Paris, the U.S. government's disdain for the idea of a European monarch in Mexico was demonstrated by the absence of Dayton from a glittering reception for Maximilian attended by all other members of the diplomatic corps. Seward had ordered that, if Maximilian appeared in Paris "with any assumption of political authority or title in Mexico, you will entirely refrain from intercourse with him. . . . We do not hold formal or informal communications with political agents or representatives of revolutionary movements in countries with which we maintain diplomatic intercourse."[58] One historian remarked that this was the first time a Hapsburg had been described as a "revolutionary."

On March 23 Seward sent Dayton a revised draft resolution by Senator McDougall stating that "the occupation of Mexico, or any part thereof, by the Emperor of France, or by the person indicated by him as Emperor of Mexico, is an offense to the people of the republic of the United States of America."[59] The House of Representatives unanimously declared its opposition to monarchy in Mexico by approving on April 4 a resolution moved by Congressman Henry Winter Davis:

> The Congress of the United States are unwilling by silence to leave the nations of the world under the impression that they are indifferent spectators of the deplorable events now transpiring in the republic of Mexico and . . . declare that it does not accord with the policy of the United States to acknowledge any monarchical government erected on the ruins of any republican government in America under the auspices of any European power.[60]

Although Senator Sumner refused to allow the House resolution to reach the Senate floor, Seward sent it to Dayton with a comment that "the resolution truly interprets the unanimous sentiment of the people of the United States with regard to Mexico."

When Dayton saw Drouyn de Lhuys on April 22, the foreign minister's first words were "Do you bring us peace, or bring us war?" Dayton explained that the congressional resolutions did not mean that the

U.S. government was about to make war on France, although it had always said that any interference by France in the form of government in Mexico would be viewed with great dissatisfaction in the United States.[61] A few days later Seward reaffirmed his faith that "the destinies of the American continent are not to be permanently controlled . . . in the capitals of Europe."[62]

Maximilian was on his way to Mexico when the Republican national convention met in Baltimore in early June 1864 to renominate Lincoln for a second term. The convention adopted a resolution declaring that the displacement of republican government in Mexico was a threat to the United States:

> The people of the United States can never regard with indifference the attempt of any European power to overthrow by force or to supplant by fraud the institutions of any republican government on the Western continent, and . . . they will view with extreme jealousy, as menacing to the peace and independence of their own country, the efforts of any such power to obtain new footholds for monarchical governments, sustained by foreign military force in close proximity to the United States.[63]

In his letter accepting the nomination, Lincoln reserved his freedom to maintain his cautious policy toward Mexico as long as it was necessary:

> While the resolution in regard to supplanting of republican government upon the western continent is fully concurred in, there might be misunderstanding were I not to say that the position of the government in relation to the action of France in Mexico . . . will be faithfully maintained so long as the state of facts shall leave that position pertinent and applicable.[64]

Lincoln told General John M. Thayer that there was nothing the United States could do about Maximilian until after the Union was restored:

> Napoleon has taken advantage of our weakness in our time of trouble, and has attempted to found a monarchy on the soil of Mexico in utter

disregard of the Monroe doctrine. My policy is, attend to only one trouble at a time. If we get well out of our present difficulties and restore the Union, I propose to notify Louis Napoleon that it is about time to take his army out of Mexico. When that army is gone, the Mexicans will take care of Maximilian.[65]

Meanwhile, Lincoln's policy was to say as little as possible about Mexico and the French intervention. His annual message to Congress in December 1864 contained only two sentences regarding that country: "Mexico continues to be a theatre of civil war. While our political relations with that country have undergone no change, we have, at the same time, strictly maintained neutrality between the belligerents."[66] The message did not mention the presence in Mexico of a French army or an Austrian archduke posing as emperor of Mexico.

But Lincoln could not prevent a number of statements that, once the American Civil War was over, Americans would drive the French out of Mexico. The idea of a postwar American expedition to Mexico had been mentioned from time to time since the beginning of the French intervention. Postmaster General Montgomery Blair told Romero, the Mexican chargé, on May 5, 1862, that "as soon as the Southern insurrection is defeated . . . the United States will send an army to Mexico to throw the French out."[67] John J. Crittenden, chairman of the House Foreign Affairs Committee, made a nearly identical promise to Romero a few days later.[68] In 1864, just after his nomination as Lincoln's new vice president, Andrew Johnson warned Napoleon in a speech in Nashville that "the day of reckoning is coming":

> It will not be long before the Rebellion is put down. . . . And then we will attend to this Mexican affair, and say to Louis Napoleon, "You cannot found a monarchy on this Continent." An expedition into Mexico would be a sort of recreation to the brave soldiers who are now fighting the battles of the Union, and the French concern would be quickly wiped out.[69]

The idea of a joint expedition to Mexico of Northern and Southern troops was suggested by James Gordon Bennett's *Herald* in January 1864:

As for Mexico, we will, at the close of the rebellion, if the French have not left there before, send fifty thousand Northern and fifty thousand Southern troops, forming together a grand army to drive the invaders into the Gulf. That is the way we shall tolerate a French monarchy in Mexico.[70]

During the election campaign in 1864, when Lincoln needed the support of the influential editor, he promised to nominate Bennett to succeed Dayton as minister to France. Bennett had often visited France and spoke French. In February 1865, after Dayton's death, Lincoln offered Bennett the post. A U.S. minister who had advocated American intervention in Mexico would hardly have been welcome in France. Expecting that Bennett would decline, Lincoln may have been sending a message to Napoleon that he was considering a tougher line on the French intervention in Mexico. Bennett did decline the post, and John Bigelow, the U.S. consul general in Paris, was named minister to France.[71]

After Mercier's departure late in 1863, the French government had only a chargé d'affaires, M. de Geofroy, in Washington. A visiting French journalist wrote his wife that the gentlemen of the French legation "live among themselves, see nobody, and never speak to any native."[72]

∓ ∓ ∓

In January 1865 Francis P. Blair Sr. visited Jefferson Davis in Richmond and suggested that he lead an expedition to Mexico to drive out the French. The elder Blair had edited the administration paper during Andrew Jackson's presidency, had known every subsequent president, and had been on friendly terms with Jefferson Davis before the war. His son, Montgomery Blair, was Lincoln's postmaster general. Blair's initial letter to Davis said he was "entirely unaccredited except . . . by having permission to pass our lines and to offer to you my own suggestions."[73] He arrived in Richmond on January 12, 1865. Blair was cordially received by his old friend, and Mrs. Davis embraced the "dear old rascal."

Blair read Davis a paper containing the following statement:

Jefferson Davis . . . can . . . deliver his country from the bloody agony now covering it in mourning. He can drive Maximilian from his American throne, and baffle the designs of Napoleon. . . . President Lincoln has opened the way in his amnesty proclamation and the message which looks to armistice. Suppose the first enlarged to embrace all engaged in the war; suppose secret preliminaries to armistice enable President Davis to transfer such portions of his army as he may deem proper for this purpose to Texas. . . . If more force were wanted . . . would not multitudes of the army of the North . . . be found ready to embark in an enterprise vital to the interests of our whole republic. . . . He who expels the Bonaparte Hapsburg dynasty from our Southern flank . . . will ally his name with those of Washington and Jackson . . . If in delivering Mexico he should model its States in form and principle to adapt them to our Union and add a new Southern constellation while rounding our possession on the continent at the Isthmus, he would complete the work of Jefferson.[74]

This and other language in Blair's paper indicates that he was thinking of an enterprise in Mexico carried out after a Confederate surrender (although called an "armistice"), an amnesty accorded to all Confederates, and the restoration of the Union. But two accounts by Confederates state that Blair had proposed a joint operation in Mexico during an armistice, without restoration of the Union. Confederate envoy James Mason, citing a letter from Benjamin to Duncan F. Kenner, told Lord Palmerston that Blair had proposed negotiations on the following basis: "leave all questions in dispute open and undecided; an armistice to take place; and a league offensive and defensive entered into to drive the French out of Mexico."[75] Mrs. Davis described the Blair proposal in similar terms in her memoirs: "After the Monroe Doctrine is restored to the continent, the two governments could sit down in common victory to work out a peace."[76]

It is hardly conceivable that Blair, who was undoubtedly familiar with Lincoln's total rejection of all options except reunion, encouraged Davis to think that Lincoln might agree to an armistice without a commitment to the restoration of the Union. It is less unlikely that Davis thought Blair's idea of an expedition to Mexico just might offer a last straw of hope for the survival of the Confederacy—or at least for Davis's own continuing freedom. Nicolay and Hay wrote in 1890 that Davis "took little pains to disguise his entire willingness to enter upon the wild scheme of military conquest and annexation which could easily be read between the lines of a political crusade to rescue the Monroe Doctrine from its present peril."[77]

Seward described the results of Blair's visit in a dispatch to Adams:

> He brought back a letter which had been addressed to him by Jefferson Davis, in which he said that he would waive formalities and send or receive commissioners to confer with the President concerning peace between the two countries. Mr. Blair returned to Richmond with a letter which he had received from the President, in which he said that he would informally receive any persons who should come from Davis . . . to treat for a restoration of peace between the people of our one common country.[78]

On January 29 Alexander H. Stephens, R. M. T. Hunter, and John A. Campbell arrived at Union lines below Richmond as Confederate peace commissioners. Lincoln decided that he and Seward should meet with the Confederates on a Union warship at Hampton Roads. Stephens's description after the war of the proposal he made during the four-hour shipboard meeting on February 3 resembled the previously cited Confederate versions of Blair's idea:

> Could not both Parties . . . in our contest come to an understanding and agreement to postpone their present strife until [the Monroe Doctrine] is maintained in behalf of Mexico, and might it not, when successfully sustained there, . . . almost inevitably lead to a peaceful and harmonious solution of their own difficulties. . . . Mr. Lincoln replied with considerable earnestness that he could entertain no proposition for ceasing active military operations which was not based upon a pledge first given for the ultimate restoration of the Union. . . . These pointed and emphatic responses seemed to put an end of the Conference.[79]

Seward's dispatch to Adams on the Hampton Roads meeting did not indicate that Stephens had proposed an expedition to Mexico:

What the insurgent party seemed chiefly to favor was a postponement of the question of separation, upon which the war is waged, and a mutual direction of efforts of the government as well as those of the insurgents to some extrinsic policy or scheme for a season, during which passions might be expected to subside, and the armies be reduced, and trade and intercourse between the people of both sections resumed. It was suggested by them that through such postponement we might now have immediately peace, with some not very certain prospect of an ultimate satisfactory adjustment of political relations between the government and the States, section, or people now engaged in conflict with it. This suggestion, though deliberately considered, was nevertheless regarded by the President as one of armistice or truce, and he announced that we can agree to no cessation or suspension of hostilities, except on the basis of the disbandment of the insurgent forces and the restoration of the national authority throughout all States of the Union.[80]

Lincoln's insistence on the restoration of the Union shattered Davis's hope for peace between the "two countries." But the idea of an American expedition to Mexico lived on for more than a year. On his way back to Washington from Richmond in January, Blair stopped at General Grant's headquarters and told him of the plan to oust Maximilian and the French from Mexico. Although unwilling to consider any such plan before a Confederate surrender, Grant liked Blair's idea of a joint postwar force of Union and Confederate veterans to drive the Europeans out of Mexico. His attempts to implement this idea after Lee's surrender are reviewed in Epilogue I.

On April 14 the newly arrived British minister, Sir Frederick Bruce, reported to London that the United States was preparing to oust Maximilian from Mexico.[81] But the previous week the marquis de Chambrun, who was with the president during a visit to Grant's headquarters at City Point, asked Lincoln about the possibility of a U.S. military intervention in Mexico. "There has been war enough," the president replied; "during my second term there will be no more fighting."[82]

A War with America as Soon as She Makes Peace

Union Relations with Britain and Canada, 1864–1865

As the third anniversary of the firing on Fort Sumter approached, the British government's policy of neutrality in the American conflict had become well established. But there were many sources of tension between the U.S. and British governments, and the hostility of the ruling classes in Britain toward the North remained unchanged. Seward reviewed Lincoln's outlook on U.S.-British relations in a dispatch to Adams on February 13, 1864:

> Great Britain regards the insurgents as a lawful naval belligerent; we do not. . . . The dealings of British subjects with the insurgents . . . are continually producing controversies and claims upon which the two governments cannot agree. . . . It already begins to be a cause of a painful apprehension in both countries that, if peace should come today, it would be very difficult to adjust the controversies already ripened between the two nations. . . . It is the earnest desire of the President that both governments may improve the present hour by a common preparation for a peaceful, friendly, and beneficent future.[1]

Neither the American minister in London, Charles Francis Adams, nor the British minister in Washington, Lord Lyons, was optimistic

239

about chances for improved relations. Adams was convinced that the most important reason for the continuing hostility of the British ruling classes was fear of popular democracy:

> Efforts are . . . steadily made in *The Times* and other newspapers following that lead to . . . sustain the public mind in the confidence of our ultimate failure. There is no longer any sort of disguise maintained as to the wishes of the privileged classes. Very little genuine sympathy is entertained for the rebels. The true motive . . . is the fear of the spread of democratic feeling at home in the event of our success.[2]

Lyons was equally convinced of the hostility of most Americans toward Britain: "There can unhappily be no doubt that three-fourths of the American people are eagerly longing for a safe opportunity of making war with England."[3] His exaggerated view of American hostility toward Britain led Lyons to write several dispatches expressing concern for the safety of the British colonies in Canada.

In the early 1860s the area of present-day Canada was known as British North America; it contained seven separate British colonies as well as vast areas of unsettled wilderness. A British governor general in Quebec governed present-day Quebec and Ontario directly and three maritime provinces on the Atlantic through lieutenant governors. A new governor general, Viscount Monck, arrived in November 1861.[4] Two British colonies on the Pacific were ruled by a separate governor. The unsettled area between Lake Superior and the Pacific was the responsibility of the Hudson's Bay Company.

Canada had no national government and no diplomatic relations with the United States except through the British government. If the U.S. Department of State wished to bring up any issue related to Canada, it sent a note to the British minister in Washington, who might pass it on directly to the governor general in Quebec or refer it to the Foreign Office in London.

The pattern of Canadian attitudes toward the United States was similar to that in Britain. The middle and laboring classes tended to favor the North, while governing officials, conservative provincial leaders, and the press tended to favor the South. Robin Winks wrote that in Canada "much of the conservative opposition to the North stemmed from the fact that the English Radicals often had pointed to the United States as an example of success of democracy."[5] The Canadian press usually followed the anti-Northern line of *The Times* in London.

In the 1840s Canadians and Britons had watched Americans invade their southern neighbor and eventually sign a treaty transferring to the United States one-half of Mexico's territory before the Texas revolution. In the 1860s the British feared that the United States would eventually attempt to annex some or all of the territory of its northern neighbor. Biographer Jasper Ridley observed that "Palmerston's chief anxiety, as far as the Americans were concerned, was that they would invade and conquer Canada; and this remained a great source of anxiety to him all his life."[6] During most of the Civil War period the government and people of the United States showed little interest in Canada. But Lyons took seriously every hint of possible American interest in the postwar acquisition of Canada.

Lyons's dispatch in May 1861 about the danger of war with the United States, cited in chapter 4, included a comment that the Americans "undoubtedly look upon Canada as our weak point" and a reminder that in 1860 Seward had advocated "the annexation of Canada as a compensation for any loss which might be occasioned by the disaffection of the South."[7] Just before the first major battle of the war, at Bull Run, Lyons reported that the *Herald* in New York had proposed that "the North and South should agree to an armistice for two or three years, and shall turn the military preparations which they have made against each other to account by conquering British and Russian North America, Cuba, Jamaica, and the other West Indian Islands and Central America."[8]

During the *Trent* crisis, at the end of 1861, preparations for a possible war with the United States convinced British leaders that the three-thousand-mile Canadian border could not be defended in the event of a determined attack from the United States. British worries about the vulnerability of Canada receded in 1862 and the first half of 1863, but arose again after Union victories at Gettysburg and Vicksburg in July 1863. Lyons's participation in August in the "diplomatic excursion" to several Empire State cities near the Canadian border and his subsequent visit to Canada probably contributed to his conviction that Canada was vulnerable.

In the early spring of 1864 the British Admiralty sent a Royal Navy captain, James G. Goodenough, to America to visit dockyards and shipbuilding companies and report on U.S. preparations "for a war afloat against a maritime power." Lyons wrote Russell that Goodenough's report confirmed "my impression that the Americans are very seriously preparing for a Foreign War."[9] He reiterated this view in a confidential dispatch on April 25:

> This report . . . shows that the Government of the United States is steadily making preparations to enable it to engage with advantage in foreign war, and that its means of carrying on a naval war are becoming every day more formidable. . . . There can be no doubt that these preparations are made mainly with a view to a war with England, and that . . . advantage would be eagerly taken of any conjuncture or circumstances which would enable a declaration of war against England to be made with tolerable safety. . . . They believe that they could throw an overwhelming force into Canada, and that sudden attacks on some of the British Colonies in this hemisphere, and in particular on Bermuda and the Bahamas, would in all probability be successful.[10]

Although Goodenough's report contained impressive evidence of the rapid expansion of the U.S. Navy, it provided little support for Lyons's conclusion that the United States was preparing for a naval war with Britain. Lyons offered no other evidence to support his conclusions. His dispatch, circulated in London in the Foreign Office Confidential Print, gave cabinet members and senior officials an utterly false view of the outlook and plans of U.S. officials.

Lyons's conclusion that the United States was preparing for a naval war with Britain was totally unfounded. The secretary of the navy noted repeatedly in his diary his belief that the president and secretary of state were unnecessarily apprehensive about the possibility of war with Britain. Welles scoffed at the idea that the United States needed warships suitable for a naval war with a European power:

> What we needed for this war and the blockade of our extensive coast was many vessels of light draft and good speed, not large, expensive ships, for we had no navy to encounter but illicit traders to capture. . . .

A war with one or more of the large maritime powers would require an entirely different class of vessels. . . . We wanted not heavy navy-built ships but such vessels as could capture neutral unarmed blockade runners. There was no navy, no fighting craft, to encounter.[11]

The same week that Lyons wrote Russell about U.S. preparations for a foreign war, Seward wrote Adams that "the president earnestly desires not only a continuance of peace but also to preserve our long existing friendship with Great Britain. He is therefore indisposed to complain of injuries on part of British subjects whenever he can refrain consistently with the safety, honor, and dignity of the United States."[12]

In late July, William Lindsay asked in Parliament whether the government planned any effort to bring about a suspension of hostilities in America. Palmerston replied in the negative:

Her Majesty's government deeply lament the great sacrifice of life and property in America and the distress which that war has produced in this country. But we have not thought that in the present state of things there was any advantage to be gained by entering into concert with any other powers for the purpose of proposing or offering mediation, or of negotiating with the government of the United States or of the Confederate States to bring about a termination of this unhappy war.[13]

Palmerston defended the government's neutrality policy in a speech to his constituents at Tiverton on August 23:

There is much diversity of opinion as to the merits of the contending parties. Some are for the north on the ground of their hatred of slavery; some are for the south on the ground of their love of freedom and independence. . . . We may hope that time and reflection . . . and the fact of the immense losses that have been sustained, and the slight hopes of success which appear on the part of the North [will lead to] some progress . . . toward healing that tremendous breach which now exists.[14]

After more than three years of civil war in America, Palmerston still thought that the North could not win and that the only chance for peace in America lay in some type of accommodation between North and South.

෴   ෴   ෴

Lincoln was renominated by a National Union convention in June, but by late summer his conflict with the Radical Republicans over post-war reconstruction policies was so serious that many political leaders and editors thought Lincoln could not win reelection. In mid-August, even before the Democrats had selected a candidate, Lyons reported that "Mr. Lincoln's chance of the Presidency for a second term seems vanishing," although he thought "the fall of Atlanta or even that of Mobile might however change this." The following week he wrote that "Mr. Lincoln's star is very pale."[15]

On August 29 the Democratic National Convention in Chicago nominated General George McClellan, former commander of the Union army, to oppose Lincoln. Ignoring a recent statement by Jefferson Davis that he would consider no peace proposal that did not include Confederate independence, the badly divided Democratic convention adopted a resolution demanding that "immediate efforts be made for a cessation of hostilities" and for the restoration of peace "on the basis of the Federal Union." McClellan rejected an unconditional armistice and insisted that reunion must be a precondition for any peace settlement. British newspapers that had scoffed at McClellan's ineffective leadership of the Union army in 1862 probably wondered in 1864 how effective the young ex-general, who had no experience as a civilian official, would be as president. Yet Dayton noted from Paris that the English and French press "yet entertain a hope of the death of the administration."[16]

Prospects for Lincoln's reelection brightened during the fall as a result of Sherman's capture of Atlanta and Sheridan's successes in the Shenandoah Valley of Virginia. James M. McPherson described the impact of these military successes on public opinion in the North:

> As late as the summer of 1864, when the war seem to be going badly for the North, . . . Lincoln came under enormous pressure to negotiate peace with the Confederacy. . . . Lincoln resisted this pressure, but at

what appeared to be the cost of his reelection to the Presidency. If the election had been held in August 1864 instead of November, Lincoln would have lost. . . . Events on the battlefield, principally Sherman's capture of Atlanta and Sheridan's spectacular victories over Jubal Early in the Shenandoah Valley . . . turned Northern opinion from deepest despair in the summer to confident determination by November.[17]

On election day, November 8, Lincoln carried every state except Kentucky, Delaware, and New Jersey, winning 212 of the 233 electoral votes. Of the slightly more than 4 million votes cast, about 2.2 million (55 percent) were for Lincoln, while nearly 1.8 million were for McClellan.

General Grant viewed the success at the polls as "a victory worth more to the country than a battle won. Rebeldom and Europe will so construe it."[18] Lincoln told a crowd at the White House that the election in wartime demonstrated to the world the viability of popular republican government:

We cannot have free Government without elections; and if the rebellion could force us to forgo or postpone a national election, it might fairly claim to have already conquered and ruined us. . . . The election . . . has demonstrated that a people's Government can sustain a national election in the midst of a great civil war. Until now, it has not been known to the world that this was a possibility.[19]

But Lincoln's electoral victory had little positive effect on the opinions of European leaders. "The English don't like the reelection of Mr. Lincoln," Adams's secretary, Benjamin Moran, noted in his diary on November 22, "and grieve over it as if it were a disaster to themselves."[20] *The Times* thought Lincoln's reelection had shattered hopes for an early end to the terrible war in America:

The country has heard the worst that can be said against the President. It knows of his arbitrary arrests, his Emancipation edicts, his appointment of military dictators, his ceaseless demand for men. . . . But everything has been—to use the American expression—endorsed by the popular vote. The President may conduct the war as he pleases for four years more. . . . The expectation of a speedy peace has not accompanied the reelection of Mr. Lincoln.[21]

Before the fall of Atlanta, *The Times* thought Sherman could not escape "a disastrous fate" in Georgia.[22] During his audacious march to the sea, the European press was sure his army would be surrounded and captured. "The journals of Great Britain and France," the U.S. legation in Paris reported, "have almost universally predicted the destruction of General Sherman in his retreat from Atlanta, as they call it."[23] After Sherman's capture of Savannah, Lincoln hoped the success of his campaign in Georgia would "bring those who sat in darkness to see a great light."[24]

As the British gradually began to understand that these Union victories could lead to the total defeat of the Confederate armies, they began to worry again about the possibility of an American attack on Canada— perhaps by a joint army from North and South—after the war. These fears were intensified by U.S. reactions to a mid-October raid on a Vermont community by Confederate agents operating in Canada.

On October 18 twenty Confederates secretly crossed the border from Canada and proceeded by stagecoach in small groups to St. Albans, a Vermont community of about five thousand people about twenty-five miles south of the Canadian border, near Lake Champlain. They stayed that night in several hotels in St. Albans. The next morning the Confederates robbed three banks of more than $200,000 and set fire to several buildings. Citizens of St. Albans fired on them, and several residents were killed in the return fire. The raiders fled back across the border on stolen horses.[25]

When General John A. Dix, Federal commander in the Northeast, heard about the raid, he sent a telegram to the commanding officer at Burlington, Vermont: "Send all the efficient force you have to St. Albans, and try to find the marauders who came from Canada this morning. . . . In case they are not found on our side of the line, pursue them into Canada, if necessary, and destroy them."[26]

Lord Russell recalled later "the very just remark of President Lincoln that these inroads and depredations were organized with a view to bring on a war between Great Britain and the United States [and] that both Governments were bound to do everything in their power to frustrate so wicked a design."[27] Lord Monck, the governor general of Canada, sent assurances to Seward that "there exists among the British authorities in Canada the most earnest desire to use all the powers which the laws confer upon them . . . for the repression and punishment of outrages such as that which has just occurred at St. Albans."[28]

Twelve of the raiders were captured in Canada. Seward requested their extradition on October 26 pursuant to the Webster-Ashburton Treaty of 1842.[29] Monck replied that the men would be delivered to U.S. authorities "as soon as I shall have been advised that the proofs required by the treaty of extradition have been made."[30] The case against the men was presented to a police magistrate named Coursol in Montreal. In mid-November the legal process was suspended for a month to allow messengers to be sent to Richmond for proof of the defense claim that the raid was an act of war authorized by the Confederate government. Both Monck and Lincoln refused to give the messengers safe conduct to Richmond.

Meanwhile, the U.S. government had taken the first of several diplomatic steps intended to increase pressure for more effective enforcement of British neutrality in Canada. A few days after the raid, Seward instructed Adams to give notice to the British government, as allowed by the Rush-Bagot Treaty of 1817 on naval armaments on the Great Lakes, that "at the expiration of six months . . . the United States will deem themselves at liberty to increase the naval armaments upon the lakes, if, in their judgment, the condition of affairs in that quarter shall then require it." Seward clearly linked action on naval armaments to British enforcement of its neutrality policy: "The policy of neutrality which her Majesty has proclaimed has failed . . . and . . . must continue to fail more conspicuously every day so long as asylum is allowed there to active agents of the enemies of the United States, and they are in any way able . . . to use British ports and British borders as a base for felonious depredations against the citizens of the United States."[31]

For a month after the raid it seemed, as Adams remarked to Russell, that the British authorities in Canada were making "faithful and diligent efforts to bring these disturbers of the public peace to account."[32] This belief was shattered on December 14 by the astonishing news that Coursol had released the Confederate prisoners. When the case was resumed, the defense challenged the jurisdiction of the magistrate on the technical ground that the governor general had not issued a warrant required by British law. Coursol accepted the argument, ordered the discharge of the prisoners, and returned to them the stolen money that was in their possession when they were captured. Although Vermont attorneys hurriedly obtained a new warrant, the Montreal chief of police, Lamothe, stalled until the prisoners had escaped.[33]

Seward was furious: "It is impossible to consider these proceedings as either legal, just, or friendly toward the United States." But Adams was instructed to assure Russell that the U.S. government "nevertheless most earnestly desires and constantly aims to remain in peace and friendship and fraternal intercourse with the British provinces and with the British empire."[34] On December 17 Seward issued an order, directed by the president, that any traveler entering the United States from the neighboring British provinces would henceforth require a passport issued by the competent Canadian authority and counter-signed by a U.S. diplomatic agent or consul.[35]

Robin Winks described the angry reaction of the U.S. press to the release of the St. Albans raiders:

> The Canadas found themselves bearing the brunt of a newspaper attack nearly as intense as that during the *Trent* affair. . . . The *Chicago Tribune* hysterically shouted that the North should take Canada by the throat and throttle her "as a St. Bernard would throttle a poodle pup.". . . The *New York Times* felt that henceforth Canadian territory was entitled to no more respect than was that of Virginia or South Carolina. "It may be said that this will lead to a war with England," the *Times* admitted, and added, "But if it must come, let it come. . . . We were never in bet-ter condition for a war with England."[36]

The most significant reaction in Congress was the abrogation of the Reciprocity Treaty of 1855 with Britain. It provided for free trade in a series of enumerated products between the United States and Canada but allowed the imposition of tariffs on U.S.-manufactured goods entering Canada. The treaty's benefits to the United States had been debatable before the war and had eroded during the war due to increased domestic demand for the enumerated products. After the treaty had been in force for ten years, it could be canceled by either party with a year's notice. Agitation for abrogation when allowed in 1865 had begun before the war on commercial grounds and gained momentum during the war as a means of punishing Britain for her recognition of Confederate belligerency and other actions benefiting the Confederates.[37] A resolution calling for abrogation of the treaty was passed by the House on December 14 by a vote of 85 to 57, and was approved by the Senate on January 12 by a vote of 38 to 8.[38] Seward informed the British legation that the present attitudes of the British government, especially the recognition of Confederate belligerency, prevented the negotiation of a new treaty on U.S.-Canadian trade.[39]

¤⁄ɔ   ¤⁄ɔ   ¤⁄ɔ

During the first three months of 1865 the government and the public in Britain were very fearful that the end of the American Civil War, which seemed to be approaching, would be followed by an American attack on Canada. This fear was derived from many influences—U.S. annexation of vast new territories from Mexico only thirteen years before the Civil War, Seward's prewar interest in the acquisition of Canada, references to the future annexation of Canada in several newspapers, Palmerston's long-standing expectation of an eventual American attempt to annex Canada, Lyons's exaggerated reports of American hostility toward Britain and his unfounded claims that the United States was preparing for a naval war with Britain, angry government and public reactions to the release of the St. Albans raiders, abrogation of the treaties on naval armament on the Great Lakes and reciprocal trade with Canada, the belief in Britain that the United States would not demobilize its large army and navy after the war until it achieved its assumed annexationist goals, and speculation that a joint Union-Confederate expedition to Canada or Mexico might be a feature of an agreement ending the Civil War.

On January 20 Palmerston wrote the queen that fear of a war with the United States was the main reason for the cabinet's rejection of a motion by Gladstone, Chancellor of the Exchequer, to reduce the budget for the Royal Navy:

> The great majority of the Cabinet were against such a measure, considering the very hostile spirit towards England which pervades all classes

in the Federal States, and looking to the probability that, whenever the civil war in America shall be ended, the Northern States will make demands upon England which cannot be complied with, and will either make war against England or make inroads into your Majesty's North American possessions which would lead to war.[40]

Queen Victoria noted in her diary a conversation on February 12 with a cabinet minister, Sir Charles Wood: "Talked of America and the danger, which seems approaching, of our having a war with her as soon as she makes peace, of the impossibility of our being able to hold Canada, but we must struggle for it."[41]

In the second week of February there were rumors in Britain of a meeting of Confederate and Union delegates in Virginia. The owners of blockade running ships and high-priced cotton were appalled at the prospect of peace. Adams described the British reaction to his son on February 17:

> The consternation was extraordinary. . . . You would have thought that a great calamity had befallen the good people of England. . . . Happily for the distressed nerves of our friends, the next day brought them a little relief. A steamer had come with . . . later news. It was not so bad as they had feared. . . . There would be no peace. Hurrah. The papers of this morning are all congratulating the public that the war will go on indefinitely.[42]

"The impression is now very general," Adams wrote to Seward on February 23, "that peace and restoration at home are synonymous with war with this country. . . . The impression is sedulously kept up that your own feelings are strongly hostile to this country. I find this to prevail even among a large class of persons wholly friendly to us. I have combated it with them in vain."[43]

On March 1 Seward sent Adams an unequivocal message from the president:

> European politicians do not now mistake in supposing that the people of the United States are indulging a profound sense of injury. . . . Demands for redress are very apt to culminate in schemes of conquest.

This, however, is not the policy of the President. . . . The President does not for a moment think of sending armies or navies with such a purpose . . . into Canada, or the West Indies, or Mexico.[44]

Adams replied that, although he had "taken some pains to ridicule the notion that we have the smallest desire to appropriate Canada by conquest," belief in American aggressive intentions persisted:

The ill-founded and unfortunate opinion expressed by Lord Russell in the early part of the contest, that on our side it was waged for empire, has been twisted to confirm an impression that we intend to spread our armies not merely over the slaveholding States but over Canada on the one side and Mexico on the other. It is of no avail to represent to them that even were . . . our policy to acquire those countries, the true way to bring it about would be by patience, conciliation, and the establishment of a harmony of interests. . . . These are not European ideas, and therefore stand no chance of being appreciated. The sense of the presence of a half a million of men in arms and of a powerful naval armament, with nothing to do, is much more distinctly defined in the imagination.[45]

On March 17 Adams formally notified Lord Russell that, pursuant to the congressional resolution of January 18, the U.S. government was abrogating the Reciprocity Treaty of 1855. But by then Lincoln and Seward had taken two other steps to ease U.S.-British tensions. The order requiring passports for Canadians entering the United States was rescinded. Adams was instructed to inform Russell that, although the U.S. government had reserved the right to increase naval armaments on the Great Lakes, it had no plans to do so. Seward thought these moves had "relieved Canada of apprehensions of hostile intentions on our part" and hoped they would have a "soothing influence in England."[46]

British concern about a U.S. attack on Canada waned just as the British press was reacting to Lincoln's second inaugural address on March 4, 1865. *The Times* struck a somber note: "The President . . . knows too well the difficulties of the task which still lies before his Government. . . . His address appears to be intended to repress the more sanguine expectations of the Northern people, and to intimate to them that fresh exertions and sacrifices will be necessary."[47] The most positive comment was in *The Spectator*. It thought that during his first term Lincoln had been "visibly growing in force of character, in self-possession, and in magnanimity, till . . . we can detect no longer the rude and illiterate mold of a village lawyer's thought, but find it replaced by a grasp of principle, a dignity of manner, and a solemnity of purpose."[48]

Relations with the United States and the defense of Canada were debated at length in Parliament on March 13 and 23. Palmerston declared on the thirteenth "that it is less likely than many suppose that the United States will, when their war is over, attack Canada."[49] Ten days later he assured the House of Commons that "there is no danger of war with America. Nothing that has recently passed indicates any hostile disposition on the part of the United States toward us."[50]

On April 10, 1865, the Department of State sent two circulars to U.S. ministers in Europe. The first announced the surrender of Lee's army:

> The past week has been characterized by a rapid and uninterrupted series of military successes more momentous in their results than any that proceeded them during the war. Richmond and Petersburg . . . have been captured by our armies. The insurrection has no longer a seat for its pretended government. Its so-called officials are fugitives. Its chief army . . . had been retreating closely pursued and hemmed in by the victorious forces of the Union . . . until the triumph of the national armies finally culminated in the surrender of General Lee and the whole insurgent army of northern Virginia to Lieutenant General Grant yesterday afternoon at half past four o'clock.[51]

A second circular informed U.S. ministers that Seward had been seriously injured in an accident during a carriage ride.[52] The coachmen stopped to repair a door latch and the horses bolted. Seward attempted to gather the reins and fell from the coach. His injuries included a jaw fractured on both sides, a broken arm, and a dislocated shoulder.

On April 15 the State Department sent another momentous communication to U.S. ministers. It was signed by "W. Hunter, Acting Secretary." William Hunter was chief clerk of the department:

The sad duty devolves upon me to announce the assassination of the President at Ford's theater, last night by a pistol-shot from a person who entered his box for the purpose. The assassin escaped, but it is supposed has since been arrested. The President died at seven and a half o'clock this morning. Vice President Johnson has assumed the functions of President, having been sworn in by the Chief Justice. At about the same time, an attempt was made by . . . a different person to assassinate Mr. Seward, but the murderer only succeeded in inflicting painful and severe wounds, principally upon his face. Mr. F. W. Seward was beaten over the head with a heavy weapon in the hands of the person who attacked his father, and is grievously hurt.[53]

The assassination of a head of state shocked leaders and ordinary people around the world and prompted an outpouring of reactions from all levels in many countries. A thousand-page memorial volume containing a collection of these speeches, editorials, and resolutions was published by the Department of State in 1866. The extensive British reactions in this volume clearly demonstrate the persistent misjudgment of Lincoln by the British upper classes.

Lord Russell's remarks in the House of Lords on the assassination are the only public statement he ever made about the characteristics and roles of Abraham Lincoln. The Lincoln traits he mentioned were integrity, sincerity, straightforwardness, kindness, generosity, and concern for the suffering of others. The only references to Lincoln as commander in chief were that "he always felt disinclined to harsh measures" and that commanders complained that he always wanted to temper the severity of court-martial sentences. Russell did not mention the Emancipation Proclamation; he only noted that Lincoln had thought at first that he had no constitutional right to interfere with slavery and had later proposed a constitutional amendment to abolish it. The foreign secretary made no reference to Lincoln's role in foreign affairs.[54] Palmerston was not in the House of Commons when it took note of Lincoln's assassination. The government spokesman, Sir George Grey, said little about Lincoln himself and focused on the shock of the assassination and the sympathy of the British people for the loss suffered by the American people.

Lord Derby, Conservative leader in the House of Lords, reiterated the widely held British view that the Civil War had been conducted by the Union for "empire" and by the Confederates for independence. But Derby described Lincoln as "a man who conducted the affairs of a great nation, under circumstances of great difficulty, with singular moderation and prudence" and stated that his death was "a serious misfortune" for the United States. Benjamin Disraeli, Conservative leader in the House of Commons, referred to the "homely and inno-cent" character of the president and stated that "in one of the severest trials which ever tested the qualities of man, he fulfilled his duty with simplicity and strength." The future prime minister concluded with the only remarks in either House that gave a positive vision of a reunit-ed America:

> Let us express a fervent hope that from out of the awful trials of the last four years . . . the various populations of North America may issue ele-vated and chastened, rich with the accumulated wisdom and strong in the disciplined energy which a young nation can only acquire in a pro-tracted and perilous struggle. Then they will be enabled not merely to renew their career of power and prosperity, but they will renew it to contribute to the general happiness of mankind.[55]

Editorials from twenty-eight British newspapers were included in the memorial volume. These editorials, presumably the most positive comments that appeared in the British press, indicate the cool reac-tions of British editors to Lincoln even after his assassination.[56]

The dominant common theme was the unanimous feeling of shock in Britain at the assassination of a head of state. It was described as "a dastardly crime," an "appalling tragedy," "a deed scarcely paralleled in the world's history for brutal atrocity or wicked-ness," and "an act . . . which the world will regard with feelings of unutterable horror." These reactions were independent of opinions on Lincoln; the British would have been appalled by the assassination of any head of state.

Most of the editorials emphasized Lincoln's personality and charac-ter, and said little about his vision, leadership, or accomplishments. "Now that he is dead," observed the *Evening Standard*, "the good qualities of the unfortunate Lincoln seem to come into the foreground. We remember his honesty, . . . manliness, . . . consistency [and] spirit of conciliation; . . . we almost excuse his obstinacy in the prosecution of the war." The *Daily News* mentioned his "honesty and sagacity, . . . simple integrity of purpose, firmness of will, patience, humanity, [and] deep sense of accountability." In Dublin, the *Daily Express* noted his "homely common sense" and "homely honesty." Glasgow's *Herald* thought that as president "Honest Abe" was just "as blunt and unaffected, as simple-hearted, kindly, and playful . . . as ever he had been when . . . he drove his team through the forests of Illinois."

Only a few papers made positive general comments about Lincoln's leadership. The *Mercury*, in Leeds, thought Lincoln had been "a man of great good sense and cool judgment" who had shown "unflinching firmness of purpose" as well as a "truly patriotic and Christian spirit." The *Bradford Review* said "he possessed great grasp and force of intellect, honesty and singleness of purpose, unsullied integrity, unshaken perseverance, firmness in authority, and ambition utterly unselfish." Liverpool's *Daily Post* opined that "the memory of his statesmanship, . . . wise above the average, . . . will live in the hearts and minds of the whole Anglo-Saxon race."

The Times, which had attacked Lincoln throughout the war, remained critical in two editorials after his death. The first noted the "mixed strength and weakness of his character" and opined that Lincoln had "felt himself of late a mere instrument engaged in working out a great cause . . . which he was powerless to control." The second, which was not included in the memorial publication, stated that "he did not personally illustrate any principle upon which either Union could be enforced or separation justified. . . . He brought no policy to a position of almost absolute power and fearful responsibility except a stubborn determination worthy of an old English Conservative. . . . He gave himself up to the one instinct of keeping together the Union at any cost."[57]

Only a few editorials mentioned Lincoln's role as emancipator of the slaves. The *West Coast Advertiser* merely observed that "his name will ever be associated with the freedom of the slave." The *Caledonia Mercury* noted only that his "firmness and fearlessness against the slaveholding faction . . . has endeared him to the thoroughgoing emancipationists of both north and south." The *Daily Express* in Dublin thought he had "yielded to pressure from behind" when there arose "a fierce, loud cry for abolition." The *Renfrewshire Independent* was almost alone in directly praising Lincoln's role as emancipator. "Those Englishmen who in reality abhor slavery have had reason to regard President Lincoln as in some measure the scourge of the curse, raised up to crush it. . . . How wisely, how humanely, and how effectually he has fulfilled his beneficent duty, his bitterest enemies have at last been obliged to declare."

None of the twenty-eight newspapers noted Lincoln's role as commander in chief and war strategist, and only one paper mentioned Lincoln's role in foreign relations. The *Morning Star* noted that "Lincoln was our steady friend. Assailed by the coarsest attacks on this side of the ocean . . . Abraham Lincoln calmly and steadfastly maintained a policy of peace with England and never did a deed, never wrote or spoke a word, which was unjust or unfriendly to the British nation." No other public recognition in Britain of Lincoln's efforts throughout the war to maintain peaceful relations with Britain has been discovered during the research for this book.

Despite the restrained reaction of political leaders and the press, many groups and individuals in Britain expressed their shock and sympathy with deep feeling and great sincerity. One of these was a lonely British widow who wrote to Mrs. Lincoln:

> Dear Madam: Although a stranger to you, I cannot remain silent when so terrible a calamity has fallen upon you and your country, and must express personally the deep and heartfelt sympathy with you under the most shocking circumstances of your present misfortune. No one can better appreciate than I can, who am myself utterly brokenhearted by the loss of my own beloved husband, what your sufferings must be; and I earnestly pray that you may be supported by Him to Whom alone the sorely stricken can look for comfort, in this hour of heavy affliction! With the renewed expression of true sympathy, I remain, dear Madam, your sincere friend, Victoria R.[58]

CHAPTER 18

Government by the People Shall Not Perish

The International Lincoln

The national Lincoln—political leader, antislavery debater, chief executive, commander in chief, defender of the Union, and emancipator—has received more attention from historians and biographers than any other figure in American history. But no contemporary, biographer, or previous historian has painted a full and accurate portrait of the international Lincoln. His role in establishing U.S. foreign policies and in the conduct of U.S. foreign relations during the Civil War has remained almost unknown.

There are many reasons for the neglect of the international Lincoln. Compared to the very extensive record of his national leadership, evidence of Lincoln's important role in U.S. diplomacy has been relatively scarce, scattered, and inaccessible. Until now the fragments of evidence on this role, which are scattered through the extensive Lincoln literature and diplomatic documentation, have not been assembled and evaluated. Many of the fragments seem to have limited significance unless they are studied alongside other evidence from the same period.

Diaries and recollections by contemporaries provide important evidence on Lincoln's reactions to foreign policy issues, but most of these men talked to Lincoln about only one or two foreign issues. The only man who knew how much Lincoln contributed to U.S. foreign policy was William Henry Seward, but he left no diary or reminiscences of his four years as Lincoln's secretary of state.

Historians and biographers discussing Lincoln's role in foreign affairs usually cite three actions in 1861—his rejection of Seward's "foreign war panacea," his removal of the most belligerent language from Seward's dispatch to Adams in May 1861, and the decision to release Mason and Slidell. References to his role in U.S. diplomacy in the subsequent three years of his presidency are rare.

My search in the Lincoln literature for generalizations about Lincoln's role in foreign affairs by historians and biographers yielded little except statements that his role was very limited. The inaccuracy of these statements has, I trust, been demonstrated in the preceding chapters. I have quoted many historians and biographers on specific topics but found no scholarly quotation that provided an accurate overview of Lincoln's participation in Union diplomacy. My evaluation of the international Lincoln is based entirely on my examination of the evidence I have assembled.

This evidence indicates that Lincoln consulted regularly with Seward on foreign affairs and contributed substantially to the content and tone of the most important dispatches to U.S. ministers abroad. He was much more diplomatic by nature than Seward. His calm judgment, judicious view of U.S. priorities and interests, and extensive previous experience as an advocate and negotiator complemented Seward's greater knowledge of foreign countries and diplomatic practices and restrained Seward's initial tendencies to be indiscreet, impetuous, and temperamental. These two men of very different backgrounds and personalities forged one of the most effective partnerships in the history of U.S. diplomacy. They determined U.S. responses to diplomatic developments with few significant inputs from cabinet, bureaucracy, Congress, press, or public.

Lincoln's first foreign policy decision was to reject the "foreign war panacea" suggested by Seward and others in 1861 as a way to reunite the nation. The importance of this decision was stressed in an editorial by Horace Greeley in the *Tribune* in New York on April 24, 1865, the day the Lincoln funeral train arrived in New York:

Mr. Lincoln . . . stubbornly refused to utter a word calculated to embroil us in a contest with any foreign power. "One War At a Time"—the words with which he decided the *Trent* case—were the keynote of his entire official career. He never proposed the idea, once so popular, of getting out of our domestic struggle by plunging into one with a European power. . . . It would have been easy and popular to plunge the country into a great foreign war; but that would have been to ensure its permanent disruption and overthrow. Mr. Lincoln saw the right from the outset, and had the courage and patriotism to pursue it.[1]

Lincoln's paramount diplomatic goal was to avoid European meddling in the American Civil War, which he believed would lead to war between the United States and the interfering nation or nations. As Bruce Catton noted, this goal was fully achieved:

Considering the course of the war as a whole . . . Northern diplomacy was highly successful and . . . Southern diplomacy was a flat failure. At the time, most Northerners bitterly resented what they considered the unfriendly attitude of Britain and France, but neither country did much that would give the South any real nourishment. . . . The open recognition, the active aid, the material and financial support which the South needed so greatly were never forthcoming. Europe refused to take a hand in America's quarrel. North and South were left to fight it out between themselves.[2]

But this crucial Union foreign policy objective was not achieved without great tensions in U.S. relations with Britain and France and great misunderstanding in Europe of Lincoln's actual intentions. A man of peace, he had to use the threat of war at times to achieve his peaceful objectives.

Lincoln made a number of important presidential decisions that were based primarily on his very strong desire to avoid a war with Great Britain. In the spring of 1861 he eliminated Seward's most warlike rhetoric in a crucial dispatch to the U.S. minister in London. He decided in the spring and reaffirmed in the summer that the United States should maintain a blockade under international law rather than act unilaterally to close the Southern ports despite strong British protests. In December he released Confederate envoys whose removal from a British packet by a U.S. Navy captain had been strongly protested by the British government. His decision in the summer of

1862 to issue an emancipation proclamation was motivated in part by his belief that it would prevent the British from extending diplomatic recognition and support to the Confederacy, an action he thought would inevitably lead to war between the United States and Britain. In the spring of 1863 he resisted pressure from Congress to retaliate against construction of warships for the Confederacy in Britain by commissioning privateers to operate against British blockade runners. That spring and summer he eased U.S.-British tensions arising from the blockade by releasing the mail captured on the British steamer *Peterhoff*, removing the admiral who was causing unnecessary tensions with the British in the Caribbean, and restricting the U.S. Navy's use of Caribbean ports in its operations against the blockade runners. In the fall of 1863, after the British detained two ironclad rams built for the Confederacy, he made several other conciliatory gestures toward Britain. In the fall of 1864 he canceled General Dix's order to pursue across the Canadian border any Confederates raiding American territory from Canada. Early in 1865 he denied that he had any desire to annex Canada, canceled an order requiring passports for Canadians entering the United States, and promised that the United States would not increase naval armaments on the Great Lakes.

In all of these cases there is clear evidence of Lincoln's strong desire to maintain peaceful relations with Great Britain. But he got little credit in Britain for these efforts. Throughout the war the perception of Lincoln by important British leaders was skewed by the antidemocratic and anti-Union prejudices of the British upper classes, the editorial diatribes of *The Times* and other British newspapers, the negative and distorted diplomatic reporting of the British minister in Washington, and the aggressive image of Lincoln and Seward remaining from their early efforts to demonstrate that British intervention in the American conflict would lead to war between the United States and Britain. Although the threat of British intervention receded after 1862, the hostility of British leaders toward the Union leadership did not. But no one in Britain thought Lincoln had played a very important role in U.S. diplomacy. Most of the comments by British leaders and editors about Lincoln just after his assassination ignored his role in foreign affairs.

A British biographer of Lincoln, Lord Charnwood, wrote in 1917 that Lincoln's changes in the dispatch to Adams early in 1861 showed "his strange, untutored diplomatic skill and the general soundness of his view of foreign affairs." He thought Lincoln had "forced Seward to work for peace and friendly relations with Great Britain, and made that minister the agent . . . of a peaceful resolution [of the *Trent* affair] which in its origin was his own."[3] But even Charnwood's excellent biography contains nothing on Lincoln's efforts to maintain peaceful relations with Britain during the last three years of the Civil War. In his impressive study of Anglo-American relations, Oxford professor H. C. Allen hardly mentions Lincoln's role in foreign affairs, gives Seward the entire credit for the decision to release the envoys taken from the *Trent*, and expresses doubt about Lincoln's interest in the overseas impact of the Emancipation Proclamation.[4]

Another group of Lincoln's decisions provided important moral support to the republican government of Mexico while avoiding any major U.S. commitment in that country, withheld U.S. recognition of Maximilian's imperial regime in Mexico, and applied increasing U.S. pressure on Napoleon to withdraw his troops from Mexico. Lincoln's cautious approach to Mexico was greatly influenced by his critical analysis in 1848 of James K. Polk's brash policies in that country. During the Civil War it was necessary to convince the French that the United States might provide important financial and/or military assistance to the republicans in Mexico even though, in fact, Lincoln was determined to avoid any such commitment. Seward's adroit diplomatic bluffing and Lincoln's adept parrying of domestic political pressures for a more aggressive policy in Mexico left a tangled web of confusion that has not been unraveled by previous historians.

Lincoln thought U.S. diplomatic pressure and a veiled threat of U.S. intervention in Mexico, combined with Mexican resistance to the French intervention and European and domestic pressures on Napoleon, would eventually force the French emperor to withdraw his army from Mexico and allow the Mexican republicans to dispose of Maximilian's imperial government. His policy in Mexico was continued by Seward and President Johnson, and his goal was achieved—approximately as he had envisioned it—two years after his death.

ↄ   ↄ   ↄ

Most of Abraham Lincoln's foreign policy was necessarily negative—to prevent or minimize foreign interference and to avoid foreign entanglements. But he also established a very positive international
objective—to maintain and expand the role of the United States as a
successful example of democratic government for all men everywhere.

Lincoln's prepresidential speeches contained many references to the
unique role of the United States as a demonstration to the world of the
viability and effectiveness of democratic government. The founding
fathers, he observed in 1837, "aspired to display before an admiring
world a practical demonstration of the truth of a proposition which
had hitherto been considered at best no better than problematical—
namely, the capability of a people to govern themselves."[5] He remarked
in 1842 that "our political revolution of '76 has given us a degree of
political freedom far exceeding that of any other of the nations of the
earth. In it the world has found a solution to the long mooted problem
as to the capability of man to govern himself. In it was the germ which
has vegetated, and still is to grow and expand into the universal liberty
of mankind."[6]

Resolutions Lincoln drafted for a meeting in Springfield in 1852
declared that "the sympathies of this country . . . should be exerted in
favor of the people of every country struggling to be free; and while we
meet to do honor to Kossuth and Hungary, we should not fail to pour
out the tribute of our praise and approbation to the patriotic efforts of
the Irish, the Germans, and the French, who have unsuccessfully
fought to establish in their several governments the supremacy of the
people." Lincoln returned to this theme in his eulogy of Henry Clay at
the Illinois capitol in 1852: "Mr. Clay's predominant sentiment . . .
was a strong sympathy for the oppressed people everywhere. [His]
efforts in behalf of the South Americans, and afterward in behalf of the
Greeks, in times of their respective struggles for civil liberty, are among
the finest on record."[7]

"The monstrous injustice of slavery," Lincoln declared in 1854,
"deprives our republican example of its just influence in the world,
enables the enemies of free institutions, with plausibility, to taunt us

as hypocrites [and] causes the real friends of freedom to doubt our sincerity."[8]

By proclaiming that "all men were created equal," Lincoln asserted in 1857, the founding fathers "meant to set up a standard maxim for a free society which could be . . . constantly spreading and deepening its influence and augmenting the happiness and value of life to people of all colors everywhere."[9] The struggle to implement the principles of the Declaration, he noted in his last debate with Senator Douglas in 1858, would affect "the whole great family of man."[10] Lincoln wrote in 1859 that the Declaration contained "an abstract truth applicable to all men and all times."[11] On the way to Washington early in 1861 he told the New Jersey Senate that the U.S. Constitution and political system "held out a great promise to all the people of the world." At Independence Hall in Philadelphia the next day he said the Declaration of Independence gave "hope to the world for all future time."[12]

Stephen B. Oates wrote that President Lincoln saw the Civil War "in a world dimension":

He defined and fought it according to his core of unshakable convictions about America's experiment and historic mission in the progress of human liberty. The central issue of the war, he told Congress on Independence Day, 1861, was whether a constitutional republic—a system of popular government—could preserve itself. There were Europeans who argued that anarchy and rebellion were inherent weaknesses of a republic and that a monarchy was the more stable form of government. Now, in the Civil War, popular government was going through a fiery trial for its very survival. If it failed in America, if it succumbed to the forces of reaction represented by the slave-based Confederacy, it might indeed perish from the earth. The beacon of hope for oppressed humanity the world over would be destroyed.[13]

President Lincoln extended a friendly hand to existing republican governments, nearly all of which were in Latin America. Alfred and Kathryn Hanna wrote that "Lincoln's instructions to U.S. ministers and other officials in Spanish America constituted an emotionally earnest crusade for the survival of free institutions."[14] His support for democracy and republican government in Latin America was evident in his welcoming remarks to newly arrived ministers from Latin American countries:

> The republican system of government, which has been adopted so generally on this continent, has proved its adaptation to what is the first purpose of government everywhere—the maintenance of national independence. It is my confident hope and belief that this system will be found, after sufficient trials, to be better adapted everywhere than any other to the great interests of human society—namely, the preservation of peace, order, and national prosperity. [To minister from Granada, June 4, 1861][15]
>
> The United States has no enmities, animosities, or rivalries, and no interests which conflict with the welfare, safety, and rights or interests of any other nation. . . . While the United States are thus a friend to all other nations, they . . . cherish especial sentiments of friendship for, and sympathies with, those who, like themselves, have founded their institutions on the principles of the equal rights of men. [To minister of Peru, March 4, 1862][16]
>
> Republicanism is demonstrating its adaptation to the highest interest of society—the preservation of the State itself against the violence of faction. Elsewhere on the American continent it is struggling against the inroads of anarchy, which invites foreign intervention. Let the American States . . . prove to the world that . . . we are . . . capable of completing and establishing the new [system] which we have now chosen. On the results largely depends the progress, civilization, and happiness of mankind. [To minister of San Salvador, April 24, 1862][17]

Lincoln's moral and diplomatic support for the embattled republican government of Mexico has been reviewed in chapters 8 and 16.

Lincoln was very aware that the world was watching the struggle in America and that its outcome would have a profound impact on the future prospects for freedom and democracy in other countries. On a number of occasions he linked the conflict in America with the hopes for freedom and democracy of people around the world:

> The central idea pervading this struggle is the necessity . . . of proving that popular government is not an absurdity. We must settle this ques-

tion now, whether in a free government the minority have the right to break up the government whenever they choose. If we fail it will go far to prove the incapability of the people to govern themselves. [To John Hay, May 7, 1861][18]

This issue embraces more than the fate of these United States. It presents to the whole family of man the question whether a constitutional republic or a democracy—a government of the people, by the same people—can or cannot maintain its territorial integrity against its own domestic foes. . . . It is now for [us] to demonstrate to the world that those who can fairly carry an election can also suppress a rebellion—that ballots are still the rightful and peaceful successors of bullets. [To Congress, July 4, 1861][19]

This country . . . maintains, and means to maintain, the . . . capacity of man for self-government. [To minister of Sweden, November 8, 1861][20]

[The Civil War] involves . . . not only the civil and religious liberties of our own dear land, but in a large degree the civil and religious liberties of mankind in many countries through many ages. [To Evangelical Lutheran churchmen, May 13, 1862][21]

Our common country is in great peril. . . . Once relieved, its form of government is saved to the world. [To border state congressmen and senators, July 12, 1862][22]

Fourscore and seven years ago our fathers brought forth on this continent a new nation, conceived in liberty, and dedicated to the proposition that all men are created equal. Now we are engaged in a great civil war, testing whether that nation, or any nation so conceived and so dedicated, can long endure. . . . We here highly resolve that . . . this nation, under God, shall have a new birth of freedom—and that government of the people, by the people, for the people, shall not perish from the earth. [Gettysburg Address, November 19, 1863][23]

James G. Randall observed that, by ending his address at Gettysburg with these words, Lincoln "associated the deepest of patriotic emotions with his dominant political idea—that is, the imperative obligation . . . to prove to other nations that the American experiment of government by the people was no failure."[24]

Seward told Francis Carpenter, who was painting the famous picture of Lincoln reading the Emancipation Proclamation to the cabinet, that "the central and crowning act of the Administration . . . is the preservation of the Union, and in that, the saving of popular government for the world."[25] Several historians have regarded this goal as equal in importance to the preservation of the American union and the elimination of slavery in America. Pauline Maier noted Lincoln's conviction that "the North fought not only to save the Union, but to save a form of government."[26] Merrill Peterson wrote that Lincoln gave the war "a third purpose, beyond preserving the Union and emancipating the slaves; it was about saving the democratic experiment in America."[27] H. C. Allen observed that Lincoln "set the aims of the North not merely of preserving the Union but of ensuring the future of free democratic government, not only in America, but throughout the world."[28]

ↄ   ↄ   ↄ

By 1865 Abraham Lincoln had became a symbol of government by and for the people. His death just after the Union victory left his image unsullied by postwar involvement with the intractable problems of reunification and reconstruction. Harry S. Truman observed that "there never was a man in the White House who was more thoroughly and completely mistreated than [President Andrew] Johnson. . . . If Lincoln had lived, he would have had the same experience, but . . . heroes know when to die."[29] Arthur Schlesinger Jr. recalled John F. Kennedy's question: "Would Lincoln have been judged so great a President if he had lived long enough to face the almost insoluble problem of Reconstruction?"[30]

Walt Whitman noted the curious paradox "of all the kings and queens and emperors of the earth . . . sending tributes of condolence and sorrow in memory of one raised through the commonest average of life—a rail-splitter and flatboatman."[31] Yet, as his former secretaries noted, "it was among the common people of the entire civilized world that the most genuine and spontaneous manifestations of sorrow and appreciation were produced. . . . He was canonized, as he lay on his bier, by the irresistible decree of countless millions."[32]

The victory in the American Civil War of the symbol of popular government spurred the development of more democratic institutions around the world, beginning with historic changes in Britain and France only a few years after Lincoln's death. In 1867, after decades of fruitless debate on electoral reform, the British Parliament passed a reform bill that increased the middle-class vote in rural counties and extended the vote to artisans and better-paid workers in the towns. British historians regard the victory of popular republican government in America as a major contributor to the long-delayed electoral reform in Britain. G. M. Trevelyan wrote that "Lincoln's victory gave a shattering blow to the domestic conservatism which Palmerston had so long imposed on the English Liberals."[33] H. C. Allen observed that "the impact of the Civil War and Reconstruction upon British life and liberalism cannot be seriously doubted, and the main weight of it was felt in the advancement of British democracy."[34]

Lincoln's victory also gave new hope to the democrats in France. "It is difficult to exaggerate the enthusiasm which his name inspires among the masses of Europe," Bigelow reported from Paris in 1865.[35] Five years later, when Napoleon III was captured by German invaders, a democratic Third Republic arose from the ashes of Napoleon's Second Empire.

Stephen B. Oates wrote that Abraham Lincoln embodies "the mystical genius of our nation":

> He possesses what Americans have always considered their most noble traits—honesty, unpretentiousness, tolerance, hard work, a capacity to forgive, a compassion for the underdog, a clearsighted vision of right and wrong, a dedication to God and country, and an abiding concern for all. . . . The Lincoln of mythology carries the torch of the American dream, a dream of noble idealism, of self-sacrifice and common humanity, of liberty and equality for all.[36]

This mystical Lincoln has carried the torch of freedom, democracy, and equality to all men everywhere. David Lloyd George, prime minister of Britain during World War I, asserted in 1917 that the Allies fought to secure Lincoln's democratic principles in Europe: "The democracy for which he stood was now the hope of mankind."[37] After

the war, Lloyd George wrote a moving tribute to the influence of the
international Lincoln:

> I doubt whether any statesman who ever lived sank so deeply into the
> hearts of the people as Abraham Lincoln did. . . . His courage, forti-
> tude, patience, humanity, clemency, his trust in the people, his belief in
> democracy . . . will stand out forever as beacons to guide troubled
> nations.[38]

A Source of Apprehension and Danger

U.S. Pressures for French Withdrawal from Mexico, 1865–1867

In the years following the Civil War, two major international legacies of the war dominated U.S. diplomacy—American disapproval of the French intervention and imperial government in Mexico, and American grievances arising from British actions and reactions during the war. U.S. efforts to encourage Napoleon to withdraw his troops from Mexico are described in this epilogue. The protracted diplomatic process that ultimately produced a settlement of American grievances against Britain is reviewed in Epilogue II.

ↄ   ↄ   ↄ

William Henry Seward remained as secretary of state during the presidential term of Lincoln's successor. President Andrew Johnson was preoccupied throughout his term with a massive struggle with the Radical Republicans in the Congress over reconstruction policies in the South. Despite pressures from General Grant and some congressional leaders for a more aggressive policy in Mexico, Seward was able to maintain Lincoln's policy of persistent diplomatic pressure for French withdrawal coupled with the avoidance of any military or economic intervention in Mexico.

After the Confederate surrender, European leaders assumed the United States government would be too preoccupied with reconstruction of the Union to interfere with Maximilian's French-backed regime in Mexico. The United States "will be so busy reorganizing their vast territories and repairing the calamities following the disastrous war," Lord Palmerston wrote Maximilian, "that it is more than likely that they will refrain from disturbing your Majesty and that you will be granted the time firmly to establish the Mexican Empire."[1] Although the United States made no direct effort to disturb Maximilian, it refused to recognize the legitimacy of his government in Mexico and maintained pressure on Napoleon to withdraw the French troops that provided essential support for Maximilian's imperial government.

This U.S. policy was reaffirmed by Seward soon after he returned to work following the attempt on his life the night Lincoln was killed:

> The United States are not prepared to recognize a monarchical and European power in Mexico. . . . The United States have maintained the strict line of forbearance and neutrality which their relations to the several belligerent parties dictated. . . . They desire peace, and would cheerfully restore their traditional relations with France. It will remain to France to say whether for these relations shall be substituted an alienation whose consequences might involve an arrest of the march of civilization throughout the world.[2]

General Grant thought the United States should provide active military support for the republican government in Mexico. Three weeks after Lee's surrender, the Mexican minister, Mattias Romero, reported that Grant had told him that "although he is tired of war, his major desire is to fight in Mexico against the French, that the Monroe Doctrine has to be defended at any price." A week later Grant told Romero that "60,000 veterans from the United States would march to Mexico as soon as they were mustered out, and this government would not oppose the action."[3] Grant ordered General Sheridan to the Rio Grande for the joint tasks of regarrisoning the state of Texas and increasing the pressure on the French to leave Mexico. By midsummer Sheridan had assembled an occupation force of more than fifty thousand men in southern Texas.

Several explanations of Grant's motives have been offered by contemporaries and biographers. Welles noted in June that some cabinet members thought Grant was mainly interested in an excuse "to retain a large military force in service."[4] Bates recorded in December that the Radical Republicans "were extremely anxious to have the war continued as long as possible, for without a pretense of war, they may find it hard to continue for much longer the use of martial law," which they needed to carry out their harsh reconstruction policies in the South. They argued that "the Empire in Mexico is part of the rebellion, and until it is put down the war continues, and so long as we are at war, we must have martial law."[5] Grant had argued in a letter to Johnson that "the empire is a part of the rebellion."

Grant's biographers offered other explanations. Brooks D. Simpson wrote that Grant wanted to send to Mexico an army composed of both Union and Confederate veterans: "One way to facilitate reunion might be to reforge the bonds of brotherhood in the furnace of combat against a common foe."[6] William S. McFeeley felt Grant was remembering the slump in his career after his service in the war with Mexico: "Another war . . . had ended, leaving him with no life to lead. . . . He had to keep his life going. . . . Ulysses Grant was reluctant to let go of war."[7]

Seward strongly opposed any type of U.S. intervention in Mexico. He maintained that persistent U.S. diplomatic pressure, combined with domestic and European pressures on Napoleon, would force a French withdrawal. Welles described the opposing positions taken by Grant and Seward in a cabinet meeting on June 16, 1865:

> General Grant came in to press upon the government the importance of taking decisive measures in favor of the republic of Mexico. Thought that Maximilian and the French should be warned to leave. . . . Seward was emphatic in opposition to any movement. Said the Empire was rapidly perishing and, if let alone, Maximilian would leave in less than six months . . . [but] if we interfered it would prolong his stay and the Empire also. Seward acts from intelligence, Grant from impulse.[8]

Welles recorded that a letter from Grant urging "prompt action against the imperial government" was read to the cabinet on June 23 but that "there was not a general concurrence" in Grant's apprehensions.[9] On July 14 the cabinet discussed a letter from Sheridan, endorsed by Grant, that was very hostile to the French and Maximilian. Seward reviewed the history of the U.S. war with Mexico in the 1840s: "If we got into a war and drove out the French, we could not get out ourselves."[10] Sir Frederick Bruce reported later to London that Secretary of War Stanton told him that "he considered the prospects of organizing the country under Maximilian hopeless, that France would get tired of the pecuniary sacrifice it entailed for no object and would give up the cause, and that it would be absurd to go to war for a matter which will terminate of itself."[11]

Unable to convince the cabinet to approve direct U.S. intervention in Mexico, Grant came up with a new version of the Blair plan. He wrote Johnson on July 15 that he regarded "the French occupation of Mexico as part and parcel of the late rebellion in the United States and a necessary part of it to suppress before entire peace can be assured." He proposed that "a leave of absence be given to one of our general officers for the purpose of going to Mexico to give direction to such emigration as may go to that country."[12]

This vague language covered a more specific plan that Grant had developed in cooperation with the Mexican minister. Major General John M. Schofield, a former Union corps and army commander, would recruit both Union and Confederate volunteers for an army corps to be commissioned by the government of Mexico. Sheridan would furnish arms and equipment for men to be released from the Union army to join Schofield's corps. But Seward convinced Johnson to send Schofield on a trip to Europe. The general claimed later that Seward had told him to "get your legs under Napoleon's mahogany, and tell him he must get out of Mexico," but Seward's instructions to Bigelow did not indicate that Schofield had been given any specific mission. The general spent six pleasant months in Europe and met Napoleon only once at a soiree. But Schofield became convinced that the emperor would withdraw his troops as quickly as he could. Some years later Seward told Bigelow that the only purpose of sending Schofield to Europe had been to "squelch the wild scheme" of Grant in Mexico.[13]

☙   ☙   ☙

In a September 6 dispatch to Bigelow, which was shown to Drouyn de Lhuys, Seward reaffirmed the U.S. refusal to recognize Maximilian's empire in Mexico:

> France appears to us to be lending her great influence, with a considerable military force, to destroy the domestic republican government in Mexico and to establish there an imperial system under the sovereignty of a European prince. . . . We do not insist or claim that Mexico and the other states on the American continent shall adopt the political institutions to which we are so earnestly attached, but we do hold that the people of those countries are entitled to exercise the freedom of choosing and establishing institutions like our own, if they are preferred. In no case can we in any way associate ourselves with efforts of any party or nation to deprive the people of Mexico of that privilege.[14]

The dispatches of the French minister in Washington, Montholon, reporting the growing public resentment in the postwar United States of the presence of French troops in Mexico, also contributed to Napoleon's growing conviction that he must remove his troops before his Mexican intervention led to war with the United States.[15]

There were other major pressures on Napoleon to withdraw the French troops from Mexico. The Mexican adventure had always been very unpopular in France; the French people wanted the troops brought home as soon as possible. Maintaining a large army in Mexico was expensive; Maximilian had promised to pay all of the expenses of the French occupation but had been unable to do so. Napoleon was beginning to worry about the growing power of Prussia and thought the forty thousand French troops in Mexico might be more useful on the Rhine.

Jasper Ridley wrote that Napoleon had made three major miscalculations about Mexico:

> He had not expected the resistance of the guerrillas to be so stubborn. . . . His second miscalculation had been about Maximilian, who he now realized was not a suitable choice. . . . Napoleon's third and most serious miscalculation had been about the United States. He had

believed that the South would win the American Civil War and that Maximilian would have as his northern neighbor not a powerful United States of America but a weakened Confederate States of America. He had hoped at the least that Maximilian would be firmly established in Mexico before the Civil War ended, and that once French troops had withdrawn from Mexico, the United States would accept and recognize Maximilian. He had also underestimated how successful Romero and the liberals would be in rousing public opinion in the United States to a sense of solidarity with Juárez.[16]

In October 1865 Napoleon offered to withdraw all French forces from Mexico in exchange for U.S. recognition of Maximilian's government in Mexico.[17] Seward quickly rejected this quid pro quo:

> The United States . . . still regard the effort to establish permanently a foreign and imperial government in Mexico as disallowable and impracticable. . . . They are not prepared to recognize . . . any political institutions in Mexico which are in opposition to the republican government with which we have so long and so constantly maintained relations of amity and friendship.[18]

Bigelow read this dispatch to Drouyn de Lhuys, who admitted that "he derived neither pleasure nor satisfaction from its contents."[19]

On November 14, 1865, President Johnson nominated General John A. Logan as U.S. minister to the Juárez government, even though the location of that migratory government was uncertain. "Black Jack" Logan, who had been one of Sherman's corps commanders and later commander of the Army of the Tennessee, was a bitter critic of France and of Maximilian. Welles thought he would not be "a very intelligent or cultured diplomat."

The apparent purposes of this nomination were to increase French apprehensions about a possible U.S. military intervention in Mexico in order to accelerate French withdrawal, and to mollify Grant, who resented the diversion of General Schofield from the proposed expedition to Mexico.[20] Seward told Welles that the French minister was "scared out of his wits" by the Logan appointment.[21] Having served these purposes, the nomination was withdrawn.

Sir Frederick Bruce, the British minister, reported in December that President Johnson had two strong opinions on U.S. foreign policy:

> One is the Monroe Doctrine, . . . hostility to monarchy on the Southern frontier of the United States and hostility to all attempts by the European powers to seize territory in the American continents or to interfere by force in its internal administration. In these views he will be supported by all parties in this country. . . . The second is a profound distrust and aversion to the European Napoleon as the head of a great scheme or conspiracy for extending imperialism. . . . The President stated . . . that he would not recede one step on the Mexican question and that if France forced a quarrel upon him on that ground he would spend the last dollar and the last man in the contest.[22]

In mid-December Bigelow was instructed to tell Drouyn de Lhuys that the traditional U.S. friendship with France would be jeopardized unless France desisted "from the prosecution of armed intervention in Mexico to overthrow the domestic republican government existing there and to establish upon its ruins [a] foreign monarchy."[23]

In October, Napoleon had offered to withdraw from Mexico in return for U.S. recognition of Maximilian, but the offer had been rebuffed. In January, Napoleon offered withdrawal in return for a pledge that the United States would not intervene in Mexico.[24] Seward rejected this proposal along with the French claim that Maximilian's government had been established with the consent of the Mexican people:

> The United States have not seen any evidence that the people of Mexico have . . . accepted the so-called empire. . . . Such an acceptance could not have been freely procured or lawfully taken at any time in the presence of the French army of invasion. . . . The presence of European armies in Mexico, maintaining a European prince with imperial attributes, without her consent and against her will, is deemed a source of apprehension and danger . . . to the United States.[25]

In March, Grant urged President Johnson to approve the sale of surplus arms and ammunition to the Mexican republicans, stressing that without this aid "their cause is in great danger and an ultimate war between this government and the usurpers [is] imminent."[26] "All we do to keep the republican government of Mexico going," he wrote to Secretary of War Stanton, "will save us men and money in the end."[27]

The United States was notified of French plans to withdraw from Mexico in a dispatch dated April 5, 1866. Napoleon had ordered the withdrawal of French troops in three detachments—the first in November 1866, the second in March 1867, and the third in November 1867.[28] This schedule would have allowed all the troops to embark at Vera Cruz during winter months and to avoid departures in the summer "sickly season," when the risk of yellow fever in the coastal areas was highest. Although the withdrawal plan was announced unilaterally by the French, Seward and Johnson subsequently referred to it as an "agreement" with the United States.

But reports that several ships were en route to Mexico with fresh French troops soon raised doubts about the French promises to withdraw. In mid-May, Seward took two steps to increase U.S. pressure for French withdrawal. He wrote Bigelow on May 12 that "it would not be a matter of surprise if Congress should adopt some proceeding which might entirely change the attitude of this government in regard to the war between France and Mexico."[29] A few days later he told Sir Frederick Bruce that it was "not unlikely" that the Mexican loan would be brought forward in Congress. "I should not be surprised," the British minister reported to London, "if this government were to take advantage of any plausible ground for abandoning their neutrality in the Mexican question. No doubt Sonora or Lower California were pledged as security for the loan."[30] There is no other evidence that Seward was thinking about reopening the question of a loan to Mexico.

Grant never understood Seward's skillful efforts to step up pressure on Napoleon to withdraw from Mexico while carefully maintaining U.S. neutrality in the war between France and Mexico. Grant wrote Sheridan in July that Seward was "a powerful practical ally of Louis Napoleon."[31] Sheridan thought Seward's cautious policy in Mexico was attributable to "butt-headedness or the indifference or vanity of old age."[32]

❦   ❦   ❦

Soon after the French plan to withdraw from Mexico was made public, Johnson appointed a new minister to the republican government of Mexico. Lewis D. Campbell had been a newspaper editor in Ohio, a member of Congress, and a political crony of Andrew Johnson. Juárez was still in northwestern Mexico, and the promised French withdrawal was not scheduled to be completed for another year and a half. This early appointment demonstrated to France and to Juárez's supporters in the United States that the administration was preparing for closer ties with the Juárez government. The new minister was in no hurry to begin his mission and remained in the United States until November 1866.

By the fall of 1866 there were many indications that Maximilian's empire in Mexico was tottering. Empress Carlotta went to Europe in August and pleaded with Napoleon to keep his troops in Mexico, but he refused. During an audience with the pope in September, Carlotta suffered a mental breakdown from which she never recovered. Bigelow reported in October that the new French foreign minister, the marquis de Moustier, had assured him that "there was nothing the Emperor desired more than to disembarrass himself of all his engagements with Mexico as soon as he could with dignity and honor."[33] There were many indications that the French withdrawal would force Maximilian to abdicate and return to Europe. Bigelow was told by Napoleon that he had "invited" Maximilian to abdicate.[34]

In October, Johnson and Seward concocted a plan to send Campbell to Mexico accompanied by General Grant as military adviser. This scheme offered political as well as diplomatic advantages. Grant strongly opposed President Johnson's reconstruction policies in the South. Johnson wanted to appoint General Sherman as secretary of war, replacing Stanton, but Grant was unwilling to take orders from his former subordinate. Ordering Grant to Mexico with Campbell would remove him from Washington for some weeks but appease the Radical Republicans, who had been pushing for a more aggressive policy in Mexico. Grant refused to accept the Mexican mission on the ground that the president could not compel a military officer to take a diplomatic assignment. Sherman declined the cabinet post but offered to go on the mission to Mexico with Campbell in order to release Grant from a difficult situation.[35]

Campbell's instructions stated that he should confer with Juárez concerning the possibility that "some disposition might be made of the land and naval forces of the United States, without interfering with the jurisdiction of Mexico or violating the laws of neutrality, which would be useful in favoring the restoration of law, order, and republican government in that country."[36] How U.S. forces could assist the republican government of Mexico without entering Mexican territory or violating the neutrality laws was not explained. This language was apparently intended to convince Napoleon to implement the "agreement" for the speedy withdrawal of his troops from Mexico. Seward sent Bigelow a copy of the instruction with a suggestion that he show it to the French foreign minister.

Seward and Welles thought the deteriorating military situation would make the planned phased withdrawal very hazardous. Welles noted in his diary that Napoleon "cannot withdraw his troops by detachments. . . . They must all go at once or the last remnant [will] be sacrificed."[37] This military consideration was apparently used by Seward as the basis for a politically useful assertion that the withdrawal of all French troops was imminent.

He wrote Campbell that "the President expects that within the next month a portion, at least, of the French expeditionary forces will leave Mexico and [he] thinks it not improbable that the whole expeditionary force may be withdrawn at or about the same time."[38] Grant told Romero on November 3 that Seward had asserted in the cabinet that "the whole French army will assuredly have withdrawn from Mexico before the [American] mission arrives at [Vera Cruz], thus leaving open the road to Mexico City where the [Juárez] government would already be established."[39] Seward's statement that the French would have left Vera Cruz by the time Campbell and Sherman arrived there was also recorded by Welles. Sherman thought the departing French might want to turn the fortress of San Juan d'Ulloa over to temporary American custody, pending the arrival in Vera Cruz of Juárez's forces.[40]

None of these expectations was warranted by the facts known to Seward in early November. The announced French plan was to complete their withdrawal by the fall of 1867; Seward could not have expected the French to give up their port of debarkation before the last French ship was ready to sail. He seems to have deliberately misrepresented the situation in Mexico in order to justify a mission that would serve his diplomatic and domestic objectives.

Campbell and Sherman sailed from New York on November 9 on a U.S. warship, the *Susquehanna*. During a stopover in Havana, they heard that Vera Cruz was still in French hands and that Maximilian was expected there shortly en route to Europe. Nonetheless, they proceeded to that port. Upon their arrival in the harbor on November 29, they learned that the Mexican capital was still occupied by the French. Maximilian had left Mexico City on October 21 for Orizaba, a mountain city only about seventy-five miles from Vera Cruz. During a month there he was persuaded by Mexican conservatives to abandon his plan to abdicate. On December 1, Sherman wrote in his memoirs, "we received the proclamation made by the Emperor Maximilian at Orizaba in which . . . he declared his purpose to remain and 'shed the last drop of his blood in defense of his dear country.' "[41]

The American envoys did not get off the warship during its four-day stay at Vera Cruz. There were conflicting rumors about the whereabouts of Juárez. "It seems to be the general impression," Campbell wrote Seward on December 1, "that he is now in the neighborhood of the city of San Luis Potosí." It could be reached from Tampico, a port on the Gulf of Mexico that was held by the republicans.[42] So the *Susquehanna* steamed north to Tampico. There Campbell and Sherman were told that imperial forces still held San Luis Potosí and that Juárez was probably still in Chihuahua.[43] Campbell sent a letter to Juárez's foreign minister, Sebastian Lerdo de Tejada, indicating that he hoped to reach Juárez soon because action on Mexican affairs might be required by the present Congress before its term expired on March 4. The letter gave no hint of the purpose of his mission or the type of congressional action that was contemplated.[44]

On December 5 Campbell and Sherman arrived at the mouth of the Rio Grande. Sherman wrote his brother that Juárez was probably still in Chihuahua: "I have not the remotest idea of riding on mule back a thousand miles in Mexico to find its chief magistrate."[45] After hearing that Juárez had still been in Chihuahua as recently as November 24, Campbell decided to abandon the effort to reach Juárez.[46] He wanted to return to Ohio, but Seward insisted that he remain in New Orleans "while events ripen in Mexico."[47] The nominal U.S. minister to Mexico waited there for six months. Meanwhile, Juárez was moving south, following his armies, which had been regaining control over most of central Mexico. By January the French, who were preparing for withdrawal, held only Vera Cruz, two major cities on routes to the capital (Orizaba and Puebla), Mexico City, and Querétaro, a city about 125 miles north of the capital.[48]

If considered a serious effort to establish closer relations with Juárez, the Campbell-Sherman mission must be judged a total failure. By Christmas, Welles had concluded that the mission had been "a *faux pas*, a miserable bungling piece of business."[49] But it is not likely that Seward so completely misjudged the timing and geography of a mission to Juárez. The only apparent explanation for the otherwise ludicrous trip is that Seward wanted to send a strong message to Napoleon that the United States was considering military aid to Juárez but Seward also wanted to avoid any actual commitment to the Mexican president. The evidence strongly suggests that Seward did not want the envoys to reach Juárez and was only using the Campbell-Sherman mission to support his diplomatic bluffing.

છ   છ   છ

While Campbell and Sherman were on their way to Vera Cruz, Seward had received a dispatch from Bigelow saying that Napoleon now planned to withdraw all his forces from Mexico in the spring of 1867—six months before the withdrawal of the last French contingent under the previous plan. Although the military reasons for a single withdrawal movement were understood in Washington, Seward was furious that Napoleon had not kept his promise to begin his withdrawal in November. Welles recorded that Seward read the cabinet "a thunder-and-lightning dispatch, a sort of ultimatum, full of menace."[50] No one in the cabinet supported the draft except Postmaster General Montgomery Blair. The next day Seward brought a milder draft, which was accepted by the cabinet.

The dispatch was sent to Bigelow via the new transatlantic cable, completed a few months earlier. It was the first, or nearly the first, transatlantic cable sent by the U.S. Department of State and began a new era of transatlantic diplomacy by cable. Bigelow was instructed to inform the French government that the U.S. government was very disappointed by the French failure to withdraw the first contingent of troops in November. The cable contained the following vague but ominous statement: "Instructions will be issued to the U.S. military forces of observation to await in every case special directions from the President."[51]

Bigelow cabled Drouyn de Lhuys's reply on December 3: "The resolutions of the French government are not changed, but from military considerations it has thought it ought to substitute a collective repatriation to one by divisions, and our corps of occupation is to embark in the month of March next."[52]

Despite American doubts, Napoleon kept his promise. The French forces evacuated the Mexican capital on February 5, and the last French ship left Vera Cruz on March 16. Maximilian rejected Marshal Bazaine's invitation to accompany the departing French troops.

On April 6, 1867, the Austrian minister in Washington, Count Wydenbruck, informed Seward that Emperor Franz Joseph had heard that his brother was surrounded by Juárez's troops at Querétaro. Wydenbruck said he had been instructed by cable to ask Seward to "use your influence with Juárez to urge him to respect the person of my Emperor's brother."[53] Seward immediately sent a telegram to Campbell, who was still waiting in New Orleans:

> The capture of Prince Maximilian . . . seems probable. The reported severity practiced upon the prisoners taken at Zacatecas excites apprehensions that similar severity may be practiced in the case of the prince and his alien troops. Such severity would be injurious to the national cause of Mexico and to the republican system throughout the world. You will communicate to President Juárez, promptly and by effectual means, the desire of this government, that in case of his capture the prince and his supporters may receive the humane treatment accorded by civilized nations to prisoners of war.[54]

Campbell sent John White, who was recommended by General Sheridan, with a letter to Juárez's foreign minister, Lerdo de Tejada, who Campbell now thought was finally at San Luis Potosí. White went to Galveston by train and steamer, took a U.S. dispatch steamer to Tampico, reached San Luis Potosí by April 20, and found there Juárez and Lerdo de Tejada. White delivered Campbell's letter and returned to New Orleans on May 15 with the foreign minister's reply. Lerdo de Tejada wrote that the Mexican government "holds to the obligation of considering, according to the circumstances of the cases, what the principles of justice demand, and the duties which the Mexican people hold it to fulfill toward them."[55] Although White had reached Juárez from New Orleans in only fourteen days, neither Campbell nor Seward raised the possibility that Campbell might make a similar trip to reach the government to which he had been accredited.

Seward learned on May 26 that Querétaro had fallen to the republican forces and that Maximilian and his principal generals were prisoners. The news flashed to Europe by cable. On May 29 Wydenbruck received another cable from Vienna instructing him to "renew earnestly the demand of a warm intercession of the American government for release."[56] Seward did not want to offend Austria and other European monarchies by appearing insensitive to the fate of the ex-emperor. But he feared that a further U.S. intervention on behalf of Maximilian would offend Juárez and his supporters in the United States and lessen Maximilian's chance for survival. He summoned the Mexican minister, Romero, who reported that Seward "feared very much that a hasty mediation might produce . . . some results contrary to those wished for, and that he consequently thought . . . that the Mexican government might see things in the same light . . . and that it was useless to intervene."[57]

On June 1 Seward instructed Campbell by telegram to "proceed with as much dispatch as possible to the residence of President Juárez of Mexico, and enter upon your mission. Earnestly urge clemency to Maximilian and other prisoners of war, if necessary."[58] But during the next two weeks Campbell and Seward exchanged a series of telegrams that demonstrate that neither man was eager for the mission in Mexico to begin.

Juárez had told White in April that he expected to return to the Mexican capital "in three or four months"—in July or August.[59] But Campbell wired Seward on June 3 that "presuming that President Juárez is now, or very soon will be in the city of Mexico, I propose to go there via Vera Cruz unless you instruct otherwise." Campbell asked if the revenue cutter *Wilderness* or the U.S. steamer *De Soto*, which were in New Orleans, could be ordered to take him to Vera Cruz.[60] Seward replied that no U.S. ship could be spared and that Campbell should "proceed by whatever conveyance or route you might find most speedy or practicable."[61] Yet a week later Seward promised to send home Mrs. Juárez, who had been living in the United States, in a U.S. warship; the *Wilderness* took her from New Orleans to Vera Cruz in July,[62] and it was sent to Charleston in October to take Romero to Vera Cruz. Seward's refusal to provide Campbell with transport indicates that he did not want him to reach Juárez until Maximilian's fate had been determined.

"Shall I go to the city of Mexico via Vera Cruz, or to San Luis Potosí via Monterrey?" Campbell asked on June 6.[63] Seward ignored the San Luis Potosí option, presumably because Juárez might still be there. Campbell was told that if he could find no ship to take him directly to Vera Cruz, he should go first to Havana and then take an English or French steamer to Vera Cruz. Since Havana is about as far from Vera Cruz as New Orleans, it was hardly a logical route for an envoy on an ostensibly urgent mission. Campbell protested that voyages from Havana to Vera Cruz were prohibited by quarantine rules; Seward responded only with the statement that "the President desires you to proceed to Mexico without delay according to the previous instructions."[64]

Campbell's mission to Mexico was aborted by an exchange of telegrams on June 15. The first was from Campbell to Seward: "Since the . . . 11th I have been confined to my room by severe bilious attack. My physician says I cannot now go without hazarding my life, especially via Havana and Vera Cruz where yellow fever prevails. If government considers it important to send minister immediately, I will tender my resignation, if desired."[65] The claim of illness seems to have been an excuse to terminate a frustrating mission. Seward immediately replied that "it is important that the minister to Mexico should proceed at once. Your resignation will, therefore, be accepted, with thanks for your service and regret for your retirement."[66] Seward knew Campbell's resignation would delay the arrival of a U.S. minister in Mexico and allow him to maintain the facade of urgent U.S. concern without actually becoming involved in the fate of Maximilian.

On the day he accepted Campbell's resignation, Seward summoned Juárez's minister again and told him that the emperor of Austria, the emperor of France, and the queen of England had appealed to the United States "to use any legitimate good offices within their power to avert the execution of the Prince Maximilian." He feared another effort to make this point might embarrass Juárez and be counterproductive.[67] Seward was relaying the concerns of European monarchs without adding to the previous U.S. pressure. This message did not reach Juárez while Maximilian was still alive.

Several biographers of Maximilian and Juárez have ignored or misrepresented Seward's response to the issue of Maximilian's fate. Joan Haslip, biographer of Maximilian, did not mention any U.S. effort on Maximilian's behalf.[68] Ralph Roeder, a biographer of Juárez, wrote that Seward made only a "perfunctory gesture" and that Campbell "decided to disregard it rather than court an inevitable rebuff."[69] Jasper Ridley, who wrote on both Maximilian and Juárez, was closer to the truth. He wrote that many statesmen "thought Seward, not wishing to offend the European powers by refusing to intervene for Maximilian and not wishing to offend Juárez by doing so, was deliberately keeping Campbell in New Orleans so that he would reach Juárez too late to save Maximilian."[70]

A direct U.S. appeal to Juárez to save Maximilian's life would not have been effective. The capture and execution of Maximilian were the inevitable results of Napoleon's decision to withdraw his troops and Maximilian's refusal to leave Mexico with them. Juárez believed that the honor and national interest of Mexico required the death of the man who had attempted to destroy its legitimate government and impose a European-style monarchy backed by European troops. Maximilian was tried by a military court and was sentenced to die. He was executed by a firing squad on June 19, 1867.

Ralph Roeder wrote that Seward had made a significant contribution to Juárez's eventual triumph in his long struggle with the French and Maximilian:

> The new ties with the United States...broke the bonds of the past and coupled the two countries in common interest. The influence of Washington had been brought to bear on the struggle with belated but powerful effect. Seward had assisted him parsimoniously but successfully, refusing to recognize any other government or pretender, forcing the evacuation of the French by a diplomatic pressure that increased steadi-

ly as Napoleon weakened, . . . and reducing the American Emperor to his own resources. It was due in no small measure to [Seward's] management, acting as umpire and timekeeper, that the field was cleared for the final event.[71]

Despite pressure from Grant and others for a more aggressive policy in Mexico, Seward had maintained Abraham Lincoln's policies of persistent diplomatic pressure for French withdrawal combined with persistent refusal to recognize the legitimacy of Maximilian's "empire" in Mexico. A Seward biographer, Frederick Bancroft, wrote that Seward's handling of the French intervention in Mexico was "his most perfect achievement in diplomacy."[72]

The Massive Grievance

*The "*Alabama *Claims" Against Britain,*
1865–1872

For nearly eight years after the Civil War, Americans in the North nursed a set of grievances against the British for their actions and reactions during the American Civil War. These included the unfriendly attitudes of British leaders toward the Union cause (chapter 3), the British government's recognition of Confederate belligerency (chapter 4), the British preparations for war during the *Trent* crisis (chapter 5), the large purchases of Confederate bonds by Britons (chapter 6), the prolonged threat of British diplomatic recognition and support of the Confederacy (chapter 9), the warships built for the Confederacy in Britain (chapters 10 and 13), the supplies provided to the Confederate raiders at British colonial ports (chapter 10), and the predominant role of British ships and crews in the blockade running operation (chapter 11).

Within this spectrum of grievances, the depredations of the *Alabama* and other British-built commerce raiders had the greatest impact on individual Americans—the owners of ships and cargoes and the crews of the captured ships—and created a large collection of claims against the British government. The settlement of these specific and direct individual claims was greatly complicated and delayed by the question whether the British should also compensate the United States for a number of other costs and impacts arising from British actions during the war.

Several of Seward's dispatches to Adams and Adams's letters to Russell during the war were intended to lay the foundation for postwar claims for the losses resulting from the operations of the raiders built in Britain for the Confederacy. Lincoln told Grant and others in 1865 that "after ending our war successfully we would be so powerful that we could call [Britain] to account for the embarrassments she had inflicted on us."[1]

Postwar British governments consistently refused to admit that Britain had failed to meet the obligations of a neutral government under international law and, until 1871, expressed no sense of regret for the depredations of the British-built raiders. These British governments were composed mainly of men who had been cabinet members or opposition leaders during the Civil War. After the death of Palmerston in October 1865, Lord Russell became prime minister and Lord Clarendon, a former diplomat who had been foreign secretary from 1853 to 1858, again headed the Foreign Office. Allan Nevins described Russell's unwillingness to yield on the "*Alabama* claims": "He and most Englishmen believed the government had been truly neutral. Stiff, narrow, and apprehensive of the political consequences of yielding, he declined to budge."[2]

In June 1866 Russell's Liberal government was succeeded by a Conservative government headed by Lord Derby with his son Lord Stanley, a prewar colonial secretary, as foreign secretary. In August, Seward sent the new British government a long list of claims by American citizens for damages suffered from the depredations of the Confederate raiders "built, manned, armed, equipped, and fitted out in British ports and . . . harbored, sheltered, provided, and furnished . . . in British ports." He stated that settlement of these claims had become "urgently necessary to a re-establishment of entirely friendly relations between the United States and Great Britain."[3]

The Tory government would have welcomed the elimination of the dangerous precedent created by the construction of warships for the Confederacy in Britain if it could have been done without opening a Pandora's box of other issues. As Samuel Flagg Bemis noted, thoughtful Englishmen had begun to realize that the previous British government had blundered by "creating a precedent for the fitting out of warships by Britain's enemies in neutral ports. . . . In future wars a power like Germany, Russia, or Japan . . . would be free by Great Britain's own pronouncements of policy to build cruisers in time of war in American neutral harbors. . . . The seas would swarm with new *Alabamas* to destroy British commerce everywhere or drive it under cover of the neutral American flag."[4]

After the attempt by Radical Republicans to impeach President Andrew Johnson had failed by only one vote in May 1868, Seward hoped to resolve the last major diplomatic issue remaining from the war. That spring Charles Francis Adams resigned the post as U.S. minister in London that he had held since 1861. President Johnson appointed a former Maryland senator, Reverdy Johnson, to succeed Adams.

In November 1868 Johnson and Stanley signed a draft agreement providing that all claims by individual Americans against the British government and by British subjects against the U.S. government would be submitted to two American and two British commissioners aided by an umpire selected by the commissioners. Several weeks later the Liberals returned to power in Britain with William Gladstone as prime minister and Lord Clarendon again as foreign secretary. Clarendon had grown old and tired, was primarily interested in European issues, and cared little for U.S.-British relations. Lord Russell, an influential member of the House of Lords, was still adamantly opposed to any acceptance of British responsibility for the depredations of the *Alabama*. But the new government was anxious to eliminate the dangerous precedent of shipbuilding in a neutral country for a belligerent.

On January 14, 1869, a somewhat modified version of the Johnson-Stanley agreement was signed by Johnson and Clarendon. No action was taken by the U.S. Senate on the Johnson-Clarendon agreement until after the inauguration of Ulysses S. Grant as president on March 4, 1869. Grant appointed a wealthy New Yorker, Hamilton Fish, as his secretary of state. Fish had been a congressman, governor of New York, and senator. Allan Nevins, biographer of Fish, wrote that he "was preeminent for the clarity and soundness of his judgment, for his perfect moderation and self control, and for his quiet dignity and indomitable firmness. . . . He was in the highest sense a gentleman and a man of principle. . . . He always insisted upon American rights within the framework of international law, and always maintained them."[5]

Fish did not defend an agreement made by the previous administration that was widely regarded as a totally inadequate response by Britain to American grievances.

Senator Sumner's speech against the treaty in the Senate on April 13, 1869, was described by his biographer, David Donald:

> The Johnson-Clarendon Convention failed to remove "the massive grievance which under our country suffered for years." . . . The original British offense . . . was committed on May 13, 1861, when the Queen issued her proclamation of neutrality recognizing the belligerent status of the Confederacy. . . . Without it "no rebel ship could have been built in England . . . nor could any munitions of war have been furnished" to the South. . . . The British government compounded this first error by permitting the *Alabama* and her consort "pirate" ships to be built and fitted out in British ports. These raiders which looted and burned American shipping were "not only British in origin, but British in equipment, British in armament, and British in crews." The welcome, hospitality, and supplies subsequently given to these Confederate cruisers in British ports added a third degree of British complicity. . . . The Johnson-Clarendon Convention contained no acknowledgment of wrong or even of liability, not "one soothing word for a friendly power deeply aggrieved."[6]

Sumner stressed that the treaty provided only for the adjudication of claims of shipowners and other individuals and made no provision for major "national" losses—including increased insurance on American vessels, the reduction in the tonnage of exports and imports carried by American ships, and the costs of the blockade. He asserted that "through British intervention, the war was doubled in duration" and hinted that since the total cost of the Civil War was around $4 billion, the total "bill" to the British should be $2 billion![7] This extraordinary position, although never carefully analyzed, was widely supported in the Senate and in the country. Only one senator voted for the ratification of the Johnson-Clarendon Treaty.

Adams, in retirement in Massachusetts, thought Sumner's speech had raised "the scale of our demands of reparation so very high that there is no chance of negotiation left unless the English have lost all their spirit and character."[8] Samuel Flagg Bemis wrote that by asserting the huge "indirect" claims Sumner hoped "to sink into the popular mind in both the United States and England a claim so big that it could be satisfied only by the cession of Canada to the United States."[9] Allan Nevins also thought Sumner hoped for "the fame of annexing Canada."[10] Many Americans were not pleased that the Canadian Confederation established in 1867 had remained in the British Empire, and they still hoped for the eventual U.S. annexation of Canada. It soon became apparent, however, that the Canadians did not want to be annexed. The British minister stated in June 1869 that Britain did not insist on keeping Canada, but "could not part with it without the consent of the inhabitants."[11]

Grant and Fish reluctantly accepted Sumner's recommendation that his friend John Lothrop Motley, the historian who had been U.S. minister to Austria during the war, be appointed to succeed Reverdy Johnson as U.S. minister to Britain. Motley had lived in Britain, had many highly placed British friends, and seemed well qualified for the post. But he was also very passionate in his beliefs, intolerant, and impetuous.

Hoping that the claims issue could be reconsidered later, after a period for tempers to cool, Fish instructed Motley to avoid discussion of the issue.[12] But Motley felt free to explain and defend Sumner's speech on the *Alabama* claims. Fish's instructions had clearly stated that the president did not want to make an issue of the royal proclamation in 1861 recognizing Confederate belligerency. But in his first meeting with Clarendon, Motley complained that the proclamation had been "the fountainhead of the disasters which had been caused to the American people."[13]

Grant was shocked at Motley's insubordination, but Fish convinced him to avoid a head-on collision with Sumner. Motley was allowed to remain in London for another year, but discussion of claims issues was transferred to Washington. Fish began secret negotiations with the British minister, Sir Edward Thornton, that continued for twenty months. On several occasions Fish and Grant made statements that resembled Sumner's assertion of the "massive grievance" against Britain. In a dispatch to Motley in September 1869, Fish stated that during the war Great Britain had been "the arsenal, the navy-yard, and the treasury of the insurgent Confederates."[14] In his annual message to Congress in December 1869, Grant approved the Senate's rejection of the Johnson-Clarendon agreement:

> The injuries resulting to the United States by reason of the course adopted by Great Britain during our late Civil War—in the increased rates of insurance, in the diminution of exports and imports and other obstructions to domestic industry and production, in its effects upon the foreign commerce of the country, in the decrease and transfer to Great Britain of our commercial marine, in the prolongation of the war, and the increased cost (both in treasure and lives) of its suppression— could not be adjusted and satisfied as ordinary commercial claims.[15]

David Donald noted that "the voice was Grant's, the pen was Fish's, but the thought was Sumner's."[16]

In June 1870 Grant ordered Motley's recall. Several potential nominees declined the post in London, and it was not filled until the appointment in December of Robert C. Schenck. He had been an Ohio congressman from 1843 to 1851, U.S. minister to Brazil from 1851 to 1853, president of a railway company, and a major general during the war.

The removal of Motley led to very strained relations between Sumner and Fish. Sumner refused to talk to Fish at social functions, although there was still official communication between the chairman of the Senate Foreign Relations Committee and the secretary of state. Meanwhile, Lord Clarendon died and Lord Granville succeeded him at the Foreign Office. Nevins wrote that "Granville had more youth, more vigor, more imagination, and he comprehended the profound importance of Anglo-American amity."[17]

That summer British interest in a settlement of the *Alabama* claims was greatly increased by the outbreak of a war between France and Prussia. After six weeks of war, Napoleon III surrendered with 81,000 men at Sedan on September 3, the Second Empire collapsed, and the Third French Republic was proclaimed. Marshal Bazaine, former commander of Napoleon's army in Mexico, delivered 150,000 men and the fortress of Metz into Prussian hands in October. Paris remained under siege from mid-September until its surrender on January 28.

Three biographers have given their subjects the credit for the suggestion for a comprehensive settlement that would cover all U.S.-British issues, including the "*Alabama* claims," other issues arising from the American Civil War, and ongoing fishing and boundary issues. Allan Nevins wrote that Fish suggested the idea in a September 26 talk with Thornton.[18] William S. McFeeley stated that President Grant told Fish in November 1870 that he wanted the U.S.-British issues settled before the next presidential election.[19] E. Fitzmaurice gave the credit to his subject, Lord Granville.[20] Whatever its origin, the proposal was quickly approved by the British cabinet, and a former British official in Canada, Sir John Rose, was sent to Washington for secret preliminary conversations. Rose arrived in Washington on January 9 and had a six-hour talk that night with Fish at his home. He left at 3 A.M. with the outline of an agreement to submit all U.S.-British issues to a Joint High Commission of five Americans and five Britons.

During a meeting with Fish and in a subsequent memorandum, Senator Sumner insisted that the only adequate compensation for all of the damages suffered by the United States would be the withdrawal of the British flag from North America, including Canada and the island colonies. Fish subsequently used Sumner's outrageous memorandum to convince senators that Sumner should be relieved of his chairmanship of the Foreign Relations Committee and to convince the British government to move quickly, while there was a chance for a settlement they could accept.[21]

The British commissioners arrived in Washington in late February 1871. In addition to Thornton, the British commissioners included a member of Gladstone's cabinet (the earl de Grey and Ripon), a senior member of the Tory opposition (Sir Stafford Northcote), the prime minister of Canada (Sir John McDonald), and an Oxford professor of international law (Montague Bernard). The American commissioners inluded Fish, Schenck, a justice of the Supreme Court (Samuel Nelson), a former attorney general (E. Rockwood Hoar), and a former senator from Oregon (George H. Williams).

The ten commissioners met in Washington in thirty-seven sessions beginning on February 27. On May 8, 1871, they signed the Treaty of Washington, which dealt with a wide range of navigation, fisheries, trade, and boundary issues and established a procedure for the settlement of the "*Alabama* claims." They were to be submitted to an international tribunal consisting of arbitrators appointed by the president of the United States, the queen of England, the emperor of Brazil, the king of Italy, and the president of the Swiss Confederation. A treaty protocol expressed the British government's regret "for the escape, under whatever circumstances, of the *Alabama* and other vessels from British ports, and for the depredations committed by those vessels."[22] But the British did not accept responsibility for the escape or for the depredations.

The treaty included three new rules proposed by the British government. They provided that a neutral government was required:

> 1. To use due diligence to prevent the fitting out, arming, or equipping, within its jurisdiction, of any vessel which it had reasonable ground to believe was intended to cruise or to carry on war against a Power with which it was at peace; and also use like diligence to prevent the departure from its jurisdiction of any [such] vessel.
>
> 2. Not to permit or suffer either belligerent to make use of its ports or waters as the base of naval operation against the other, or for the purpose of the renewal or augmentation of military supplies or arms, or the recruitment of men.
>
> 3. To exercise due diligence in its own ports and waters . . . to prevent any violation of the foregoing obligations and duties.[23]

The treaty also stated that arbitrators "should assume that Her Majesty's Government had undertaken to act upon the principles set forth in these rules" during the American Civil War.

During the negotiations the Americans had repeatedly bought up the question of "national" or "indirect" claims, including losses due to the transfer of merchant ships to the British flag, increased premiums for marine insurance, the prolongation of the war, and the resulting increased cost of the war.[24] But the indirect claims were not mentioned in the treaty. Allan Nevins wrote that "the question should have been definitely . . . cleared away. It was not, and the penalty was paid later in months of controversy, resentment, and anxiety. . . . [A] tacit exclusion should have been clearly understood by both sides, and it was not. The British commissioners thought they had obtained it, but the

Americans never for a moment thought they had given it."[25] But the absence of any reference in the treaty to indirect claims undoubtedly contributed to the speedy ratification of the treaty in both countries.

Fish convinced Grant to appoint Charles Francis Adams as the American member of the international tribunal. It convened in Geneva on December 15, 1871, to receive the elaborate written presentation of the American grievances against Britain. The American brief was prepared by the designated U.S. agent, Assistant Secretary of State J. C. Bancroft Davis. Most of the lengthy "United States Case" focused on claims directly related to the *Alabama* and its sister raiders. But the British were shocked to discover that it also included a long litany of other American complaints about British actions and inactions during the American war. These included the anti-Union animus of British public men, British recognition of Confederate belligerency, British rejection of the U.S. application to join the Declaration of Paris, British preparations for war during the *Trent* affair, and negotiations by a British consul with the Confederate government.[26] Adams thought that the American case had been "advanced with an aggressiveness of tone and attorney-like smartness more appropriate to the wranglings of a quarter sessions court than to pleadings before a grave international tribunal."[27]

The most astonishing aspect of the U.S. case, however, was that it again asserted U.S. claims for four categories of national or indirect costs, including the cost of the pursuit of the Confederate cruisers, increased costs of insurance for U.S. merchant ships, losses due to the transfer of registry of merchant ships to the British flag, and costs due to the alleged prolongation of the war. The latter claim consisted of the entire cost of the war after the battle of Gettysburg—*plus seven percent interest*! Martin B. Duberman, biographer of Adams, wrote that Fish "was not actually seeking a money reward for the claims, but an adverse judicial decision on them which would at once put an end to public demands at home and establish a vital international precedent abroad."[28] This conclusion is supported by a private letter Fish wrote in 1872:

> It is not [in] the interest of the United States, who are habitually neutrals, to have it decided that a neutral is liable for the indirect injuries

consequent upon an act of negligence. We have too large an extent of
coast and too small a police, and too much of the spirit of bold speculation and adventure, to make the doctrine a safe one for our future. The
"indirect claims" had . . . been too prominent in the history of the
Alabama Claims to be unnoticed. . . . To have omitted them from the
Case would not have been fair to either party. . . . It is in the interest of
both governments that they be passed upon by the Tribunal, and in the
interest of both that the Tribunal decide that a neutral is not liable to
pecuniary damages for the indirect consequences of a breach of its own
neutral obligations resulting not from intentional wrong, but from accident or negligence.[29]

The American claim of British responsibility for prolongation of
the war has never been examined critically—at Geneva or later by historians. The brief justification for this huge claim in the U.S. case contained a number of sweeping statements that are contradicted by
evidence presented in previous chapters of this book:

The 4th day of July, 1863, saw the aggressive forces on land of the
insurrection crushed. From that day its only hope lay in prolonging a
defense until . . . the United States should become involved in a war
with Great Britain. The insurgents . . . counted, not without reason,
upon inflaming popular passion in the United States . . . until the people should force the Government into a retaliation upon Great Britain,
the real author of their woes. In pursuance of this policy they withdrew
their military forces within the lines of Richmond, and poured money
into Bulloch's hands to keep afloat and increase his British-built navy,
and to send it into the most distant seas in pursuit of the merchant
marine of the United States. Thus the Tribunal will see that, after the
battle of Gettysburg, the offensive operations of the insurgents were
conducted only at sea, through the cruisers; and observing that the war
was prolonged for that purpose, will be able to determine whether
Great Britain ought not, in equity, to reimburse the United States the
expenses thereby entailed upon them.[30]

The assertion that after Gettysburg the Confederates were hopeful
of war between the United States and Britain conflicts with evidence in

chapter 15 that by then the Confederate leadership had abandoned hope of British assistance, withdrawn their envoy from London, and expelled British consuls from Confederate cities. The assertion that after Gettysburg the Confederates poured money into Bulloch's hands to build more raiders in Britain conflicts with evidence in the same chapter that in the fall of 1863 Bulloch was thoroughly discouraged by the British decision to detain the ironclad rams, described in chapter 12, and was transferring the Confederate shipbuilding program entirely to France. The assertion that after Gettysburg the Confederates withdrew their military force "within the lines of Richmond" grossly misstates the military history of the second half of the war. The implication that a defensive strategy on land was adopted in order to emphasize offensive operations at sea suggests a military significance of the operations of the Confederate commerce raiders that was never claimed by Confederates or by historians.

The claim that British actions doubled the length of the war was not supported in the brief justification quoted above or anywhere else in the four-volume record of the Geneva tribunal. Evidence that Confederate commerce raiders prolonged the war was not presented because it did not exist. The autobiography and biographies of Captain Semmes demonstrate that the cargoes of the ships captured and burned by the *Sumter* and the *Alabama* were rarely of any military value. Of the forty-eight ships burned by the *Alabama* whose cargoes were identified in John M. Taylor's biography of Semmes, eleven were whalers, twelve carried agricultural products and foodstuffs, fourteen were loaded with other bulk commodities (coal, salt, lumber, and fertilizer), five had mixed cargoes, and four were in ballast. Most of the cargoes were bound for other countries, not the United States. The cargoes of only two of the ships—one carrying a partial load of saltpeter used in gunpowder and one carrying masts, spars, and rigging for a U.S. warship—appeared to have had any military or naval value.[31] Since no captured cargo reached the Confederacy, the captures made no contribution to the Confederate war effort. The operations of the raiders raised Confederate morale, but they also increased Union determination to maintain the struggle.

The massive British roles in the blockade running operation, reviewed in chapter 11, contributed far more significantly to the prolongation of the war than the random burning of Union merchant ships by the Confederate commerce raiders. Arms and supplies brought from Britain in British ships enabled the Confederates to continue the war for a year or two longer than would have otherwise been possible. In 1866 the British minister in Washington reported that "the country at large attributed to our blockade-runners the prolongation of the war."[32]

Yet neither the British government nor the American government was willing to challenge the right of a belligerent to maintain a blockade of enemy ports or the right of citizens of neutral nations to attempt to evade it. Each of the contending governments was reluctant to make any protest or commitment regarding blockades or blockade running that would limit its options in future wars. Although the British role in blockade running operations offered the only substantial justification for the American claim of British responsibility for prolonging the war, no such justification was presented during the long *"Alabama* claims" controversy. Lacking a justification for the huge indirect claims that they were willing to present, the Americans were glad to keep the discussion of such claims on a very general level. In order to protect their option to maintain a blockade during a future war in Europe, the British made no claims for the loss of British ships captured while attempting to evade the U.S. blockade. Samuel Flagg Bemis noted that during World War I Britain "profited beyond measure by her far-sighted decision not to protest the blockade during the Civil War."[33]

The British government's took the position that "it is not within the province of the Tribunal of Arbitration at Geneva to decide upon the claims for indirect losses and injuries put forward by the United States."[34] By refusing to be drawn into substantive discussion of the indirect claims, the British officials at Geneva missed the opportunity to demonstrate the fallacy of the claim that the raiders built in Britain for the Confederacy had prolonged the war. The "British Counter Case," presented in the spring of 1872, merely stated that "the estimates of losses, public and private, presented by the United States are so loose and unsatisfactory, and so plainly excessive in amount, that they cannot be accepted as furnishing a *prima facie* basis of calculation."[35]

"We must be insane," Prime Minister Gladstone declared, "to accede to demands which no nation with a spark of honour or spirit left could submit to even at the point of death."[36] A British official at Geneva, Lord Blachford, thought "the American Government are just as much alive to the enormity of their indirect claims as we are. . . . They do not dare to give them up themselves, but wish to ride off upon an adverse decision of the arbitrators and . . . have an answer to anyone who charged them with abandoning what the popular sentiment required them to maintain."[37]

The issue of the indirect claims delayed the Geneva arbitration for five months and nearly caused the total failure of the arbitration process. The U.S.-British diplomatic correspondence between February and June on the issue of indirect claims ran to 118 dispatches, notes, and telegrams and covered 154 printed pages in the records of the arbitration sent to Congress in December. Yet this extensive correspondence contained little additional substantive justification from the Americans for the indirect claims.

On April 22 Lord Russell introduced a resolution in the House of Lords calling for British withdrawal from the Geneva tribunal until the indirect claims were withdrawn by the United States; debate on the motion was postponed until early June. The British government proposed on May 10 that the controversy be resolved by adding a new article to the Treaty of Washington under which the United States would withdraw the claims for indirect losses and both countries would agree to refrain from making similar claims in the future.[38] Grant submitted the proposed article to the Senate, but it insisted on adding ambiguous language. The British government rejected the American revisions but suggested others. This process was still under way on June 6, when the House of Lords debated Lord Russell's resolution. Granville read a somewhat ambiguous note from Schenck, authorized by Fish, which seemed to indicate U.S. acceptance of the latest British revisions. Russell declared himself satisfied and withdrew his motion.[39] But the events of the preceding weeks had demonstrated that resolution of the issue by an amendment to the treaty would be a complex, time-consuming, and hazardous process.

The difficult issue of the indirect claims was resolved a fortnight later at Geneva by a courageous action by the American member of the tribunal, Charles Francis Adams. Granville wrote a friend on June 12 that Adams had been secretly working for a declaration by the arbitrators that they were "individually and collectively convinced that the indirect claims are untenable, and cannot be entertained by them."[40] Adams convinced the other arbitrators to agree to this way out of the impasse. H. C. Allen wrote that "it was a brave and noble act . . . and formed a fitting culmination to his role in the history of Anglo-American relations. . . . Adams justly said: 'I should be assuming a heavy responsibility; but I should do so, not as an arbitrator representing my country, but as representing all nations.' "[41] "That an Adams should have assumed the responsibility," observed James Thurslow Adams, "was in line with the whole family precedent and tradition."[42]

On June 19 the five arbitrators unanimously declared that they had arrived, individually and collectively, at the conclusion that "these [indirect] claims do not constitute, upon the principles of international law applicable to such cases, good foundation for an award of compensation or computation of damages between nations, and should . . . be wholly excluded from the consideration of the tribunal in making its award."[43] Fish cabled Davis on June 22 that the president accepted the declaration of the tribunal "as its judgment upon a question of public law which he had felt that the interests of both Governments required should be decided."[44]

These actions cleared the way for the decision by the tribunal on September 14, 1872, that Great Britain should pay the United States $15 million as compensation for the direct damages of the *Alabama* and the *Florida*. Although the British member of the tribunal, Sir Alexander Cockburn, dissented vigorously and Gladstone thought the settlement was "harsh in its extent and unjust in its basis,"[45] the British public reluctantly accepted the settlement and the British government promptly paid the money awarded by the tribunal. Richard Shannon, the most recent biographer of Gladstone, wrote that Gladstone had concluded by 1880 that his initial objections to the settlement were "as dust in the balance compared with the moral example set" of two proud nations going "in peace and concord before a judicial tribunal" rather than resorting "to the arbitrament of the sword."[46]

Oxford professor H. C. Allen wrote that the settlement was well worth the price: "The Treaty of Washington banished once more the

fear of fratricidal war. . . . It was a triumph for the policy of concession
and conciliation. . . . It also strengthened the tradition of negotiating
and arbitrating even the most serious disputes between the two states,
until it became eventually unbreakable."[47] Roy Jenkins, a member of
recent British governments and a biographer of Gladstone, observed
that "the settlement not only was the greatest nineteenth-century triumph of rational internationalism over shortsighted jingoism, but also
marked the breakpoint between the previous hundred years of
Anglo-American strain and the subsequent century . . . of two world
wars fought in alliance."[48]

$\mathcal{N}$OTES

Abbreviations

E. D. Adams: Ephraim D. Adams, *Great Britain and the American Civil War* (New York, 1925).

Barnes: James J. and Patience P. Barnes, *Private and Confidential: Letters from British Ministers in Washington to the Foreign Secretaries in London, 1844–67* (Selingsgrove, Pa., 1993).

BDFA: Kenneth Bourne and D. Cameron Watt, eds., *British Documents on Foreign Affairs: Reports and Papers from the Foreign Office Confidential Print*, Part 1, Series C, North America, 1837–1914, (Bethesda, Md., 1986), volumes 5 and 6: *The Civil War, 1859–1865.*

BL: British Library, London.

Coll. Works: Roy P. Basler, ed., *Collected Works of Abraham Lincoln* (New Brunswick, N.J., 1953).

FR-61 to FR-72: *Foreign Relations of the United States* ("Papers Relating to Foreign Affairs Accompanying the Annual Message of the President"), December 1861 to December 1872 (Reprint: New York, 1965).

Hendrick: Burton J. Hendrick, *Statesmen of the Lost Cause: Jefferson Davis and His Cabinet* (New York, 1939).

NA: National Archives, College Park, Maryland.

ORA: *The Official Record of the Union and Confederate Armies in the War of the Rebellion* (Washington, 1880–1900).

ORN: *The Official Records of the Union and Confederate Navies in the War of the Rebellion* (Washington, 1894–1914).

Owsley: Frank Owsley, *King Cotton Diplomacy* (Chicago, 1959).

PRO: Public Record Office, London.

Recollected Words: Don E. and Virginia Fehrenbacher, *Recollected Words of Abraham Lincoln* (Stanford, Calif., 1996).

Richardson: James D. Richardson, ed., *The Messages and Papers of Jefferson Davis and the Confederacy* (New York, 1966).

Welles Diary: Gideon Welles, *Diary of Gideon Welles, Secretary of the Navy Under Lincoln and Johnson* (Boston, 1911), 3 vols.

Chapter 1: Holding Watch Against Foreign Intrusion

1. David H. Donald, *Lincoln* (London, 1995), 320.
2. Philip S. Paludan, *The Presidency of Abraham Lincoln* (Lawrence, Kans., 1994), 88–89.
3. Jasper Ridley, *Lord Palmerston* (New York, 1971), 551.
4. Charles Francis Adams Jr., *Charles Francis Adams* (Boston, 1890), 146.
5. Moran Diary, December 26, 1861, and November 19, 1862, in S. A. Wallace and F.

E. Gillespie, eds., *The Journal of Benjamin Moran* (Chicago, 1949), II, 930, 1092.

6. James G. Randall and Richard N. Current, *Lincoln the President: Last Full Measure* (New York, 1955), 84.

7. Motley letter, June 1861, in Lord Charnwood, *Abraham Lincoln* (New York, 1917), 237.

8. Rudolf Schleiden to Government of Bremen, March 1861, in R. H. Lutz, "Rudolph Schleiden and the Visit to Richmond, April 25, 1861," *Annual Report of the American Historical Association for the Year 1915* (Washington, 1917), 209–16.

9. Randall and Current, 83.

10. Lincoln debate with Douglas, October 15, 1858, in Donald, 223–24.

11. John M. Taylor, *William Henry Seward: Lincoln's Right Hand* (New York, 1991), 201.

12. Lincoln to Congress, Decemer 6, 1864, FR-64, I, 6.

13. John Hay, *Century Magazine*, November 1890, in Paul M. Angle, ed., *The Lincoln Reader* (Rutgers, N.J., 1947), 437.

14. John J. Duff, *A. Lincoln: Prairie Lawyer* (New York, 1960), 15–17.

15. George Borrett, "In Carpet Slippers," October 1868, in Charles M. Segal, ed., *Conversations with Lincoln* (New York, 1961), 346.

16. Lincoln, "Resolutions in Behalf of Hungarian Freedom," in Carl Van Doren Stern, ed., *The Life and Writings of Abraham Lincoln* (New York, 1940), 336.

17. Lincoln notes for debates in 1858, in Carl Sandburg, *Abraham Lincoln: The Prairie Years and the War Years* (New York, 1953), 150.

18. Glyndon G. Van Deusen, *William Henry Seward* (New York, 1961), 105.

19. Taylor, 144–45.

20. Lyons to Russell, January 7, 1861, in Lord Newton, *Lord Lyons: A Record of British Diplomacy* (London, 1913), I, 80.

21. John G. Nicolay and John Hay, *Abraham Lincoln: A History* (New York, 1890), VI, 234–36.

22. Van Deusen, 283–84.

23. Newcastle to Head, June 5, 1861, in George Warren, *Fountain of Discontent: The Trent Affair and Freedom of the Seas* (Boston, 1981), 57.

24. E. D. Adams, II, 114.

25. Robin Winks, *Canada and the United States: The Civil War Years* (Baltimore, 1960), 79.

26. Frederick W. Seward, *Reminiscences of a War-Time Statesman and Diplomat, 1830-1915* (New York, 1916), in *Recollected Words*, 398.

27. Carl Schurz, *The Autobiography of Carl Schurz* (New York, 1961), 177.

28. Ida Tarbell, *The Life of Abraham Lincoln* (New York, 1900), II, 32.

29. Francis Fessenden, *Life and Public Services of William Pitt Fessenden*, (Boston, 1907), I, 242.

30. Randall and Current, 80.

31. Benjamin Thomas, *Abraham Lincoln: A Biography* (New York, 1952), 353.

32. Norman B. Ferris, *The Trent Affair: A Diplomatic Crisis* (Knoxville, 1977), 102.

33. Adams to Charles Francis Adams Jr., June 25, 1861, in Norman B. Ferris, *Desperate Diplomacy: William H. Seward's Foreign Policy, 1861* (Knoxville, 1976), 58.

34. Seward to Montholon, February 12, 1866, FR-65, II, 813–22.

35. Seward to Dayton, May 11, 1863, in George E. Baker, ed., *The Works of William H. Seward* (Boston, 1884), V, 383.

36. Seward to Sanford, March 26, 1861, FR-61, 53.

37. Seward to Dayton, September 26, 1863, FR-63, II, 710.

38. Seward to Dayton, June 17, 1861, FR-61, 224.

39. Seward to Adams, November 30, 1861, *ORA*, 2nd ser., II, 1108.

40. Hendrick, 147.

Chapter 2: To Be Treated as Other Independent Nations

1. William C. Davis, *Jefferson Davis: The Man and His Hour* (New York, 1991), 128.

2. James M. McPherson, *Battle Cry of Freedom: The Civil War Era* (New York, 1988), 104

3. Davis, 252.

4. Clement Eaton, *Jefferson Davis* (New York, 1977), 164, 172.

5. Hendrick, 69.

6. George C. Rable, *The Confederate Republic* (Chapel Hill, N.C., 1994), 71–72.

7. William C. Davis, *A Government of Our Own: The Making of the Confederacy* (New York, 1996), 371.

8. Eli N. Evans, *Judah P. Benjamin: The Jewish Confederate* (New York, 1988), 103, 156.

9. Robert D. Meade, *Judah P. Benjamin: Confederate Statesman* (New York, 1943), 96–97.

10. Evans, 45, 93, 96.

11. William H. Russell, *My Diary North and South* (New York, 1954), 96.

12. Hendrick, 171–73.

13. Davis, *A Government of Our Own,* 200.

14. Hudson Strode, *Jefferson Davis: Tragic Hero* (New York, 1964), 77.

15. Emory M. Thomas, *The Confederate Nation: 1861–65* (New York, 1979), 169.

16. Hunter to Slidell and Hunter to Mason, September 23, 1861, *ORN*, 2nd. ser., III, 262, 264.

17. Benjamin to Mason, April 12, 1862, in Richardson, II, 227.

18. Jefferson Davis to Confederate Congress, January 12, 1863, in Richardson, I, 280.

19. Jefferson Davis, *The Rise and Fall of the Confederate Government* (New York, 1881), II, 370.

20. Charles P. Cullop, *Confederate Propaganda in Europe, 1861–65* (Coral Gables, Fla., 1969), 18.

21. Slidell to Thouvenel, July 21, 1862, in Richardson, II, 288.

22. Adams to Seward, July 31, 1862, FR-62, 160.

23. Cullop, 28–29.

24. Ibid., 55.

25. Benjamin to Slidell, April 12, 1862, in Richardson, II, 230.

Chapter 3: A Powerlessness to Comprehend

1. Baron de Brunow to Prince Gortchakov, January 1, 1861, in B. B. Sideman and Lillian Friedman, eds., *Europe Looks at the American Civil War* (New York, 1960), 20.

2. *The Times* (London), September 26, 1861, in Norman B. Ferris, *Desperate Diplomacy: William H. Seward's Foreign Policy, 1861* (Knoxville, 1976), 132.

3. Russell to Lyons, January 10, 1861, Russell Papers, PRO 30/22/96, item 418, PRO.

4. Russell to Lyons, May 6, 1861, in E. D. Adams, I, 88.

5. *The Economist* (London), May 15, 1861, in Owsley, 194.

6. Palmerston to Queen Victoria, December 29, 1861, in Sideman and Friedman, 119.

7. *The Times* (London), July 18 and August 27, 1861, in Owsley, 196.

8. G. M. Trevelyan, *British History in the Nineteenth Century, 1782–1901* (London, 1922), 331–32.

9. David Thompson, *England in the Nineteenth Century, 1815–1914* (London, 1950), 74, 117.

10. Adams to Seward, June 9, 1864, FR-64, II, 89.

11. Lord Charnwood, *Abraham Lincoln* (New York, 1917), 313.

12. Rufus Sears, ed., *Selected Writings of Lord Acton* (Indianapolis, 1985), I, 363.

13. Edward Dicey, *Spectator of America* (Chicago, 1971), 288.

14. Russell speech, Newcastle, October 14, 1861, in James D. Bulloch, *The Secret Service of the Confederate States in Europe* (New York, 1959), II, 312.

15. Charnwood, 257.

16. Lyons to Russell, May 22 and July 23, 1860, in Barnes, 233–34.

17. W. H. Russell, *My Diary North and South* (New York, 1954), 22.

18. Dicey, 91.

19. Ibid.

20. Alexander J. Beresford-Hope, *A Popular View of the American Civil War* (London, 1861), in Sideman and Friedman, 32.

21. Nicholas C. Edsal, *Richard Cobden: Independent Radical* (Cambridge, Mass., 1986), 399.

22. Karl Marx, "On the Civil War and Lincoln," *Die Presse*, Vienna, October 12, 1862, in Sideman and Friedman, 190.

23. W. H. Russell, 24.

24. Martin Crawford, *The Anglo-American Crisis of the Mid-Nineteenth Century* (Athens, Ga., 1987), 123–27.

25. Staff of *The Times* (London), *History of The Times: The Tradition Established, 1841–1884* (London, 1939), 359.

26. *Dispatch* (London), in Carl Sandburg, *Abraham Lincoln: The Prairie Years and the War Years* (New York, 1954), 339.

27. Charnwood, 257.

28. Mark E. Neeley, Jr. *The Last Best Hope of Earth: Abraham Lincoln and the Promise of America* (Cambridge, Mass., 1993), 114.

29. Lincoln, Inaugural Address, March 4, 1861, in Maureen Harrison and Steve Gilbert, eds., *Abraham Lincoln in His Own Words* (New York, 1994), 293.

30. Francis B. Carpenter, *Six Months at the White House with Abraham Lincoln: The Story of a Picture* (New York, 1866), 76-77, in *Recollected Words*, 83–84.

31. Jasper Ridley, *Lord Palmerston* (New York, 1971), 587–88.

32. Ibid., 549.

33. John Morely, *The Life of William Edward Gladstone* (London, 1908), I, 535.

34. Welles Diary, September 18, 1863, I, 437.

35. Hendrick, 264–65.

36. G. P. Gooch, *The Later Correspondence of Lord John Russell* (London, 1925), lxiii.

37. Hendrick, 278.

38. Carl Schurz, *The Autobiography of Carl Schurz* (New York, 1961), 179-80.

39. Thomas A. Bailey, *A Diplomatic History of the American People* (New York, 1946), 341–42.

40. H. C. Allen, *Great Britain and the United States: A History of Anglo-American Relations, 1783–1952* (New York, 1955), 455.

41. Seward to Adams, February 13, 1864, FR-64, I, 171.

42. Russell to Lyons, May 21 and June 22, 1861, Russell Papers, PRO 30/22/96, PRO.

43. *The Times* (London), February 16, 1864, FR-64, I, 176.

44. Adams to meeting of Americans, *Evening Star* (London), May 2, 1865, in FR-65, Appendix, 278.

45. Lord Newton, *Lord Lyons* (London, 1913), I, 148.

46. Lyons to Russell, October 21, 1861, in Ferris, 199.

47. Ferris, 8.

48. Lyons to Russell, May 2 and July 22, 1860, in Barnes, 233–34.

49. James G. Randall and Richard N. Current, *Lincoln the President: Last Full Measure* (New York, 1955), 81.

50. Lyons to Russell, April 15, 1861, in Newton, I, 37.

51. Lyons to Russell, May 20, 1861, in E. D. Adams, I, 128.

52. Schuler Colfax reminiscence in Allen Thorndike Rice, ed., *Reminiscences of Abraham Lincoln* (New York, 1888), 346–47.

53. Randall and Current, 83.

54. Ferris, 55.

55. Ibid., 200.

56. Lyons to Russell, December 22, 1862, in Barnes, 312.

57. Eugene H. Berwanger, *The British Foreign Service and the American Civil War* (Lexington, Ky., 1994), 170.

58. Russell to Lyons, April 8, 1861, PRO 30/22/96, item 418, PRO.

59. Russell to Lyons, March 25, 1865, in Newton, I, 142.

60. Lincoln to Queen Victoria, March 28, 1865, FR-63, I, 309.

Chapter 4: Recognition Would Be Intervention

All dates are in 1861 unless otherwise noted.

1. Thaddeus Stevens interview, *Herald* (New York), July 8, 1867, *Recollected Words*, 423.

2. Lincoln to Welles, March 18, in *Coll. Works*, IV, 292.

3. Lyons to Russell, March 26, in Lord Newton, *Lord Lyons* (London, 1913), I, 31.

4. Lyons to Russell, April 15, Newton, I, 36.

5. Diary of W. H. Russell, April 4, in W. H. Russell, *My Diary North and South* (New York, 1954), 36.

6. Philip S. Paludan, *The Presidency of Abraham Lincoln* (Lawrence, Kans., 1994), 90–91.

7. Gerald Ford, *A Time to Heal* (New York, 1979), 52.

8. Allen Thorndike Rice, ed., *Reminiscences of Abraham Lincoln* (New York, 1888), iv.

9. Argyll to Motley, May 14, in Dowager Duchess of Argyll, ed., *George Douglas, Eighth Duke of Argyll: Autobiography and Memoirs* (London, 1906), II, 170.

10. *The Times* (London), March 24, 1865, FR-65, I, 263–64.

11. Edward Channing, *A History of the United States* (New York, 1927), VI, 491.

12. H. C. Allen, *Great Britain and the United States: A History of Anglo-American Relations, 1783–1952* (New York, 1955), 463.

13. Spencer Walpole, *The Life of Lord John Russell* (London, 1891), II, 369.

14. Yancey, Rost, and Mann to Toombs, May 21, in Philip Van Doren Stern, *When the Guns Roared: World Aspects of the Civil War* (Garden City, N.Y, 1965), 56.

15. Adams to Seward, May 21, FR-61, 91.

16. Dairy of Charles Francis Adams, June 10, in James Thurslow Adams, *The Adams Family* (New York, 1930), 264.

17. Adams to Seward, June 14, FR-61, 104.

18. Seward to Adams, May 21, FR-61, 87.

19. E. D. Adams, I, 264.

20. Lyons to Russell, May 20, *BDFA*, V, 223–25.

21. Lyons to Russell, May 24, in Barnes, 251–52.

22. Donald, 20.

23. Seward to Adams, July 6, in John M. Taylor, *William Henry Seward: Lincoln's Right Hand* (New York, 1991), 180.

24. Lyons to Russell, July 20, in Barnes, 255; Seward to Adams, July 21, FR-61, 118.

25. Allen, 462.

26. *The Times* (London), May 30, in E. D. Adams, I, 97.

27. Benjamin Perley Poore reminiscence, in Rice, 229.

28. Lyons to Russell, July 30, *BDFA*, V, 276.

29. Henry Adams to Charles Francis Adams Jr., August 6, in J. C. Levenson, ed., *The Letters of Henry Adams* (Cambridge, Mass., 1982), I, 248.

30. Lincoln, Memorandum on Military Policy, July 23, in Carl Van Doren Stern, ed., *The Life and Writings of Abraham Lincoln* (New York, 1940), 677.

31. Lyons to Russell, June 14, in Barnes, 209.

32. Lyons to Russell, July 12, *BDFA*, V, 267.

33. Lyons to Russell, July 20, in Barnes, 255.

34. Lyons to Russell, July 24, *BDFA*, V, 267.

35. Browning diary, July 28, in T. C. Pease and J. G. Randall, eds., *The Diary of Orville Hickman Browning* (Springfield, Ill., 1933), I, 489.

36. Seward to Adams, July 20, FR-61, 118.

37. Lyons to Russell, August 12, *BDFA*, V, 294.

38. Howard Jones, *Union in Peril: The Crisis Over British Intervention in the Civil War* (Chapel Hill, N.C., 1992), 40–41, 66.

39. Adams to Russell, August 23, *BDFA*, V, 289–91.

40. Russell to Adams, August 28, *BDFA*, V, 292–94.

41. Seward to Adams, September 7, FR-61, 142.

42. Adams to Russell, September 3, *BDFA*, V, 298.

43. Russell to Adams, September 9, *BDFA*, V, 301.

44. Bunche to Lyons, August 16, *BDFA*, V, 303–04.

45. Eugene H. Berwanger, *The British Foreign Service and the American Civil War* (Lexington, Ky., 1994), 51.

46. Yancey, Rost, and Mann to Hunter, August 7, *ORN*, 2nd ser., III, 236.

47. Russell to Yancey, Rost, and Mann, August 24, *BDFA*, V, 291–92.

48. Walpole, II, 355.

49. Ibid., II, 356.

50. Palmerston to Layard, October 30, in Jasper Ridley, *Lord Palmerston* (New York, 1971), 552.

Chapter 5: A Gross Outrage

Unless otherwise noted, all dates cited are in 1861. The account of the removal of the Confederate envoys from the *Trent* is drawn from *The Official Records of the Union and Confederate Navies in the War of the Rebellion (ORN)*, 1st ser., I, 129–148, and from George F. Warren, *Fountain of Discontent: The Trent Affair and Freedom of the Sea* (Boston, 1981).

1. Martin Crawford, ed., *William Howard Russell's Civil War: Private Diary and Letters, 1861-62* (Athens, Ga., 1992), 178.

2. Wilkes to Welles, November 16, in *ORN*, lst ser., I, 144.

3. Bates Diary, November 18, in Howard K. Beale, ed., *The Diary of Edward Bates* (Washington, 1933), 202.

4. Norman B. Ferris, *The Trent Affair: A Diplomatic Crisis* (Knoxville, 1977), 24.

5. Virginia Mason, *The Public Life and Diplomatic Correspondence of James M. Mason* (New York, 1906), 216–17.

6. Ferris, 24.

7. William H. Russell, November 16, *My Diary North and South* (New York, 1954), 361.

8. Henry W. Temple, "William H. Seward," in Samuel F. Bemis, ed., *The American Secretaries of State and Their Diplomacy* (New York, 1958), VII, 63.

9. Lincoln to Edward Everett, December 18, in *Coll. Works*, V, 26.

10. Benson J. Lossing, *Pictorial History of the Civil War in the United States* (Hartford, 1868), II, 165–67.

11. Gideon Welles, *The Galaxy*, May 1873, 647, in John G. Nicolay and John Hay, *Abraham Lincoln: A History* (New York, 1890), V, 265.

12. Welles Diary, May 12, 1863, I, 288–89.

13. Thornton K. Lothrop, *William Henry Seward* (Boston, 1896), 325.

14. McClellan to wife, November 17, in Stephen W. Sears, ed., *The Civil War Papers of George B. McClellan* (New York, 1989), 135.

15. Lothrop, 327.

16. Seward to Thurlow Weed, March 7, 1862, in Nicolay and Hay, V, 31.

17. W. H. Russell, 261.

18. Seward to Adams, November 30, in Lothrop, 328.

19. Welles Diary, August 10, 1862, I, 74.

20. Richard S. West, *Gideon Welles: Lincoln's Navy Department* (Indianapolis, 1943), 133–35.

21. John Niven, *Gideon Welles: Lincoln's Secretary of the Navy* (Baton Rouge, 1973), 417.

22. Welles to Wilkes, November 30, *ORA*, 2nd ser., II, 1109.

23. Welles Diary, May 12, 1863, I, 288–89.

24. Glyndon G. Van Deusen, *William Henry Seward: Lincoln's Secretary of State* (New York, 1961), 309.

25. Lyons to Russell, November 29, in Barnes, 296.

26. Lincoln, Annual Message to Congress, December 3, in Carl Van Doren Stern, ed., *The Life and Writings of Abraham Lincoln* (New York, 1940), 686.

27. Lyons to Russell, December 6, in Barnes, 271; Galt Memorandum, December 5, in Charles M. Segal, ed., *Conversations with Lincoln* (New York, 1961), 147.

28. Browning Diary, December 6, in Theodore C. Pease and James G. Randall, eds., *The Diary of Orville Hickman Browning* (Springfield, Ill., 1925), 513–14.

29. Yancey, Rost, and Mann to Hunter, December 1, *ORN*, 2nd ser., III, 304.

30. Warren, 96.

31. Palmerston to Delane, November 11, in E. D. Adams, I, 208.

32. Palmerston to Queen, November 13, in John Bigelow, *Retrospections of an Active Life* (New York, 1909), I, 404.

33. Bigelow draft for General Scott, December 2, in Bigelow, I, 388.

34. Warren, 69.

35. *Morning Chronicle* (London), November 28, in B. B. Sideman and L. Friedman, eds., *Europe Looks at the Civil War* (New York, 1960), 101.

36. Charles Francis Adams Jr., *Charles Francis Adams* (Boston, 1890), 218–19.

37. Henry Adams to Charles Francis Adams Jr., December 13, in J. C. Levenson, ed., *The Letters of Henry Adams* (Cambridge, Mass., 1982), I, 266.

38. David Thomson, *England in the Nineteenth Century* (London, 1978), 155.

39. Adams to Seward, March 30, 1865, FR-65, I, 298.

40. Gladstone to Argyll, December 8, in Bigelow, I, 428.

41. Gladstone Diary, November 30, in H. G. C. Matthews, ed., *The Gladstone Diaries* (Oxford, 1978), VI, 77.

42. Palmerston to Queen, November 29, in Bigelow, I, 404.

43. Prince Albert to Palmerston, November 30, in Philip Van Doren Stern, *When the Guns Roared: World Aspects of the Civil War* (Garden City, N.Y., 1965), 92.

44. *The Times* (London), December 3 and 10, in Temple, VII, 68.

45. Lyons to Russell, November 19, in Lord Newton, *Lord Lyons* (London, 1913), I, 55.

46. Lyons to Russell, November 19, Russell papers, PRO 30/22/55, PRO, in Ferris, 88.

47. Bright speech at Rochdale, December 4, in Sideman and Friedman, 102.

48. Adams to Seward, December 6, *ORA*, 2nd ser., II, 1119–20.

49. Ferris, 92–93.

50. Weed to Bigelow, December 5, in Bigelow, I, 403.

51. Adams to Charles Francis Adams Jr., December 20, in W. C. Ford, ed., *A Cycle of Adams Letters* (Boston, 1920), I, 88.

52. Adams to Charles Francis Adams Jr., December 27, in Ford, I, 91.

53. Lewis to friend, December 10, in Ferris, 57.

54. Robin Winks, *Canada and the United States: The Civil War Years* (Baltimore, 1960), 83.

55. Warren, 126.

56. Stern, 93.

57. Adams to Seward, December 12, *ORA*, 2nd ser., II, 1123–24.

58. Adams to Seward, December 20, *ORA*, 2nd ser., II, 1137.

59. Russell to Palmerston, December 16, in E. D. Adams, I, 215.

60. *The Times* (London), March 14, 1865, FR-65, I, 240.

61. Adams Diary, January 4, 13, and 14, 1862, in Martin B. Duberman, *Charles Francis Adams* (Boston, 1960), 283.

62. D. Jordan and E. J. Pratt, *Europe and the American Civil War* (Boston, 1931), 43–45.

63. Browning Diary, December 15, in Pease and Randall, I, 515.

64. W. H. Russell, 262.

65. W. H. Russell to Delane, December 12, in Martin Crawford, ed., *William Howard Russell's Civil War* (Athens, Ga., 1992), 207.

66. W. H. Russell, December 20, in W. H. Russell, 262.

67. Russell to Lyons, November 30, *ORN*, lst ser., I, 156–60.

68. Russell to Lyons, December 1, 1861, in Newton, I, 62.

69. Lyons to Russell, December 19, *ORA*, 2nd ser., II, 1135.

70. Ibid.

71. James R. Gilmore, *Personal Recollections of Abraham Lincoln and the Civil War* (Boston, 1898), 57–58.

72. Titan J. Coffey recollection in A. T. Rice, ed., *Reminiscences of Abraham Lincoln* (New York, 1888), 245.

73. Bright to Sumner, December 6, in Ferris, 175.

74. Browning Diary, December 21, in Pease and Randall, I, 516–17.

75. Nicolay and Hay, V, 33–34.

76. Russell to Napier, January 10, 1862, *BDFA*, VI, 17.

77. Lyons to Russell, December 23, *ORA*, 2nd ser., II, 1142.

78. Sumner to Francis Lieber, December 24, in Beverly W. Palmer, ed., *The Selected Letters of Charles Sumner* (Boston, 1990), II, 89.

79. Sumner to Bright, December 23, in Ida Tarbell, *The Life of Abraham Lincoln* (New York, 1900), 74.

80. Lyons to Russell, December 23, *ORA*, 2nd ser., II, 1142.

81. Horace Porter, *Campaigning with Grant* (New York, 1897), in Segal, 380.

82. Frederick W. Seward, *Reminiscences of a War-Time Statesman and Diplomat, 1861–72* (New York, 1891), 189–90, in *Recollected Words*, 399.

83. Seward to Lyons, December 26, *ORN*, lst ser., I, 177–87.

84. Bright to Sumner, December 6, in Carl Sandburg, *Abraham Lincoln: The War Years* (New York, 1939), I, 366.

85. Nicolay and Hay, V, 35.

86. Warden, *Life of Chase*, 394, in Lothrop, 332.

87. Porter, in *Recollected Words*, 407-8.

88. Sumner to Cobden, December 31, in Palmer, II, 94.

89. Russell to Lyons. January 10, 1862, *ORN*, lst ser., I, 189.

90. John Stuart Mill, *Fraser's Magazine*, February 1862, in Frank Friedel, ed., *Union Pamphlets of the Civil War Era* (Cambridge, Mass., 1967), 327–28.

91. Adams Diary, January 8, 1862, in Duberman, 284.

92. Seward to Bertinatti, February 19, 1862, FR-62, 581.

93. *Richmond Examiner*, December 1861, in Frank L. Alfriend, *The Life of Jefferson Davis* (Cincinnati, 1868), 329.

94. Lee to wife, December 25, in Robert E. Lee Jr., *Recollections and Letters of General Robert E. Lee* (Garden City, N.Y., 1904), 59.

95. Alfriend, 323.

Chapter 6: Cotton Is King

1. Edward Channing, *A History of the United States*, (New York, 1927), VI, 335.
2. Owsley, 4–5.
3. Channing, VI, 336.
4. Hudson Strode, *Jefferson Davis: Confederate President* (New York, 1959), 75.
5. Strode, 75.
6. Benjamin to Slidell, April 8, 1862, in Richardson, II, 221–22.
7. Hay Diary, November 7, 1862, in Tyler Dennett, ed., *Lincoln and the Civil War in the Diaries and Letters of John Hay* (New York, 1939), 33.
8. Mejan to Thouvenel, May 30, 1862, FR-62, 421.
9. Bunch to Russell, August 13, 1862, *BDFA*, VI, 84.
10. Peter Sinclair, *Freedom or Slavery in the United States* (London, 1862), in B. B. Sideman and L. Friedman, eds., *Europe Looks at the Civil War* (New York, 1960), 180.
11. Owsley, 136.
12. John Watts, *The Facts of the Cotton Famine* (London, 1866), 227–28, in Owsley, 147.
13. Stuart to Russell, July 29, 1862, in Barnes, 294.
14. Browning Diary, July 25, 1862, in J. G. Randall and T. Pease, eds., *The Diary of Orville Hickman Browning* (Springfield, Ill., 1933), 563–64.
15. Granville to Palmerston, September 25, 1862, in E. Fitzmaurice, *Life of Granville George Leveson Gower, Second Earl of Granville* (London, 1905), I, 442.
16. Owsley, 544.
17. W. Baring Pemberton, *Lord Palmerston* (London, 1954), 313.
18. Frenise A. Logan, "India—Britain's Substitute for Cotton," *Journal of Southern History*, V, 24 (November 1958), 474.
19. William S. Thayer to Seward, November 12, 1862, and February 17, 1863, FR-63, II, 1102–1103, 1109.
20. E. Joy Morris to Seward, November 11, 1862, FR-63, II, 1084.
21. Seward to Thayer, December 15, 1862, FR-63, II, 1107.
22. James S. Pike to Seward, February 18, 1863, FR-63, II, 809.
23. Owsley, 137.
24. Adams to Seward, June 11, 1863, FR-63, I, 273.
25. Eli N. Evans, *Judah P. Benjamin: The Jewish Confederate* (New York, 1988), 116.
26. Benjamin to Slidell, April 12, 1862, in Robert D. Meade, *Judah P. Benjamin: Confederate Statesman* (New York, 1943), 254–55.
27. Slidell to Benjamin, July 25, 1862, *ORN*, 2nd ser., III, 484–86.
28. Owsley, 266.
29. James W. Daddysman, *The Matamoros Trade* (Newark, N.J., 1984), 38.
30. M. B. Hammond, *The Cotton Industry* (New York, 1897), in Owsley, 263.
31. Seward to Lyons, August 8, 1864, FR-64, II, 673.
32. *The Index* (London), December 1863, FR-64, I, 80–81.
33. Meade, 269–70; Evans, 195.
34. Hendrick, 232.
35. Adams to Seward, April 8, 1864, FR-64, I, 582.
36. Stephen H. Wise, *Lifeline of the Confederacy: Blockade Running During the Civil War* (Columbia, S.C., 1988), 147.

37. Ibid., 95.
38. General Q. A. Gilmore to General Halleck, February 21, 1865, FR-65, I, 180.
39. Adams to Seward, February 17, 1865, FR-65, I, 178.
40. Adams to Seward, April 20, 1865, FR-65, I, 323.
41. Adams to Seward, February 17, 1855, FR-65, I, 178.
42. Seward to Adams, March 13, 1865, FR-65, III, 205.

Chapter 7: A War with America Would Hamper My Operations

1. Serge Garonsky, *The French Liberal Opposition and the American Civil War* (New York, 1968), 246–47.
2. David H. Pinkey, "France and the Civil War," in H. M. Hyman, ed., *Heard Around the World: The Impact Abroad of the Civil War* (New York, 1969), 100.
3. Henry Kissinger, *Diplomacy* (New York, 1994), 107.
4. Owsley, 305; Beckles Willson, *John Slidell and the Confederates in Paris* (New York, 1932), 54.
5. Drouyn de Lhuys to Pennington, December 3, 1864, FR-65, II, 201.
6. Adams to Seward, December 2, 1864, FR-65, I, 13.
7. Seward to Dayton, April 22 and May 4, 1861, FR-61, 200, 207.
8. Dayton to Seward, May 22, 1861, FR-61, 209.
9. Seward to Dayton, June 8, 1861, FR-61, 221.
10. Seward to Mercier, June 8, 1861, in L. M. Case and W. F. Spencer, *The U.S. and France: Civil War Diplomacy* (Philadelphia, 1970), 61.
11. *La Patrie*, Paris, July 21, 1861, in Herbert Mitgang, ed., *Lincoln as They Saw Him* (New York, 1956), 273.
12. Dayton to Seward, June 1861, FR-61, 218.
13. Dayton to Seward, December 6, 1861, FR-62, 307.
14. Dean B. Mahin, *Olive Branch and Sword: The United States and Mexico, 1845–1848* (Jefferson, N.C., 1997), 47–49, 52–53, 72.
15. Louis M. Sears, *John Slidell* (Durham, N.C., 1925), 108–12.
16. Ibid., 73; Samuel Flagg Bemis, *A Diplomatic History of the United States* (New York, 1942), 370.
17. Slidell to Mason, March 28, 1862, in Sears, 189.
18. Slidell memorandum, in Virginia Mason, *The Public Life and Diplomatic Correspondence of James M. Mason* (New York, 1906), 367.
19. Seward to Dayton, January 4, 1864, FR-64, III, 15.
20. John G. Nicolay and John Hay, *Abraham Lincoln: A History* (New York, 1890), VI, 83.
21. Owsley, 271.
22. Mercier to Thouvenel, April 13, 1862, in Owsley, 283.
23. Benjamin to Mason, July 19, 1862, in Mason, 299.
24. Benjamin to Slidell, July 16, 1862, *ORN*, 2nd ser., III, 463.
25. Bemis, 365–66.
26. Lindsay memorandum, in Mason, 423.
27. Slidell to Benjamin, July 25, 1862, *ORN*, 2nd ser., III, 484–86.
28. Slidell to Benjamin, July 15, 1862, *ORN*, 2nd ser., III, 486–87.

29. Bigelow to Seward, August 1862, in John M. Taylor, *William Henry Seward: Lincoln's Right Hand* (New York, 1991), 196.

30. Eduard Laboulaye, *Journal de Debats*, Paris, in B. B. Sideman and L. Friedman, eds., *Europe Looks at the Civil War* (New York, 1960), 164–65.

31. Slidell to Benjamin, October 28, 1862, in Richardson, II, 345–47.

32. Case and Spencer, 347–50.

33. Dayton to Seward, November 6, 1862, FR-62, 405.

34. Drouyn de Lhuys to Mercier, January 9, 1863, in Case and Spencer, 386–88.

35. Seward to Dayton, Feburary 6, 1863, in R. J. Bartlett, ed., *The Record of American Diplomacy* (New York, 1954), 292–93.

36. Mann to Benjamin, March 13, 1863, in Gavronsky, 171.

37. Slidell to Mason, June 15, 1863, and Slidell to Benjamin, June 21, 1863, in Owsley, 446–47.

38. Owsley, 544.

39. Warren F. Spencer, *The Confederate Navy in Europe* (Tuscaloosa, Ala., 1983), 213.

Chapter 8: Maintaining the Independence of Mexico

1. Dean B. Mahin, *Olive Branch and Sword: The United States and Mexico, 1845–1848* (Jefferson, N.C., 1997), 75–76.

2. Lincoln, "Autobiographical Sketch," in Carl Van Doren Stern, ed., *The Life and Writings of Abraham Lincoln* (New York, 1940), 606.

3. Mahin, 183–86.

4. Lincoln speech in House of Representatives, January 12, 1848, in Stern, 306.

5. Donald Riddle, *Congressman Abraham Lincoln* (Urbana, Ill., 1957), 34, 41.

6. Mahin, 137–51.

7. Henry B. Parkes, *A History of Mexico* (Boston, 1970), 223, 243.

8. Parkes, 247.

9. Alfred J. Hanna and Kathryn A. Hanna, *Napoleon III and Mexico* (Chapel Hill, N.C., 1971), 22.

10. Parkes, 247.

11. Ocampo to Romero, December 22, 1860, *Coll. Works*, IV, 178.

12. Romero to Ministry, January 23, 1861, in Charles M. Segal, ed., *Conversations with Lincoln* (New York, 1961), 6.

13. Jack K. Bauer, *The Mexican War—1846–1848* (New York, 1974), 276–77, 363.

14. Lyons to Russell, March 25, 1861, FO 115/252, item 211, PRO.

15. Corwin to Seward, July 29, 1861, in Hanna and Hanna, 49–50.

16. Benjamin Moran Diary, August 31, 1861, in S. A. Wallace and F. E. Gillespie, eds., *The Journal of Benjamin Moran, 1857–1865* (Chicago, 1949), II, 870.

17. Corwin to Seward, July 29, 1861, in Ruhl J. Bartlett, ed., *The Record of American Diplomacy* (New York, 1954), 298.

18. Seward to Corwin, August 24, 1861, draft, M77, NA.

19. Bates memorandum to cabinet, August 27, 1861, in Howard K. Beale, ed., *The Diary of Edward Bates, 1859–1866: Annual Report of the American Historical Association for 1930* (Washington, 1933), 188–89.

20. Romero to Ministry of Foreign Affairs, September 9, 1861, in Thomas D. Schoonover, *Mexican Lobby: Mattias Romero in Washington, 1861–1869* (Lexington, Ky., 1986), 9.

21. Romero to Ministry, August 31, 1861, in Schoonover, 9.

22. Seward to Corwin, September 2, 1861, in Bartlett, 299–300.

23. Bates memorandum, August 27, 1861, in Beale, 188–89.

24. Adams to Seward, September 28, 1861, in Norman B. Ferris, *Desperate Diplomacy: William H. Seward's Foreign Policy, 1861* (Knoxville, 1976), 158–59.

25. Corwin to Seward, November 29, 1861, M97, NA.

26. Moran Diary, September 28, 1861, in Wallace and Gillespie, II, 884.

27. Corwin to Seward, September 7, 1861, M97, NA.

28. Seward to Corwin, October 2, 1861, M77, NA.

29. Dayton to Seward, September 27, 1861, in Owsley, 111.

30. Seward to Spanish, French, and British ministers, December 4, 1861, in Bartlett, 300–01.

31. Corwin to Seward, November 29, 1861, M97, NA.

32. Ibid.

33. "Draft of Treaty Proving for a Loan to Mexico," November 1861, and "Treaty between the United States of America and the Mexican Republic for a Loan to the Latter," April 6, 1862, in Christian L. Wiktor, ed., *Unperfected Treaties of the United States of America, 1776–1976* (Dobbs Ferry, N.Y., 1976), 219–22, 224–29.

34. Corwin to Seward, September 7, 1861, M97, NA.

35. Lincoln to Senate, December 17, 1861, in *Coll. Works*, V, 74.

36. Browning Diary, December 21, 1861, 516.

37. Lincoln to Senate, January 24, 1862, in *Coll. Works*, V, 110.

38. Seward to Corwin, February 15, 1862, M77, NA.

39. Corwin to Seward, March 24, 1862, FR-62, 732.

40. Sumner to Seward, February 20, 1862, in Beverly Palmer, ed., *The Selected Letters of Charles Sumner* (Boston, 1990), II, 102.

41. Moorfield Story, *Charles Sumner* (Boston, 1900), 221.

42. Bates Diary, February 21, 1862, in Beale, 35.

43. Lincoln to Senate, February 22, 1862, in *Coll. Works*, V, 136.

44. Romero to Ministry, February 24, 1862, in Schoonover, *Mexican Lobby*, 22–23.

45. Senate resolution, February 25, 1862, in *Coll. Works*, V, 109.

46. Lincoln to Senate, February 27, 1862, in *Coll. Works*, V, 138.

47. Seward to Corwin, February 28, 1862, NA, 397.

48. Wiktor, 223–29.

49. Slidell to Benjamin, July 15, 1863, ORN, 2nd ser., III, 486–87.

50. Seward to Corwin, May 28, 1862, FR-62, 747.

51. Seward to Corwin, June 7, 1862, FR-62, 748.

52. Lincoln to Senate, June 23, 1862, in *Coll. Works*, V, 281.

53. Seward to Corwin, June 24, 1862, FR-62, 749.

54. Romero to Ministry, July 3, 1862, in Schoonover, *Mexican Lobby*, 26.

55. Wythe to Russell, June 11, 1862, PRO 30/22/74, item 153, PRO.

56. Corwin to Seward, Auust 28, 1862, FR-62, 767–68.

57. Seward to General N. P. Banks, November 28, 1863, FR-63, II, 1341.

58. Thomas D. Schoonover, *Dollars Over Dominion: The Triumph of Liberalism in Mexican–United States Relations, 1861–67* (Baton Rouge, 1978), 117.

59. Juárez to family, April 1865, in Ralph Roeder, *Juárez and His Mexico* (New York, 1947) II, 598.

Chapter 9: We May Wait a While

All dates are in 1862 unless otherwise noted.

1. William C. Davis, *Jefferson Davis: The Man and the Hour* (New York, 1991), 386; Eli N. Evans, *Judah P. Benjamin: The Jewish Confederate* (New York, 1988), 88; Gordon Warren, *Fountain of Discontent: The Trent Affair and Freedom of the Sea* (Boston, 1981), 6–7.

2. Hendrick, 251; James M. Callahan, *Diplomatic History of the Southern Confederacy* (New York, 1964), 141–42.

3. Palmerston to Queen, February 6, in George E. Buckle, ed., *The Letters of Queen Victoria* (New York, 1926), 2nd ser., I, 17.

4. Mason to Hunter, February 22, in Virginia Mason, *The Public Life and Diplomatic Correspondence of James M. Mason* (New York, 1906), 260.

5. Palmerston to Queen, March 7, in Buckle, I, 22–23.

6. Adams to Seward, May 2, FR-62, 79.

7. Martin Duberman, *Charles Francis Adams* (Boston, 1960), 290–91.

8. Howard Jones, *Union in Peril: The Crisis Over British Intervention in the Civil War* (Chapel Hill, N.C., 1992), 133–35.

9. Russell to Mason, July 24, in Richardson, II, 302–03.

10. Lyons to Russell, April 25, in Barnes, 283–84.

11. E. D. Adams, II, 30.

12. Stuart to Russell, July 1, in Barnes, 291.

13. Seward to Adams, August 2, in Charles Francis Adams Jr., *Charles Francis Adams* (Boston, 1890), 285–86.

14. Adams to Seward, September 4, FR-62, 184.

15. Herbert C. F. Bell, *Lord Palmerston* (London, 1936), 326–27.

16. Lincoln to Greeley, August 22, in Herbert Mitgang, ed., *Lincoln as They Saw Him* (New York, 1956), 301.

17. Palmerston to Russell, September 14, in Spencer Walpole, *Life of Lord John Russell* (London, 1891), II, 361.

18. Russell to Palmerston, September 14, in E. D. Adams, II, 38.

19. Russell to Palmerston, September 17, in Walpole, II, 360–61.

20. Palmerston to Russell, September 23, in Walpole, II, 362.

21. Granville to Russell, September 27, in E. Fitzmaurice, *Life of Granville George Leveson Gower, Second Earl of Granville, K.G.* (London, 1905), I, 442–43.

22. Palmerston to Russell, October 2, in E. D. Adams, II, 43.

23. Russell to Palmerston, October 4, in E. D. Adams, II, 46.

24. Stuart to Russell, September 23, in E. D. Adams, II, 47.

25. Jones, 182.

26. H. C. Allen, *Great Britain and the United States: A History of Anglo-American Relations, 1783–1952* (New York, 1955), 480.

27. Adams to Seward, October 17, FR-62, 222.

28. Charles Francis Adams Jr., 287.

29. E. D. Adams, II, 92.

30. Carl Schurz, *Reminiscences*, II, 30-39, in E. D. Adams, II, 92.

31. John G. Nicolay and John Hay, *Abraham Lincoln: A History* (New York, 1890), VI, 155.

32. Lincoln to Chicago clergy, September 13, in *Coll. Works*, V, 422.

33. Woodrow Wilson, *Division and Reunion, 1829–1889* (New York, 1905), 227.

34. Jones, 174.

35. Winston Churchill, *The Great Democracies* (New York, 1958), 90.

36. Jenkins, II, 158.

37. Yancey, Mann, and Rost to Russell, August 14, 1861, *BDFA*, V, 1861.

38. Lyons to Russell, January 20, in E. D. Adams, II, 80.

39. Russell to Gladstone, January 26, in E. D. Adams, II, 80; Jones, 176.

40. Seward to Adams, May 28, FR-62, 101–05.

41. Adams to Seward, July 3, FR-62, 122.

42. E. D. Adams, II, 96.

43. Bright to Sumner, October 10, in B. B. Sideman and L. Friedman, eds., *Europe Looks at the Civil War* (New York, 1960), 189.

44. *Post* (London), October 8, in John Hope Franklin, *The Emancipation Proclamation* (Garden City, N.Y., 1963), 71.

45. Stuart to Russell, September 26, in Barnes, 300.

46. *The Times* (London), October 21, in D. Jordan and E. J. Pratt, *Europe Looks at the Civil War* (Boston, 1931), 192.

47. Russell to cabinet, October 13, in Walpole, II, 363.

48. E. D. Adams, II, 51.

49. Clarendon to Palmerston, October 16, in E. D. Adams, II, 51–52.

50. Palmerston to Russell, October 22, in H. C. Allen, *Great Britain and the United States: A History of Anglo-American Relations, 1783-1952* (New York, 1955), 481.

51. Duberman, 296.

52. Gladstone to cabinet, October 24, in Philip Guedalla, *Gladstone and Palmerston* (London, 1926), 239–41.

53. Russell to Lewis, October 26, in Owsley, 353.

54. Gray to Russell, October 27, in G. P. Gooch, *The Later Correspondence of Lord John Russell, 1840–1878* (London, 1925), II, 329–33.

55. Russell to Palmerston, November 3, in E. D. Adams, II, 62.

56. E. D. Adams, II, 271.

57. Owsley, 339.

58. Jones, 109, 181, 185, 196.

59. E. D. Adams, II, 63.

60. Lewis to Clarendon, November 12, in E. D. Adams, II, 64.

61. W. Baring Pemberton, *Lord Palmerston* (London, 1954), 313.

62. Russell to Cowley, November 13, *BDFA*, VI, 112.

63. Duberman, 297–98.

64. Lyons to Russell, November 28, *BDFA*, VI, 121.

65. Lincoln to Congress, December 1, in Carl Van Doren Stern, ed., *Life and Writings of Abraham Lincoln* (New York, 1940), 745.

66. Seward to Pike, December 23, FR-63, II, 802.

67. Pike to Seward, December 31, FR-63, II, 804.
68. Henry Adams to Charles Francis Adams Jr., January 23, 1863, in J. C. Levenson, ed., *The Letters of Henry Adams* (Cambridge, Mass., 1982), I, 327.
69. Cobden to Sumner, January 3, 1863, in Jordan and Pratt, 222.
70. Gregory to Mason, March 17, 1863, in Owsley, 440.
71. Mason to Benjamin, February 9, 1863, *ORN*, 2nd ser., II, 686.
72. Russell to Lyons, February 14, 1863, in E. D. Adams, II, 155.
73. Thomas A. Bailey, *A Diplomatic History of the American People* (New York, 1946), 370.
74. Bruce Catton, *The Civil War* (New York, 1971), 111.
75. Seward to Pike, March 9, 1863, FR-63, II, 813.
76. Bates Diary, February 6, 1863, in Howard K. Beale, ed., *The Diary of Edward Bates* (Washington, 1933), 282.
77. Lincoln, "Resolution on Slavery," with Sumner to Bright, April 17, 1863, in *Coll. Works*, VI, 177.

Chapter 10: The Wolf from Liverpool

All dates are in 1862 unless otherwise noted.

1. Hendrick, 374–75.
2. Joseph T. Durkin, *Stephen R. Mallory: Confederate Navy Chief* (Chapel Hill, N.C., 1954), 169.
3. Ibid., 156.
4. John M. Taylor, *Confederate Raider: Raphael Semmes of the Alabama* (Washington, 1994), 56.
5. James D. Bulloch, *The Secret Service of the Confederate States in Europe; Or How the Confederate Cruisers Were Equipped* (New York, 1959), I, 48.
6. Ibid., I, 67.
7. Ibid., I, 68.
8. Ibid., I, 56.
9. Sir Hugh Cairns, Court of Exchequer, November 18, 1863, *The Times* (London), November 19, 1863, FR-63, II, 1302.
10. Stuart to Russell, August 16, *BDFA*, VI, 80.
11. Bulloch, I, 61.
12. Adams to Russell, June 23, FR-62, 129.
13. Commissioners of Customs to Russell, July 1, FR-62, 130.
14. Opinion of R. P. Collier, July 16, FR-63, 151.
15. Opinion of Mr. Adams, Geneva Tribunal Records, FR-72, Part 2, IV, 174–75.
16. Opinion of Sir Alexander Cockburn, Geneval Tribunal Records, FR-72, Part 2, IV, 455.
17. Opinion of Mr. Adams, Geneva Tribunal Records, FR-72, Part 2, IV, 177.
18. Charles Francis Adams Jr., *Charles Francis Adams* (Boston, 1890), 311.
19. Hamilton to Layard, July 22, FR-72, Part 2, I, 319–20.
20. "Position and Duties of the Law Officer of the Crown in England," in Counter Case of Great Britain, Geneva Tribunal Records, FR-72, Part 2, II, 409–10.
21. Adams to Russell, July 22, FR-62, 151.

22. Layard to Law Officers, July 23, in Counter Case of Great Britain, Geneva Tribunal Records, FR-72, Part 2, I, 320.

23. Adams to Seward, July 31, FR-72, Part 2, III, 91.

24. Squarry to Adams, July 23, FR-62, 153.

25. Layard to Law Officers, July 23, in Counter Case of Great Britain, Geneva Tribunal Records, FR-72, Part 2, I, 323.

26. Opinion of R. P. Collier, July 23, FR-62, 152.

27. Opinion of Mr. Adams, Geneva Tribunal Records, FR-72, Part 2, IV, 175.

28. Russell to Adams, September 22, FR-62, 200, and December 19, FR-63, I, 63.

29. John Earl Russell, *Recollections and Suggestions, 1813–1873* (Boston, 1875), 235.

30. Atherton and Palmer to Russell, July 29, *BDFA*, VI, 68–69.

31. Spencer Walpole, *The Life of Lord John Russsell* (London, 1891), II, 366–67.

32. Bulloch, I, 238.

33. Charles Francis Adams Jr., 311.

34. Adams to Seward, November 21, in E. D. Adams, II, 120.

35. Gordon Waterfield, *Layard of Nineveh* (New York, 1968), I, 230, 235.

36. Russell to Queen, November 14, in G. P. Gooch, ed., *The Later Correspondence of Lord John Russell* (London, 1925), II, 284.

37. Lord Newton, *Lord Lyons: A Record of British Diplomacy* (London, 1913), I, 99.

38. Russell, *Recollections*, 334.

39. Morgan to Edwards, July 30, *BDFA*, VI, 71–72.

40. Opinion of Sir Alexander Cockburn, Geneva Tribunal Records, FR-72, Part 2, IV, 461.

41. Bulloch, I, 236–42.

42. Adams to Seward, August 7, FR-62, 169.

43. Layard to Rogers, July 31, *BDFA*, VI, 69.

44. Layard to Treasury, August 2, *BDFA*, VI, 39.

45. Argyll to Russell, December 5, 1872, in Dowager Duchess of Argyll, ed., *George Douglas, Eighth Duke of Argyll: Autobiography and Memoirs* (London, 1906), II, 201.

46. Russell to Admiralty, January 31, *BDFA*, VI, 41–42.

47. J. C. Bancroft Davis, "Report of the Agent of the United States," September 21, 1872, Geneva Tribunal Records, FR-72, Part 2, IV, 12.

48. Sir Roundell Palmer, British Supplemental Argument, July 29, 1872, Geneva Tribunal Records, FR-72, Part 2, III, 433-38.

49. Raphael Semmes, *Service Afloat, or the Remarkable Career of the Confederate Cruisers Sumter and Alabama* (Baltimore, 1887), 315.

50. Taylor, 72, 92, 148, 173, 187.

51. Norman B. Ferris, *Desperate Diplomacy: William H. Seward's Foreign Policy, 1861* (Knoxville, 1976), 188.

52. Taylor, 132–34; Ronckendorf to Welles, November 21, *ORN*, lst ser., I, 549–51.

53. Welles Diary, December 29, 1862, I, 207.

54. Taylor, 154.

55. Hendrick, 375.

56. Richard Cobden in House of Commons, May 12, FR-64, II, 19.

57. Adams to Seward, June 17, 1864, FR-64, II, 125–72.

58. Adams to Russell, April 7, 1865, FR-65, I, 317.

59. Bulloch to Mallory, February 18, 1864, in George W. Dalzell, *The Flight from the Flag: The Continuing Effect of the American Civil War on American Shipping* (Chapel Hill, N.C., 1940), 243,

60. W. E. Forster in House of Commons, May 12, 1864, FR-64, II, 15.

61. Seward to Adams, October 6, FR-63, I, 395.

62. Palmerston in House of Commons, March 27, 1863, FR-63, II, 1303.

63. Welles Diary, July 5, 1864, II, 67.

Chapter 11: No Obligation to Stop a Contraband Trade

1. David Thomson, *England in the Nineteenth Century* (London, 1950), 121, 124.

2. Adams to Seward, June 18, 1863, FR-63, I, 276.

3. Russell to Adams, April 2, 1863, FR-63, 205.

4. Russell to Adams, May 10, 1862, FR-62, 93.

5. *Morning Star* (London), March 28, 1863, I, 168.

6. Russell to Stuart, September 22, 1862, FR-62, 305.

7. Cobden to Sumner, May 2, 1863, in Nicholas C. Edsal, *Richard Cobden: Independent Radical* (Cambridge, Mass., 1986), 395.

8. Bruce to Stanley, July 6, 1866, in Barnes, 389.

9. Russell to Lyons, December 20, 1861, in E. D. Adams, I, 255.

10. Richard S. West, *Gideon Welles: Lincoln's Navy Department* (Indianapolis, 1943), 182–83.

11. John Niven, *Gideon Welles: Lincoln's Secretary of the Navy* (Baton Rouge, 1973), 507.

12. Lincoln to Congress, December 8, 1863, in *Coll. Works*, VII, 43.

13. Niven, 447.

14. Stephen R. Wise, *Lifeline of the Confederacy: Blockade Running During the Civil War* (Columbia, S.C., 1988), 113, 145.

15. Peter Sinclair, *Freedom or Slavery in the United States,* in B. B. Sideman and L. Friedman, eds., *Europe Looks at the Civil War* (New York, 1960), 182–83.

16. Adams to Seward, April 23, 1864, FR-63, I, 222.

17. Wise, 285–328.

18. British Foreign Office, "Return of claims against the U.S. Government from the commencement of the Civil War to the 31st of March, 1864," FR-64, I, 736–63.

19. Lincoln to Congress, December 8, 1863, in *Collected Works*, VII, 43.

20. Report of Secretary of War to Congress, 1865, House Executive Document No. 1, 39th Congress, 1st session, in Niven, 507.

21. Seward to Lyons, January 25, 1864, FR-64, II, 507.

22. Seward to Lyons, March 31, 1864, FR-64, II, 621.

23. Richard Goff, *Confederate Supply* (Durham, N.C., 1969), 43.

24. Mason to Benjamin, September 5, 1863, *ORN*, 2nd ser., III, 867.

25. Hotze to Benjamin, December 26, 1863, *ORN*, 2nd ser., III, 982.

26. Richard E. Beringer et al., *Why the South Lost the Civil War* (Athens, Ga., 1986), 61.

27. Hamilton Cochran, *Blockade Runners of the Confederacy* (Indianapolis, 1958), 51.

28. Gorgas Diary, August 3, 1863, in Sarah W. Wiggins, ed., *The Journals of Josiah Gorgas, 1857–1878* (Tuscaloosa, Ala., 1995), 77.

29. Welles Diary, August 10, 1862, I, 74.

30. Ibid.

31. Russell to Stuart, September 22, 1862, FR-62, 305.

32. Beringer et al., 58.

33. Barnes, 339.

34. Wise, 226.

35. Ibid., 196.

36. Ibid., 166.

37. Emory M. Thomas, *The Confederate Nation* (New York, 1979), 201.

38. Goff, 183.

39. Ibid., 184.

40. Gorgas Diary, January 12, 1865, in Wiggins, 148.

41. Cochran, 133.

Chapter 12: A Thing to be Deprecated

All dates are in 1863 unless otherwise noted.

1. Welles Diary, April 2, I, 255; Welles to Seward, March 31, in Welles Diary, I, 253.

2. Seward to Lyons, March 9, in E. D. Adams, II, 126.

3. Lyons to Russell, March 10, in Barnes, 319.

4. Lyons to Russell, March 24, in Barnes, 319–20.

5. Adams to Seward, March 13, FR-63, I, 143.

6. Welles Diary, March 31, I, 250.

7. E. D. Adams, II, 128.

8. *The Times* (London), March 28, FR-63, I, 164–82.

9. E. D. Adams, II, 136.

10. Adams to Seward, June 25, FR-63, I, 279.

11. *Morning Star* (London), March 28, FR-63, I, 175.

12. Frank K. Merli, *Great Britain and the Confederate Navy, 1861–1865* (Bloomington, Ind., 1970), 182.

13. James D. Bulloch, *The Secret Service of the Confederate States in Europe* (New York, 1959), I, 400.

14. Ibid., 426.

15. Adams to Russell, July 11, FR-63, I, 315, and *BDFA*, VI, 159.

16. Law Officers to Russell, July 24, *BDFA*, VI, 161–62.

17. Seward to Adams, July 11, FR-63, I, 309.

18. Adams to Seward, February 11, 1864, FR-64, I, 166.

19. Adams to Charles Francis Adams Jr., July 24, in W. C. Ford, ed., *A Cycle of Adams Letters, 1861–1865* (Boston, 1920), II, 63.

20. Argyll to Gladstone, September 4, in Dowager Duchess of Argyll, ed., *George Douglas, Eighth Duke of Argyll: Autobiography and Memoirs* (London, 1906), II, 204–05.

21. Argyll to Gladstone, September 10, in Dowager Duchess of Argyll, II, 205.

22. Adams to Russell, August 14, FR-63, I, 348–49.

23. Colquohon to Russell, August 28, *BDFA*, VI, 173–74.

24. Russell to Adams, September 1, FR-63, I, 363.

25. Layard to Home Office, September 1, in W. D. Jones, *Confederate Rams at Birkenhead* (Tuscaloosa, Ala., 1961), 72.

26. Russell to Layard, September 2, Layard Papers, 38989, item 299, BL.

27. Layard to Russell, September 2, Layard Papers, 38989, item 295, BL.

28. Russell to Layard, September 3, Layard Papers, 38989, item 303, BL.

29. Layard to Treasury, September 3, in Jones, 72.

30. Russell to Palmerston, September 3, in Spencer Walpole, *The Life of Lord John Russell* (London, 1891), 359n.

31. Palmerston to Russell, September 4, PRO 30/22/22, item 343, PRO.

32. *The Times* (London), February 24, 1864, in FR-64, I, 212, 219.

33. Adams to Russell, September 3, FR-63, I, 357.

34. Adams to Russell, September 4, FR-63, I, 361.

35. Charles Francis Adams Jr., *Charles Francis Adams* (Boston, 1890), 342.

36. Adams to Russell, September 5, FR-63, I, 367.

37. Layard to Stuart, September 5, Layard Papers, 38989, item 320, BL.

38. Moran Diary, October 5, in Sarah Wallace and Frances E. Gillespie, eds., *The Journal of Benjamin Moran* (Chicago, 1949), II, 1218.

39. Russell to Adams, September 8, FR-63, I, 368.

40. Adams Diary, September 8, in Charles Francis Adams Jr., 344.

41. Adams to Seward, September 10, FR-63, I, 370.

42. W. Bering Pemberton, *Lord Palmerston* (London, 1954), 314.

43. Martin Duberman, *Charles Francis Adams* (Boston, 1960), 316.

44. Ibid., September 17, I, 435.

45. Welles Diary, August 29, I, 429.

46. Seward to Adams, September 5, FR-63, I, 365.

47. Seward to Adams, September 19, FR-63, I, 381.

48. Seward to Adams, September 28, FR-63, I, 383.

49. Seward to Adams, June 8, 1864, FR-64, II, 100.

50. Mallory to Slidell, March 27, in Bulloch, I, 398.

51. Mallory to Bulloch, April 7, 1864, in Bulloch, I, 434.

52. Thomas A. Bailey, *A Diplomatic History of the American People* (New York, 1946), 373.

53. Bulloch to Mallory, July 9, *ORN*, 2nd ser., I, 456.

54. Warren F. Spencer, *The Confederate Navy in Europe* (Tuscaloosa, Ala., 1983), 116–19.

Chapter 13: Questions of Great Intricacy and Importance

All dates are in 1863 unless otherwise noted.

1. Henry Adams to Charles Francis Adams Jr., in J. C. Levenson et al, eds., *Letters of Henry Adams* (Cambridge, Mass., 1982), I, 343–44.

2. Milne to Lyons, March 23, FR-63, 484.

3. Lincoln to Welles, July 25, in Welles Diary, October 1, I, 448.

4. Seward to Lyons, May 12, FR-63, I, 536.

5. Lyons to Seward, May [n.d.], FR-63, I, 534-35.

6. Russell to Lyons, January 1862, FR-62, 252.

7. Welles Diary, April 10, I, 267.

8. Welles Diary, April 18, I, 275–76.

9. Welles Diary, April 28, I, 286–87.

10. Adams to Seward, March 27, 1862, FR-62, 54.

11. Adams to Seward, April 1, 1862, FR-62, 60.

12. Russell to Lyons, January 17, in Carl Sandburg, *Abraham Lincoln: The War Years* (New York, 1939), I, 23.

13. Sumner to Cobden, April 26, in Beverly W. Palmer, ed., *The Selected Letters of Charles Sumner* (Boston, 1990), II, 161.

14. Sumner to Duchess of Argyll, April 25, 1865, and Duchess of Argyll to Sumner, May 12, 1865, in Palmer, II, 295–96.

15. Sumner to Bright, May 24, 1865, in Palmer, II, 297.

16. *The Index*, London, May 28, in E. D. Adams, II, 165.

17. Adams to Seward, July 9, FR-63, I, 305.

18. Adams to Seward, January 31, 1862, FR-62, 20.

19. Stanley Weintraub, *Disraeli: A Biography* (New York, 1993), 399.

20. E. D. Adams, I, 79.

21. Mason to Benjamin, May 28, in Richardson, III, 489–91.

22. Adams to Charles Francis Adams Jr., June 25, in W. C. Ford, ed., *A Cycle of Adams Letters, 1861–1865* (Boston, 1920), II, 40.

23. Mason to Benjamin, June 20, in Richardson, II, 510.

24. Slidell to Benjamin, June 25, *ORN*, 2nd ser., III, 820.

25. Slidell to Benjamin, June 12, in Richardson, II, 506.

26. E. D. Adams, II, 171.

27. James M. McPherson, *Battle Cry of Freedom: The Civil War Era* (New York, 1988), 651.

28. Adams to Seward, July 3, FR-63, I, 303.

29. E. D. Adams, II, 174–76.

30. Welles Diary, July 17, I, 374.

31. Lincoln to Welles, July 25, in Welles Diary, October 3, I, 451.

32. Seward to Adams, July 30, FR-63, I, 328.

33. Adams to Seward, July 30, FR-63, I, 329

34. Adams to Seward, August 20, FR-63, I, 346.

35. Welles Diary, August 11, I, 398.

36. Welles Diary, Agust 21, I, 409.

37. John M. Taylor, *William Henry Seward: Lincoln's Right Hand* (New York, 1991), 221.

38. Tyler Dennett, ed., *Lincoln and the Civil War in the Diaries and Letters of John Hay* (New York, 1939), 76.

39. David Donald, *Charles Sumner and the Rights of Man* (New York, 1970), 129.

40. Russell to Lyons, October 23, in Lord Newton, *Lord Lyons: A Record of British Diplomacy* (London, 1913), I, 119.

41. Argyll to Gladstone, September 28, in Dowager Duchess of Argyll, ed., *George Douglas, Eighth Duke of Argyll: Autobiography and Memoirs* (London, 1906), II, 207.

42. Seward to Adams, September 23, FR-63, I, 383.

43. Welles to Lincoln, September 30, in Welles Diary, October 3, I, 452.

44. Lyons to Russell, November 3, in E. D. Adams, II, 183.

45. James G. Randall, *Lincoln the President: Midstream* (New York, 1952), 338.

46. Lincoln to Congress, December 8, in *Coll. Works*, VII, 36.

47. Seward to Adams, December 17, FR-64, I, 45.

48. Welles Diary, December 25, I, 495.

49. Moran Diary, December 31, in Sarah A. Wallace and Frances E. Gillespie, eds., *The Journal of Benjamin Moran, 1857–1865* (Chicago, 1949), II, 1250.

50. Seward to Adams, January 15, 1864, FR-64, I, 99.

Chapter 14: To Make Europeans Understand

1. Schurz to Seward, September 14, 1861, in Frederic Bancroft, ed., *Speeches, Correspondence, and Political Papers of Carl Schurz* (New York, 1913), I, 185.

2. Sanford to Seward, November 25, 1864, FR-64, IV, 265.

3. Motley to Seward, June 26, 1864, FR-64, IV, 153.

4. Fogg to Seward, October 25, 1862, FR-63, I, 775.

5. Seward to Fogg, June 1861, in Heinz K. Meier, *The United States and Switzerland in the Nineteenth Century* (The Hague, 1963), 72.

6. Seward to Harvey, August 13, 1862, FR-62, 587.

7. Seward to Sanford, May 10, 1862, FR-62, 654.

8. Bancroft to Seward, February 29, 1969, in John Hawgood, "The Civil War and Central Europe," in Harold Hyman, ed., *Heard Around the World: The Impact Abroad of the Civil War* (New York, 1969), 149–50.

9. Hawgood, 151.

10. Gorchakow to Taylor, October 1862, in B. B. Sideman and L. Friedman, eds., *Europe Looks at the Civil War* (New York, 1960), 184.

11. E. D. Adams, II, 129.

12. Samuel Flagg Bemis, *A Diplomatic History of the United States* (New York, 1942), 366–67.

13. *New York Times*, October 26, 1861, in Lewis Coe, *The Telegraph* (Jefferson, N.C., 1993), 87.

14. Lincoln to Congress, December 6, 1864, in *Coll. Works*, VIII, 138–39.

15. A. R. Tyrner-Tyrnauer, *Lincoln and the Emperors* (New York, 1962), 32.

16. Jordan and Pratt, 195.

17. Thomas A. Bailey, *A Diplomatic History of the American People* (New York, 1946), 377.

18. Welles Diary, February 2, 1864, I, 520.

19. Perry to Seward, October 28, 1864, FR-65, II, 465.

20. Seward to Perry, April 4, 1865, FR-65, II, 522.

21. Seward to Canisius, October 10, 1862, FR-62, 567.

22. Ibid.

23. J. G. Randall and Richard N. Current, *Lincoln the President: Last Full Measure* (New York, 1955), 78–79.

24. Garibaldi to Marsh, October 7, 1862, in Sideman and Friedman, 68–74.

25. Pike to Seward, September 3, 1862, FR-62, 617.

26. Murphy to Seward, May 27, 1861, FR-61, 349.

27. Seward to Pike, October 4 and 9, 1861, FR-61, 374–75.

28. Pike to Seward, October 12, 1861, FR-61, 377.

29. Pike to Seward, January 6, 1864, FR-64, III, 306–307.

30. Seward to Sanford, October 31, 1867, FR-67, I, 644.

31. Sanford to Seward, September 15, 1864, FR-64, IV, 262.
32. Seward to Sanford, October 4, 1864, FR-64, IV, 231.
33. Seward to Fogg, May 15, 1861, FR-61, 330.
34. Fay to Seward, July 2, 1861, FR-61, 337.
35. Fogg to Seward, December 24, 1863, FR-64, IV, 391.

Chapter 15: Alone on the Earth

1. Beckles Willison, *John Slidell and the Confederates in Paris* (New York, 1932), 101-102.
2. Hudson Strode, *Jefferson Davis: Confederate President* (New York, 1959), 349.
3. E. Merton Coulter, *The Confederate States of America* (Baton Rouge, La., 1950), 191.
4. Ibid.
5. Benjamin to Lamar, June 11, 1863, in Richardson, II, 405.
6. Jefferson Davis, *The Rise and Fall of the Confederate Government* (New York, 1881), II, 370.
7. Benjamin to Slidell, August 17, 1863, *ORN*, 2nd ser., III, 873.
8. Mason to Benjamin, August 6, 1863, *ORN*, 2nd ser., III, 856.
9. Slidell to Benjamin, August 5, 1863, *ORN*, 2nd ser., III, 855.
10. Mason to Russell, September 21, 1863, FR-64, I, 811.
11. Virginia Mason, *The Public Life and Diplomatic Correspondence of James M. Mason* (New York, 1906), 467.
12. Moran Diary, September 22, 1862, in S. A. Wallace and F. E. Gillespie, eds., *The Journal of Benjamin Moran, 1857–1865* (Chicago, 1949), II, 1212.
13. Eugene H. Berwanger, *The British Foreign Service and the American Civil War* (Lexington, Ky., 1994), 14.
14. Benjamin to Mason, June 6, 1863, FR-64, I, 825.
15. Moore to Caldwell, May 5, 1863, in Berwanger, 114.
16. Berwanger, 114–16.
17. Benjamin to Fullerton and Walker, October 8, 1863, in Berwanger, 117.
18. Benjamin to Davis, October 8, 1863, in Berwanger, 120.
19. Willison, 186–201.
20. Hudson Strode, *Jefferson Davis: Tragic Hero* (New York, 1964), 27.
21. Hendrick, 382.
22. Owsley, 414–17.
23. Ibid, 422–24.
24. James D. Bulloch, *The Secret Service of the Confederate States in Europe* (New York, 1959), II, 41.
25. Bulloch to Mallory, February 18, 1864, in Bulloch, II, 41.
26. Ibid., II, 46.
27. Owsley, 426.
28. Bulloch to Mallory, June 10, 1864, in Bulloch, II, 48.
29. Hendrick, 385.
30. John Bigelow, *France and the Confederate Navy* (New York, 1888), 107–108, 165.
31. John Bigelow, *Retrospections of an Active Life* (New York, 1909–1913), in Willison, 211–12, 223.

32. Slidell to Benjamin, September 1864, in Willison, 229.

33. Benjamin to Slidell, December 27, 1864, in R. J. Bartlett, ed., *The Record of American Diplomacy* (New York, 1954), 295–96.

34. Eli N. Evans, *Judah P. Benjamin: The Jewish Confederate* (New York, 1988), 275.

35. Ibid., 279.

36. Mason to Benjamin, March 31, 1865, in Richardson, II, 714.

37. Evans, 279; Mason, 560.

Chapter 16: This Government Avoids Intervention

1. Lyons to Malmesbury, May 14 and 30, 1859, in Lord Newton, *Lord Lyons* (London, 1913), 13, 15.

2. Adams to Seward, November 1, 1861, in Norman B. Ferris, *Desperate Diplomacy: William H. Seward's Foreign Policy, 1861* (Knoxville, 1976), 167.

3. Adams to Seward, September 12, 1862, FR-62, 190.

4. Corwin to Seward, June 29, 1861, in Owsley, 107.

5. Romero to Seward, May 4, 1861, FR-65, III, 537; Seward to Romero, May 7, 1861, FR-65, III, 538.

6. Toombs to Pickett, May 17, 1861, in James M. Callahan, *Diplomatic History of the Southern Confederacy* (New York, 1964), 71.

7. Hunter to Slidell, September 23, 1861, *ORN*, 2nd ser., III, 271.

8. Michel Chevalier, *la France, le Mexique et la Etates-Confederes* (Paris, 1863), in Alfred J. Hanna and Kathryn A. Hanna, *Napoleon III and Mexico* (Chapel Hill, N.C., 1971), 65.

9. Benjamin to Preston, January 7, 1864, *ORN*, 2nd ser., III, 988–89.

10. Napoleon III to General Forey, July 3, 1862, in John G. Nicolay and John Hay, *Abraham Lincoln: A History* (New York, 1890), VI, 33–34.

11. Leopold I to Maximilian, October 25, 1861, in A. R. Tyrner-Tyrnauer, *Lincoln and the Emperors* (New York, 1962), 69.

12. Palmerston to Russell, January 19, 1862, in D. P. Crook, *The North, the South, and the Powers, 1861–1865* (New York, 1974), 184.

13. Seward to Dayton, March 3, 1862, in Tyrner-Tyrnauer, 47.

14. Seward to Corwin, June 24, 1862, FR-62, 749.

15. Seward to Dayton, August 23, 1862, FR-62, 377.

16. Welles Diary, July 27, 1863, I, 385.

17. Arroyo to Seward, July 20, 1863, FR-63, II, 704–705.

18. Motley to mother, September 22, 1863, and Motley to O. W. Holmes, September 22, 1863, in George W. Curtis, ed., *The Correspondence of John Lothrop Motley* (New York, 1889), I, 1389, and II, 143.

19. Dayton to Seward, August 21, 1863, FR-63, II, 689.

20. Dayton to Seward, September 7, 1863, in Owsley, 514.

21. Seward to Dayton, September 21, 1863, FR-63, II, 703.

22. Harvey to Seward, October 17, 1863, FR-64, IV, 273.

23. Fogg to Seward, October 2, 1863, FR-64, IV, 389.

24. Huelseman to Rechberg, January 20, 1863, in Tyrner-Tyrnauer, 29.

25. Welles Diary, July 31, 1863.

26. Seward to Dayton, September 21, 1863, in George E. Baker, ed., *The Diplomatic History of the War for the Union, Being the Fifth Volume of the Works of William H. Seward* (Boston, 1884), V, 403.

27. B. B. Sideman and L. Friedman, *Europe Looks at the Civil War* (New York, 1960), 162.

28. Motley to Seward, September 21, 1863, FR-64, IV, 116

29. Dayton to Seward, March 11, 1864, FR-64, III, 51.

30. Lincoln to Stanton, July 29, 1863, in *Coll. Works*, VI, 374.

31. Lincoln to Banks, August 5, 1863, in *Coll. Works,* VI, 364.

32. John Hay Diary, August 6, 1863, in Tyler Dennett, ed., *Lincoln and the Civil War in the Diaries and Letters of John Hay* (New York, 1939), 77.

33. Lincoln to Grant, August 9, 1863, in John G. Nicolay and John Hay, *Abraham Lincoln: A History* (New York, 1890), VII, 401.

34. Halleck to Banks, August 10, 1863, *ORA*, lst ser,, XXVI, 673.

35. Grant to Lincoln, August 23, 1863, *ORA*, lst ser., XXVI, 673.

36. Halleck to Grant, January 8, 1864, in Ludwell H. Johnson, *The Red River Campaign* (Baltimore, 1958), 42

37. Bruce Catton, *Never Call Retreat* (New York, 1965), 232–33.

38. Joseph H. Parks, *General Edmund Kirby Smith C.S.A.* (Baton Rouge, 1954), 314; Kirby Smith to Slidell, September 1, 1863, *ORA*, 1st ser., XXII, 993–94.

39. Slidell to French Foreign Office, December 4, 1863, *ORN*, 2nd ser., III, 978.

40. Seward to Banks, November 28, 1863, FR-53, II, 1341.

41. Seward to Bigelow, May 21, 1864, in John Bigelow, *Retrospections of an Active Life* (New York, 1909–1913), II, 788–89.

42. Seward to General E. R. S. Canby, September 30, 1864, FR-64, III, 155.

43. Slidell to Thouvenel, July 21, 1862, *ORN*, 2nd ser., III, 467–79.

44. Slidell to Benjamin, July 25, 1862, *ORN*, 2nd ser., III, 484.

45. Hendrick, 309.

46. Slidell to Benjamin, December 3, 1863, in Nicolay and Hay, VII, 413.

47. Davis to Confederate Congress, December 7, 1863, in Richardson, I, 360.

48. Benjamin to Preston, January 7, 1864, *ORN*, 2nd ser., III, 988–89.

49. Joan Haslip, *The Crown of Mexico* (New York, 1971), 197–98.

50. Motley to Seward, September 21, 1863, FR-63, I, 115.

51. Slidell to Benjamin, March 16, 1864, in Nicolay and Hay, VII, 413.

52. Mann to Benjamin, March 11, 1864, *ORA*, 2nd ser., II, 1057–59.

53. Slidell to Benjamin, March 16, 1864, in Nicolay and Hay, VII, 413; Owsley, 523.

54. Seward to Adams, February 25, 1864, FR-64, I, 201.

55. Thomas D. Schoonover, *Mexican Lobby: Mattias Romero in Washington, 1861–1867* (Lexington, Ky., 1986), xiii.

56. Nicolay and Hay, VII, 407.

57. Lyons to Russell, February 23, 1864, in E. D. Adams, II, 198.

58. Seward to Dayton, February 27, 1864, FR-64, II, 45.

59. Seward to Dayton, March 23, 1864, FR-64, III, 56.

60. House resolution, April 4, 1865, in Nicolay and Hay, VII, 408.

61. Dayton to Seward, April 22, 1864, FR-64, III, 76.

62. Seward to Dayton, April 30, 1864, FR-64, III, 80.

63. Resolution of Republican National Convention, June 1864, in Nicolay and Hay, VII, 421.

64. Jay Monaghan, *Diplomat in Carpet Slippers: Abraham Lincoln Deals With Foreign Affairs* (New York, 1945), 370.

65. John H. Thayer reminiscence, *New York Sun*, in Clifton M. Nichols, *Life of Abraham Lincoln* (New York, 1896), 317.

66. Lincoln to Congress, December 6, 1864, FR-64, I, 3.

67. Romero to Foreign Ministry, May 5, 1862, in Schoonover, 24–25.

68. Romero to Foreign Ministry, May 12, 1862, Ibid.

69. Johnson speech in Nashville, in Thomas A. Bailey, *A Diplomatic History of the American People* (New York, 1946), 383.

70. *Herald* (New York), January 21, 1864, in Bailey, 381.

71. J. G. Randall and Richard Current, *Lincoln the President: Last Full Measure* (New York, 1955), 44, 282–83; James L. Crouthamel, *Bennett's New York Herald* (Syracuse, N.Y., 1989), 148–49.

72. Chabrun to wife, April 10, 1865, in Sideman and Friedman, 276.

73. Nicolay and Hay, X, 95.

74. Blair report, January 1865, in Nicolay and Hay, X, 97–102.

75. Mason memorandum, March 14, 1865, in Richardson, II, 711.

76. Varina H. Davis, *Memoirs*, II, 575–78, in Eli Evan, *Judah P. Benjamin: The Jewish Confederate* (New York, 1988), 277.

77. Nicolay and Hay, X, 107.

78. Seward to Adams, January 30, 1865, FR-65, I, 105.

79. Alexander Stephens, *War Between the States*, II, 600–04, in Charles M. Segal, ed., *Conversations with Lincoln* (New York, 1961), 369–70.

80. Seward to Adams, February 7, 1865, FR-65, I, 130.

81. Marquis de Chambrun, "Personal Recollections of Mr. Lincoln," *Scribner's Magazine*, XIII (January 1893), 26–38.

82. Bruce to Russell, April 14, 1865, in E. D. Adams, II, 155.

Chapter 17: A War with America as Soon as She Makes Peace

1. Seward to Adams, February 13, 1864, FR-64, I, 171–72.

2. Adams to Seward, June 9, 1864, FR-64, II, 89.

3. Lyons to Russell, April 19, 1864, in Lord Newton, *Lord Lyons* (London, 1913), I, 129; Lyons to Russell, April 25, 1864, *BDFA*, VI, 303–304.

4. Robin Winks, *Canada and the United States: The Civil War Years* (Baltimore, 1960), 72.

5. Ibid., 215.

6. Jasper Ridley, *Lord Palmerston* (New York, 1971), 263.

7. Lyons to Russell, May 20, 1861, *BDFA*, VI, 223–25.

8. Lyons to Russell, July 1, 1861, *BDFA*, V, 259.

9. Lyons to Russell, April 19, 1864, in Barnes, 341.

10. Lyons to Russell, April 25, 1864, *BDFA*, VI, 303–04.

11. Welles Diary, December 26, 1863, I, 496–97.

12. Seward to Adams, April 22, 1864, FR-64, I, 639.

13. *The Times* (London), July 26, 1864, in FR-64, II, 229.

14. *The Times* (London), August 24, 1864, FR-64, II, 284.

15. Lyons to Russell, August 15 and 23, 1864, in Barnes, 347.

16. Dayton to Seward, November 17, 1864, FR-64, III, 195.

17. James M. McPherson, *Drawn with the Sword* (New York, 1996), 133.

18. Grant to Stanton, November 24, 1864, *ORA*, 3rd ser., XXXXI, 581.

19. John G. Nicolay and John Hay, *Abraham Lincoln: A History* (abridged edition, Chicago, 1966), 286.

20. Moran Diary, November 22, 1864, in S. A. Wallace and F. E. Gillespie, eds., *The Journal of Benjamin Moran, 1857-1865* (Chicago, 1949), ii, 1351.

21. *The Times* (London), November 15, 1864, in Herbert Mitgang, ed., *Lincoln as They Saw Him* (New York, 1956), 420-21.

22. *The Times* (London), August 8, 1864, in E. D. Adams, II, 232.

23. W. S. Pennington to Seward, December 30, 1864, FR-65, II, 204.

24. Lincoln to Sherman, December 1864, in Paul M. Angle, ed., *The Lincoln Reader* (New Brunswick, N.J., 1947), 475.

25. Winks, 299–300.

26. *Evening Post* (New York), FR-64, II, 75.

27. Russell to Lyons, December 29, 1864, *BDFA*, VI, 329.

28. Monck to Burnley, October 26, 1864, FR-64, II, 755.

29. Seward to Burnley, October 25, 1864, FR-64, II, 752–53.

30. Monck to Burnley, October 31, 1864, FR-64, II, 762.

31. Seward to Adams, October 24, 1864, in Russell to Lyons, November 26, 1864, FR-65, II, 18.

32. Adams to Russell, November 25, 1864, FR-65, I, 5.

33. Winks, 314.

34. Seward to Adams, December 19, FR-65, I, 49–50.

35. Department of State Order, December 17, 1864, FR-66, I, 54.

36. Winks, 318.

37. Samuel Flagg Bemis, *A Diplomatic History of the United States* (New York, 1942), 302; Winks, 342.

38. Adams to Seward, March 23, 1865, FR-65, I, 259.

39. Seward to Adams, March 10, 1865, FR-65, I, 201.

40. Palmerston to Queen Victoria, January 20, 1865, in George Buckle, ed., *The Letters of Queen Victoria*, 2nd ser. (New York, 1926), I, 249.

41. Queen Victoria Diary, February 12, 1865, in Buckle, I, 250.

42. Charles Francis Adams to Charles Francis Adams Jr., February 17, 1865, in W. C. Ford, ed., *A Cycle of Adams Letters, 1861–1865* (Boston, 1920), II, 256–57.

43. Adams to Seward, February 23, 1865, FR-65, I, 182–83.

44. Seward to Adams, March 1, 1865, FR-65, I, 191.

45. Adams to Seward, March 16, 1865, I, 246.

46. Seward to Adams, March 8 and 20, 1865, FR-65, I, 197, 252.

47. *The Times* (London), March 17, 1865, in Mitgang, 444.

48. *The Spectator* (London), March 25, 1865, in Mitgang, 446–47.

49. Palmerston to Queen, March 13, 1865, in Buckle, I, 262.

50. *The Times* (London), March 24, 1865, FR-65, I, 292.

51. Seward to Adams (circular), April 10, 1865, FR-65, I, 307.

52. F.W. Seward to Adams, April 10, 1865, FR-65, I, 307–308.

53. Hunter to Adams, April 15, 1865, FR-65, I, 321.

54. *The Times* (London), May 2, 1865, FR-65, I, 338–39.

55. *The Times* (London), May 2, 1865, FR-65, I, 343.

56. FR-65 Appendix, 360-418.

57. *The Times* (London), April 28, 1861, in Mitgang, 485–87.

58. Queen Victoria to Mrs. Lincoln, April 29, 1865, in Buckle, I, 267.

Chapter 18: Government by the People Shall Not Perish

1. *Tribune* (New York), April 24, 1865, in Herbert Mitgang, *Lincoln As They Saw Him* (New York, 1956), 482.

2. Bruce Catton, *The Civil War* (New York, 1971), 113.

3. Lord Charnwood, *Abraham Lincoln* (New York, 1917), 262, 264.

4. H. C. Allen, *Great Britain and the United States: A History of Anglo-American Relations, 1783–1952* (New York, 1955), 471, 485.

5. Lincoln speech, Springfield, Ill., January 27, 1837, in Maureen Harrison and Steve Gilbert, eds., *Abraham Lincoln in His Own Words* (New York, 1994), 45, 52.

6. Lincoln speech, Springfield, Ill., February 22, 1842, in Harrison and Gilbert, 81–82.

7. James G. Randall, *Lincoln the Liberal Statesman* (New York, 1947), 199–200.

8. Lincoln speech, Peoria, Ill., October 16, 1854, in Randall, 115.

9. Lincoln speech, Springfield, Ill., June 26, 1857, in Randall, 180–181.

10. Webb Garrison, *The Lincoln No One Knows* (Nashville, 1993), 241–42.

11. Lincoln to H. L. Pierce, April 6, 1859, in *Coll. Works*, IV, 168–69.

12. Lincoln to New Jersey Senate, February 21, 1865, and Lincoln speech at Independence Hall, February 22, 1861, in Paul M. Angle and Earl S. Miers, eds., *The Living Lincoln* (New York, 1992), 378–79.

13. Stephen B. Oates, *Abraham Lincoln: The Man Behind the Myths* (New York, 1984), 90.

14. Alfred J. Hanna and Kathryn A. Hanna, *Napoleon III and Mexico* (Chapel Hill, N.C., 1971), 57.

15. Lincoln to Marcelino Hurtado, June 4, 1861, in *Coll. Works*, IV, 393.

16. Lincoln to Frederico Barrenda, March 4, 1862, in *Coll. Works*, V, 142–43.

17. Lincoln to Lorenzo Montufar, April 24, 1862, in *Coll. Works*, V, 198.

18. Lincoln to John Hay, May 7, 1861, in Mario M. Cuomo and Harold Holzer, eds., *Lincoln on Democracy* (New York, 1990), 215.

19. Lincoln to Congress, July 4, 1861, in *Coll. Works*, IV, 426, 438–39.

20. Lincoln to Count Edward Piper, November 8, 1861, in *Coll. Works*, V, 18.

21. Lincoln to Evangelical Lutheran churchmen, May 13, 1863, in Angle and Miers, 474.

22. Lincoln to Border State Congressmen and Senators, July 12, 1862, in *Coll. Works*, V, 317.

23. Lincoln, Gettysburg Address, November 19, 1863, in *Coll. Works*, VII, 23.

24. Randall, 201.

25. John Hay Diary, July 24, 1864, in Tyler Dennett, ed., *Lincoln and the Civil War in the Diaries and Letters of John Hay* (New York, 1939), 197.

26. Pauline Maier, *American Scripture: Making the Declaration of Independence* (New York, 1997), 207.

27. Merrill D. Peterson, *Lincoln in American Memory* (New York, 1994), 385.

28. H. C. Allen, "Civil War, Reconstruction, and Great Britain," in Harold Hyman, ed., *Heard Around the World: The Impact Abroad of the Civil War* (New York, 1969), 49.

29. William E. Leuctenberg, *In the Shadow of FDR* (Ithaca, N.Y., 1983), 40.

30. Arthur Schlesinger Jr., *A Thousand Days* (Boston, 1975), 675.

31. Walt Whitman reminiscence in Allen Thorndike Rice, ed., *Reminiscences of Abraham Lincoln* (New York, 1888), 475.

32. John G. Nicolay and John Hay, *Abraham Lincoln: A History*, abridged ed. (Chicago, 1966), 378–79.

33. G. M. Trevelyan, *British History in the Nineteenth Century, 1782–1901* (London, 1922), 339.

34. H. C. Allen, in Hyman, 96.

35. Bigelow to Seward, May 31, 1865, FR-65, II, 300.

36. Oates, 15–16.

37. Merrill Peterson, *Lincoln in American Memory* (New York, 1994), 199.

38. David Lloyd George, "A Tribute," in John Wesley Hill, *Abraham Lincoln: A Man of God* (New York, 1920), v.

Epilogue I: A Source of Apprehension and Danger

1. Jasper Ridley, *Lord Palmerston* (New York, 1971), 517.

2. Seward to Bigelow, June 12, 1865, FR-65, III, 393.

3. Romero to Ministry, April 30 and May 8, 1865, in Thomas D. Schoonover, *Mexican Lobby: Mattias Romero in Washington, 1861–1867* (Lexington, Ky., 1986), 58–59.

4. Welles Diary, June 23, 1865, II, 322.

5. Bates Diary, December 12, 1865, in Howard K. Beale, *The Diary of Edward Bates, 1859-1866, Annual Report of the American Historical Association for 1930* (Washington, 1933), 523.

6. Brooks D. Simpson, *Let Us Have Peace* (Chapel Hill, N.C., 1991), 112.

7. William S. McFeeley, *Grant: A Biography* (New York, 1981), 221.

8. Welles Diary, June 16, 1865, II, 317.

9. Welles Diary, June 23, 1865, II, 322.

10. Welles Diary, July 14, 1865, II, 333.

11. Bruce to Clarendon, January 14, 1866, in Barnes, 370.

12. Grant to Johnson, July 15, 1865, in Paul Bergeron, ed., *Papers of Andrew Johnson* (Knoxville, 1989), VIII, 410.

13. Seward to Bigelow, December 9, 1896, in Alfred J. Hanna and Kathryn A. Hanna, *Napoleon III and Mexico* (Chapel Hill, N.C., 1971), 241–47.

14. Seward to Bigelow, September 6, 1865, FR-65, III, 413.

15. John M. Taylor, *William Henry Seward: Lincoln's Right Hand* (New York, 1991), 252; Joan Haslip, *The Crown of Mexico* (New York, 1971), 321.

16. Jasper Ridley, *Maximilian and Juárez* (New York, 1992), 212–13.

17. Drouyn de Lhuys to Montholon, October 18, 1865, in Hanna and Hanna, 153.

18. Seward to Bigelow, November 6, 1865, FR-65, III, 422.

19. Bigelow to Seward, November 30, 1865, FR-65, III, 427.

20. Hanna and Hanna, 264.

21. Welles Diary, December 20, 1865, II, 401.
22. Bruce to Clarendon, December 18, 1865, in Barnes, 369.
23. Seward to Bigelow, December 16, 1865, FR-65, III, 429.
24. Drouyn de Lhuys to Montholon, January 6, 1866, FR-65, III, 805–806.
25. Seward to Montholon, Feburary 12, 1866, FR-66, II, 813.
26. Grant to Johnson, March 3, 1866, in John Y. Simon, ed., *The Papers of Ulysses S. Grant* (Carbondale, Ill., 1988), XVI, 322.
27. Grant to Stanton, March 24, 1866, in Simon, XVI, 137.
28. Drouyn de Lhuys to Montholon, April 5, 1866, FR-66, III, 28.
29. Seward to Bigelow, May 12, 1865, FR-66, I, 306.
30. Bruce to Clarendon, May 15, 1866, in Barnes, 381.
31. Grant to Sheridan, July 30, 1866, in Simon, XVI, 267.
32. Sheridan to Grant, October 31, 1866, in Simon, XVI, 323.
33. Bigelow to Seward, October 12, 1866, FR-66, I, 360.
34. Bigelow to Seward, November 8, 1866, FR-66, I, 364.
35. James T. Merrill, *William Tecumseh Sherman* (New York, 1971), 312.
36. Seward to Campbell, October 25, 1866, in George E. Baker, ed., *The Works of William H. Seward* (Boston, 1884), 47.
37. Welles Diary, November 22, 1866, II, 623.
38. Seward to Campbell, October 25, 1866, in Baker, 472–73.
39. Romero to Ministry, November 3, 1866, in Schoonover, 144.
40. Sherman to Grant, November 3, 1866, in Simon, XVI, 341.
41. Sherman, 909.
42. Campbell to Seward, December 1, 1866, FR-66, III, 13.
43. Campbell to Seward, December 13, 1866, FR-67, III, 335.
44. Campbell to Lerdo de Tejada, December 5, 1866, FR-67, II, 335.
45. W. T. Sherman to Sen. John Sherman, December 7, 1866, in Hanna and Hanna, 288.
46. Campbell to Seward, December 13, 1866, FR-67, II, 335.
47. Seward to Campbell, January 8, 1867, FR-67, II, 344.
48. Ridley, *Maximilian and Juárez*, 254.
49. Welles Diary, December 24, 1866, II, 649.
50. Welles Diary, November 22, 1864, II, 623.
51. Seward to Bigelow, November 23, 1866, FR-66, I, 366–67.
52. Bigelow to Seward, December 3, 1866, FR-66, I, 368–69.
53. Wydenbruck to Seward, April 6, 1867, FR-67, I, 564.
54. Seward to Campbell, April 6, 1867, FR-67, II, 388.
55. Lerdo de Tejada to Campbell, April 22, 1867, FR-67, II, 404.
56. Beust to Wydenbruck, May 29, 1867, FR-67, I, 566.
57. Romero memorandum, May 29, 1867, FR-67, II, 554.
58. Seward to Campbell, June 1, 1867, FR-67, II, 411.
59. Campbell to Seward, May 15, 1867, FR-67, II, 404.
60. Campbell to Seward, June 3, 1867, FR-67, II, 411.
61. Seward to Campbell, June 5, 1867, FR-67, II, 411.
62. Margarita Juárez to Seward, June 17, 1867, FR-67, II, 560.
63. Campbell to Seward, June 6, 1867, FR-67, II, 412.

64. Campbell to Seward and Seward to Campbell, June 11, 1867, FR-67, II, 417.

65. Campbell to Seward, June 15, 1867, FR-67, II, 418.

66. Seward to Campbell, June 15, 1867, FR-67, II, 419.

67. Romero memorandum, June 15, 1867, FR-67, II, 560.

68. Haslip, 279–80.

69. Ralph Roeder, *Juárez and His Mexico* (New York, 1947), II, 670–72.

70. Ridley, *Maximilian and Juárez*, 273.

71. Roeder, II, 662.

72. Frederick Bancroft, *Life of William H. Seward* (New York, 1900), II, 419,

Epilogue II: The Massive Grievance

1. Horace Porter, *Campaigning with Grant* (New York, 1897), 407–08.

2. Allan Nevins, *Hamilton Fish: The Inner History of the Grant Administration* (New York, 1936), 147.

3. Seward to Adams, August 27, 1866, FR-66, I, 177–78.

4. Samuel Flagg Bemis, *A Diplomatic History of the United States* (New York, 1942), 406.

5. Nevins, 905–07.

6. David Donald, *Charles Sumner and the Rights of Man* (New York, 1970), 374–76.

7. Ibid.

8. Donald, 386.

9. Bemis, 407.

10. Nevins, 152.

11. J. Bartlet Brebner, *Canada: A Modern History* (Ann Arbor, 1960), 149.

12. Donald, 407.

13. Ibid., 408.

14. Fish to Motley, September 25, 1869, FR-72, Part 2, I, 122.

15. Grant to Congress, December 1869, FR-72, Part 2, II, 196.

16. Donald, 413.

17. Nevins, 429.

18. Ibid., 426.

19. William S. McFeeley, *Grant: A Biography* (New York, 1981), 348.

20. E. Fitzmaurice, *Life of Granville George Leveson Gower, Second Earl of Granville, K.G.* (London, 1905), II, 83.

21. Donald, 484–88.

22. Protocol, Conference on the Alabama Claims, FR-72, Part 2, I, 12.

23. Bemis, 409–10.

24. Fitzmaurice, II, 87.

25. Nevins, 386–87.

26. Case of the United States, FR-72, Part 2, I, 189.

27. James Thurslow Adams, *The Adams Family* (New York, 1936), 317.

28. Martin Duberman, *Charles Francis Adams, 1807–1886* (Boston, 1960), 347.

29. Fish to Storer, April 5, 1872, Fish Papers, in Nevins, 528.

30. Case of the United States, FR-72, Part 2, I, 189.

31. John M. Taylor, *Confederate Raider: Raphael Semmes of the Alabama* (Washington, 1994).

32. Bruce to Stanley, October 22, 1866, in Barnes, 390.

33. Bemis, 413.

34. Schenck to Granville, March 21, 1872, Part 2, III, 459.

35. Counter Case of Great Britain, FR-72, Part 2, II, 392–93.

36. H. C. Allen, *Great Britain and the United States: A History of Anglo-American Relations, 1783–1952* (New York, 1955), 516.

37. Blachford to Granville, February 11, 1872, in Fitzmaurice, II, 94.

38. Schenck to Fish, May 10, 1872, Part 2, II, 500.

39. Fitzmaurice, II, 96–97.

40. Granville to Bright, June 12, 1872, in Fitzmaurice, II, 98–99.

41. Allen, 514.

42. James Thurslow Adams, *The Adams Family* (New York, 1930), 317.

43. Geneva Tribunal, Protocol V, June 19, 1872, FR-72, Part 2, V, 20.

44. Fish to Davis, June 22, 1872, FR-72, Part 2, II, 579.

45. Richard Shannon, *Gladstone: Heroic Minister, 1865–1898* (London, 1999), 113–14.

46. Ibid.

47. Allen, 517.

48. Roy Jenkins, *Gladstone: A Biography* (New York, 1995), 356.

INDEX

$\mathcal{A}BOUT$ $\mathcal{T}H\mathcal{E}$ $\mathcal{A}UTHO\mathcal{R}$

Dean B. Mahin was born in 1925 and served in the U.S. Army in France, Germany, and Austria during World War II. After the war he received an undergraduate degree in history and a graduate degree in international affairs.

He worked for forty years as an employee or contractor for U.S. international agencies—the Department of State, the U.S. Information Agency, and the U.S. Agency for International Development. His positions included coordinator of a large program of visits to the United States by German leaders, director of the U.S. Information Center in Germany's Ruhr region, director of the largest staff programming international visitors for the Department of State, coordinator of U.S. programs for multiregional international groups of professionals in the energy, urban affairs, economic, and educational fields, and editor of a series of publications on international energy projects.

Mr. Mahin is the author of *Olive Branch and Sword*, a study of the diplomatic history of the U.S. war with Mexico from 1846 to 1848. He and his wife, Ursula, live in Charlotte, North Carolina.